Franz Kafka

The Necessity of Form

ALSO BY STANLEY CORNGOLD

BOOKS

*The Commentators' Despair: The Interpretation of Kafka's
"Metamorphosis"*

The Fate of the Self: German Writers and French Theory

EDITED WORKS

Aspekte der Goethezeit (with Michael Curschmann and Theodore
Ziolkowski)

Ausgewählte Prosa by Max Frisch

The Metamorphosis by Franz Kafka

Thomas Mann, 1875–1975 (with Richard Ludwig)

Franz Kafka

The Necessity of Form

by Stanley Corngold

CORNELL UNIVERSITY PRESS · ITHACA AND LONDON

First published 1988 by Cornell University Press.

International Standard Book Number 0-8014-2199-3
Library of Congress Catalog Card Number 88-47721

Printed in the United States of America

*Librarians: Library of Congress cataloging information
appears on the last page of the book.*

*The paper in this book is acid-free and meets the guidelines for
permanence and durability of the Committee on Production Guidelines
for Book Longevity of the Council on Library Resources.*

My whole being is directed toward literature; I have followed this direction unswervingly . . . , and the moment I abandon it I cease to live. Everything I am, and am not, is a result. . . . It is the earthly reflection of a higher necessity.

FRANZ KAFKA, Letters to Felice (1913)

From the West all content acquires meaning from form only, one's gaze is fixed only on form, courtesy of Flaubert. . . . It became the feature of apocalypse: the task of reality pure and simple, the transposition of all substance into form, into the formula.

GOTTFRIED BENN, "Züchtung I"

He does not live for the sake of his personal life; he does not think for the sake of his personal thoughts. It seems to him that he lives and thinks under the compulsion of a family, which, it is true, is itself superabundant in life and thought, but for which he constitutes, in obedience to some law unknown to him, a formal necessity.

FRANZ KAFKA, The Great Wall of China (1920)

Contents

Contents

Preface

To say what Kafka's work means is to say more than one can, if meanings depend on descriptions of experience, having beginnings and ends. For here, in Hölderlin's words, "beginning and end no longer allow themselves to be coupled together like rhymes."[1] Kafka himself doubted that "The Judgment"—the story he loved the best—meant anything "straightforward" and "coherent."[2] But the want of such meaning should not suggest something fugitive or arabesque about his achievement. Kafka's work is informed by a literally cabalistic stringency that draws reading after reading to itself—including readings based on experience. This is a fact about its power to invite disclosure by experience, not its need to be improved by it. Indeed, recent studies of Kafka have been less and less concerned with reproducing the description of personal experience that Kafka's work purportedly makes. In other words, Kafka is rarely read today as if he were writing in the discursive system of 1800, in which, as Friedrich

1. This sentence is Friedrich Hölderlin's description of Nature in dissolution; see *Sämtliche Werke* (Stuttgart: Kohlhammer, 1961), 5:220. Sources for the foregoing epigraphs are LF 313; Gottfried Benn, "Züchtung I," in *Gesammelte Werke: Essays, Reden, Vorträge* (Wiesbaden: Limes, 1959), 1:217; GW 269.

2. In a letter to Felice Bauer dated June 2, 1913, Kafka wrote: "Can you discover any meaning in 'The Judgment'—some straightforward, coherent meaning that one could follow? I can't find any, nor can I explain anything in it" (LF 265). Silvio Vietta notes, "In Kafka's stories 'meaning' itself is thematized"; see "Franz Kafka, Expressionism, and Reification," trans. Douglas Kellner, in *Passion and Rebellion: The Expressionist Heritage,* ed. Stephen Eric Bronner and Douglas Kellner (South Hadley, Mass.: Bergin, 1983), p. 210.

Kittler says, "all depicted events are explained in the psychological or philosophical culture of a voice in the margins of the text."[3] The power of Kafka's work consists in the many ways it suggests that literature can function without meaning—that is, without provoking substitutions or analogies that appeal to the beginnings and ends of experience. Kafka's works are the signs of a body in labor; signs of a consciousness needing to be; signs, above all, of the being who *is* literature, seeking through language the ecstatic consumption of experience.

These relations can be put into concepts and ideas, and certainly powerful formulas are found in Kafka's notebooks, in which writing is defined as "a form of prayer" (DF 312) and literature as an "assault on the last earthly frontier" (DII 202). But all such gnomes leave an irreducible remainder of startling images, suggesting that they are fragments torn from only a dream of textbook poetics. Critics' redescriptions of these relations tend to be derivative, flattened-out stories of the way Kafka's writing arose and mattered for him. His work is the braille of a being that loads the rifts beneath its runes. Kafka's sense of the continuity of poetic desire and writing is at once the ink relation of script and the blood relation of birth, and thus he acknowledged all of his live, published works in a story called "Eleven Sons."[4] What is at stake for him is not encoding meanings in fiction but, simply put, writing—his last word. He writes as one who must write, whose works enact the craving for a final breath: "There is no having, only a being, only a state of being that craves the last breath, craves suffocation" (DF 37).

The animation of Kafka's writing self proceeds from a great depth, whence it is guided "above ground" into an "incredible spate of new things" (GW 263).[5] A good deal of this novelty is produced by pecu-

3. Friedrich A. Kittler, "Ein Erdbeben in Chile und Preußen," in *Positionen der Literaturwissenschaft: Acht Modellanalysen am Beispiel von Kleists "Das Erdbeben in Chile,"* ed. David E. Wellbery (Munich: Beck, 1985), p. 27 (translation mine, as are all translations not otherwise specified). Cf. Kittler's *Aufschreibesysteme 1800 . 1900* (Munich: Fink, 1985).

4. Toward the end of his life, when Kafka despaired of publication, he declared that the relation between him and his works was precisely not that of a family. But the metaphor, whether with a positive or negative value, makes the point of the "blood bond" between Kafka and his work (DI 134).

5. In his diaries Kafka wrote of his "great longing to write my state entirely out of me, write it into the depths of the paper just as it comes out of the depths of me" (DI 173).

liar devices of literary rhetoric, which in the past have been avoided by historians, since they pose special difficulties to interpretation. Kafka's distinctive tropes and strategies, such as "metamorphosed metaphors" and "monopolized" narrative style, appear to affirm the power to excite interpretation as the warrant of literature at the same time that they prevent this activity from reaching a conclusion. Indeed, wrote Kafka, his works are "scarcely tolerable, incapable of becoming history" (GW 263–64). In this book, however, I try to show that Kafka's rhetoric can be recovered as the enactment of the project of one who had to live his life as literature, in works bearing witness to this fate.

In modern literature the threat to meaning and its overcoming have a history of their own, which Kafka's literary past helps to define. The tradition of Kafka takes readers to Cervantes, Flaubert, and Nietzsche as writers who provoke a comparable disruption by such narrative strategies as framed narration and "veiled discourse," as well as by themes related to Kafka's own: the phenomenon of unwilled self-reversal, consternation between persons, the difficulty of conceiving of an individual life as rounding to a close.

The first part of this book deals with a few short works in which the basic figures of Kafka's thought and composition can be found most clearly—figures prominently informed by principles of resemblance and difference in a state of high tension. These are chiefly the tropes of metaphor and symbol on the one hand, allegorical allusion on the other. Their principles shape, moreover, the kinds of criticism that Kafka's works have attracted. This is to say, the works themselves construct, dramatize, and reject principles generating types of interpretation.[6] The figures of sameness and strangeness found in the earliest stories recur as patterning devices within the novels.[7]

6. Metaphor is constituted by a principle of resemblance over time, which is to say, by repetition despite disparity—the conditions enabling metaphor to function are fundamentally historical. The difference constituting Kafka's allusion includes the "mere difference" of metonymy, the "double difference" of chiasm, and the "interminable difference" of allegory. At times Kafka inverts the usual order of priorities. He does not appear to use the tropes of rhetoric (and their principles) as devices for the literary representation of experience. Rather, he operates with principles of resemblance and difference as prime reality, and writing, when scrupulously done, is the occasion of their greatest freedom and comprehensiveness of interaction.

7. In an unpublished paper "On Repetition," James Rolleston singles out "the drastically foreshortened second half of Das Urteil ('The Judgment'), the uncanny

Kafka's stories raise a great many general questions, which they rain like arrows into nearby fields. Three of these questions are particularly important for this book—they concern the possibility of literary history, the effect on readers of fictively enacted shocks to understanding, and what I call "prereading" or implied reading. When I needed other examples of these topics, I sought them in writers whose relation to Kafka was already instructive. Kafka made the choice easy. He was attracted to Flaubert more than to any other author, and the work he loved most was *Sentimental Education*.[8] In writing about this novel, I spend a considerable amount of time exclusively on its closing chapters. This procedure is justified by Kafka, who, in an astonishing diary entry, gave *Sentimental Education* the importance of the fifth book of Moses by connecting their endings: both works record the failure of a man to arrive at his goal—Moses, "not because his life is too short but because it is a human life" (DII 196). Meanwhile, the figure of Don Quixote rides through Kafka's fiction—through "Spain" the Promised Land of K.'s longed-for emigration from the world of *The Castle*,[9] through the parable "The Truth about Sancho Panza," and through other aphoristic fragments from the great posthumous volume *Dearest Father*. Finally, the valuable foil among philosophers is Nietzsche, whom Kafka read early: they are both to the same degree philosophers of ethics and rhetoric—of the intimate involvement of scruples and tropes—laying weight, when the choice could be made, on the first term. The essays on other writers in the second part of this book have therefore been importantly prompted by Kafka. This middle section (chiefly Chapters Six, Seven, and Eight) deliberately repeats, though with a difference, texts

---

repetition of the whipping scene in *Der Prozeß* (*The Trial*), the culminating death-in-life of the country doctor." Equally important are odd and marginal interferences by the narrator in an otherwise uniform perspectival structure.

8. See the major study by Charles Bernheimer, *Flaubert and Kafka: Studies in Psychopoetic Structure* (New Haven, Conn.: Yale University Press, 1982), and further his "Psychopoetik: Flaubert und Kafkas *Hochzeitsvorbereitungen auf dem Lande,*" in *Der junge Kafka,* ed. Gerhard Kurz (Frankfurt am Main: Suhrkamp, 1984), pp. 154-83. Albert Mingelgrun has compiled a register of salient points of contact between the lives, themes, and aesthetic obsessions of the two writers in "Kafka à la rencontre de Flaubert," *Europe* 49 (1971):168–78.

9. Gerhard Kurz, "Die Literatur, das Leben, und der Tod: Anmerkungen zu Cervantes und Kafka," *Archiv für das Studium der neueren Sprachen und Literaturen* 212 (1975): 265.

and issues discussed in the first part of the book, with the intention of giving them new emphasis from context. Thus, "Kafka, Nietzsche, and the Question of Literary History" (Chapter Six) takes up the matter of "Kafka's Double Helix" (Chapter Five); "Consternation: The Anthropological Moment in Prose Fiction (Cervantes, Flaubert, Kafka)" (Chapter Seven) takes up "The Hermeneutic of 'The Judgment'" (Chapter Two); and "The Curtain Half Drawn: Prereading in Flaubert and Kafka" (Chapter Eight) takes up the "*The Trial* / 'In The Penal Colony': The Rigors of Writing," which for reasons of continuity actually follows as Chapter Nine. An "Excursus" considers the relation of these chapters and concerns to the institution of Kafka studies.

This book itself generates a relation between two approaches to Kafka's work. On the one hand it proposes, as a necessary but insufficient condition of reading, Kafka's intelligibility—his symbolic images, his experiences of thought, the narrative of a life, a developing discourse—in individual works and in Kafka's career as a whole. On the other hand it lingers on Kafka's characteristic figures, the constituents of his rhetorical imagination—such as metamorphosed metaphors, fictive perspectives, and chiastic reversals—considering always the disruptive bearing, on the usual tale of a tale told, that such figures have. What effect, in other words, do Kafka's rhetorical decisions have on the reader's desire to read Kafka's work as an intelligible whole, modeled on a life story?

The outcome is not, and should not be, a single field or principle. Kafka described, typically, his attempts to write as seeking "that freedom of true description which releases one's foot from experience [*die einem den Fuß vom Erlebnis löst*]" (DI 100; Ta 104), but Gustav Janouch also records Kafka as asking, "The material must be worked on by the spirit [before it can develop into eternal art]? What does that mean? It means to experience, nothing else except to experience and to master what is experienced. That is what matters" (J 159). It therefore comes as no surprise that for Kafka "the point of view of art and that of life are different even in the artist himself" (DF 86)—a difference that I understand as itself varying. My chapters make various attempts to define the main modes of this relation, stressing on the one hand the sheer disparateness of art from human life and the deadly estrangement which that difference required Kafka to live, and on the other the exemplary wholeness of Kafka's life and the perfection and truthfulness of its representation in his work. The first mode stresses the impossibility of grasping Kafka's life and work in a systematic way; the second, the assured possibility of their recovery. But this is not to suggest that the major pattern of such a life lies in the therefore monotonous binary of Kafka's thought about art and life, its mainly two tones. Hölderlin's poetry of poetry (to take a counterexample) was, as Hölderlin perceived, too "regulated" in its tonality, consisting only of an upper and a subordinated tone. Kafka's "poetry" of writing—a poetics explicit in his letters and journals, and all-present though hidden in his stories—is one of the richest, most intricate, and varied ever composed, an entire diapason of values and connections ranging from the metaphysical heights of writing as a "new Kabbalah" to the technological flatlands of writing as a kind of strenuous use of the "parlograph" (a primitive dictaphone).[10] I try to reflect some of this variety within Kafka's continual thought about literature.

This book is rather parsimonious in the number of works of Kafka treated. That is because its choice of texts is determined by my previous work on Kafka's early stories and aphorisms—work done originally from the desire to begin at the beginning and to which I return in the hope of getting a better grasp. I have decided, however, not to add on many new chapters in the name of an unattainable comprehensiveness. Work done "a long time ago" promises the unity of whatever belongs to the past. Equally, in bringing older and newer essays together, I can generate something they never displayed in the past: namely, a common perspective—one which, I realize, has needed a good deal of rewriting to achieve. While doing this I regis-

10. Gerhard Neumann, "'Nachrichten vom "Pontus"': Das Problem der Kunst im Werk Franz Kafkas," *Franz Kafka Symposium—1983: Akademie der Wissenschaften und der Literatur zu Mainz,* ed. Wilhelm Emrich and Bernd Goldmann (Mainz: V. Hase & Koehler, 1985), p. 115. Neumann's discussion is indebted to Kittler, whose *Aufschreibesysteme* distinguishes between *Dichtung* and *Literatur*—the latter practice being importantly preoccupied with the materiality of script, especially the technical character of the modern writing medium, involving dictation, typewriting, telegraphy, etc. Kafka was fascinated with technological innovations; he is the author of the first published description of modern airplanes in German literature. See Joachim Unseld, *Franz Kafka—Ein Schriftstellerleben* (Frankfurt am Main: Fischer, 1984), p. 29.

tered, at first with alarm, the number of times certain passages from Kafka's confessional writings recur. More than twice I have set down his description of how his organism withered for the sake of writing and how his writing could treat of truthful things only "allusively." These apothegmatic rumors from the life of literature are elaborated and inserted into arguments dealing with the intensity of Kafka's devotion to writing as a way of being and his belief that, as a way of being, his writing could and did tell the truth. But couldn't these repetitions be eliminated? Kafka is eloquent on the subject of his writing, and it should not be difficult to satisfy the reader's reasonable expectation of novelty and inclusiveness by substituting other passages for ones already used.[11] I have finally decided to let them stand. There are too many advantages in doing so.

First, repetitive citation could be reckoned a fact about Kafka himself, whose sense of identity was, to an extraordinary extent, a constant. His "being," which he called by the unwonted *Schriftstellersein*, "being [as] a writer" (Br 385; L 333), was determined by the decision to write—a decision he described as not his to make but made for him. His fate obliged him to be the same thing always: the being who has to write and in many ways cannot, for he can never write well enough—cannot write with the wholeheartedness that writing requires, so as to say, having written: I am entirely that sentence.

Second, in having to reread the same passages, the patient reader will be rewarded, I think, by the consciousness of how inexhaustibly interesting they are. The effect of their recurrence in a variety of contexts is intensified power: they ray out light in more and more directions.

My final reason for keeping them is personal: this selection of citations necessarily has my signature—even though, as the mark of a collector and based on taste, it could sign equally, as Benjamin noted, ignorance as to how these objects were actually produced. Still, they sank into me when I first began to write about Kafka twenty years ago, and they keep returning. I cannot now imagine life without

11. In his letters and diary entries but not in his fiction. See Gerhard Neumann's elaboration of this distinction in his "Nachrichten vom 'Pontus.'" For a useful compilation of Kafka's texts on his own writing, see *Dichter über ihre Dichtungen: Kafka*, ed. Erich Heller and Joachim Beug (Munich: Heimeran, 1969).

them, and I want to see them again in all the places where they come up.

Like Hölderlin's persona in his early poem "To Quietness" ("An die Ruhe"), who builds with this very poem an "altar of thanks" to Rousseau, I would be happy if *mutatis mutandis* this book could mark my gratitude to Kafka. If there is anything good in it at all, that is what my gratitude to him is for.

STANLEY CORNGOLD

Princeton, New Jersey

Acknowledgments

The following material is used with permission. A short version of Chapter One appeared in *European Judaism* 8 (Summer 1974): 16–21. Chapter Two was published in slightly different form in *The Problem of "The Judgment": Eleven Approaches to Kafka's Story*, ed. Angel Flores (New York: Gordian Press, 1977), pp. 39–62. Chapter Three introduced Stanley Corngold, *The Commentators' Despair: The Interpretation of Kafka's "Metamorphosis"* (Port Washington, N.Y.: Kennikat Press, 1973), pp. 1–38; I have made a few changes. An early version of Chapter Four was published in the *Journal of the Kafka Society of America* 5 (December 1981): 23–31. Chapter Five originally appeared in *Literary Review* 26 (Summer 1983): 521–33, and is here much elaborated. A shorter version of Chapter Six was published in *Nietzsche: Literature and Values*, ed. Volker Duerr, Reinhold Grimm, and Kathy Harms, *Monatshefte* Occasional Volume no. 6 (Madison: University of Wisconsin Press, 1988), pp. 153–66. Chapter Seven appeared, much abbreviated, in *Literature and Anthropology*, ed. Jonathan Hall and Ackbar Abbas (Hong Kong: Hong Kong University Press, 1986), pp. 156–88. Chapter Eight was published in *The Comparative Perspective on Literature*, ed. Clayton Koelb and Susan Noakes (Ithaca: Cornell University Press, 1988), pp. 263–83. Several pages of Chapter Nine appeared as "The Question of the Law, The Question of Writing," in *Twentieth Century Interpretations of "The Trial,"* ed. James Rolleston (Englewood Cliffs, N.J.: Prentice-Hall, 1976), pp.

Acknowledgments

100–104. The substance of Chapter 12 was published as "Perspective, Interaction, Imagery and Autobiography: Recent Approaches to Kafka's Fiction," *Mosaic* 8, Special Issue on Literature and Ideas (Winter 1975): 149–66.

A chapter that is not included in this book but is of some importance to the argument is "The Author Survives on the Margin of His Breaks: Kafka's Narrative Perspective," in my *Fate of the Self: German Writers and French Theory* (New York: Columbia University Press, 1986), pp. 161–79.

I wish to thank my editors at Cornell University Press—especially Bernhard Kendler and Patricia Sterling—for having made the task of publishing this book so interesting.

> Ella si va, sentendosi laudare,
> Benignamente d'umiltà vestuta.

S.C.

Abbreviations for
Kafka Citations

The following abbreviations are used throughout the text and notes, followed by the appropriate page numbers.

A   *Amerika: A Novel*, trans. Edwin and Willa Muir. New York: Schocken, 1962. See R.

B   *Beschreibung eines Kampfes*, ed. Max Brod. Frankfurt am Main: Fischer, 1954. See DS and GW.

BF   *Briefe an Felice*, ed. Erich Heller and Jürgen Born. Frankfurt am Main: Fischer, 1967. See LF.

BM   *Briefe am Milena*, ed. Willi Haas. New York: Schocken, 1952. See LM.

Br   *Briefe, 1902–1924,* ed. Max Brod. Frankfurt am Main: Fischer, 1958. See L.

C   *The Castle,* trans. Willa and Edwin Muir. Harmondsworth, Middlesex: Penguin, 1966. See R.

DI   *The Diaries of Franz Kafka, 1910–1913,* trans. Joseph Kresh. New York: Schocken, 1948. See Ta.

DII   *The Diaries of Franz Kafka, 1914–1923,* trans. Martin Greenberg. New York: Schocken, 1949. See Ta.

DF   *Dearest Father,* trans. Ernst Kaiser and Eithne Wilkins. New York: Schocken, 1954. See H.

DS   *Description of a Struggle,* trans. Tania and James Stern. New York: Schocken, 1958. See B.

Abbreviations

E *Erzählungen*, ed. Max Brod, Frankfurt am Main: Fischer, 1946. See S.

GW *The Great Wall of China*, trans. Willa and Edwin Muir. New York: Schocken, 1960.

H *Hochzeitsvorbereitungen auf dem Lande und andere Prosa aus dem Nachlaß*, ed. Max Brod. Frankfurt am Main: Fischer, 1953. See DF.

J Gustav Janouch, *Conversations with Kafka*, trans. Goronwy Rees. New York: New Directions, 1971.

L *Letters to Friends, Family, and Editors*, trans. Richard and Clara Winston. New York: Schocken, 1977. See Br.

LF *Letters to Felice*, trans. James Stern and Elizabeth Duckworth. New York: Schocken, 1973. See BF.

LM *Letters to Milena*, ed. Willi Haas, trans. Tania and James Stern. New York: Schocken, 1953. See BM.

M *The Metamorphosis*, ed. and trans. Stanley Corngold. New York: Bantam Books, 1972. See E.

PP *Parables and Paradoxes*. German and English. New York: Schocken, 1961.

R *Die Romane: Amerika, Der Prozeß, Das Schloß*. Frankfurt am Main: Fischer, 1972.

S *The Complete Stories*, ed. Nahum Glatzer. New York: Schocken, 1971. See E.

SE *Sämtliche Erzählungen*, ed. Paul Raabe. Frankfurt am Main: Fischer, 1970.

T *The Trial*, trans. Willa and Edwin Muir. New York: Modern Library, 1956. See R.

Ta *Tagebücher*, ed. Max Brod. Frankfurt am Main: Fischer, 1951. See DI, DII.

Franz Kafka

The Necessity of Form

Introduction

Suppose Max Brod had executed Kafka's last will and testament.[1] His novels (*Amerika*, *The Trial*, and *The Castle*) and his confessional writings (his diaries, notebooks, and many letters) would have been lost forever. Kafka might be remembered as the author of seven very slim volumes of short stories and novellas. Or would he be remembered at all, and would his stories have achieved greater prominence than the prose of such contemporaries as Friedrich Adler, Wilhelm Schäfer, and Emil Strauß, whom Kafka read and admired?[2] Precision in cruelty and the impassive connection of the routine with the terrible, extraordinary event are qualities of other Expressionist writers and in general of the sensibility of central European literature in the first two decades of this century. As early as 1907, Max Brod assigned to Kafka a place alongside Heinrich Mann, Frank Wedekind, Gustav Meyrink, and Franz Blei in a "sacred group" of German writers "who adorn the

1. The immense irony of Kafka's last behest, asking Max Brod to destroy all the published work and many of the unpublished manuscripts, is that Kafka knew it would fall on deaf ears. Of all the faithless literary executors in the world, Kafka could have found no one less likely than Max Brod to execute such a will. In this matter Brod figures as Abraham: he defies the moral order of keeping faith with mankind in order to respond to what he takes to be a divine injunction to value supremely Kafka's poetic personality. To him Kafka incarnates at once the human and the sacred order.

2. At various places throughout his diaries, Kafka acknowledges the value of these writers and their works.

most varied sides of existence with their art and their cruelty."[3] It is easy to perceive the logic of this grouping, but the qualities that Kafka shares with Heinrich Mann and Gustav Meyrink do not go far toward explaining how the modern sensibility has become Kafkaesque[4] and how—as we learn to see more of what is in Kafka—modern literature, writing, and thought about writing will be grasped as Kafkaesque.[5]

Is Kafka's distinction, then, due chiefly to the salvaging of three unfinished novels whose transparency is the fortuitous result of the great horror of modern history—the technical application of political terror? This would be a standard and, I think, irreproachable literary judgment. In one's gratitude to Max Brod, one would slight his editorial liberties, pass swiftly over his allegorical and sentimental misreadings of the novels, and praise him for the rescue of *Amerika, The Trial, The Castle*: for holding up to the world a mirror of its cruelty, its deadly evasions, its crazy syntax, its hatred of ecstasy— and its only mute aspiration, for its voice speaks from the cage.

To hold to this view, however, is to restrict Kafka's work to the most accessible features of its scene and its rhetoric. Such bad dreams then predominate as the mechanical frenzy of the Hotel Occidental, the anaerobic antechambers of the Court, the brutish miasma of the taverns in the precincts of the Castle. We hear mainly the tergiversating rhetoric, the devilish confusions and hesitations of the officials, covering impatience and murder. These worlds, meanwhile, are registered with an odd attentiveness to detail and bewilderment at large

3. This sentence appeared in Brod's review of Franz Blei's play *Der dunkle Weg* (The dark way) in the Berlin newspaper *Die Gegenwart*, February 7, 1907. Gerhard Kurz assembles valuable information about the way modern central European writing begins in a mood empowering writing—the mood of the aesthetic movement; see *Traum-Schrecken: Kafka's literarische Existenzanalyse* (Stuttgart: Metzler, 1980). But Kafka's art serves not the adornment of the empirical person but rather its total reduction and extinguishing.

4. To what extent should Kafka be understood as having created his own reception? Or is his distinction more nearly the lucky harvest of a world grown exceptionally fertile in terror? Neither one. Kafka helps create the "description" of an experience of terror whose existence thereupon confirms his work for its clairvoyance. For further discussion of this question of authors and literary movements, see Chapter Ten.

5. Kafka's most marked contribution to modern art and culture is to the way in which the subject of writing has become Writing, the way in which reflection on the act of writing has become ontological, not psychological, ranging from metaphysical reference to technical aspects of its production.

2

by the hero in whose perspective the reader is lost; his wandering gaze creates a mood of anxious distraction.

If this is the usual account of Kafka's importance, it excludes too many features even of the work published in his lifetime, for many of his stories are (in Martin Greenberg's helpful definition) thought stories, not dream stories;[6] and the intensity with which ontological distinctions are made in a piece like "Josephine the Singer" would disappoint the reader of good will who had come to Kafka's last volume for a final arraignment (say) of judicial murder.

The standard picture of Kafka's achievement omits qualities different from his flair for bureaucracy, his ear for family language, and his *flaneur*'s sense of the humbling ugliness of places where city business is done; it omits more than his skill, as an obsessive exegete of his own constructions, in parodying aporias. These other, essentially moral and—in the perspective of an Unamuno, a Benjamin, or a Levinas—"anti-philosophical" powers[7] are vivid in the confessional writings, which suggest the *esprit de finesse* of a Jewish Pascal. Kafka's exertions as a judge of his experience are inspired by an "inner commandment [*das innere Gebot*]" not unlike a dream (DF 92–93; H 111). He is required to be the seriousness that reads his life as the instance or violation of a law of which he has only gleams. This seriousness informs what Elias Canetti calls Kafka's "compulsive sacralization" of places and states of mind—which amounts to a "sacralization of man. Every place, every moment, every aspect, every step of the way is serious and important and unique."[8] Kafka's life is required reading no matter how inauspicious and even when it mainly yields "filth." His great concern, transparent through his disclaimer, is to strive to answer to a supreme tribunal.[9]

He is always more, however, than the upright creature noting his

---

6. Martin Greenberg, *The Terror of Art: Kafka and Modern Literature* (New York: Basic Books, 1968).

7. I am grateful to Michael Metteer for this aperçu.

8. Elias Canetti, *Der andere Prozeß: Kafkas Briefe an Felice* (Munich: Hanser, 1969), p. 36.

9. Kafka wrote in a letter to his fiancée Felice Bauer, meaning to excoriate his own deceit, "I do *not* actually strive to be good, to answer to a supreme tribunal" (LF 545; my italics). That is because, he says, he really means to become the sole sinner who can parade his meanness before all the world without losing its love. But this premise belongs to the rhetoric of a letter aiming to drive Felice away..

own evasions. He is the writer who intends to bring to light a depth or hiddenness of background to experience—the irreducible strangeness of that other law. "Can it be," wrote Nietzsche, "that all our so-called consciousness is a more or less fantastic commentary on an unknown, perhaps unknowable, but felt text?"[10] Kafka's literary works constitute a commentary on the text of the law, embodying his life in them only as it comes under its jurisdiction. "Free command of the world at the expense of *its* laws," he wrote. "Imposition of *the* law. The happiness in obeying the law" (DII 199; my italics). "Mankind," he said to Gustav Janouch, "can only become a gray, formless, and therefore nameless mass through a fall from the Law which gives it form" (J 172). Kafka felt a quite audacious responsibility for establishing this law. Of his persona, called "He," he wrote: "He does not live for the sake of his personal life; he does not think for the sake of his personal thoughts. It seems to him that he lives and thinks under the compulsion of a family, which, it is true, is itself superabundant in life and thought, but for which he constitutes, in obedience to some law unknown to him, a formal necessity" (GW 269). Kafka's concern as a writer is the felt text supporting the palimpsest of experience, like the truth that Walter Benjamin saw, not as spread out in a fan but as lodged in its folds. In this sense Kafka's writing is the erasure of experience from the living letter of the law.

Canetti observed that "instead of offering his fiancée at least the promise of a body in place of his actual, unavailable body, Kafka puts in its place something [he calls] more truly his own: the fullness of things he has seen, things seen in the person he is courting: this fullness [of the seen] is his body."[11] To which must be added, above all, things written. In writing things seen—better, in writing what he sees through things—Kafka sublimates his body to a nakedness of breath and light. Writing to uncover the pure textual body of the law, Kafka grows beautiful. In an early diary entry, he glimpses this I: "Already, what protected me seemed to dissolve here in the city. I was beautiful in the early days, for this dissolution takes place as an apotheosis, in which everything that holds us to life flies away, but even in flying away illumines us for the last time with its human

10. Friedrich Nietzsche, *Morgenröte*, in *Werke in drei Bänden,* ed. Karl Schlechta (Munich: Hanser, 1954–56), 1:1095.
11. Canetti, *Der andere Prozeß,* p. 28.

light" (DI 28). The work of writing dissolves the complex of experience: art, says Kafka, is "a way of being dazzled by truth" (DF 41). The light set free by such "constructive destruction" (DF 103) of experience is the light of essential human life—the law: "The Man from the Country" comes "in the darkness . . . [to] perceive a radiance that streams inextinguishably from the door of the Law" (T 269). From such a light source the writer might powerfully snatch and focus a few gleams (DF 87), for, wrote Kafka, "by means of the strongest possible light one can dissolve the world" (DF 295).

It is, then, as the writer—writing in a condition of greatest anxiety and conscious always of the shame of distraction—that Kafka becomes the Bellarmin of his corpus.[12] At heightened moments even his inattentiveness is proof against banality; whatever he writes has exactly the kind and degree of rhetorical elegance signing spiritual beauty and force: "When I arbitrarily write a single sentence," Kafka noted, "for instance, 'He looked out of the window,' it already has perfection" (DI 45). Kafka makes live the lost question of genius: since it is not from labor, whence does this unflawed body of language and spirit come which fits a Kantian definition of beauty? It owes its distinction to the play of a style—and more: Kafka's prose uncovers the lost luminousness of the spiritual body; his writing is the music of the dissolution of what obstructed it. This work of clearing is quickly rewarded by Kafka's love of the word as a beautiful body—the sign, the letter, the printed text.[13]

*   *   *

Is there a coherent corpus of information constituting the law, a knowledge that could be recovered from Kafka's work as a whole? If there were one, how could it be obtained without reference to the longings of Kafka's physical body—in short, to events irreducibly personal and precisely for this reason inaccessible to "introspection"? Perhaps they can be recovered from events accessible to Kafka's biographers. Yet readers of Kafka's life tend to come away with a sense of gaping disproportion between the story of his empirical body and the

12. Bellarmin, the beautiful Arminius (or Hermann), is the idealized recipient of letters written by Hyperion, the eponymous Greek hero of Hölderlin's epistolary novel (1799).
13. Kafka was particularly preoccupied with the appearance—above all, with the print, the type-face—of his books.

language of its desires. His real life, it seems, has no other story to tell than the search for circumstances propitious for the leap out of it into the uncanny world of writing. At the beginning of this struggle, however, is the curse of one who from the start found himself outside the human stall while craving a simplicity of vision and nourishment within it. Kafka found consolation in thinking of himself as the "formal necessity" of a great family "superabundant in life" (GW 269). But what is it to be the merely formal condition of such abundance? Life, to be valued as "splendid" (DII 195), must be seen—and so it must be held off at a distance. But at that remove from the family table, a body could starve.

So strong, however, was Kafka's loyalty to the truth of separation that to a remarkable degree, for one who felt himself to be forever starving in the world and would indeed starve, he did not have to spend his life disengaging himself from involvements—professional, political, or erotic—into which he fell through the distractions of his body.[14] Between 1908 and his retirement in 1922 because of sickness, he worked in only one office (as a high-ranking civil servant at the Workmen's Accident Insurance Institute for the Kingdom of Bohemia in Prague). He did not join and then resign from parties or societies. If he did make and break marriage engagements, he twice broke off from the same woman—Felice Bauer—and his parting from her meant essentially only a change of addressee for his letters.[15] His biography is a repetition, a "marching double-time in place" (DI 157), of the longing for physical bliss within a mute social ritual—a longing at cross-purposes with the ascetic restraint of the writer's task that he had to take on almost from birth.[16] In this sense Kafka lived and believed he lived under the sign of a single metamorphosis, which

14. He mentions having admired six girls in a single summer and feeling guilty toward all of them. He was reproached, however, in only one instance—through a third person.

15. When, after a fashion, Kalka broke off relations with Felice in September 1913, he began writing letters of very much the same kind to Felice Bauer's friend Grete Bloch. His last letter to Felice is dated October 16, 1917; his splendid correspondence with Milena Jesenská began two years later. In 1919 he was also very briefly engaged to Julie Wohryzek, several months after meeting her in a pension in Silesia. His father's bitter opposition to the marriage contributed to Kafka's growing doubt and anxiety.

16. See Gerhard Neumann, *Franz Kafka, Das Urteil: Text, Materialien, Kommentar* (Munich: Hanser, 1981), p. 89.

finally condemned his body to the autonomy of starvation, and of which writing was the goad and exemplification. This is the story told by *The Metamorphosis* and "The Hunger Artist."[17]

Kafka's metamorphosis was continual and phased: it produced ascetic and participatory modes of life, varying the value and use of each of these for literature. But the revelation of contrary possibilities occurs so swiftly, oscillation is so much a constant, that through it Kafka achieves the consistency of a spinning top. "The constant variety of the forms it takes, and once, in the midst of it all, the affecting sight of a momentary abatement in its variations" (DII 229). If Kafka's writing and physical life do finally achieve the unity of a constantly humming strife, is it on the strength of their common estrangement from the norms of family? This is a compelling view—and one that has shaped the critical interpretation of Kafka's life and work.

Here, the consistency of both types of estrangement (of the life and of the work) and of their relation to one another suggests the possibility of a coherent recovery of Kafka. One could disclose, in Nietzsche's words, "the secret alphabet-script" of Kafka's bodily self in his work, especially in its literal aspect—its play with the body of the letter.[18] It is true that Kafka's physical life and work occur as types of separation, which, in their opposition to ordinary experience, could also appear to assert their unrecoverable strangeness. But a "German Romantic" way of dignifying such strangeness is to link it, by virtue of a Romantic horror of the ordinary, to a higher sort of life: "The world must be romanticized," writes Novalis, "so its original meaning will again be found. . . . By investing the commonplace with a lofty significance, the ordinary with a mysterious aspect, the familiar with the prestige of the unfamiliar, the finite with the semblance of infini-

---

17. Starvation frees the bourgeois body from its dependency on a nourishment doled out by others as part of a training in social unfreedom, whose hearth is the family table. Starving while it lives, the body is its own nourisher. The complementary illustration of such a freedom might be the vanishing of Kafka the artist—desireless, extinguished—into the perfection of a literary sign "free" of social purposes, aiming neither to explain the world nor otherwise to serve it. I have drawn such reflections from the lustrous and innovative work of Gerhard Neumann: e.g., "'Nachrichten vom "Pontus"': Das Problem der Kunst im Werk Franz Kafkas," in *Franz Kafka Symposium—1983: Akademie der Wissenschaften und der Literatur zu Mainz*, ed. Wilhelm Emrich and Bernd Goldmann (Mainz: V. Hase & Koehler, 1985).

18. Nietzsche, *Werke*, 1:1090.

ty, thereby I romanticize it."[19] In this sense literature is a raid on the absolute—what Kafka called an "assault on the last earthly frontier" (DII 202). Literature's estrangement from familiar life might therefore be an exact measure of its proximity to another but genuine life—a finer modulation of the lamentations of his body.

This idea, however, which assumes the goal of *Bildung*, is also the belief about which Kafka was most unsure. He did not know whether the other life to which writing "alluded" was the Promised Land or a precipice. This doubt identifies the main topic of his work: namely, the only questionable passage of literature to an authentic life, to an authenticity Kafka often translates, like Nietzsche, into a biologistic category—the life of an improved body. Gerhard Neumann's essay on the field of Kafka's "sliding paradox" discloses fundamentally different directions in the matter of the relation of this field to life: on the one hand it means to be the passage to an authentic life, on the other hand it carves out its own domain—a wilderness or borderland (*Grenzland*; T 548) of sheer strangeness.[20] Charles Bernheimer's *Flaubert and Kafka* makes an eminent contribution to this discussion by distinguishing between two kinds of writing or views of writing in Kafka: one, producing metaphors, generates an unstable field disrupting the vital, anaclitic bond; another aims to restore this lost connection.[21] Kafka's gnome can serve as a summary: "The point of view of art and that of life are different even in the artist himself" (DF 86).

Kafka, however, will make another, equally potent substitution for the extraordinary life that writing is about: writing is about death; it is the prayer of a dead man for "a real death"; it is eternal dying. But this death is conceived by writing, and hence, finally, writing is about the relation of writing . . . to itself. Tzvetan Todorov observes (following Blanchot): "When we write, we do merely that—the importance of the gesture is such that it leaves room for no other experi-

19. Novalis, *Fragmente des Jahres 1798*, no. 879, in *Gesammelte Werke*, 3:38. Quoted in *European Romanticism: Self-Definition*, ed. Lilian R. Furst (London: Methuen, 1980), p. 3.

20. Gerhard Neumann, "Umkehrung und Ablenkung: Franz Kafkas 'Gleitendes Paradox,'" in *Franz Kafka*, ed. Heinz Politzer (Darmstadt: Wissenschaftliche Buchgesellschaft, 1973).

21. Charles Bernheimer, *Flaubert and Kafka: Studies in Psychopoetic Structure* (New Haven, Conn.: Yale University Press, 1982).

ence. At the same time, if I write, I write about something, even if this something is writing. For writing to be possible, it must be born out of the death of what it speaks about; but this death makes writing itself impossible, for there is no longer anything to write. Literature can become possible only insofar as it makes itself impossible."[22]

The purpose of my chapters is to explore the various forms of life and of a lifelike death which Kafka's literary language enacts. Like the substrates of knowledge and morality in the transcendental ground of Kant's aesthetic judgment, they are in their root "intimately and obscurely" connected.[23]

22. Tzvetan Todorov, *The Fantastic: A Structural Approach to a Literary Genre*, trans. Richard Howard (Cleveland, Ohio: Press of Case Western Reserve University, 1973), p. 175.
23. Immanuel Kant, *The Critique of Judgement,* trans. James Creed Meredith (Oxford: Clarendon, 1952), p. 224.

PART I

Kafka's Career

Chapter One

"'You,' I Said . . .":
Kafka Early and Late

If Kafka was to such an extent entirely himself, even in the monotonous sense of having nothing in common with himself, this is even truer of the writer of the *Diaries*.[1] His language there neither develops nor declines: from the start it has found its voice, an elegant, otherworldly literalism; from the start it has closed with its own great themes, so that the relation of early to later parts of the *Diaries* is not the serial relation of beginning and end in narrative but the prefigurative relation of part to whole in the hermeneutic circle.

Kafka's intensity is present in an early diary entry, which reveals powers of analysis (especially the analysis of the inner life of writing) of so formidable a moral and metaphysical tendency that they can be assumed to inform the novels as well, although they are occulted there by different feats of social invention and rhetoric.[2] The entry, written sometime between July 19 and November 6, 1910, when Kafka was twenty-seven, is found on the seventh page of Kafka's German diaries (DI 22). It begins "'You,' I said" and consists mainly of a dialogue between speakers called "I" and "he" ("he" is later termed "this bachelor"). The venue is an open city street or alley, and the time, "really very late." Despite the fact that these voices issue out

1. Kafka warned Felice against "the monotonous blur of . . . [his] personality" (LF 211).
2. I find striking the distinction between the spiritual brilliance of the confessional writings and the novels' travesties of grayness.

of human bodies, it is hard to conceive of the speakers as empirical personalities; the relation of intention to bodily gesture is too odd or incoherent.

> "You," I said and gave him a little shove with my knee (at this sudden utterance some saliva flew from my mouth as an evil omen), "don't fall asleep!"
> "I'm not falling asleep," he answered, and shook his head while opening his eyes. . . .
> "It's really very late," I said. I had to smile a little and in order to conceal it I looked intently into the house. [DI 22–23]

This house will be crucial: there a gathering is taking place which "I" wishes to join. The possibility of his "ascending" is the first important subject of the conversation. The bachelor declares that "I" could try to go up the stairs, but it is pointless; if he does go up, he will soon enough find himself back on the street. On the other hand, he says that "I" should not hesitate on his account.

"I" does, however, hesitate; it matters enormously to him whether or not the bachelor is telling the truth. The bachelor has specified the danger of the ascent, and "I" may be identified and rejected from a place of ineffable splendor. When the bachelor next reveals that, indeed, he has not been telling the truth, "I" finds his voice. He speaks the speech that dominates the entire dialogue—an articulation of the differences between the bachelor and himself, elaborated in a web of images and categories powerfully prefiguring the discourse of existential thought.[3] To this harangue the bachelor replies with a feeble

---

3. I write this *pace* Theodor Adorno, who in "Notes on Kafka," *Prisms,* trans. Samuel and Shierry Weber (London: Spearman, 1967), pp. 245, 248, considers as "existentialism" and of little account most of what has been written on Kafka, for it fails to respond to "the principle of literalness as criterion." Gerhard Neumann, too, in "Umkehrung und Ablenkung: Franz Kafkas 'Gleitendes Paradox,'" in *Franz Kafka,* ed. Heinz Politzer (Darmstadt: Wissenschaftliche Buchgesellschaft, 1973), p. 508, identifies as a "misunderstanding" the view that "Kafka's work belongs in the sphere of Existenzphilosophie." He does, however, suggest that its concern for a "more primordial logic" of reversal and slippage might "show the traces of existential thought." An important thrust of Gerhard Kurz's *Traum-Schrecken: Kafka's literarische Existenzanalyse* (Stuttgart: Metzler, 1980) is, as its title suggests, the fundamental kinship of Kafka's work with existentialist thought and Expressionist poetry. This is a view I share. See my "Angst und Schreiben in einer frühen Aufzeichnung Kafkas," in *Franz Kafka Symposium,* ed. Maria Luise Caputo-Mayr (Berlin: Agora, 1978), p. 60: "From the outset Kafka's work is saturated with fundamental existentialist themes like anxiety, guilt, selfhood, interpretation, fiction."

complaint about his solitude. "I" thereupon withdraws from the dialogue. At the close, his words appear without quotation marks; the I has become a persona virtually identical with the narrator. And it is this persona that plainly declares the bachelor to be a menace to life.

What is the light that glances off this grimacing text?[4] What can it be if not, in part, rays scattered from the source of Kafka's greatest concern in 1910: the possibility—indeed, the necessity—of his destiny as a writer, his great intimation, his hope?[5] For in 1910 Kafka could look back on at least a dozen years of literary activity that had not gone entirely without recognition. In 1907 he had written the novel-fragment "Wedding Preparations in the Country"; and before 1908 he had composed various prose sketches, several of which appeared in the magazine *Hyperion* in 1908 and were subsequently to appear in the volume *Meditation* in 1912. Some pieces mentioned in his diaries as part of a "mountain," a "mass," were avowedly destroyed by Kafka, and others have been lost. But enough of his literary ambition had been realized for Max Brod to assign Kafka in 1907—before he had published a line, yet not as a joke—that "sacred" place alongside Heinrich Mann, Wedekind, Meyrink, and Blei.

For Kafka, however, writing was always an ordeal. Not to write was to risk going mad from the vapidness of experience, but to write was perhaps to discover that here too lay only a devilish seduction. It was crucial to contend with literature. Thus, in 1910, after "five months of my life during which I could write nothing that would have satisfied me . . . it occurs to me to talk to myself again" (DI 12). With these words (preceded by a few paragraphs) Kafka begins the *Diaries*. The purpose of his diaries is therefore marked out from the start: to articulate a self in order to liberate writing, but only that self and as much of that self fitted to the purpose of liberating writing. "My condition is not unhappiness . . . not weakness, not fatigue, not another interest—so what is it then? That I do not know this is probably connected with my inability to write." To get to the bottom of it, Kafka determines that "every day at least one line should be trained on me, as they now train telescopes on comets. And if then I

4. This light is Kafka's image for what is true. "Our art is a way of being dazzled by truth: the light on the grotesquely grimacing retreating face is true, and nothing else" (DF 41).

5. Kafka wrote his fiancée several years later: "I have no literary interests, but am made of literature. I am nothing else, and cannot be anything else" (LF 304).

should appear before that sentence once, lured by that sentence . . ." (DI 12).

These passages constitute a starting point. In one sense Kafka—an "I"—already possesses himself (he identifies the "I" as perplexed, as ignorant of its state). But in a more important sense, he does not possess himself (he does not know what this state is). Now it is at "me"—the unknown state—that lines shall be aimed; and as aiming implies an aimer, the initial division is repeated: at an obscure astral referent a detective authorial consciousness aims sentences. Its purpose is to draw into existence a new modality of itself as a reader, a watcher of the skies, which will instantly vanish into the writer.

These sentences, it is important to stress, do originate from an "I." The subject exists apart from the writing self if only as the consciousness of a lack—of an empirical state that is not yet evident. It exists practically as the intention to deploy words to shape this lack or lure shape into it. The purposive character of this language distinguishes it from the language that is supposed to arise after this need has been filled in. This first language, the psychological language of the ego, has a purely instrumental value. The literary language that this tool means to liberate has no assigned use value except to attest unavoidably to the history that precedes it—namely, to the merely instrumental and incomplete character of its precondition of empirical self-possession. Literary language here asserts the insufficiency of the existential (*existentiell*) project, never mind that the project is successful in luring hither the empirical personality and even in incorporating it.[6] On the other hand, the state of mind Kafka suffers or enjoys in

6. "Literature does not fulfill a plenitude but originates in the void that separates intent from reality. The imagination takes its flight only after the void, the inauthenticity of the existential project, has been revealed; literature begins where the existential demystification ends" (Paul de Man, *Blindness and Insight: Essays in the Rhetoric of Contemporary Criticism*, rev. 2d ed. [Minneapolis: University of Minnesota Press, 1983], pp. 234-35). During most of his life, Kafka regarded empirical self-reflection as by and large a vacuous enterprise—especially from the standpoint of writing fiction. In empirical self-reflection, language is used as a tool. Where its use breaks off is a matter of chance, since what is certain is that it cannot achieve its end. To do so would be to coincide with its object, but it cannot coincide with the empirical or any other kind of self, which is not an object but an agency of transformation. "With respect to language," writes Claude Vigée, "one can hold two positions. . . . Either one views language as a tool for doing work—in this sense, language, exactly like other things, will, in a certain finite sense, work and even work very well, but at this point it is done with. That is the finitude of language, which makes no further claim; at the end of the

poetic activity has a nonintentional character: in a word that he will invent later, it is a state of being, *Schriftstellersein*, being as a writer; but it falls out of an order of uses. The diary text cited above, which just precedes the story "'You,' I said . . . ," is exemplary: it shows Kafka wishing to be cured of his "neurasthenia" in order to write; he does not write stories for self-help.

It therefore becomes inevitable to connect the "I" of the story "'You,' I said . . ." to the subject that, knowing its ignorance of its hidden side, employs dialogical language in order to precipitate a language of fiction meant to exceed itself. Its task is metamorphosis. The genre of the story is therefore mixed—and modern: via the act of writing it enacts in fact and in its topic fictively reenacts the difficulty of a subject cut off from knowledge of its state—a self that then gradually identifies its state and frees itself to write. I connect the "you" or bachelor figure to the unknown factor, a negative hidden possibility of the "I." Certainly, the "I" of the story does consistently project its interlocutor as unknown. Thus "I" says to the bachelor: "If I just knew definitely that you were being sincere with me [were telling me the truth, *daß du aufrichtig zu mir bist*]. . . . But how could I even tell whether you were sincere with me [were telling me the truth, *ob du aufrichtig zu mir bist*]?" (DI 24; Ta 18). Furthermore, since the "I" aims to liberate writing by overcoming the resistance of its anti-self, it follows that the basic sense of the bachelor must be that mode of the self which hinders (genuine) writing, whose being is resistant to articulation.[7] He cannot literally be part of writing, even of the language of introspection; he might be glimpsed through the telescope, but he is not part of the telescope. The bachelor can thus enter writing only as a paradox or a lie, as something basically unin-

---

day, one stands there with it, alone, like a beggar. . . . Or one can use the entire structure of a language as a means of resurrection. A means too, but for another end: the resurrection of ourselves from out of this finitude—this immobility" (*Heimat des Hauches: Gedichte und Gespräche* [Bühl-Moos: Elster, 1985], pp. 139-40). That is why Kafka's diary, which confessedly arises as the project to get hold of the empirical self and hence to use language as a tool, intends to abandon its project as swiftly as possible so as to become literature. It wishes to become a site in which work arises that is precisely not "psychology." Kafka had a horror of psychology, which he likened to a dog chasing its tail. Psychologizing, the hunter Gracchus becomes a butterfly.

7. Chapters Four and Twelve discuss further the question of the necessary distortion of the truth of whatever can emerge in Kafka's narrative perspective.

telligible. And indeed these characteristics of the bachelor are evident in the piece: the bachelor is defined as a being frozen in the obliviousness of an early event—an experience of his "depth"—and the persistence with which he remains unconscious of his depth defines him as a "patched-up existence," as "no better than some sort of vermin" (DI 25, 23).

These images define the bachelor—but of course they do so only elliptically and allusively. For, as Kafka wrote, nothing outside the phenomenal world can be named even approximately by metaphors (*vergleichsweise*; H 40). The obstacle to writing precedes phenomenality, is intrinsically hidden, and hence cannot come to light except as what it is not. It appears as an excessively distorted figure. Thus the "I" hastens to add: "But forgetting [or obliviousness] is not the right word here" (DI 26), conjuring, then, other qualities of the bachelor. These images, however, together with earlier ones, all converge on the meaning of radical isolation, heterogeneousness, and obscurity. The man who without any choice in the matter "lie[s] here in the gutter . . . stowing away the rain water" (DI 23), "avoid[ing] the influence of other people," with "teeth only for his own flesh and flesh only for his own teeth" (DI 24), is finally proscribed; he is declared to stand "once and for all outside our people, outside our humanity . . . he has only the moment, the everlasting moment of torment" (DI 26). By the end of the piece he has become a "parasite" and then, finally, a "corpse" (DI 28).

Consider again this identification of the bachelor as the opaque obstacle to the life of writing. One is at once reminded of the kindred nonbeings who will afterward figure in Kafka's stories—the crossbred lambcat and Odradek and especially the "monstrous vermin" of *The Metamorphosis*. The latter is indeed radically unintelligible: he is not meant to conjure a creature of some definite kind. This would be to experience the vermin the way the cleaning woman does who calls him "old dung beetle" But "to forms of address like these Gregor would not respond; they do not reflect his uncanny identity, which cannot be grasped in an image" (M 45). Indeed, the bachelor of "'You,' I said . . ." is a prefiguration of the transmogrified Gregor Samsa; he too is described as requiring for his existence certain "ceremonies amid which I can barely keep on crawling," again, "no better than some sort of vermin" (DI 23).

Other details of the piece confirm this analysis. Interesting evidence comes from the text that Max Brod prints as a variant of this diary entry (Ta 691–92). The variant distributes differently the characteristics of the speakers. To the bachelor's question, "How long have you been in the city?" "I" replies, "*Five* months" (DI 29; my italics). Now it is not incidental that it has also been for five months that Kafka has existed as his anti-self, the nonwriter (this fact, we recall, prompted him to begin his journal). Thus the "I," an explicit projection of Kafka's will to liberate writing, has spent five months in the city, the habitat of the bachelor, where writing cannot survive.

What emerges is that the bachelor—and by implication the bachelor figure abounding in Kafka's work around this period—is by no means an immediate portrait of Kafka's social personality, the alleged futile outcast from the joys of family. The bachelor is a figurative constellation, born out of anxiety and steeped in anxiety, a monster produced from the copulation of writing and nonwriting. It can be understood only as part of a general structure necessarily entailing anxiety—the existence of literature as a domain altogether different from life, inscribing into resistant nature the hollow cipher of its itinerary: signature, womb, or wound. Literature gives birth to a new mode of being and—more visibly in this story—to a new mode of nonbeing, its own intrusive negation, the horrible complement of *Schriftstellersein*: namely, *Nicht-Schriftstellersein-können*.

Strange and mostly negative as these formulations may sound, they are compelled by the imagery with which in "'You,' I Said . . ." Kafka describes the genesis of the bachelor. This genesis is not to be understood as the metaphor of an empirical event but as the narrative of a structure of relations. The bachelor is defined by his blockage of a primordial situation corresponding to the origin of literature. The situation is one of the discovery of the "depth" of a literary existence, "the way one suddenly notices an ulcer on one's body that until this moment was the least thing on one's body—yes, not even the least, for it appeared not yet to exist and now is more than everything else that we had bodily owned since our birth" (DI 26).

The experience of the nonbeing of bodily life is the dialectical adjunct of literature, which Kafka will later call "the tremendous world I have in my head" (DI 288). The original assertion of literature displaces the empirical self: "If until now our whole person had been oriented upon the work of our hands, upon that seen by our eyes, heard by our ears, upon the steps made by our feet, now we suddenly turn ourselves entirely in the opposite direction [into an element wholly opposed, *ins Entgegengesetzte*], like a weather vane in the mountains" (DI 26; Ta 21).[8] With this revelation of what may well be seen as the "guilt" that Heidegger too defines as the "null basis of existence," everything is terribly changed.[9] One's course henceforth can be only to initiate an act arising from this experience. If it were only to have "run away . . . even in this latter direction," it would still be to move in a way requiring a sort of exquisite balance—in Kafka's phrase, forever after being "on the tips of one's toes" (DI 16). But here the bachelor originates as the negative of this response: he is the primordial failure to respond to this experience except in a way that Kafka describes figuratively as a lying-down, a freezing, a submission, and a forgetfulness. The bachelor's new element is a nullity proportional to writing; he exists as the refusal to acknowledge his initial failure. He beds down, oblivious, in the nothingness that results from the original dislocation of literature: he domesticates anxiety.

The equation of literature with a basic dislocation of bodily life, originating a hollowness "now more than everything else that we had bodily owned since our birth" (DI 26), is confirmed by a later diary entry that explicitly links the ideal of writing with continual withering:

> When it became clear in my organism that writing was the most productive direction for my being to take, everything rushed in that direction and left empty all those abilities which were directed toward the joys of sex, eating, drinking, philosophical reflection and above all music. I atrophied in all these directions. This was necessary because the totality of my strengths was so slight that only collectively could they even halfway serve the purpose of my writing. Naturally, I did not find this purpose independently and consciously, it found itself. [DI 211]

The bachelor is the figure for the refusal to acknowledge the ontological guilt of atrophy in all directions.

8. See Chapter Five.

9. Martin Heidegger, *Being and Time*, trans. John MacQuarrie and Edward Robinson (New York: Harper & Row, 1962), p. 331.

If Kafka is to live, it is crucial for him to conceive his own emptiness not as sheer sacrifice but as potential exchange. His ability to sustain the superior self as anything except erosion, however, is uncertain. As such the bachelor grows more menacing. Two years later Kafka writes:

> My talent for portraying my dreamlike inner life has thrust all other matters into the background; my life has dwindled dreadfully, nor will it cease to dwindle. Nothing else will ever satisfy me. But the strength I can muster for that portrayal is not to be counted upon: perhaps it has already vanished forever, perhaps it will come back to me again, although the circumstances of my life don't favor its return. Thus I waver, continually fly to the summit of the mountain, but then fall back in a moment. Others waver too, but in lower regions, with greater strength; if they are in danger of falling, they are caught up by the kinsman who walks beside them for that very purpose. But I waver on the heights; it is not death, alas, but the eternal torments of dying. [DII 77]

This hesitation, this wavering, stripped of its moments on the heights, is the life of the bachelor: a perpetual nostalgia for what has been lost. What he succeeds in recapturing this way is "his former property only in seeming"—once his and lost. He thus exacerbates the process of universal dissolution, is perpetually in pursuit of what a dissolving world has ineluctably dissolved of him. "He has only one thing always: his pain; in all the circumference of the world no second thing that could serve as a medicine; he has only as much ground as his two feet take up, only as much of a hold as his two hands encompass, so much the less, therefore, than the circus trapeze artist . . . who still has a safety net hung up for him below" (DI 26–27).

The predicament of the writer is that he cannot muster strength from literature as the immediate clarity of a sensation. "The inner world can only be experienced, not described" (DF 65). The "depth" does not assure the plenitude of literature but an anxious absence or nullity confirmed by its image: "And this depth I need but feel uninterruptedly for a quarter of an hour and the poisonous world flows into my mouth like water into that of a drowning man" (DI 25). This sense of nullity is identical with anxiety. Years later, in 1922, in a letter to Max Brod, Kafka will write a definitive testament to literature: Writing is "the reward for serving the devil," a service that "take[s] place in the nether parts which the higher parts no longer know, when one writes one's stories in the sunshine. Perhaps there are other forms of writing, but I know only this kind; at night, when fear [anxiety, *Angst*] keeps me from sleeping" (L 333–34; Br 384). After twelve years of service the connection of writing and anxiety, except for the somewhat darker tonality, has not changed; for in 1910 Kafka wrote to Max Brod, a few months after composing "'You,' I said . . .": "This being on my own heels is still a joy that warms me— for it stirs in me that general excitement [anxiety, *Unruhe*] which produces the only possible equilibrium" (L 70; Br 68). This joy and activity nevertheless import a turn from life so radical that Kafka will name it again and again with the imagery of death. Thus he writes to Felice Bauer: "My attitude to my writing . . . is unchangeable; it is a part of my nature, and not due to temporary circumstances. What I need for my writing is seclusion, not 'like a hermit,' that would not be enough, but like the dead. Writing, in this sense, is a sleep deeper than that of death" (LF 279). Accompanying a movement so deeply turned away from life is the anxiety that can be experienced as the pure signature of literature or else be allowed its frigid spawn—a being whose whole meaning is to resist further metamorphosis. This is principally the bachelor, the figure for the misery of nonbeing.

Given this exegetic structure, many other elements of the story come into focus. The house into which the "I" is reluctant to enter cannot but mean, in Henry James's phrase, the house of art: "From that company," says the "I," "I promise myself everything that I lack, the organization of my strength, above all" (DI 24). The phrase almost certainly prefigures the passage above (DI 211) in which Kafka speaks of writing as the organizing principle of his powers. Quite consistently, the "I" terms this scene a place of metamorphosis. That the bachelor, but not the "I," sees the house and its society as a party—its joy the tipsiness of wine, its light the brilliance of chandeliers—is a grand joke and one that makes perfect sense. To see writing as a kind of superior public life, as glory and power in reward for lesser sacrifices, is exactly the perspective best calculated to hinder this commitment. The bachelor exacerbates and arrests every anxiety generated in the self by the movement of literature.

Kafka battles for a stand. To choose literature over life is in principle to risk empowering its anti-self, anxiety at an excruciating standstill. But we know the outcome, as he then did not: "The tremendous world that I have in my head. But how free myself and free it without being torn to pieces. And a thousand times rather be torn to pieces than retain it in me or bury it. That, indeed, is why I am here, that is quite clear to me" (DI 288). At the close of this story, the "I" breaks off from his anti-self, the task of definition having been accomplished, for a time. I cannot agree with Heinz Politzer's reading of this conclusion as a fatigued merging of the figures of artist and bachelor.[10] The project should not be denied its momentary elation: the possibility of a "little attempt at independence" is realized; Kafka recognizes the bachelor for the death he implies. This victory emerges in the gradual concentration throughout the story of powers of language in the "I" and of an ever drearier everyday rhetoric in the bachelor. This movement comes to a head at the close. Here it is no longer the ruminating ego but literature that finds its voice. It conceives an ecstatic image to celebrate itself amid the devastation it inflicts or, more, amid the tribute it obtains even from the life it devastates: "Already, what protected me seemed to dissolve here in the city. I was beautiful in the early days, for this dissolution takes place as an apotheosis, in which everything that holds us to life flies way, but even in flying away illumines us for the last time with its human light" (DI 28).

*   *   *

What Kafka states in his confessional writing—information about his desire for an inhuman bliss—he enacts and evokes in writing fiction. Confessional writing is the immediate form of his flight from anxiety; fiction comes about as the transformation of anxiety into ecstasy. This instant marks the metamorphosis of one sort of self-loss into another.

10. Heinz Politzer, *Franz Kafka: Parable and Paradox* (Ithaca: Cornell University Press, 1962), p. 45.

Chapter Two

The Hermeneutic
of "The Judgment"

> For he and his property are not one, but two, and whoever destroys
> the connection destroys him at the same time.
>
> FRANZ KAFKA, *Diaries* (1910)

"The Judgment" is the only prose work of ten pages in world literature which, though not belonging to a sacred or classical canon, has
inspired in the West alone nearly two hundred visible commentaries.[1]
The scandal of "The Judgment" prompts reflection on its distinctive
power to compel interpretation. This power emerges as a paradoxical
indifference and generosity. As the story draws readings to itself, it
makes room in every instance for one more reading; its precincts are
crowded, but no interpreter has ever been turned away for lack of a
gate kept open uniquely for him or her.

To read "The Judgment" is to experience a force like that (for
Adorno) of an onrushing locomotive. "Each sentence of Kafka's says
'interpret me . . . ,'" and this is nowhere so much the case as in the
story whose title "Das Urteil" means (in philosophical language)
"The Sentence." "Through the power with which Kafka commands
interpretation," Adorno writes, "he collapses aesthetic distance. He

---

1. Doubling, in ten years, my 1977 count, this statistic is in line with the claim
that more critical literature is published on Kafka each year than on any other writer
except Shakespeare.

24

demands a desperate effort from the allegedly 'disinterested' observer of an earlier time, overwhelms him, suggesting that far more than his intellectual equilibrium depends on whether he truly understands; life and death are at stake."[2]

Precisely this demand, and these stakes, make up the subject matter of "The Judgment." The force with which the story exacts interpretation is the force with which a sentence strikes the hero, Georg Bendemann. Powerless to interpret his sentence—to swerve—he accedes and is driven out of his father's room into the street and to his death by drowning. This cautionary fable identifies the force it produces as the force that here destroys the overwhelmed subject. It warns, as it were, against a like submission: the assaulted reader must turn and sentence what in himself or herself is the willing accessory to the verdict. Readers who seize their freedom to interpret execute the naive reader in themselves and approximate the narrator of "The Judgment," who survives the execution he has arranged—survives specifically in identifying the joy and brute power of the *Verkehr*, the erotic upsurge and infinite traffic of the concluding sentence.[3]

The other side of the force compelling interpretation is a certain poverty that begs for this supplement. "The Judgment," wrote Kafka to Felice, six weeks after he had finished the story, "is somewhat wild and meaningless" (LF 86–87). The following year he wrote, "Can you discover any meaning in 'The Judgment'—some straightforward, coherent meaning that one could follow? I can't find any, nor can I explain anything in it" (LF 265). The work displays to Kafka its

2. Theodor W. Adorno, "Notes on Kafka," *Prisms*, trans. Samuel and Shierry Weber (London: Spearman, 1967), p. 246.

3. For one instant, in the words of George Steiner, "eros and language mesh: . . . intercourse and discourse, copula and copulation . . . , the seminal and the semantic functions" (*After Babel: Aspects of Language and Translation* [New York: Oxford University Press, 1975], p. 39). Steiner, thinking generally about the interpenetration of "human sexuality and speech," declares, "Eros and language mesh *at every point*" (my italics). The aim of Kafka's story, however, is to project a voice that speaks with ejaculatory pride only at a special moment and from a special place, upon the death of the protagonist. According to Max Brod, Kafka said that while writing the last line of the story he "had thought of a strong ejaculation" (*Franz Kafka: A Biography*, trans. G. Humphreys Roberts [New York: Schocken, 1947], p. 129). The word "thought" here is, however, as important as "ejaculation." For a rich discussion of sexuality and writing in "The Judgment" and in *The Castle*, see Charles Bernheimer, *Flaubert and Kafka: Studies in Psychopoetic Structure* (New Haven, Conn.: Yale University Press, 1982), pp. 139-227.

restless, unsettled character, its anxiety, as it wavers in what Adorno calls the "abyss" between literal and signifying moments. Its anxiety will not permit it—as Edouard Mörike wrote of a work of art—to shine and seem ecstatic in itself.[4] A story that invites so much interpretation can have inspired the production of meaning only as a function of its avoidance of meaning. It produces in every case a reading self who, like the narrator, must interpret to survive—a self that does so by executing the naive reader in itself. Beyond this the story produces a theorist reader who interprets the story on the very basis of its unsettled character.

If, though, "The Judgment" stages the force with which it exacts interpretation, it cannot identify its avoidance of meaning so directly. It does approach an indication of this kind through its allegory of character. There is a sort of refusal of meaning in the stubborn silence and withdrawal of the Russian friend.[5] Such a refusal is also implied, though privatively, in Georg's bad faith and in the lies he writes to his friend. But no single character in the work can communicate the strong sense of a refusal of meaning, for—according to at least one important critical tradition—such a withholding is conceivable only as the intention of a *literary* text: that is, as the act of a consciousness wholly transparent to itself which knows that as a consciousness it cannot express itself.[6] There can be no such consciousness dramatized in this work, however, because, with the exception of the final sen-

4. Edouard Mörike, "Auf eine Lampe," *Sämtliche Werke* (Munich: Hanser, 1964), p. 85.

5. Bernheimer has plainly identified the Russian element of the friend, via a diary entry of Kafka's, as "the very absence of representation." Kafka wrote: "The infinite attraction of Russia. It is best represented not by Gogol's troika but by the image of a vast, unoverseeable river of yellowish water on which waves—but not too high ones—are everywhere tossing. Wild, desolate heaths upon its banks, blighted grass. But nothing can represent it; rather everything effaces it" (DII 115). Bernheimer notes: "Just as [in a letter to Felice of June 2, 1913] Kafka speaks of the friend as 'hardly a real person,' so he sees the blighted grass of the Russian heaths as an image obscuring an essential absence. The friend's existence is Russian only insofar as his image is effaced" (*Flaubert and Kafka*, p. 170).

6. This critical tradition is neo-Kantian, which is concerned with marking out a unique domain for aesthetic language apart from cognitive and moral language on the strength of the analogy it posits between a literary text and a type of consciousness. See, e.g., Georg Lukács's "Die Subjekt-Objekt Beziehung in der Ästhetik," esp. as discussed by Paul de Man in *Blindness and Insight: Essays in the Rhetoric of Contemporary Criticism*, rev. 2d ed. (Minneapolis: University of Minnesota Press, 1983), pp. 41–44.

tence, the leading perspective is supplied by Georg, who simply takes for granted the expressiveness of his meaning. He does not know the "feeling of falsity . . . while writing" which Kafka painfully registered some months before composing "The Judgment" and which prompted him to long "to write all my anxiety entirely out of me, write it into the depths of the paper just as it comes out of the depths of me" (DI 173). Instead, Georg speaks glibly of "real news [authentic communication, *eigentliche Mitteilungen*]" (S 78; E 54), even as something he will not exchange with his friend. His concern is not the truth of what one could say but the shrewdness of what one ought to say. For him, the impossibility of communication is a question of social tact. Yet it is precisely Georg who, in the course of writing his meaning to his friend and then stating his meaning to himself, tells lies.

He lies to himself that "there was nothing to hinder" his friend from returning home and renewing all his old friendships (S 77). For Georg has registered his friend's own statement that "he was now out of touch with commerce in his native country," and Georg has also noted the possibility that his friend would be oppressed at home "through force of circumstances"—the circumstance especially that he would no longer find himself in an easy relation with his old acquaintances (S 78). Georg lies once again when he writes his friend that he will acquire in Georg's fiancée a "genuine friend" and when he adds with conviction that "there are many reasons" to prevent his friend from visiting the couple even briefly (S 80). Indeed, he lies even to his father when he agrees that he has "changed [his] mind" as a result of "thinking . . . over" the matter of informing his friend of his engagement; in fact he has reacted directly to the importunities of his fiancée (S 82).

Later on in the book, de Man writes: "Unmediated expression is a philosophical impossibility . . . [but] literature . . . is the only form of language free from the fallacy of unmediated expression. . . . A work of fiction asserts, by its very existence, its separation from empirical reality, its divergence, as a sign, from a meaning that depends for its existence on the constitutive activity of this sign. . . . These texts . . . this kind of consciousness . . . does not result from the absence of something, but consists of the presence of a nothingness. Poetic language names this void with ever renewed understanding. . . . This persistent naming is what we call literature" (pp. 9, 11, 17-18).

The father, meanwhile, is no more lucid, to himself and to the reader, than the son. He is presented in the convulsed perspective of Georg; the father's consciousness is inscrutable.

"The Judgment" therefore withholds any direct presentation of the knowledge that it is "repudiating expression" (Adorno's phrase). It keeps inexplicit, maintains as the inexplicit, the noncoincidence of truth and language—the view that truth uttered is language and hence no longer truth. The story allegorizes its silencing of whole meaning mainly in the noisy figure of the lie. The lie, however, is central.

In its fullest sense, as the solicitation of falsity, the lie is another name for the "peculiar relation that had developed between [Georg and his Russian friend] in their correspondence [*das besondere Korrespondenzverhältnis*]" (S 79; E 56). Their writing never comes close to truth telling; the point is dramatically illustrated in the father's image of the friend crumpling Georg's letters unopened. But their failure is otherwise apparent. For whether or not the friend reads these letters, he could not understand a writing that does not make sense, and Georg's text, a literature of self-justification, aims to conceal and suppress sense. Georg's meaning remains rigorously hidden from himself, the correspondent. But if there is to be such a thing in principle as a coherent interpretation of this story, one must conclude that it is exactly this meaning which rises up in the scene that issues from its suppression, even if only virtually, as that sense which is death to hide.

The field of the interpretation of "The Judgment" is the force with which it exacts interpretation and the abyss of the meaning it conceals. These terms have degraded counterparts within the story in Georg's inability to oppose his sentence and in his dissimulation. The latter terms are related as types of interpretative activity. The meaning that Georg's letter masks compels his intricate though dishonest reflection on his motives. His writing is again submitted to interpretation within the story. Georg tells his father that he has written to his friend with the aim of creating for the friend the very happiness Georg has experienced in his engagement. His father hears in the statement a manner of writing to his friend—a treacherous writing—and comes swiftly and violently to his verdict. It is to declare his son punishably guilty of deceit, of blindness, of doing devil's work.

Georg, his gaze open only to his father, cannot resist taking over this verdict as his own (DI 279).

Only because "The Judgment" is explicitly conscious of such acts as reading and writing, telling the truth and lying, repression and deception—of the order of phenomena called hermeneutic—does it produce so forceful an interpretative activity in the reader. And indeed by its own dramatization of hermeneutic force, it appropriates in advance the force with which it each time compels interpretation. In thus focusing on the power produced by acts of writing, justifying, and sentencing, the story assumes a distance from its immediate life— the clash of desires, the craving for intimacy, the suspension of the will, the refusal of individuation, as they compose the family romance. Here again "The Judgment" is exemplary: it discourages readers from taking direct access to the life that comes to light with ostensible self-evidence in their first reading. It encourages them to displace that reading as in fact a made and influenced and interested object (though one not made by them!). Its subtle shaping belongs to the play of force exerted by the history of reading, not negligibly, the way in which Kafka has been read during the seventy-five-year history of "The Judgment." The story thus implicitly asks readers to consider the history of its own commentaries, if they are to bring any measure of freedom into its domain.

* * *

Readers of "The Judgment," when they have not despaired of coherence, have traditionally pursued an idea of coherence that now seems restrictive. Interpretation aims to motivate the events that follow Georg's entering his father's room in terms of what has been revealed of Georg the letter writer; the final test of such theory is to motivate Georg's execution. To the elements of the dynamic field of son, friend, fiancée, father, and mother, readers assign values, the outcome of whose interaction is plausibly the casting out of the fiancée and the extinction of the son. This necessarily means, for example, ascribing to the father a value that will make his authority irresistible to Georg. Thus Walter Sokel describes the father as "the man who [unlike Georg] had enjoyed and been capable of true love." He thus prereads his sense of the conclusion as Georg's gaining "the

29

nourishment which fulfills him . . . unification with the will of the father."[7]

For all such readings, which define coherence as the consistency of mimetic reference, the value of each of the agonists has to be held constant and the logic of their interaction maintained as one of progressive intensification. For example, the negative value assigned early to Georg—that he blindly conceals motives aiming at power and possession—is held to inform all his interactions. If his kisses in the first section aim to cover up awareness of how inconclusive his feelings for his fiancée are, then the fact that he does not bother to defend her against his father's abuse in the second section is taken as further evidence of his indifference—even though on its own terms his silence of course imports nothing of the kind.

Typically, the repetition of an original motive is held to strengthen the motive, so that the cumulative force of a number of such repetitions can begin plausibly to motivate the violence of Georg's suicide. In fact, there has been not a number of repetitions but only the repeated ascription of an intensified value to a number of unknowns. The original value is allowed to change only to the extent that its stability is not threatened, and each change or repetition is said to reinforce its initial identity.

Consider another example. If Georg is revealed early as a deluded writer—and there can be no doubt on this point—he is held in this perspective to be a deluded speaker throughout the second part: what he states to his father as the expression of a motive can be only a dissimulation. The reproaches he makes to himself for having neglected his father, for example, are said to be merely the workings of his intent to dispossess him. And thus (although commentators are inconsistent on this point), Georg cannot always have loved his parents, as he declares an instant before letting himself drop from the bridge.

But which of these propositions about Georg's or his father's psychological character are in fact plausible? Is Georg the devilish wastrel his father declares him to be? Surely not for having wanted to shroud from his friend's eyes his own brilliant success. Can it be that Georg is the dissimulator of ultimately irreproachable motives? Doubts multi-

7. Walter Sokel, *Franz Kafka: Tragik und Ironie, Zur Struktur seiner Kunst* (Munich: Albert Langen, 1964), pp. 48, 76.

ply. Can a single value be attributed in good conscience to any of these characters? Georg has lied to his friend. Is his friend therefore a sign of genuine existence, what Sokel calls a "pure self"?[8] Why should jaundice, passivity, and the slide into bachelorhood suggest the attributes of authenticity? Whence has such a friend the authority through Georg's father, his "representative," to sentence Georg to drowning? The same doubts hover over even the less problematic figure of the fiancée. Why, as is often asserted, is Georg's fiancée accurate in saying that since Georg has such friends as the Russian bachelor, he ought never to have become engaged? It is not obvious that he admits the charge by responding, "Well, we're both to blame for [this state of affairs]" (S 80). He can be saying ironically but generously that it is only because his fiancée is so splendid that his embittered friend has become so burdensome. Nothing Georg has said or done earlier suggests that he has ever considered his friend a serious obstacle to his engagement. Indeed, the outcome of the story implies that it is not his friend but the father who drives off the fiancée: Georg is crushed by his father's colluding with the friend. His fiancée should have said that it is because he has a father like Mr. Bendemann and not because he has a friend like the Russian business-man that he should never have become engaged. Georg's father is therefore vicious but not entirely inaccurate in calling her a "nasty creature [or worse: *widerliche Gans*]" (S 85; E 64). Her notion may be stupid and indeed calculated to torment Georg. But of course we do not initially know enough about her to assign her any value, let alone insist that she stick to her first identity, especially within the play of perspectives that Kafka saw as constituting the piece.[9]

In no reading that I know has it been possible to assign to these characters values drawn from lived experience, to hold these values fast throughout their interaction, and to motivate Georg's execution. Walter Sokel's reading is among the strongest, but his version reveals inconsistencies that jeopardize the whole. In general, his reading seeks to make plausible a psychoanalytical drama: a specious ego masking libidinal and aggressive instincts is destroyed by a strong, uncon-

---

8. Ibid, p. 45.

9. "The story is perhaps a journey around father and son, and the changing figure of the friend is perhaps the perspectival change of the relations between father and son" (LF 267).

scious ego-ideal imaged in the alliance of friend (authentic self) and father (superego). This story aims to counter the reading that sees the father as senile or insane, for in that case "Georg's execution of the death sentence would be either inexplicable or an example of the hypnotic effect of the irrational. But then the part of the story dealing with the father would in no way be related to those parts dealing with the fiancée and the friend, and we would have before us a completely incoherent story, one unworthy of an artist of the rank of Franz Kafka."[10] The question is whether coherence must mean psychological plausibility.

Sokel supplies motives plausible for the psychic subagencies: superego, ego, and id. That the superego here operates with a murderous logic, a "barbaric law," will not seem strange after Freud's *The Ego and the Id*. But one must be ready thereafter to give up believing in the murderous *father*—for the father, according to Sokel, is the character who knew true love. Instead, we have in place of the father a projection of conscience. If this is so, however, what does it mean when Sokel says at the close that Georg is aware that his life has gone astray and that it is guilty of having "cut itself off and detached itself from the roots from which it has emerged"? These roots are perhaps in some physical metaphor the father, but in what sense are they in or part of conscience? "Georg sought to neglect and suppress the essential connection to the origin, to the parents and the friend."[11] What has happened to the psychoanalytic drama? In what sense and for what psychic agency is the alliance of ego and superego the "origin"? In what way does the sick, celibate, floundering friend embody the ego as the integrity of the psychic field? If the price of innocence before the father's law is to "follow the call" of the friend to a wasting death in Russia, why does the friend desire an alliance with the father? Georg declares that he has at least twice before "denied" to the father the friend's presence in their house, since the father had no particular liking for him. The proposition makes sense, but what moment in the psychoanalytic drama does it illustrate? Evidently Sokel's reading makes the interesting sense it does only by its rapid (and inevitable) shifting from one metaphorical plane to another.

10. Sokel, *Franz Kafka*, p. 53.
11. Ibid., p. 45.

As a result of such shifts between hermeneutic levels, initially posited values are not held constant. The authority of the father cannot stem at once from his benevolence as a character and his fierceness as a superego. To the extent that Georg's execution is explained, it is explained only figuratively, as a sort of death in the service of psychic integration. But indeed these psychoanalytic correlations are purely contingent, since a Kleinian or Abrahamian perspective, say, would suggest different correlations between textual terms and the various psychic subagencies generated from the Freudian triad by further schism and exchange.

There would seem to be no plausible motivation for Georg's death, where plausibility means the consistency of empirical reference. This is not—as used to be maintained—because Georg's suicide is psychologically unconvincing. Neither psychological realism nor any other system taking the suicide as a kind of death can repeat in its own terms a work of such preponderant complexity of interrelation and poverty of firm signification, can correlate with empirical or theoretical chains held to be meaningful so intricate a play of elliptical and fugitive elements. The name Georg does not signify at the beginning what it signifies at the end; the name of the father does not designate at all times during their interview the same law. For intelligibility's sake the initial posit as to their value must in both cases be changed, but that is the end of consistency.

To describe one more impossible strategy of motivating "The Judgment" is only, of course, to join a chorus of interpreters. The cry that dimensions of this story are irreducibly obscure has been part of every faithful response. This obscurity has no sooner been asserted, however, than it is invaded. The horror of the implausible swiftly introduces a second strategy—that of radical intention. In despair of consistency yet in pursuit of meaning, critics call the second half a *Wunschtraum*, a wish-dream; here, in effect, Kafka's father joins forces with the "friend"—with the sickly, solitude-seeking, incomprehensible second self of the son whom in life he has consistently derided—to condemn to death the self that in life he wished Franz Kafka to be. I have been alone among critics, I think, in writing of the second half not as a *Wunschtraum* but as an *Alptraum*, a nightmare, in which the surreptitious alliance of the father with the figure of the writer implies the death of Kafka's pursuit of autonomous language.[12] No one meanwhile has had the audacity, however justifiable, to say that the first half of the story is either a wish-dream or a nightmare, as if for a sensibility of Kafka's stringency the description of ordinary consciousness applied to the task of self-justification were not sufficiently horrible (although John Ellis has rightly perceived some of the bizarre and morbid fractures in this sensibility right from the outset).[13] But it is obvious that to motivate the second half of the text radically, by the appeal to an extrinsic intention like wishing or abjuring, is to allow in principle the irregular application of extrinsic intention, which wraps individual elements at will in the veils of bliss or nightmare. Thus drowning no longer means suffocation but "rebirth"; the collusion of father and friend is a joyous confirmation of true identity, and so on. The pursuit of coherence among elliptical elements turns into the chaos of arbitrary revaluations applied from the outside—the unsettling free play of the psychoanalyst without a patient.

To declare at intervals, meanwhile, that the characters have changed is only to replace the irregular extrinsic intention with an equally arbitrary intrinsic fluctuation of perspective. What is left for the critic to do? What else, after having identified the disturbance—the story's punishing meagerness of determination and its inverse, the unsettling freedom it offers to interpretation—but to double the critical consciousness, to identify in the frankest way the types of substitution in which his or her criticism engages? The values we associate with the figures in this story may of course originate elsewhere—in the text of Freud, in the text of Kafka's confessional writings (thus there may be extrinsic reference). These values may indeed change (as a play of intrinsic intention), and the optic in which the reader views and feels them may change (as a play of extrinsic intention); nothing can restrict their number and combination. Thus we cannot and need not hold to a linear and progressive, end-oriented pattern in which the end has the power of organizing retrospectively everything that has preceded it; this is evident forever. It is Heinz Politzer's achievement to have seen the father's attack on the son—"an innocent child, yes, that you were truly, but still more truly have you been a devilish

---

12. Stanley Corngold, "Introduction" (M iv–xvi).

13. John Ellis, "Kafka: 'Das Urteil,'" in *Narration in the German Novelle: Theory and Interpretation* (London: Cambridge University Press, 1975), pp. 118–211.

human being" (S 87)—for the revolution in modes of order which it imports. "Here," writes Politzer, "innocence and wickedness are no longer presented as consecutive stages in Georg's development from child to man. Rather, the judgment, leaving psychology behind, speaks of the close interconnection in every human of good and evil, of promise and betrayal."[14] Kafka asks us to take seriously the differential character, the implicit multivalence of his figures. But if undecidability is not to be degraded either to mystery or despondency, we must continue to read; and here we will not be wrong to reintroduce a notion of the writer's intention which rotates the text of "The Judgment" toward the whole text of Kafka. The sense in the story which is death to hide—which occurs through Georg and all around Georg but not to Georg—is the punishment of the writer who would write to enthrall the world.

*   *   *

Kafka's own commentary on "The Judgment" focuses on the figure of the Russian friend—"the greatest bond" between father and son. Interpreters were helpless to identify this mysterious mask until Kate Flores offered the inspired suggestion that the friend's isolation, exile, and idealism reflect Kafka's identity as a writer. The idea has since been elaborated by Martin Greenberg, Eric Marson, and Jürgen Demmer, among others.[15] It now seems most reasonable to say of the friend that if he is this kind of figure, he does not stand purely and simply for the writing destiny but for that destiny pursued under the condition of bachelorhood which in 1912 had been Kafka's sole experience of writing.

This way of stating the identification makes more evident the complexity and polyvalence of the friend. The friend can represent bachelorhood as a set of empirical circumstances under which writing might best be pursued. As a bachelor he can also stand for the intrin-

---

14. Heinz Politzer, *Franz Kafka: Parable and Paradox* (Ithaca: Cornell University Press, 1962), p. 59.

15. Kate Flores, "The Judgment," in *Franz Kafka Today*, ed. Angel Flores and Homer Swander (Madison: University of Wisconsin Press, 1964), p. 13; Martin Greenberg, "The Literature of Truth," in *The Terror of Art: Kafka and Modern Literature* (New York: Basic Books, 1968), pp. 47–68; Eric Marson, "Franz Kafka's 'Das Urteil,'" *AUMLA* 16 (November 1961): 167–78; Jürgen Demmer, *Franz Kafka: Der Dichter der Selbstreflexion* (Munich: Fink, 1973).

sic "purity" of writing—its idealism, its longing for autonomy, its rigorous self-reflexiveness. Finally, as the condition in which Kafka has written hitherto, bachelorhood can represent all the (contradictory) values that belong to Kafka's writing to this point—briefly, its ecstasy and diabolism, its power and its sterility. Kafka hoped to write well and despaired at having written impurely, and he felt all the complex tones of this failure. He saw his writing as insufficiently wholehearted, insufficiently sustained, and—*as* the act of writing— intrinsically insufficient. The friend is thus a complex sign, but he is not therefore unbounded: he is a sign of writing in one form of its empirical existence, in its transcendental determination, and in its character as moral experience. The story modulates the meaning of the friend throughout the range of these significations and in their depth of analogy and disjunction. My reading profiles the possibilities of analogy between the transcendental, moral, and empirical dimensions of Kafka's conception of writing. This is not to rule out, however, a reading of "The Judgment" that focuses on the disjunction of these planes.

The authority for assigning connections between the characters in "The Judgment" and aspects of Kafka's own life comes from his diary entry itself. Here Kafka associates Georg Bendemann with himself and Frieda Brandenfeld with Felice Bauer, the woman he had recently met and would detain as his fiancée for the next five years. Very little stress has been laid, however, on the fact that in this story Georg Bendemann is also a writer—of a letter to be sure, but to say this is only to specify the kind of writing he does. This writer is, as "Bendemann," inescapably a "Bindemann," the man who forms ties. According to Max Brod, Kafka knew a good deal of etymology; and the old Indo-Germanic root *bhendh* yields the modern *Binde-* or "binding-."[16] Indeed the reflexive form *sich binden* yields the precise meaning of "to become engaged." Georg's writing aims explicitly to bind his friend to himself and to affirm his engagement to his fiancée, to continue to enjoy their abundance of contrary properties.

Several aspects of the events surrounding Kafka's first meeting with Felice Bauer strengthen this connection. On the evening of her visit to Max Brod, Kafka showed Felice pictures from his trip to Weimar, where he had fallen in love with the beautiful daughter of

16. Gerhard Wahrig, *Deutsches Wörterbuch* (Gütersloh: Bertelsmann, 1970), p. 693.

the custodian of Goethe's house; thereafter, Kafka had written postcards to the girl, which she had actually answered. In a letter to Brod, Kafka had reflected, "If I am not, in her eyes, unpleasant, I am at any rate of no more importance to her than a pot. But then why does she write as I would wish it? Do you suppose it is true that one can attach girls to oneself by writing? [*Wenn es wahr wäre, daß man Mädchen mit der Schrift binden kann?*]" (L 80; Br 97). The German is even more suggestive: "Do you suppose it is true that one could tie up girls with writing"—in the physical sense of braided signs—and hence bind them to writing?[17] At this point, of course, Kafka can be referring only to writing letters.

An event six weeks after Kafka's first meeting with Felice makes even stronger the connection between writing and getting engaged. On the day that Kafka sat down to write his first letter to Felice—a woman about whom, at their first meeting, he had formed "an unshakeable judgment [*unerschütterliches Urteil*]" (DI 269; Ta 285)—he received for the first time in his life a publisher's contract for a work he had written. Two days later he composed "The Judgment."

In this story Georg describes the fiancée merely as the daughter of a "well-to-do" family, reducing her to a token of her exchange value. When Georg so plainly writes to his friend with an acquisitive design, he uses language *vergleichsweise:* that is, to make the comparisons that underlie acts of acquisition and appropriation. But according to Kafka, language concerned with human inwardness, with something "outside the phenomenal world," must never be used in this way. For "corresponding as it does to the phenomenal world . . . [language] is concerned only with property and its relations," and to operate between the two parties *vergleichsweise* is to attempt to bring about between them a legal settlement (DF 40). To use language without respecting the difference between things invisible and things seen is forever to speak only of "property and its relations," is to confirm "writing's lack of independence of the world" (DII 201). There remains, meanwhile, the more genuine mode of using language *andeutungsweise*, allusively, by which language conjures traces of an order not its own (DF 40). Writing that aims at self-aggrandizement and self-justification does devil's work in the sense that it sinks lan-

---

17. This passage is discussed in Elias Canetti, *Der andere Prozeß: Kafkas Briefe an Felice* (Munich: Hanser, 1969), p. 11.

guage ever more deeply into that species of blank captivation which Kafka terms "the world of the senses . . . the Evil in the spiritual world" (DF 39). In writing's reflection on itself, it would not be absurd for the crime of writing badly to merit capital punishment at the hands of its own outraged authority.

The Georg Bendemann we see is a writer, and as such he writes badly. The passage above about "allusion" hints at a truer use of language, yet no use of language escapes untruth, escapes the writer's own (or its own) veering devotion to worldly interest. But the virtual impossibility of another sort of writing makes even less tolerable for Kafka the accession to the correspondence between language and the phenomenal world. Writing interestedly is writing that doubles its failure to make a difference by its defiance of the knowledge that not making a difference matters. Georg's manner of establishing connections is complacent and duplicitous and not tested against an aspiration that could diminish its fluency.

Georg's fluency is another name for his strong ego, his worldly success, and his playful consciousness of his own power. At the level of writing, this competence suggests claims not unlike Kafka's early sentiments about the power of his writing. In the year before composing "The Judgment," for example, he noted in his diaries: "When I arbitrarily write a single sentence, for instance, 'He looked out of the window,' it already has perfection" (DI 45). There is none of the fastidious longing here which was later to restrict the "perfection" that all but allusive writing could achieve.

The exegetical value of seeing Georg as a writer is considerable; in this light "The Judgment" repeats and varies the dialogical structure of a number of Kafka's early works obviously centering on writing. In the diary entry for 1910 beginning "'You,' I said," for example, an ostensible bourgeois and a bachelor embody contrary moments of *Schriftstellersein* (existence as a writer). Here the bachelor focuses negative aspects of writing, suggesting the possibility that the anxiety belonging to writing could freeze and come to a fatal standstill; the bourgeois speaker, on the other hand, is a more lucid and constructive figure whose voice merges with that of the narrator.

In "The Judgment" the distribution of properties of the writing self is very different. If we take Georg's friend as the projection of writing that arises from an avowed nonmanipulative bachelorhood, then Georg represents writing as a manipulative process for which marriage is a comprehensive figure. Marriage conveys the seductive hope of a union between the law of writing and the world of the senses in which writing could also retain its "spiritual" privilege. (The fact that in the story both Georg and his friend are "in business" authorizes the view that both are aspects of writing.)

In "The Judgment," then, the essential opposition is not between a projection of Kafka's social personality on the one hand and his hopes as a writer on the other. This dichotomy, persistently repeated in criticism, is not telling if we recall that there never was any moment in Kafka's life when he could conceive of part of himself as separate from "literature." The story makes the distinction between a self (Georg) that writes in order to continue its connection with the world, by having the world serve it, and a self that pursues literature under the condition of a possibly propitious reclusiveness. The debate opposes marriage and bachelorhood and their fine ramifications, not as either of these might second the world in its struggle with writing but as conditions of the strongest writing. Indeed, for Kafka, being engaged to be married was always to mean being engaged in the voluminous correspondence he carried on with Felice Bauer. Every thought of his fiancée belonged to the progress of their correspondence. The one mode of her absence/presence issued into letters; the mode of her absence/presence in which she was not figuring as a wife issued into fiction. But Kafka never conceived of a relation with his fiancée that implied the suspension of writing.

Georg, as a persona of Kafka's writing self, must resolve at the outset of "The Judgment" the claims of the fiancée and the friend, of a writing that takes the woman hostage and a writing that flows from solitude. When Georg decides that he will write his friend definitive news of his engagement, "The Judgment" comes into being: it will put on trial the mode of writing that issues from the alliance of the woman and the writer. Kafka's project is to test through Georg the unholy strategy of marrying in order to write well. This hypothesis is confirmed by Kafka's remark in his diary that "the bride . . . lives in the story only in relation to the friend" (DI 278–79); the friend is the only mode in which Kafka has so far known the life of literature.

The figure of Georg, however, is essentially in bad faith. He is at work suppressing consciousness of the scandal of an engagement that is bent on an increase in power, whether to the profit of the self or of the writer. Both terms are implicit in Kafka's sentence: "Since

39

[through marriage] I grow in vigor [my powers, *Kräften*, increase], I carry more [I shall stand more, *trage*]" (DF 211; H 238). Georg is the manipulator who manipulates even his own intent: he conceals it.

His anxiety emerges in the lies he tells himself—and in another significant detail. Georg dwells on the point that the friend has withheld sympathy upon learning of the death of Georg's mother. Georg does not know how to construe this lapse except to presume that grief on such an occasion is inconceivable to one who lives abroad. The "dryness" of the friend's response to the event is for Georg unintelligible, a response he cannot recognize or acknowledge (S 78). Whence this obstacle to understanding? It is plausible to think that Georg does not wish to know that he himself has not grieved for his mother's death, that he himself has suppressed consciousness of this death. The motive would be understandable. His mother's death liberates in him a mobile erotic energy; it is the precondition of his becoming engaged. This truth is troublesome to Georg for the opportunity of a vaunting triumph in the rivalry it implies with the father, but more so for the way in which it coerces him into this rivalry: he wants to think of his act of becoming engaged not as motivated but as free. (We must remember that Kafka is going through this experience with Georg, and we know his horror of determination, of compulsion, of the broken will. But what Kafka sees and dreads is what for Georg is only the blind side of a lie. This is the structure of all Kafka's novels.)

In now writing to his friend, Georg makes his engagement a *fait accompli*. His hesitation in writing obviously stems from the possibility that this will prove the ultimate breakdown of his connection with his friend. As long as he has "this friend in Saint Petersburg," he thinks he possesses the meaning of the figure; he has once before rejected the opportunity to share the friend's life, but to stay in correspondence with him is to keep this possibility open (S 82).

When Georg finally sits down to write, the act is not his own but is compelled by his fiancée. In acting he will learn his determinateness, but this experience of constraint is masked at first in his elation, which ironically and privatively prefigures the narrator's elation at the close. Georg's delight in his letter is his first suggestion of the success of his new effort at enthralling others. At the same time, he has not perceived that this delight issues from a blind play of coercions. He has induced his fiancée to place this compulsion on him. He at once forces it and distorts it by the violence with which he suppresses her argument for writing definitive news of the engagement to the friend. To send to the friend the first product of his alliance is doubtless to risk repudiation, for this product is no longer wholly Georg's but already the outcome of a play of forces, one of which belongs to the being he meant to control.

In this state of anxiety Georg enters his father's room. The turn to the father is as lucid and expectable as if it were part of a logical demonstration. Now that Georg has embarked on family life, the decision to write under the condition of marriage has to be examined in the light of a more detached writing (the friend's existence) and in the light of marriage itself (the existence of the married man par excellence, the father). To manage this enterprise would assure Georg the surplus satisfaction of beating his father at his own game of flourishing from the power ceded to him by the woman.

A tonality of dread informs this interview. The language of the story turns into a different channel: the text has so far mirrored a text (the letter) and Georg's commentary on the text; its form is now a language of primary process, family conversation—that form of language for Kafka most liable to conjure chaos and self-dispersion. "Conversations," he wrote, "take the importance, the seriousness, the truth out of everything I think" (DI 292). "In me, by myself, without human relationship, there are no visible lies. The limited circle is pure" (DI 300). Kafka's hatred of conversation is an expression of his hatred of the language wholly bent on an expansive mastering totality of the self and the world.

Not surprisingly, Georg goes to pieces. The key thrust in this exchange is his sudden perception of his friend, the writing destiny, as something failed, estranged, and wholly vulnerable. Within the mixing of elements in the friend—the empirical and the pure—the major tone of "real writers" emerges (L 82). Writing is damaged, and Georg is guilty of the harm: he has not sufficiently protected it. Writing's revenge on an impure solicitation is its withdrawal, its inaccessibility.

Georg himself is now wounded: he will not defend his fiancée even though she is abused. That the fiancée is only the name for a certain impure annexation of the world to writing has been confirmed; she is abandoned, leaving the field open for the struggle for remaining possession of the friend.

Georg cannot escape the falsehood of his original project. His dread finds its object in the horrible revelation of the intimacy between the friend and the father. The father asserts that the friend is a son after his own heart, his "ideal" offspring. The communication between the father and his correspondent is said to be one of perfect transparency: each flows into the other. Writing becomes the creature of the father—the father, the subject of writing, the representative of the writing destiny as it articulates itself. Writing is in the father and of the father; writing is his own reproduction. Writing strengthens the father, turns him against the son who would live in any fashion except solitude and self-denial. His ideal offspring is a fanatic of masochistic asceticism, an admirer of the mad priest who has carved a cross in his palm.

If the first stage of the alienation of writing is its lostness to Georg, the alliance of the father with writing conjures an even more abject image. In the poisonous atmosphere in which writing becomes the slut whom Georg has prostituted, the father's blessing is only a kiss of death. The friend is perishing of this alliance; the bond will prove as fatal to him as it will to Georg and his father. Georg's situation is impossible. He has lost the friend, he must grasp that the friend is corrupted and dying; but he has himself been defined from the start by his dependency on the friend, on the hope of a continuity with the being who is essentially writing.

The effort to keep the friend while annexing the power of the woman fails, quite as if to testify to the iron operation of a law of exclusion; the result of Georg's earlier unwillingness to make a choice between the loved mother and the friend who showed no grief for her death was the ceding of all her power to his father. Now, too, Georg's unwillingness to make a choice between the friend and the fiancée has the perverse result of ceding the power of the friend to the father.

Georg is an impossible figure; writing, this act of writing, cannot proceed through his perspective. The narrator has in fact been steadily withdrawing from his persona in moving from identification to dialogue. He must now definitively withdraw, must assert his autonomy and find its narrative form. The autonomy of the narrative is the key issue for Kafka: is writing finally and forever only the babble of the family romance? Is there no chance in the writing destiny of "a leap out of murderer's row" (DII 212)? What sort of freedom can writing assert if it knows itself to originate with the father and, like the friend, take its essential direction from the father?[18]

The collusion is constituted in part by Georg's guilty perception of this state of affairs; his perspective must be surmounted. To acquiesce in the alliance of father and friend is to call down a death sentence. The experimental figure of the union of marriage and writing conjures a state that writing cannot survive: the alliance of friend and father corrupts writing with the father's alien will, and the attempt to appropriate writing through marriage simply puts writing on a par with the acquist of power the father has gained from marriage—the power to engender a devilish son. To marry in order to write would be only to reproduce the devilish offspring that the father has produced; Georg Bendemann, who seeks to get engaged elsewhere, to leap out of his solipsism, would succeed only in reproducing himself.

The Georg of the outset, who possessed writing through a sort of Faustian devil's bargain with himself, is not the Georg of the close, who can no longer "write," cannot interpret the sentence laid on him. The father of the outset, who in Georg's confident perspective was no obstacle to his double affirmation of sexual and literary power, is allowed, as the chief representative of family, to pose the question that touches the concealed doubt of Georg's whole enterprise. If Georg marries, he no longer keeps the connection with the Russian friend, the life of writing. To mingle marriage with writing is not to repair but only to repeat the fault that Kafka saw as writing's congenital fragility—the uncertainty that it could exist in definitive separation from the dying world of organic process, of family filiation. The voice that registers the "unending [almost infinite, *geradezu unendlich*]" (S 88; E 68) traffic over the bridge is not Georg's. It is a voice that aims to conjure a trace of the universal "family animal" at its source, at an order fundamental enough to justify the effort of writing to find access to it, there to litigate and contend (L 294).

*　　*　　*

What relation does this reading have to the theory I said governed all possible readings of "The Judgment"? Whatever consistency (intelligibility) it achieves is strictly speculative and is obtained by a

18. "[My writing] was . . . something, to be sure, which you were the cause of, but which took its course in a direction determined by me" (DF 177).

deliberate process of substitution that reaches out beyond the text. I am attempting to recover unequivocal meaning from a work whose own terms resist it. If the identification of Georg as a dissumulator of texts is based on the text, certainly the link between the Russian friend and writing is not: it is based on an association of underdetermined signs (sickness, solitude, Russia) with the sense they have in Kafka's confessional writings. If we allow this, we must also allow that the significances of these signs remain consistent through each repetition. The invocation of the Saint Petersburg friend on the father's lips must also mean the writing destiny. In maintaining this continuity, however, we are merely exercising our will to coherence. The story neither allows this assertion nor disallows it. But it is wholly evident how little the act of subjectively asserting meaning is equal to the act that originates the ultimate impassiveness of the text.

The argument that the alliance between father and friend is intolerable to Kafka and must be construed as a nightmare, as a condition at all costs contrary to fact, is not given in the text but is extrinsically motivated by the intent of making meaningful the entire phenomenon Kafka. Without the existence of the confessional writings and the right to bring them into court, the motivation would be wholly arbitrary. The "nightmarish" text I read is only a moment in the autobiography of the writing consciousness in Kafka.

The irreducible reality of the work itself is its undecidability. I earlier identified this phenomenon as its "abyss of meaning," which has a degraded counterpart in the lie, the lie whose structure one can see repeated in the bad faith with which, and because of which, Georg accepts his death. One comes closer to this phenomenon, however, by considering the father's sentencing of his son.

At the outset of this chapter I envisioned Georg as a person having the status of the reader. It was then possible to declare the work cautionary, a negative example, because of Georg's simple accession to his death sentence. But in saying this I implied that Georg has good reasons, in the psychological sense, not to resist his sentence. This sort of implication is not encouraged by the text: the matter of his sentencing has to be put more appropriately.

Georg accedes to his sentence without even a velleity of resistance. The very utterance of the sentence produces its effect. To sentence

Georg to death is to set in motion a relentless process that brings about the state of affairs designated in the sentence.

The sentence is in effect a performative. It does not intend in its utterance to designate a state of affairs that is taking place and is extrinsically caused. It aims instead to bring into existence a state of affairs of which it is the sole cause. Merely as a set of signs the sentence "I sentence you to death," uttered at the appropriate moment by a judge in court, constitutes a verdict; furthermore, if the court's machinery is in place, the verdict also brings about the fatal conclusion that the sentence designates.

This point encourages critics to construe Georg's accession to the sentence as the act of the son who indeed places himself in a court of law upon entering his father's room. This theory needs the prior assumption that Georg considers himself guilty and, in effect, turns himself in for sentencing. There is no good evidence in the text, however, for either of these assumptions.

Nothing requires that the sentence be grasped as a real performative. What is crucial is that in this text the sentence operates performatively contrary to the fact, and it does so by an act of will on the part of the narrator. One might recall a passage from Kafka's abortive novel "Wedding Preparations in the Country," written five years earlier, in which this sort of arbitrary authority over events in the world is explicitly named: "The carriages and people in the street move and walk hesitantly on shining ground, for I am still dreaming. Coachmen and pedestrians are shy, and every step they want to advance they ask as a favor from me, by looking at me. I encourage them and encounter no obstacle" (DF 6).

The dream of arbitrary omnipotence is fulfilled by a writing that is self-constitutive. Earlier in this chapter I quoted the diary passage in which Kafka speaks of "the special nature of my inspiration": "I can do everything, and not only what is directed to a definite piece of work. When I arbitrarily write a single sentence, for instance, 'He looked out of the window,' it already has perfection" (DI 45). I said then that this bold claim lacked the fastidiousness of Kafka's later disclaimer of perfection in his writing. But it is clear now that this "perfection" is not to be construed empirically. It designates the eternally self-constitutive intent of fiction, its character of always mean-

45

ing to speak in the performative mode. This is the power that the beleaguered narrator, who has earlier identified his perspective with the impossible optic of Georg, must assert in order to survive.

The assertion of the narrator's will aims to put his production into the order of the undecidable, since his intent is not to duplicate empirical consistency but to declare a break with consistency. The transgressive counterpart of this intent, meanwhile, is that of the interpreter, who in pursuing coherence opposes the arbitrary will of the narrator. This is the sense in which every interpretation undoes fiction: it undermines the will of the narrator, either privatively, by adducing a different and inappropriate standard of coherence, or—more appropriately in Kafka's case—by conjuring the abysmal reality of the text. For over this reality, in which the performative figures as a mere tautology, the narrator's assertion of omnipotence is only one more metaphorical bridge.

Interpreters of Kafka must ask "as a favor" "every step" they "want to advance"—from neither the author nor the narrator, however, but from the text; here they have little ground beneath their feet and can finally pass over the abyss of meaning only by constructions of their own.

To be a writer of Kafka's order is to side neither with the narrator nor with that second narrator, the interpreter, but with the text. The writer Kafka inhabits an order of the abyss which distinguishes him from every reader questing for a site somewhere in or over the work. Kafka exists not as the reader's pathos but as the large impassiveness of his text—somewhere off to one side of that bridge over which, in "The Judgment," there passes an almost infinite traffic. That is the place of one whose being is entirely literature, who must live as the merely "formal necessity" of another family "superabundant in life and thought" (GW 269).

Chapter Three

The Metamorphosis:
Metamorphosis of the Metaphor

What *is* literature? Where does it come from? What use is
it? What questionable things! Add to this questionableness
the further questionableness of what you say, and what you
get is a monstrosity.

FRANZ KAFKA, *Dearest Father*

To judge from its critical reception, Franz Kafka's *The Metamorphosis*
(*Die Verwandlung*) is the most haunting and universal of all his stories,
and yet Kafka never claimed for it any special distinction. He never,
for example, accorded it the importance he reserved for "The Judgment," a work it resembles but which it surpasses in depth and
scope.[1] On the morning of September 23, 1912, after the night he
spent composing "The Judgment," Kafka, with a fine elation, wrote
in his diary: "Only *in this way* can writing be done, only with such
coherence, with such a complete opening out of the body and the
soul" (DI 276). But throughout the period of the composition of *The
Metamorphosis*—from November 17 to December 7, 1912—and until
the beginning of the new year, his diary does not show an entry of
any kind; and when it resumes on February 11, 1913, it is with an

---

1. Elias Canetti wrote: "In *The Metamorphosis* Kafka reached the height of his
mastery: he wrote something which he could never surpass, because there is nothing
which *The Metamorphosis* could be surpassed by—one of the few great, perfect poetic
works of this century" (*Der andere Prozeß: Kafkas Briefe an Felice* [Munich: Hanser,
1969], pp. 22–23).

47

interpretation not of *The Metamorphosis* but of "The Judgment." The diary does finally acknowledge the new story, almost a year after its composition, with this remark: "I am now reading *Metamorphosis* at home and find it bad" (DI 303).

Kafka was especially disappointed with the conclusion of the story. On January 19, 1914, he wrote, "Great antipathy to *Metamorphosis*. Unreadable ending" (DII 12), and he blamed the botched conclusion on a business trip he was obliged to make just as he was well advanced into the piece. His annoyance and remorse at having to interrupt his work is vivid in the letters written at the time to his fiancée, Felice Bauer. These letters reveal Kafka's moods all during the composition of the story—moods almost entirely negative. The story originates "in bed in my misery, and now troubles me [oppresses me with inmost intensity, *innerlichst bedrängt*]" (LF 47; BF 102). The tonality of the piece appears again as "despair" (LF 49) and "indifference" (LF 76). On November 23 the story is said to be "a little frightening [horrible, *fürchterlich*]" (LF 58; BF 116); a day later, "infinitely repulsive" (LF 58). A trace of liking and concern for *The Metamorphosis* appears in a later letter: "It's a pity that in some passages of the story my state of exhaustion and other interruptions and extraneous worries about other things are so apparent [inscribed, *eingezeichnet*]. I know it could have been done more neatly [purely, *reiner*]; this is particulary conspicuous in the more tender [sweeter, *süße*] passages" (LF 89; BF 160). But by this time Kafka has begun to consider *The Metamorphosis* more and more an interruption of the writing of the uncompleted novel that was to become *Amerika*. Finally, on the morning of December 7, he states the complaint that will recur: "My little story is finished, but today's ending does not please me at all; it really could have been done better, there is no doubt about this" (LF 91).

Kafka's own sense of *The Metamorphosis* compels us to consider the work essentially unfinished. The interruptions that set in so frequently past the midpoint of the story tend to shift the weight of its significance back toward its beginning. This view draws support from other evidence establishing what might be termed the general and fundamental priority of the beginning in Kafka's works. One thinks of the innumerable openings to stories scattered throughout the diaries and notebooks, suddenly appearing and as swiftly vanishing, leaving undeveloped the endless dialectical structures they contain. On October 16, 1921, Kafka explicitly invoked "the misery of having perpetually to begin, the lack of the illusion that anything is more than, or even as much as, a beginning" (DII 193). For Dieter Hasselblatt, Kafka's prose "is in flight from the beginning, it does not strive toward the end: *initiofugal*, not final. And since it takes the impulse of its progression from what is set forth or what is just present at the outset, it cannot be completed. The end, the conclusion, is unimportant compared to the opening situation."[2]

One is directed, it would seem, by these empirical and theoretical considerations to formulate the overwhelming question of *The Metamorphosis* as the question of the meaning of its beginning. What fundamental intention inspires the opening sentence: "When Gregor Samsa woke up one morning from unsettling dreams, he found himself changed in his bed into a monstrous vermin [*ungeheueres Ungeziefer*]" (M 3; E 71)? We shall do well to keep in mind, in the words of Edward Said, "the identity [of the beginning] as *radical* starting point; the intransitive and conceptual aspect, that which has no object but its own constant clarification."[3] Much of the action of *The Metamorphosis* consists of Kafka's attempt to come to terms with its beginning.

The opening recounts the transformation of a man into a monstrous, verminous bug; in the process, it appears to accomplish still another change: it metamorphoses a common figure of speech. This second transformation emerges in the light of the hypothesis proposed in 1947 by Günther Anders: "Kafka's sole point of departure is . . . *ordinary language*. . . . More precisely: *he draws from the resources on hand, the figurative nature [Bildcharakter], of language. He takes metaphors at their word [beim Wort]. For example*: Because Gregor Samsa wants to live as an artist [i.e. as a *Luftmensch*—one who lives on air, lofty and free-floating], in the eyes of the highly respectable, hardworking world he is a 'nasty bug [*dreckiger Käfer*]': and so in *The Metamorphosis* he wakes up as a beetle whose ideal of happiness is to be sticking to the ceiling." For Anders, *The Metamorphosis* originates in the transformation of a familiar metaphor into a fictional being having the literal attributes of this figure. The story develops as aspects of the metaphor are enacted in minute detail. Anders's evidence

2. Dieter Hasselblatt, *Zauber und Logik: Eine Kafka Studie* (Cologne: Verlag Wissenschaft und Politik), p. 61.
3. Edward Said, "Beginnings," *Salmagundi*, Fall 1968, p. 49.

for this view is furnished partly by his total understanding of Kafka: "What Kafka describes are . . . existing things, the world, as it appears to the stranger (namely strange)." Anders further adduces examples of everyday figures of speech which, taken literally, inspire stories and scenes in Kafka. "Language says, 'To feel it with your own body [*Am eignen Leibe etwas erfahren*]' when it wants to express the reality of experience. This is the basis of Kafka's *In the Penal Colony*, in which the criminal's punishment is not communicated to him by word of mouth, but is instead scratched into his body with a needle."[4]

Anders's hypothesis has been taken up in Walter Sokel's studies of *The Metamorphosis*. The notion of the "extended metaphor," which Sokel considers in an early essay to be "significant" and "interesting" though "insufficient as a total explanation of *The Metamorphosis*,"[5] reemerges in his *Writer in Extremis* as a crucial determinant of Expressionism: "The character Gregor Samsa has been transformed into a metaphor that states his essential self, and this metaphor in turn is treated like an actual fact. Samsa does not call himself a cockroach; instead he wakes up to find himself one." Expressionistic prose, for Sokel, is defined precisely by such "extended metaphors, metaphoric visualizations of emotional situations, uprooted from any explanatory context."[6] In *Franz Kafka: Tragik und Ironie*, the factual character of the Kafkan metaphor is emphasized: "In Kafka's work, as in the dream, symbol is fact. . . . A world of pure significance, of naked expression, is represented deceptively as a sequence of empirical facts."[7] Finally, in his *Franz Kafka*, Sokel states the most advanced form of his understanding of Kafka's literalization of the metaphor:

> German usage applies the term *Ungeziefer* (vermin) to persons considered low and contemptible, even as our usage of "cockroach" de-

4. Günther Anders, *Kafka—Pro und Contra* (Munich: Beck, 1951), pp. 40–41, 20, 41. For an English version (not a literal translation), see Günther Anders, *Franz Kafka*, trans. A. Steer and A. K. Thorlby (London: Bowes & Bowes, 1960). The translations here are mine.

5. Walter Sokel, "Kafka's 'Metamorphosis': Rebellion and Punishment," *Monatshefte* 40 (April–May 1956): 203.

6. Walter Sokel, *The Writer in Extremis: Expressionism in Twentieth-Century Literature* (Stanford, Calif.: Stanford University Press, 1959), pp. 47, 46.

7. Walter Sokel, *Franz Kafka: Tragik und Ironie, Zur Struktur seiner Kunst* (Frankfurt am Main: Fischer Taschenbuch, 1983), p. 110.

scribes a person deemed a spineless and miserable character. The traveling salesman Gregor Samsa, in Kafka's *Metamorphosis*, is "like a cockroach" because of his spineless and abject behavior and parasitic wishes. However, Kafka drops the word "like" and has the metaphor become reality when Gregor Samsa wakes up finding himself turned into a giant vermin. With this metamorphosis, Kafka reverses the original act of metamorphosis carried out by thought when it forms metaphor; for metaphor is always "metamorphosis." Kafka transforms metaphor back into his fictional reality, and this counter-metamorphosis becomes the starting point of his tale.[8]

The sequence of Sokel's reflections on Anders's hypothesis contains an important shift of emphasis. Initially, the force of *The Metamorphosis* is felt to lie in the choice and "extension" (dramatization) of the powerful metaphor. To support his view, Sokel cites Johannes Urzidil's recollection of a conversation with Kafka: "Once Kafka said to me: 'To be a poet means to be strong in metaphors. The greatest poets were always the most metaphorical ones. They were those who recognized the deep mutual concern, yes, even the identity of things between which nobody noticed the slightest connection before. It is the range and the scope of the metaphor which makes one a poet.'"[9] But in his later work Sokel locates the origin of Kafka's "poetry" not in the metamorphosis of reality accomplished by the metaphor but in the "counter-metamorphosis" accomplished by the transformation of the metaphor. Kafka's "taking over" figures from ordinary speech enacts a second metaphorization (*metaphero* = "to carry over")—one that concludes in the literalization and hence the metamorphosis of the metaphor.[10] This point once made, the genuine importance of Kafka's remarks to Urzidil stands revealed through their irony. In describing the poet as one "strong in metaphors," Kafka is describing writers other than himself; for he is the writer par excellence who came to detect in metaphorical language a crucial obstacle to his own enterprise.

Kafka's critique of the metaphor begins early, in the phantasmagoric story "Description of a Struggle" (1904–5). The first-

8. Walter Sokel, *Franz Kafka* (New York: Columbia University Press, 1966), p. 5.

9. Walter Sokel, "Kafka's 'Metamorphosis,'" 205. John [*sic*] Urzidil, "Recollections," in *The Kafka Problem,* ed. Angel Flores (New York: Octagon, 1963), p. 22.

10. Anders, *Kafka,* p. 42.

person narrator addresses the supplicant—another persona of the author—with exaggerated severity:

> Now I realize, by God, that I guessed from the very beginning the state you are in. Isn't it something like a fever, a seasickness on land, a kind of leprosy? Don't you feel that it's this very feverishness which is preventing you from being properly satisfied with the genuine [*wahrhaftigen*] names of things, and that now, in your frantic haste, you're just pelting them with any old [*zufällige*] names? You can't do it fast enough. But hardly have you run away from them when you've forgotten the names you gave them. The poplar in the fields, which you've called the "Tower of Babel" because you didn't want to know it was a poplar, sways again without a name, so you have to call it "Noah in his cups." [DS 60].

The weight of these accusations falls on the character who is dissatisfied with the "genuine" names of things and substitutes metaphors for them. His action is doubly arbitrary. First, the motive that prompts him to rename things—the act that generates figures—is arbitrary. His metaphors are the contingent product of a fever; or worse, they arise from deliberate bad faith, the refusal to accept the conventional bond of word and thing. Second, not a single one of his metaphors is any good, none leaves a permanent trace.

But what is also striking about this passage is its critique of "ordinary" as well as figurative names. With the irony of overstatement, the accusatory speaker calls the conventional link of name and thing "genuine," despite the fact that he does not appear to have at his disposal any such genuine names to identify the affliction of the supplicant. The speaker suffers from the same unhappy necessity of designating things by an enchainment of "any old" metaphors—such as "fever," "seasickness on dry land," "a kind of leprosy." Because (as Derrida says) "language is fundamentally metaphorical," designating, in Heidegger's phrase, the "significations to which words accrue" as the significations within words, a critique of metaphor amounts logically to a critique of naming.[11] The exact difference between ordinary names and figurative names cannot be specified. Kafka's speak-

11. Jacques Derrida, "Violence et Métaphysique," *L'ecriture et la différence* (Paris: Seuil, 1967), p. 137; Martin Heidegger, "Den Bedeutungen wachsen Worte zu," in *Sein und Zeit* (Tübingen: Klostermann, 1963), p. 161.

er, while seeing no advantage in replacing names with the figures of poetic language, at the same time cannot enact naming except by associating metaphors. Metaphors falsify, and they also invade "genuine" names.[12]

In a diary entry for December 27, 1911, Kafka recorded his despair of a particular attempt at metaphor. "An incoherent assumption is thrust like a board between the actual feeling and the metaphor of the description" (DI 201). Kafka had begun this diary entry confidently, claiming to have found an image analogous to a moral sentiment. "My feeling when I write something that is wrong might be depicted as follows": A man stands before two holes in the ground, one to the right and one to the left; he is waiting for something that can rise up only out of the hole to the right. Instead, apparitions rise, one after the other, from the left; they try to attract his attention and finally even succeed in covering up the right-hand hole. At this stage of the construction, the materiality of the image predominates; as it is developed, however, so is the role of the spectator, who scatters these apparitions upward and in all directions in the hope "that after the false apparitions have been exhausted, the true will finally appear." But precisely at the point of conjuring up "truthful apparitions," the metaphorist feels most critically the inadequacy of this figurative language: "How weak this picture is." And he concludes with the complaint that between his sentiment and figurative language there is no true coherence (though he cannot, predictably, say this without having recourse to a figure of speech). Now what is crucial here is that an image that is mainly material has failed to represent the sentiment of writing; and though it has been replaced by one that introduces the consciousness of an observer, between the moral sentiment of writing and an act of perception there is also no true connection. If the writer finds it difficult to construct metaphors for "a feeling of falsity," how

12. This suspicious critique of metaphor is proto-Expressionist. It will be taken up again and again by Expressionist writers—e.g., Carl Einstein, writing retrospectively: "Metaphor and metaphoricity refer to more than an isolated literary process; they characterize a general mood and attitude. In the metaphor one avoids repeating facts and weakens contact with reality. Metaphoricity is justified by the illusion of arbitrarily creating something new at every moment. The literati lost a sense of factual events and trusted in the empty power of their words" (*Die Fabrikationen der Fiktionen,* ed. Sibylle Penkert [Hamburg: Rowohlt, 1973], p. 283).

much greater must be his difficulty in constructing figures for genuine feelings, figures for satisfying the desire "to write all my anxiety entirely out of me, write it into the depths of the paper just as it comes out of the depths of me, or write it down in such a way that I could draw what I have written into me completely" (DI 173).

Kafka's awareness of the limitations of figurative language continues to grow. The desire to represent a state of mind directly in language—in a form consubstantial with that consciousness—and hence to create symbols cannot be gratified. "For everything outside the phenomenal world, language can only be used allusively [as an allusion, *andeutungsweise*] but never even approximately in a comparative way [as a simile, *vergleichsweise*], since, corresponding as it does to the phenomenal world, it is concerned only with property and its relations" (DF 40; H 45). But try as language will to reduce itself to its allusive function, it continues to be dependent on the metaphor, on developing states of mind by means of material analogues. On December 6, 1921, Kafka wrote: "Metaphors are one among many things which make me despair of writing. Writing's lack of independence of the world, its dependence on the maid who tends the fire, on the cat warming itself by the stove; it is even dependent on the poor old human being warming himself by the stove. All these are independent activities ruled by their own laws; only writing is helpless, cannot live in itself, is a joke and a despair" (DII 200–201). Indeed, the question arises of what truth even a language determinedly nonsymbolic—in Kafka's words, "allusive"—could possess. The parable employs language allusively, but in the powerful fable "On Parables" Kafka writes: "All these parables really set out to say merely that the incomprehensible is incomprehensible, and we know that already" (GW 258). At this point, it is clear, the literary enterprise is seen in its radically problematical character. The growing desperation of Kafka's critique of metaphorical language leads to the result—in the words of Maurice Blanchot—that at this time of Kafka's life "the exigency of the truth of this other world [of sheer inwardness determined on salvation] henceforth surpasses in his eyes the exigency of the work of art."[13] This situation suggests not the renunciation of

13. Maurice Blanchot, "The Diaries: The Exigency of the Work of Art," trans. Lyall H. Powers, in *Franz Kafka Today*, ed. Angel Flores and Homer Swander (Madison: University of Wisconsin Press, 1964), p. 207.

writing but only the clearest possible awareness of its limitations, an awareness that emerges through Kafka's perplexity before the metaphor in the work of art and his despair of escaping it.

* * *

Kafka's "counter-metamorphosis" of the metaphor in *The Metamorphosis* is inspired by his fundamental objection to the metaphor. His purpose is accomplished—so Anders and Sokel propose—through the literalization of the metaphor. But is this true? What does it mean, exactly, to literalize a metaphor? The metaphor designates something (A) *as* something (B)—something in the quality of something not itself. To say that someone is a verminous bug is to designate a moral sensibility as something unlike itself, as a material sensation—complicated, of course, by the atmosphere of loathing that this sensation evokes. With I. A. Richards, I shall call the *tenor* of the metaphor (A), the thing designated, occulted, replaced, but otherwise established by the context of the figure; and the *vehicle*, the metaphor proper, (B), that thing *as* which the tenor is designated.[14] If the metaphor is taken out of context, however, if it is taken literally, it no longer functions as a vehicle but as a name, directing us to (B) as an abstraction or an object in the world. Moreover, it directs us to (B) in the totality of its qualities and not, as does the vehicle, only to those qualities of (B) that can be assigned to (A).

This analysis will suggest the destructively paradoxical consequence of "taking the metaphor literally," supposing now that such a thing is possible. Reading the figure literally, we go to (B) as an object in the world in its totality; yet reading it metaphorically, we go to (B) only in its quality as a predicate of (A). As literalization proceeds, as we attempt to experience in (B) more and more qualities that can be accommodated by (A), we *metamorphose* (A). But if the metaphor is to be preserved and (A) and (B) are to remain unlike, we must stop before the metamorphosis is complete. If, now, the tenor—as in *The Metamorphosis*—is a human consciousness, the increasing literalization of the vehicle transforms the tenor into a monster.

This genesis of monsters occurs independently of the nature of the vehicle. The intent toward literalization of a metaphor linking a human con-

14. I. A. Richards, *The Philosophy of Rhetoric* (New York: Oxford University Press, 1936), p. 96.

sciousness and a material sensation produces a monster in every instance, no matter whether the vehicle is odious or not, whether we begin with the metaphor of a "louse" or of a man who is a jewel or a rock. It now appears that Anders is not correct in suggesting that in *The Metamorphosis* literalization of the metaphor is actually accomplished; for then we should have not an indefinite monster but simply a bug. Indeed, the continual alteration of Gregor's body suggests ongoing metamorphosis, the *process* of literalization in various directions and not its end state. Nor would Sokel's earlier formulation appear to be tenable: the metaphor is not treated "like an actual fact." Only the alien cleaning woman gives Gregor Samsa the factual, entomological identity of a "dung beetle," but precisely "to forms of address like these Gregor would not respond" (M 45). The cleaning woman does not know that a metamorphosis has occurred, that within this insect shape there is a human consciousness—one superior at times to the ordinary consciousness of Gregor Samsa. It appears, then, that the metamorphosis in the Samsa household of man into vermin is unsettling not only because vermin are disturbing, or because the vivid representation of a human "louse" is disturbing, but because the indeterminate, fluid crossing of a human tenor and a material vehicle is in itself unsettling. Gregor is at one moment pure rapture and at another very nearly pure dung beetle, at times grossly human and at times airily buglike. In shifting incessantly the relation of Gregor's mind and body, Kafka shatters the suppositious unity of ideal tenor and bodily vehicle within the metaphor. This destruction must distress common sense, which defines itself by such "genuine" relations, such natural assertions of analogues between consciousness and matter, and in this way masks the knowledge of its own strangeness. The ontological legitimation for asserting analogues is missing in Kafka, who maintains the most ruthless division between the fire of the spirit and the "filth" of the world: "What we call the world of the senses is the Evil in the spiritual world" (DF 39).

The distortion of the metaphor in *The Metamorphosis* is inspired by a radical aesthetic intention, which proceeds by destruction and results in creation—of a monster, virtually nameless, existing as an opaque sign.[15] "The name alone, revealed through a natural death,

15. Hasselblatt, *Zauber und Logik*, pp. 195, 200. This is consistent with the Expressionist desideratum par excellence: "For we are here to re-create every created thing: in language. To bring to life for the first time through ourselves: in language. *Sine*

not the living soul, vouches for that in man which is immortal."[16] But what is remarkable in *The Metamorphosis* is that "the immortal part" of the writer accomplishes itself odiously, in the quality of an indeterminacy sheerly negative. The exact sense of his intention is captured in the *Ungeziefer*, a word that cannot be expressed by the English words "bug" or "vermin." *Ungeziefer* derives (as Kafka probably knew) from the late Middle High German word originally meaning "the unclean animal not suited for sacrifice."[17] If for Kafka "writing . . . [is] a form of prayer" (DF 312), this act of writing reflects its own hopelessness. As a distortion of the "genuine" names of things, without significance as metaphor or as literal fact, the monster of *The Metamorphosis* is, like writing itself, a "fever" and a "despair."

Kafka's metamorphosis—through aberrant literalization—of the metaphor "this man is a vermin" appears to be an intricate and comprehensive act in which one can discern three orders of significance, all of which inform *The Metamorphosis*. These meanings emerge separately as one focuses critically on three facts: that the metaphor distorted is a familiar element of ordinary language; that, the distortion being incomplete, the body of the original metaphor maintains a shadow existence within the metamorphosis, and the body of *this* metaphor—a verminous bug—is negative and repulsive; and finally, that the source of the metamorphosis is, properly speaking, not the familiar metaphor but a radical aesthetic intention. Together these meanings interpenetrate in a dialectical way. For example, the aesthetic intention reflects itself in a monster but does so by distorting an initially monstrous metaphor; the outcome of its destroying a negative is itself a negative. These relations illuminate both Kafka's saying, "Doing the negative thing is imposed on us, an addition" (DF

---

verecundia. Many have tried out the criticism of language. . . . More urgent than criticism is the creation of language" (Alfred Kerr, "Sexueller Ursprung der Sprache," *Pan* 3, nos. 16-17 [1913-1914]: 280).

16. Theodore Adorno, *Prisms*, trans. Samuel and Shierry Weber (London: Spearman, 1967), p. 271.

17. Kafka studied medieval German literature at the University of Prague in 1902. Cf. Klaus Wagenbach, *Franz Kafka: Eine Biographie seiner Jugend (1883–1912)* (Bern: Francke, 1958), p. 100. He assiduously consulted Grimm's etymological dictionary. Cf. Max Brod, *Über Franz Kafka* (Frankfurt am Main: Fischer, 1966), pp. 110, 213. The citation from Grimm is discussed in depth by Kurt Weinberg, *Kafkas Dichtungen: Die Travestien des Mythos* (Bern: Francke, 1963), pp. 316–17.

36–37), and his remark to Milena Jesenská-Pollak, "But even the truth of longing is not so much its truth, rather is it an expression of the lie of everything else" (LM 200). For the sake of analysis, each of the three intents can be separated and discussed independently.

Kafka metamorphoses a figure of speech embedded in ordinary language. The intent is to make strange the familiar, not to invent the new; Kafka's diaries for the period around 1912 show that his created metaphors are more complex than "salesmen are vermin." To stress the estrangement of the monster from his familiar setting in the metaphor—the dirty bug—is to stress Gregor Samsa's estrangement from his identity in the family. Gregor harks back to, yet defiantly resists, integration into the "ordinary language" of the family. The condition of the distorted metaphor, estranged from familiar speech, shapes the family drama of *The Metamorphosis;* the *Ungeziefer* is in the fullest sense of the word *ungeheuer* (monstrous)—a being that cannot be accommodated in a family.[18]

Is it too odd an idea to see this family drama as the conflict between ordinary language and a being having the character of an indecipherable word? It will seem less odd, at any rate, to grasp the family life of the Samsas as a characteristic language. The family defines itself by the ease with which it enters into collusion on the question of Gregor. Divisions of opinion do arise—touching, say, on the severity of the treatment due Gregor—but issue at once into new decisions. The family's projects develop within the universe of their concerns, through transparent words and gestures that communicate without effort. At the end, images of family unity survive the story: the mother and father in complete union; mother, father, and daughter emerging arm in arm from the parents' bedroom to confront the boarders; mother and father "growing quieter and communicating almost unconsciously through glances" at the sight of their good-looking, shapely daughter (M 58).

Family language in *The Metamorphosis* has a precise symbolic correlative, Kimberly Sparks suggests, in the newspaper. The person in power at any moment reads or manipulates the newspaper.[19] Gregor

18. Weinberg, *Kafkas Dichtungen,* p. 317.
19. Kimberly Sparks, "Drei Schwarze Kaninchen: Zu einer Deutung der Zimmerherren in Kafkas 'Die Verwandlung,'" *Zeitschrift für deutsche Philologie* 84 (1965): 78–79.

has clipped the love object that hangs on his wall from an illustrated newspaper; his evening custom as head of the family had been to sit at the table and read the newspaper. It is a sorry comment on his loss of power and identity within the family that it is on newspaper that his first meal of garbage is served; the father, meanwhile, downcast for a while, fails to read the newspaper aloud to the family. When the boarders come to dominate the family, it is they who ostentatiously read the newspaper at the dinner table. The newspaper represents an order of efficient language from which Gregor is excluded.

The task of interpreting the monstrous noun that Gregor has become is more difficult; his transformation is essentially obscure and can be understood only through approximations. One such approximation is the *intelligible* transformation that also results in Gregor's becoming an opaque sign.

If Gregor had lost the ability to make himself understood by the others but had preserved his human shape, the family would have been inclined to interpret the change as temporary, would have encouraged Gregor to speak; the mere loss of language would not result in isolation and insignificance. But if Kafka wished to suggest the solitude resulting from the absolute loss of all significance, he had to present this condition as a consequence of the loss of the human form. The sense of Gregor's opaque body is thus to maintain him in a solitude without speech or intelligible gesture, in the solitude of an indecipherable sign. To put it another way: his body is the speech in which the impossibility of ordinary language expresses its own despair.

The conception of Gregor as a mutilated metaphor, uprooted from familiar language, brings another element of this family drama to light. The transformed metaphor preserves a trace of its original state. The consciousness of Gregor, like the uprooted metaphor, is defined by its reference to its former state: though Gregor cannot communicate, he continues to remember. This point underscores a feature of Kafka's metamorphosis which distinguishes it from the classical metamorphosis in Ovid, where a human consciousness is converted into a natural object. *The Metamorphosis* converts a word having a quasi-natural identity, the rooted and familiar identity of ordinary speech, into a word having the character of a unique consciousness. The distorted word, without presence or future, suggests a mind dominated by nostalgia for its former life—a life of obscure habit and occupation rewarded by secure family ties.

Gregor's future is mainly obstructed by a particular form of the tyranny of nostalgia, by the "consideration" he shows his family (M 23, 48). Kafka's word *Rücksicht*, with its connotations of hindsight, of looking backward, is exactly right for Gregor: his consideration arises from his clinging to a mythic past—one that is, in fact, hopelessly lost (E 96, 129). The play of Gregor's "consideration" reveals his family feeling as necessarily ambivalent, moving between extremes of solicitude and indifference.

The key passage has been pointed out by William Empson, though his interpretation of it is actually misleading. According to Empson, Kafka can only have been nodding when he wrote, in the scene of the sister's violin playing: "It hardly surprised [Gregor] that lately he was showing so little consideration for the others; once such consideration had been his greatest pride. . . . Now . . . his indifference to everything was much too deep for him to have gotten on his back and scrubbed himself clean against the carpet, as once he had done several times a day" (M 48). "After the apple incident," Empson points out, "there could surely be no question of . . . this," for the apple fired at Gregor by his father has lodged in his back and caused a festering wound.[20] But Kafka's chiding Gregor for his indifference precisely at this point is not an "inconsistency." The moment teaches us to regard Gregor's consideration for the others as an aberration, an impulse opposite to his own most genuine concern, such as it is. It is in forgetting a useless consideration and pursuing the sound of the music that Gregor is able to discover his own condition, to perceive his irreducible strangeness. The abandonment of a *Rücksicht* that is bent on reintegration into ordinary life enables him for one moment (he did not formerly "understand" music) to imagine the music of the world in a finer tone. In our perspective this moment emerges as a restitution of language to Gregor, yet of a language fundamentally

---

20. William Empson, "A Family Monster" (review of *The Metamorphosis*), *Nation* 138 (December 7, 1946): 653. Empson's surmise—"Maybe [Kafka] could never bear to read over the manuscript"—is incorrect; Kafka speaks of proofreading *The Metamorphosis* (DII 13). For the scrupulousness with which he edited his stories, see Ludwig Dietz, "Franz Kafka, Drucke zu seinen Lebzeiten: Eine textkritisch-bibliographische Studie," *Jahrbuch der deutschen Schillergesellschaft* 7 (1963): 416–57.

unlike the language he has lost. The character of the lost language is approximated by the abrupt fantasy of violence and incest following the violin music, into which Gregor's experience of music collapses. The language of music is degraded when it is made the means for the restitution of a family relationship.

*　　*　　*

Gregor's ambivalent relation to his family, inspired partly by the relationship between literary and conventional figurative language, suggests Kafka's own ambivalent feeling about intimacy. His ambivalence, centering as it does on an idea of renunciation, is spelled out in an early account of his love for the Yiddish actress Mrs. Tschissik. "A young man . . . declares to this woman his love to which he has completely fallen victim and . . . immediately renounces the woman. . . . Should I be grateful or should I curse the fact that despite all misfortune I can still feel love, an unearthly love but still for earthly objects?" (DI 139). We know that Kafka at times thought the utmost a man might achieve was to found a family; he liked to quote the words attributed to Flaubert describing a family full of children: "*Ils sont dans le vrai* [they are living the truthful life]."[21] But he also wrote to Felice Bauer, "Rather put on blinkers and go my way to the limit than have the familiar pack [*das heimatliche Rudel*] mill around me and distract my gaze" (DII 167, Ta 514). The precarious existence that Kafka maintained outside "the house of life" required vigilant curbing of his nostalgia.

The separateness and nostalgia that inform Gregor's relation to his family (and reflect Kafka's ambivalent feelings about intimate relations) dramatize still more sharply Kafka's relation to the familiar language on which he drew. In "Description of a Struggle," Kafka alluded to that fevered soul who could not be contented with the genuine names of things but had to scatter arbitrary names over familiar things. But later in the same text the same fictional persona declares, "When as a child I opened my eyes after a brief afternoon nap, still not quite sure I was alive, I heard my mother up on the balcony asking in a natural tone of voice: 'What are you doing, my dear? Goodness, isn't it hot?' From the garden a woman answered:

21. Brod, *Über Franz Kafka*, p. 89.

'Me, I'm having my tea on the lawn [*Ich jause so im Grünen*].' They spoke casually and not very distinctly, as though this woman had expected the question, my mother the answer'" (DS 62; B 44). In the model of a dialogue in ordinary language, Kafka communicates his early, intense longing for and insistence on wholeness and clarity—in Klaus Wagenbach's phrase, Kafka's "plain marveling at the magic of the simple." This is the simplicity of common speech in which names and things fit effortlessly together. Kafka's "idolatrous admiration of the truth, which grows more and more marked," Wagenbach continues, "is at the root of his decision to confine himself to the linguistic material offered him by his environment."[22] But Hermann Pongs foresees in this decision a dangerous end: the result of Kafka's confining himself to the juiceless, stilted language of Prague is Gregor Samsa's ongoing metamorphosis. "The fate of the animal voice, into which human sound is changed, becomes a terrible symptom of Kafka's being cut off from the substrata of the inner form of language. Kafka scholarship has brought to light the fact that the Prague German available to Kafka, homeless between Germans, Jews and Czechs in the region of Prague, was an already etiolated literary German, obliged to do without any forces of rejuvenation through dialect."[23]

There is some truth in this statement, to which Kafka's frequent animadversions on the German of Prague testify (but then, of course, the fate of the animal voice is not a "symptom" but a conscious reflection of Kafka's alienation). "Yesterday," writes Kafka, "it occurred to me that I did not always love my mother as she deserved and as I could, only because the German language prevented it. The Jewish mother is no 'Mutter'" (DI 111). In a letter to Max Brod composed in June 1921, Kafka discusses the predicament of the Jewish writer writing in German. The literary language of such a Jew he calls *mauscheln*, which ordinarily means "to speak German with a Yiddish accent": "This is not to say anything against *mauscheln*—in itself it is fine. It is an organic compound of bookish German [*Papierdeutsch*] and pantomime . . . and the product of a sensitive feeling for

22. Klaus Wagenbach, *Franz Kafka in Selbstzeugnissen und Bilddokumenten* (Hamburg: Rowohlt, 1964), pp. 41–56.
23. Hermann Pongs, "Franz Kafka—'Die Verwandlung': Zwischen West und Ost," in *Dichtung im gespaltenen Deutschland* (Stuttgart: Union, 1966), p. 276.

language which has recognized that in German only the dialects are really alive, and except for them, only the most individual High German, while all the rest, the linguistic middle ground, is nothing but embers which can be brought to a semblance of life only when excessively lively Jewish hands rummage through them" (L 288; Br 336-37). The middle ground of the German that Kafka heard around him was frequently not the object of his nostalgia but "clamor" (DI 220) or inanity—"in the next room . . . they are talking about vermin" (DI 258).

Now it is precisely through this act of "rummaging" about that Kafka names, elliptically and ironically, the kind of creative distortion to which he submitted the figures of the conventional idiom. That the metamorphic character of Kafka's relation to ordinary language is frequently misunderstood, however, is particularly clear from critics' speculations about the source of this act. Wagenbach suggests that Kafka's distortions are in fact the work of Prague German, which "of its own accord" provoked the counter-metamorphosis of metaphors. Kafka's native German, Wagenbach writes, "always possessed a vestige of unfamiliarity; distance, too, vis-à-vis the individual word set in of its own accord. Removed from the leveling effect of everyday usage, words, metaphors, and verbal constructions recovered their original variety of meaning, became richer in images, richer in associative possibilities. As a result, in Kafka's work too on almost every page such chains of association are found arising from taking words with strict literalness."[24]

But it is as questionable to maintain that *of its own accord* Prague German proffered its metaphors literally as it is to maintain, as Martin Greenberg does, that Kafka's sociological situation determined his use of metaphor, that "thanks to his distance as a Prague Jew from the German language, he [was] able to see it in an 'analytic' way."[25] In the seven hundred closely printed pages of Kafka's letters to Felice Bauer—letters written, of course, in Prague German—Kafka is not tempted to rummage about in the metaphors of the conventional idiom, to take them literally, or to see them in an analytic way. In these letters Kafka achieves the most palpable intimacy, the native

24. Wagenbach, *Franz Kafka in Selbstzeugnissen*, p. 56.
25. Martin Greenberg, *The Terror of Art: Kafka and Modern Literature* (New York: Basic Books, 1968), pp. 26–27.

coldness of Prague German notwithstanding; indeed, so intimate is the world he conjures up and creates through language that it becomes for him as much of the married state as he can bear. It is not Prague German that imposes on Kafka his sense of the untruthfulness of the metaphor and hence the fundamental form of his writing; the source lies prior to his reflections on a particular kind and state of language.

Kafka, writers Martin Walser, "accomplished the metamorphosis of reality prior to the work, by reducing—indeed, destroying—his bourgeois-biographical personality for the sake of a development that has for its goal the personality of the poet; this poetic personality, the *poetica personalità*, establishes the form."[26] It is Kafka's literary consciousness, reflecting itself in the destruction of all intimacy even with itself, which from the beginning puts distance between Kafka and the world of Prague German. Tzvetan Todorov, too, stresses "the difference in the hierarchy of the two ideas [of figurative language and poetic language]: figurative language is a sort of potential stock inside language, while poetic language is already a construction, a utilization of this raw material. . . . Figurative language opposes transparent language in order to impose the presence of words; literary language opposes ordinary language in order to impose the presence of things"[27]—things unheard before, new realities, reflections of the poetic self.

Kafka's attachment to the everyday language of Prague is only one impetus in the thrust of his poetic consciousness toward its own truth. His language probes the depths of the imaginary—a depth that lies concealed within ordinary language but can be brought to light through the willful distortion of the figurative underlayer of ordinary language. The primitiveness of the vermin reflects Kafka's radical thrust toward origins. His destruction of his native personality for the sake of a poetic development destroys the privilege of inherited language.

Conceiving, then, the opening of *The Metamorphosis* as the metamorphosis of a familiar metaphor, we can identify minor and major movements of Kafka's spirit: the retrospective attachment to the familiar, and the movement of the spirit toward its own reality. As

26. Martin Walser, *Beschreibung einer Form* (Munich: Hanser, 1961), p. 11.
27. Tzvetan Todorov, *Littérature et signification* (Paris: Larousse, 1967), pp. 115-17.

opposite movements, they cannot be accommodated within the metaphor that asserts an analogy between the spirit and the common life it negates. Only the metamorphosis destroying the metaphor establishes their distinction.

* * *

Our second approach to *Metamorphosis* stresses the presence in the fiction of Gregor Samsa of the residue of a real meaning, the real vermin in the conventional metaphor "the man is a vermin." This method opens a path to that whole range of criticism aiming to relate *The Metamorphosis* to empirical experiences and, by extension, to Kafka's personal life. Kafka, the approach stresses, has distorted but preserved through distortion the sense of a man debased in the way that vermin are debased. As Kafka incorporates in the story the empirical sense of a biting and sucking insect—so this argument proceeds—he incorporates as well his sense of his empirical self.[28] An essentially realistic tale of humiliation and neurosis reflects Kafka's tortured personality.

Innumerable attempts have been made to explain Gregor's debasement in terms of the ways in which a man can be humiliated. The Marxist critic Helmut Richter, for example, alludes to the deformed products of a mechanical work process, to Gregor the alienated salesman; Sokel, as a psychologist, stresses Gregor's intent to punish by means of his repulsiveness the family that had enslaved him. Hellmuth Kaiser views the metamorphosis as retribution for an Oedipal rebellion; the pathologist Wilfredo Dalmau Castañón sees it as the symptomatology of tuberculosis.[29] In most of these readings the evidence of Kafka's empirical personality is brought directly into court; the ne plus ultra of this sort of criticism is an essay by Giuliano Baioni, which sees the metamorphosis as repeating Kafka's feeling of

28. Autobiographical critics frequently attempt to force the identification of Kafka and Gregor Samsa by citing the passage (DF 195) in which Kafka has his father compare him to a stinging, bloodsucking vermin. This is done despite Kafka's explicit warning that "Samsa is not altogether Kafka" (J 55).

29. Helmut Richter, *Franz Kafka: Werk und Entwurf* (Berlin: Ruetten & Loening) pp. 112-19; Sokel, "Kafka's 'Metamorphosis,'" 213; Hellmuth Kaiser, "Franz Kafkas Inferno: Eine psychologische Deutung seiner Strafphantasie," *Imago* 17, no. 1 (1931): 41–104; Wilfredo Dalmau Castañón, "El caso clinico de Kafka en 'La Metamorfosis,'" *Cuadernos Hispanoamericanos* (Madrid) 27 (March 1952): 385–88.

guilt and absolving him of it. Kafka is guilty and must be punished simply for being himself, for being his father's son, for hating his father, for getting engaged, for not loving enough, for being incapable of loving, for being a writer who is thinking about his father, for being a factory manager and not writing, and finally, for being an imperfect creature whose body is a foreign body and stands condemned by a Hasidic ideal of unity.[30] A critical bibliography of *The Metamorphosis* compiled in 1973 describes more than one hundred published critiques of an empirical or programmatic kind.[31] Though all are plausible, they are privative; Kafka, this most highly conscious of artists, implacable skeptic of psychoanalysis, never conceived of writing as enactment of or compensation for his troubled personality.

For Kafka, personal happiness is not the goal but a stake and as such alienable—a means, functioning essentially through its renunciation, to an altogether different elation (and anxiety), which is at the heart of literature, his "real life" (DI 211). In a passage in *Amerika* written shortly before the composition of *The Metamorphosis,* Karl Rossman, as he plays the piano, feels "rising within him a sorrow which reached past the end of the song, seeking another end which it could not find" (A 88).[32] "Art for the artist," said Kafka, "is only suffering, through which he releases himself for further suffering" (J 28). In a letter to Max Brod of July 5, 1922, Kafka links his writing to the amelioration of his life in a merely concessive way: "I don't mean, of course, that my life is better when I don't write. Rather it is much worse then and wholly unbearable and has to end in madness" (L 333). But this relation between not writing and madness obtains only because he is fundamentally a writer, and a writer who does not write is an absurdity (*Unding*) that would call down madness. The only madness that writing cures is the madness of not writing.

The attempt to interpret *The Metamorphosis* through Kafka's empirical personality suffers, by implication, from the difficulty of interpreting the vermin through the residual empirical sense of the metaphor of the vermin. The author of a monograph on the story, Jürg

30. Giuliano Baioni, *Kafka: Romanzo e parabola* (Milan: Feltrinelli, 1962), pp. 81–100.

31. In Stanley Corngold, *The Commentators' Despair: The Interpretation of Kafka's "Metamorphosis"* (Port Washington, N.Y.: Kennikat Press, 1973).

32. This text mistakenly reads the word *Leid* ("sorrow") as *Lied*, (song); I have made the correction.

Schubiger, notes a concrete disparity between the form of the vermin and any bug that can be visualized:

> [The head] ends in "nostrils" and in strong jaws, which take the place of human jaws. Compared with what we are accustomed to in bugs, the head is unusually mobile. Not only can the creature lower and raise it, draw it in and stretch it out; he can even turn it so far to the side that he sees just what is going on behind him. . . . Statements about the weight of the creature . . . "two strong persons" would have been necessary to lift him out of bed [M 8] . . . are incompatible with Gregor's later ability to wander over the walls and ceiling; even with glue, a bug weighing at least seventy pounds cannot hang on the ceiling.

"And so," Schubiger concludes, "the bodily 'data' must not be understood as facts . . . they are bodily imaged questions and answers in the bug's dialogue with the world."[33] Kafka himself confirmed this conclusion when he specifically forbade his publisher to illustrate the first edition of *The Metamorphosis* with a drawing of the creature: "The insect itself cannot be depicted" (L 115).

The importance within *The Metamorphosis* of the original metaphor "this man is a vermin" is not for Kafka the empirical identity of a bug. What is paramount is the form of the metaphor as such, which is then deformed; hence, any metaphor would do, with this provision (as formulated by Jacques Lacan): "Any conjunction of two signifiers would be equally sufficient to constitute a metaphor, except for the additional requirement of the greatest possible disparity of the images signified, needed for the production of the poetic spark, or in other words for there to be metaphoric creation."[34] In the most powerful metaphor, vehicle and tenor are poles apart; this power is appropriated by the act of aesthetic distortion. Kafka's metaphor is only impoverished when the tenor, a traveling salesman, is equated with Kafka's empirical personality as factory manager.

Lacan's insight helps, moreover, to clarify another crux. Anders originally saw the metaphor underlying *The Metamorphosis* as "This man, who wants to live as an artist, is a nasty bug." Dieter Hasselblatt

---

33. Jürg Schubiger, *Franz Kafka: Die Verwandlung, Eine Interpretation* (Zurich: Atlantis, 1969), pp. 55–57.

34. Jacques Lacan, "The Insistence of the Letter in the Unconscious," *Yale French Studies* 36/37 (October 1966): 125.

has argued against this formulation, asserting, "Nowhere in the text is there any mention of the problem of the artist and society."[35] Of course it is true that Gregor Samsa is not an artist *manqué*. But as the occasion for a metamorphosis, he becomes an aesthetic object—the unique correlative of a poetic intention. Indeed, Hasselblatt's own view of *The Metamorphosis* as the response of the everyday world to the inconceivable gives the work an essential bearing on the theme of poetic language. The empirical identity of the tenor, be it artist or any other man, is inconsequential because *Metamorphosis* is dominated by an aesthetic intent. The intent to literalize a metaphor produces a being wholly divorced from empirical reality.

*　　*　　*

The third approach focuses upon this aesthetic intent, which aims, through metamorphosis of the metaphor, to assert its own autonomy. We can no longer take our bearings from the empirical sense of the vermin. Yet neither are we obliged to abandon every attempt at interpreting the signifier. For Kafka has already established a link between the bug and the activity of writing itself. In his 1907 "Wedding Preparations in the Country" (DF 2–31), of which only a fragment survives, Kafka conjures a hero, Eduard Raban, reluctant to take action in the world (he is supposed to go to the country to arrange his wedding). Raban dreams instead of autonomy, self-sufficiency, and omnipotence. For this transparent reflection of his early literary consciousness, Kafka finds the emblem of a beetle, about which there hovers an odd indeterminacy:

> And besides, can't I do it the way I always used to as a child in matters that were dangerous? I don't even need to go to the country myself, it isn't necessary. I'll send my clothed body. If it staggers out of the door of my room, the staggering will indicate not fear but its nothingness. Nor is it a sign of excitement if it stumbles on the stairs, if it travels into the country, sobbing as it goes, and there eats its supper in tears. For I myself am meanwhile lying in my bed, smoothly covered over with the yellow-brown blanket, exposed to the breeze that is wafted through that seldom aired room. The carriages and people in the street move and walk hesitantly on shining ground, for I am still dreaming. Coachmen and pedestrians are shy, and every step they want to ad-

35. Anders, *Kafka—Pro und Contra,* p. 40; Hasselblatt, *Zauber und Logik,* p. 203.

vance they ask as a favor from me, by looking at me. I encourage them and they encounter no obstacle.

As I lie in bed I assume the shape of a big beetle, a stagbeetle or a cockchafer, I think. . . .

The form of a large beetle, yes. Then I would pretend it was a matter of hibernating, and I would press my little legs to my bulging belly. And I would whisper a few words, instructions to my sad body, which stands close beside me, bent. Soon I shall have done—it bows, it goes swiftly, and it will manage everything efficiently while I rest. [DF 6–7]

The figure of the omnipotent bug is positive throughout this passage and suggests the inwardness of the act of writing rendered in its power and freedom, in its mystic exaltation, evidence of which abounds in Kafka's early diary entries:

The special nature of my inspiration . . . is such that I can do everything, and not only what is directed to a definite piece of work. When I arbitrarily write a single sentence, for instance, "He looked out of the window," it already has perfection. [DI 45]

My happiness, my abilities, and every possibility of being useful in any way have always been in the literary field. And here I have, to be sure, experienced states . . . in which I completely dwelt in every idea, but also filled every idea, and in which I not only felt myself at my boundary, but at the boundary of the human in general. [DI 58]

Again it was the power of my dreams, shining forth into wakefulness even before I fall asleep, which did not let me sleep. In the evening and the morning my consciousness of the creative abilities in me is more than I can encompass. I feel shaken to the core of my being and can get out of myself whatever I desire. . . . It is a matter of . . . mysterious powers which are of an ultimate significance to me. [DI 76]

How everything can be said, how for everything, for the strangest fancies, there waits a great fire in which they perish and rise up again. [DI 276]

But this is only one side of Kafka's poetic consciousness. The other is expressed through the narrator's hesitation in defining his trance by means of an objective correlative ("a stag-beetle . . . I think"), which suggests beyond his particular distress the general impossibility of the metaphor's naming, by means of a material image, the being of an inward state and hence a doubt that will go to the root of writing itself. After 1912 there are few such positive emblems for the inwardness and solitude of the act of writing; this "beautiful" bug[36] is projected in ignorance; the truer emblem of the alien poetic consciousness which "has no base, no substance" (L 334), which must suffer "the eternal torments of dying" (DII 77), becomes the vermin Gregor. The movement from the beautiful bug Raban to the monstrous bug Gregor marks an accession of self-knowledge—an increasing awareness of the poverty and shortcomings of writing.[37]

The direction of Kafka's reflection on literature is fundamentally defined, however, by "The Judgment," the story written immediately before *The Metamorphosis*. "The Judgment" struck Kafka as a breakthrough into his own style and produced an ecstatic notation in his diary. But later in his interpretation Kafka described the story in a somewhat more sinister tonality, as having "come out of me like a real birth, covered with filth and slime" (DI 278). The image has the violence and inevitability of a natural process, but its filth and slime cannot fail to remind the reader of the strange birth that is the subject of Kafka's next story—the incubus trailing filth and slime through the household of its family.

Two major aspects of "The Judgment," I think, inspire in Kafka a sense of the authenticity of the story important enough for it to be commemorated in the figure of the vermin. First, the figure of the friend in Russia represents with the greatest clarity to date the negativity of the "business" of writing: the friend is said by the father to be "yellow enough to be thrown away" (S 87). Second, "The Judgment," like *The Metamorphosis,* develops as the implications of a distorted metaphor are enacted: "The Judgment" metamorphoses the father's "judgment" or "estimate" into a fatal "verdict," a death "sentence."[38]

Kafka's awareness that "The Judgment" originates from the distortion of the metaphor dictates the conclusion of his "interpretation." The highly formal tonality of this structural analysis surprises the

36. Sokel, "Kafka's 'Metamorphosis,'" 81.

37. "For writing to be possible, it must be born out of the death of what it speaks about; but this death makes writing itself impossible, for there is no longer anything to write" (Tzvetan Todorov, discussing Blanchot's Kafka, in *The Fantastic: A Structural Approach to a Literary Genre*, trans. Richard Howard [Cleveland, Ohio: Press of Case Western Reserve University, 1973], p. 175).

38. Greenberg, *The Terror of Art*, p. 48.

reader, following as it does on the organic simile of the sudden birth: "The friend is the link between father and son, he is their strongest common bond. Sitting alone at his window, Georg rummages voluptuously in this consciousness of what they have in common, believes he has his father within him, and would be at peace with everything if it were not for a fleeting, sad thoughtfulness. In the course of the story the father . . . uses the common bond of the friend to set himself up as Georg's antagonist" (DI 278). This analysis employs the structural model of the metamorphosed metaphor. At first Georg considers the father as the friend, and his friend as the metaphor of the father. But Georg's doom is to take the metaphor literally, to suppose that by sharing the quality of the friend, he possesses the father in fact. In a violent countermovement the father distorts the initial metaphor, drawing the friend's existence into himself; and Georg, who now feels "what they have in common . . . only as something foreign, something that has become independent, that he has never given enough protection" (DI 279), accepts his sentence.

It is this new art, generated from the distortion of relations modeled on the metaphor, that came to Kafka as an elation, a gross new birth, and a sentence. The aesthetic intention comes to light negatively when it must express itself through so tormented and elliptical a strategem as the metamorphosis of the metaphor. The restriction and misery of this art is the explicit subject of *The Metamorphosis;* the invention that henceforth shapes Kafka's existence as a writer is original, arbitrary, and fundamentally strange. In a later autobiographical note he writes: "All that he does seems to him, it is true, extraordinarily new, but also, because of the incredible spate of new things, extraordinarily amateurish, indeed scarcely tolerable, incapable of becoming history, breaking short the chain of the generations, cutting off for the first time at its most profound source the music of the world, which before him could at least be divined. Sometimes in his arrogance he has more anxiety for the world than for himself" (GW 263–64). Kafka's pride in his separateness equals his nostalgia for "the music of the world." His tension defines the violently distorted metaphor Gregor Samsa, who, in responding to his sister's violin playing, causes this music to be broken off. That being who lives as a distortion of nature—and without a history and without a future still maintains a certain sovereignty—conjures up through the extremity of his separation the clearest possible idea of the music he cannot possess.

In the light of the beautiful beetle of "Wedding Preparations" and the trail of filth and mucus that "The Judgment" leaves behind, the vermin in *The Metamorphosis* is revealed as expressing a hermeneutical relation, as reflecting Kafka's sense of his literary destiny. But the negative character of this vermin, this judgment, still has to be clarified.[39] It is a seductive hypothesis to suppose that *The Metamorphosis* describes the fate of the writer who does not write, whose "business," like that of the Russian friend in "The Judgment," is not flourishing.

For this assumption there is a good deal of evidence in Kafka's letters. On November 1, 1912, two weeks before conceiving *The Metamorphosis,* Kafka wrote to Felice, with uncanny relevance to the story: "My life consists, and basically always has consisted, of attempts at writing, mostly unsuccessful. But when I didn't write, I was at once flat on the floor, fit for the dustbin" (LF 20).[40] It is as a wholly literary being, albeit one who is foundering, that Kafka identifies himself with the corpse that will be swept out of the bedroom. On November 18, *The Metamorphosis* becomes a "cautionary tale" for the writer at a standstill: "I am just sitting down to yesterday's story

39. *The Metamorphosis* distorts a metaphor alluding to an earlier act of writing; as such it prefigures Kafka's next published work, "In the Penal Colony." The main action of this story, the operation of a terrible machine that kills a criminal by inscribing immediately into his flesh the commandment he had disobeyed, follows from the distortion of a metaphor about writing or engraving, of the experience that engraves itself on a person's memory. The vehicle here, an act of writing, is without even a residual sense of Kafka's empirical personality. Kafka himself noted: "But for me, who believe that I shall be able to lie contentedly on my deathbed, such scenes are secretly a game" (DII 102). The more comprehensive meaning of this vehicle is supplied by Kafka's sense that in writing he was engraving his own tombstone.

40. An episode from the life of Kierkegaard parallels remarkably this sentiment and the incident from *Metamorphosis*: "Well," the cleaning woman answered, "you don't have to worry about getting rid of the stuff next door. It's already been taken care of" (M 57). Walter Lowrie, writing in his *Short Life of Kierkegaard* (Princeton, N.J.: Princeton University Press, 1971), p. 41, of the spinal trouble that eventually caused Kierkegaard's death, reports: "We have several accounts of similar attacks which were not permanent. For example, at a social gathering he once fell from the sofa and lay impotent upon the floor—beseeching his friends not to pick 'it' up but to 'leave it there till the maid comes in the morning to sweep.'" Theodore Ziolkowski noted this parallel. For a study of the relation between Kafka and Kierkegaard, see Fritz Billeter, *Das Dichterische bei Kafka und Kierkegaard* (Winterthur: Keller, 1965).

with an overwhelming desire to pour myself into it, which obviously springs from despair. Beset by many problems, uncertain of you, quite incapable of coping at the office, my novel [*Amerika*] at a standstill for a day, with a fierce longing to continue the new, equally demanding [minatory, *mahnend*] story" (LF 49; BF 105). Several days after completing *The Metamorphosis,* Kafka wrote to Felice, "And don't talk about the greatness hidden in me, or do you think there is something great about spending a two-day interruption of my writing in permanent fear of never being able to write again, a fear, by the way, that this evening has proved to be not altogether unfounded?" (LF 97).

This matter is given definite formulation in 1922, when Kafka finds an image for the danger of not writing that is powerfully reminiscent of the vermin's attempt to cling to his human past: "Since the existence of the writer is truly dependent upon his desk and if he wants to keep madness at bay he must never go far from his desk, he must hold on to it with his teeth" (L 335). Here, then, as Erich Heller writes (in his edition of the letters to Felice), is Kafka's "curse: he is nothing when he cannot write." But he is also "in a different kind of nothingness, if, rarely enough, he believes he has written well [writing does 'accept' him, *ihn 'aufnimmt'*]" (LF xvi; BF 24).

What is this "different kind of nothingness" to which a vermin image for the act of writing bears witness? Can it be grasped, as many critics believe, through Kafka's impulse to view the writer in the perspective of the nonwriter, the normal *Bürger*? In Kafka's earliest works—for example, in the developed but unfinished story beginning, "'You,' I said"—the writer appears in the eyes of others as the dim figure of the bachelor, the nonentity who must drag out his days in feeble solitude, without children or possessions (DI 22–29). "The Judgment," too, presents the writer in an alien and insulting perspective; the essential character of this relation is stressed through the alliance said to exist between the vindictive father and the friend, a transparent persona of the writer. The clearest formulation of this theme occurs in 1919, in Kafka's "Letter to His Father": "My writing was all about you," Kafka declared to his father. "All I did there, after all, was to bemoan what I could not bemoan upon your breast. It was an intentionally long-drawn-out leave-taking from you, yet, although it was brought about by force on your part, it did take its course in the direction determined by me" (DF 177).[41] In these passages, the origin of the writer appears to be fundamentally shaped by the perspective of the father; Gregor Samsa, too, needs to have his metamorphosis confirmed by the judgment of his family.

But in fact this idea is neither predominant nor even highly significant in *The Metamorphosis*. The work frequently stresses the son's defiance of the father: Gregor comes out in the open to hear the language of music despite his father's prohibition. What is more, the truth and pathos of the story stem from the reader's occupying throughout—with the exception of the "unsatisfactory" conclusion—a consciousness very nearly identical with Gregor's own. The center of gravity of the work is Gregor's sense of the world: he sees himself as a vermin, we do not see him as a vermin through the eyes of the others. Significantly, the omniscient narrator of the close of the story confirms Gregor's body to be actually verminous.

The negativity of the vermin has to be seen as rooted, in an absolute sense, in the literary enterprise itself, as coming to light in the perspective that the act of writing offers of itself. Here the activity of writing appears only autonomous enough to demand the loss of happiness and the renunciation of life. But of its own accord it has no power to restitute these sacrifices in a finer key. Over Kafka's writing stands a constant sign of negativity and incompleteness:

> When it became clear in my organism that writing was the most productive direction for my being to take, everything rushed in that direction and left empty all those abilities which were directed toward the joys of sex, eating, drinking, philosophical reflection and above all music. I atrophied in all these directions. . . . My development is now complete and, so far as I can see, thereis nothing left to sacrifice; I need only throw my work in the office out of this complex in order to begin my real life. [DI 211]

The path to Kafka's "real life" is strewn with sacrifices; and the fact that he was never able to throw off his professional work until he had become fatally ill reflects the inherent inaccessibility of his ideal.

41. I have modified this translation. The German text concludes, of Kafka's writing as a leave-taking, "daß er zwar von Dir erzwungen war, aber in der von mir bestimmten Richtung verlief" (H 203) Kaiser and Wilkins translate these clauses, "although it was brought about by force on your part, it did not [sic] take its course in the direction determined by me" (DF 177).

In a letter of July 5, 1922, to Max Brod, Kafka envisions the writer as inhabiting a place outside the house of life—as a dead man, one of those "departed," of the "Reflections," who long to be flooded back to us (DF 34). It cannot be otherwise; the writer "is insubstantial [has no genuine existence, *ist etwas nicht Bestehendes*]"; what he produces is devilish, "the reward for serving the devil. This descent to the dark powers, this unshackling of spirits bound by nature, these dubious embraces and whatever else may take place in the nether parts which the higher parts no longer know, when one writes one's stories in the sunshine. Perhaps there are other forms of writing, but I know only this kind" (L 333; Br 385).[42] "Yet," as Erich Heller remarks, "it remains dubious who this 'one' is who 'writes stories in the sunshine.' Kafka himself? 'The Judgment'—and sunshine? *Metamorphosis* . . . and sunshine? . . . How must it have been 'in the nether parts' if 'in the higher parts' blossoms like these burst forth?" (BF 22).

Kafka's art, which Kafka elsewhere calls a conjuration of spirits, brings into the light of language the experience of descent and doubt. And even this experience has to be repeated perpetually. "Thus I waver, continually fly to the summit of the mountain, but then fall back in a moment. . . . [I]t is not death, alas, but the eternal torments of dying" (DII 77). There is no true duration in this desperate flight; conjuring up his own death, Kafka writes: "Of course the writer in me will die right away, since such a figure has no base, no substance, is less than dust. He is only barely possible in the broil of earthly life, is only a construct of sensuality [the craving for enjoyment, *Genußsucht*]. That is your writer for you" (L 334; Br 385). The self-indulgence that defines the writer is that of the being who perpetually reflects on himself and others. The word "figure" in the passage above can be taken literally: the writer is defined by his verbal figures, conceived at a distance from life, inspired by a devilish aesthetic detachment with a craving to indulge itself; but he suffers as well the meaninglessness of the figure uprooted from the language of life—the dead figure. Kafka's spirit, then, does spend itself "zur Illuminierung meines Leichnams," in lighting up—but also in furnishing figural decorations for—his corpse (Br 385; L 334).

It is this dwelling outside the house of life, *Schriftstellersein*, the neg-

---

42. I have modified the Winstons' translation slightly.

ative condition of writing as such, that is named in *The Metamorphosis;* but it cannot name itself directly, in a language that designates things that exist or in the figures that suggest the relations between things constituting the common imagination of life. Instead, in *The Metamorphosis* Kafka utters a word for a being unacceptable to man (*ungeheuer*) and unacceptable to God (*Ungeziefer*), a word unsuited either to intimate speech or to prayer (E 71). This word evokes a distortion without visual identity or self-awareness—engenders, for a hero, a pure sign. The creature of *The Metamorphosis* is not a self speaking or keeping silent but language itself (*parole*)—a word broken loose from the context of language (*langage*), fallen into a void the meaning of which it cannot signify, near others who cannot understand it.

As the story of a metamorphosed metaphor, *The Metamorphosis* is not just one among Kafka's stories but an exemplary Kafkan story; the title reflects the generative principle of Kafka's fiction—a metamorphosis of the function of language. In organizing itself around a distortion of ordinary language, *The Metamorphosis* projects into its center a sign that absorbs its own significance (as Gregor's opaque body occludes his awareness of self) and thus aims in a direction opposite to the art of the symbol; for there, in the words of Maurice Merleau-Ponty, the sign is "devoured" by its signification.[43] The outcome of this tendency of *The Metamorphosis* is its ugliness. Symbolic art, modeled on the metaphor that occults the signifier to the level of signification, strikes us as beautiful: our notion of the beautiful harmony of sign and significance is one dominated by the human signification, by the form of the person which in Schiller's classical conception of art "extirpates the material reference."[44] These expectations are disappointed by the opaque and impoverished sign in Kafka. His art devours the human meaning of itself and, indeed, must soon raise the question of a suitable nourishment. It is thus internally coherent that the vermin—the word without significance—should

43. Maurice Merleau-Ponty, *Phénoménologie de la perception* (Paris: Gallimard, 1945), p. 213.
44. "Darin also besteht das eigentliche Kunstgeheimnis des Meisters, daß er den Stoff durch die Form vertilgt" (Friedrich Schiller, "Zweiundzwanzigster Brief," in *Über die ästhetische Erziehung des Menschen in einer Reihe von Briefen, Sämtliche Werke* [Munich: Carl Hanser, 1967], 5:639).

divine fresh nourishment and affinity in music, the language of signs without significance.[45]

But the song Gregor hears does not transform his suffering: the music breaks off; the monster finds nourishment in a cruder fantasy of anger and possession. This scene communicates the total discrepancy between the vermin's body and the cravings appropriate to it and the other sort of nourishment for which he yearns; the moment produces not symbolic harmony but the intolerable tension of irreconcilables. In Kafka's unfathomable sentence, "Was he an animal, that music could move him so?" (M 49), paradox echoes jarringly without end.

At the close of *The Metamorphosis* Gregor is issued a death sentence by his family which he promptly adopts as his own; he then passes into a vacant trance.

> He had pains, of course, throughout his whole body, but it seemed to him that they were gradually getting fainter and fainter and would finally go away altogether. The rotten apple in his back and the inflamed area around it, which were completely covered with fluffy dust, already hardly bothered him. He thought back on his family with deep emotion and love. His conviction that he would have to disappear was, if possible, even firmer than his sister's. He remained in this state of empty and peaceful reflection until the tower clock struck three in the morning. [M 53–54]

He is empty of all practical concerns; his body has dwindled to a mere dry husk, substantial enough to have become sonorous, too substantial not to have been betrayed by the promise of harmony in music. He suggests the Christ of John (19:30)—but not the Christ of Matthew (27:50) or Mark (15:37)—for Gregor's last moment is silent and painless. "He still saw that outside the window everything was beginning to grow light. Then, without his consent, his head sank down to the floor, and from his nostrils streamed his last weak breath" (M 54). For a moment the dim desert of Gregor's world grows luminous; his opaque body, progressively impoverished, achieves a faint translucency. Through the destruction of the specious

45. "[Music] speaks by means of mere sensations without concepts and so does not, like poetry, leave behind it any food for reflection" (Immanuel Kant, *The Critique of Judgement*, trans. James Creed Meredith [Oxford: Clarendon, 1928], p. 193).

harmony of the metaphor and the aesthetic claims of the symbol, Kafka engenders another sort of beauty and, with this, closes a circle of reflection on his own work. For in 1910, just before his mature art originated as the distortion of the metaphor, Kafka wrote in the story fragment, "'You,' I said . . .": "Already, what protected me seemed to dissolve here in the city. I was beautiful in the early days, for this dissolution takes place as an apotheosis, in which everything that holds us to life flies away, but even in flying away illumines us for the last time with its human light" (DI 28).

At the close of *The Metamorphosis*, the ongoing metamorphosis of the metaphor accomplishes itself through a consciousness empty of all practical attention and a body that preserves its opacity, but in so dwindled a form that it achieves the condition of a painless translucency, a kind of beauty. In creating in the vermin a figure for the distortion of the metaphor, the generative principle of his art, Kafka underscores the negativity of writing but at the same time enters the music of the historical world at a crucial juncture. His art reveals at its root a powerful Romantic aesthetic tradition associated with the names of Rousseau, Hölderlin, Wordsworth, and Schlegel, which criticizes symbolic form and metaphorical diction in the name of a kind of allegorical language.[46] The figures of this secular allegory do not refer doctrinally to scripture; rather, they relate to the source of the decision to constitute them. They replace the dogmatic unity of sign and significance with the temporal relation of the sign to its luminous source. This relation comes to light through the temporal difference between the allegorical sign and the sign prefiguring it; the exact meaning of the signs is less important than the temporal character of their relation. The vermin that alludes to vermin figures in Kafka's early work, and whose death amid increasing luminosity alludes casually to Christ's, is just such a figure. But to stress the temporal character of the metamorphosed metaphor of *The Metamorphosis* is to distinguish it importantly from the "extended metaphor" of Anders's and Sokel's discussion, for in this organistic conception of the figure, sign and significance coincide as forms of

46. This observation and those in the three sentences that follow it are taken from Paul de Man's "The Rhetoric of Temporality," in *Blindness and Insight: Essays in the Rhetoric of Contemporary Criticism*, rev. 2d ed. (Minneapolis: University of Minnesota Press, 1983), p. 207.

extension. And if Expressionism is to be defined by its further extension of metaphor, then *The Metamorphosis* cannot be accommodated in an Expressionist tradition. The matter should be put differently and more strongly: if Expressionism is the literary movement that takes a continual impetus from metamorphosis of the metaphor—from the allegory, critique, and deconstruction of metaphor—then Kafka is primordially Expressionist (see Chapter Ten).

* * *

The Metamorphosis alludes to a certain tradition of Romantic allegory but does so only for a moment before abruptly departing from it. The light in which Gregor dies is said explicitly to emanate from outside the window and not from a source within the subject. The creature turned away from life, facing death—and, as such, a pure sign of the poetic consciousness—keeps for Kafka its opaque and tellurian character. It is as a distorted body that Gregor is struck by the light; and it is in this light, principally unlike the source of poetic creation, that the work of art barely comes to recognize its own truth. For, wrote Kafka, "our art is a way of being dazzled by truth; the light on the grotesquely grimacing retreating face is true, and nothing else" (DF 41). Because the language of Kafka's fiction originates so knowingly from a reflection on ordinary speech, it cannot show the truth except as a solid body reflecting the light, a blank fragment of "what we call the world of the senses, [which] is the Evil in the spiritual world" (DF 39).

And so the figure of the nameless vermin remains principally opaque. More fundamental than the moment of translucency, reflected in the fact that this moment is obtained only at death and without a witness, is the horror that writing can never amount to anything more than the twisted grimace on which glances a light not its own. Here Kafka's essentially linguistic imagination joins him to a disruptive modern tradition, described by Michel Foucault:

> The literature in our day, fascinated by the being of language, . . .
> gives prominence, in all their empirical vivacity, to the fundamental
> forms of finitude. From within language experienced and traversed as
> language, in the play of its possibilities extended to their furthest point,
> what emerges is that man has "come to an end," and that, by reaching
> the summit of all possible speech, he arrives not at the very heart of

79

himself but at the brink of that which limits him; in that region where death prowls, where thought is extinguished, where the promise of the origin interminably recedes. . . . And as if this experiencing of the forms of finitude in language were insupportable . . . it is within madness that it manifested itself—the figure of finitude thus positing itself in language (as that which unveils itself within it), but also before it, preceding it, as that formless, mute, unsignifying region where language can find its freedom. And it is indeed in this space thus revealed that literature . . . more and more purely, with Kafka, Bataille, and Blanchot, posited itself . . . as experience of finitude.[47]

Postscript: Symbolic and Allegorical Interpretation

The aim of this postscript is to clarify the question of Kafka's obscurity by focusing on the rhetoric of *The Metamorphosis*. Kafka's rhetoric serves not only or chiefly to complicate descriptions of character and event to the point that fixity vanishes; rather, it defines and mobilizes types of persuasion.

Certainly, it has become the practice of many sharp readers of Kafka to try to prove his stories indecipherable.[48] The intention is admirable in a way: to call a halt to older interpretations that read into Kafka's work abundant and univocal meaning and in this way departed further and further from the writer as he read himself and as he is read by his work. Critics demythologize the figure of Kafka *homo religiosus*, of Kafka the existential philosopher—indeed, of Kafka the truth teller.[49] Instead, they offer an author of literary fictions, stressing the degree to which Kafka considered himself a purely aesthetic event. But demythologizing is that labor of the negative which must fall short of Kafka, for it ignores his view that literature intends to speak the truth—albeit figuratively, in the mode of fiction. In the end the demythologizing criticism of Kafka replaces one myth about his work with another.

---

47. Michel Foucault, *The Order of Things: An Archaeology of the Human Sciences* (a translation of *Les mots et les choses*) (New York: Pantheon, 1970), pp. 383–84.
48. E.g., Hasselblatt, *Zauber und Logik;* and Ulrich Gaier, "Chorus of Lies—On Interpreting Kafka," *German Life and Letters* 22:283-96.
49. See, e.g., Gaier, "Chorus of Lies," p. 283: "Kafka's work . . . should be taken as a challenge to find an adequate approach—not to its truth—but to its reality." But in the matter of the demythologization of Kafka *homo religiosus*, see Chapter Five.

Such is the result of insisting on the sliding multivalence of Kafka's meaning, on his intent to entangle a variety of codes that cannot be unified. This critical project ends by declaring Kafka's fiction constitutively obscure with a darkness that captivates: the loss of whole meaning wins the consolation prize of Kafka's "magic." It takes out of Kafka's work the certainty of a message, however negatively impressive that message of the entrapment by cities, the vacuousness of bureaucracy, the bloodthirstiness of family, the wounding of self-consciousness. But in its place it puts an abundance more impressive still—a fascination one can never dispel. How little this restful revelation would have contented Kafka, fabulous crow who fully meant to storm the heavens (DF 37).[50] It is Kafka, after all, who finds it "entirely conceivable that life's splendor lies in wait . . . veiled from view"—a splendor that is not itself "magic." "If you summon [this splendor] by the right word, by its right name, it will come. This is the essence of magic": namely, not to be splendid but to summon the splendor that lies beyond (DII 195).

Regulative misreadings of hermeneutic abundance and fascinating obscurity have continued to shape commentaries right up to the present moment. Bertolt Brecht saw Kafka's truth plain, amid the "mystification and nonsense," as "men being alienated from themselves by the forms of their life in society . . . [and the] dread of the unending and irresistible growth of great cities." Walter Benjamin, on the other hand, in conversation with Brecht, was determined to broach Kafka's (mysterious) depth. And so both seem like sinners at critical antipodes, with this provision: Brecht made plain that Kafka's truth is not abundant but has to be extracted technically from thickets of stunted stuff—"rubbish and waste, a lot of pure mystification"; Benjamin felt that the point of sounding the depths was not to discover mystery there but rather to identify "the important thing"—none of the above—"something else."[51]

Kafka's critics of the following generation posed cooler questions about his rhetoric and style—seminal approaches then, as now, which have taken good effect. Friedrich Beißner, Martin Walser,

50. Peter Heller, *Dialectics and Nihilism* (Amherst: University of Massachusetts Press, 1966), discusses this aphorism at length.

51. Walter Benjamin, "Conversations with Brecht," in *Aesthetics and Politics* (London: New Left Books, 1977), pp. 88–91.

Ingeborg Henel, and Rudolf Binion, for example, succeeded in clarifying a key structural dimension of *The Metamorphosis:* its narrative point of view, which is not identical but only congruent with the consciousness of the hero, masking, while keeping, a distance.[52] This perspective explains otherwise than as an effect of magic the fact that readers must attach themselves to Gregor's Samsa's optic (see Chapter Eleven). Kafka's perspective changes with the hero's death into omniscience but does not do so in order to declare the hero's metamorphosis a fascinating delusion.

Other rhetorical readings have shown the power of a more and more exact analysis of Kafka's figurative language. Max Brod, Hermann Pongs, and Kurt Weinberg, for example, have stressed the importance of the phrase *ungeheueres Ungeziefer,* the monstrous vermin designating the metamorphosis. These words do not name an insect or a bug or ultimately any natural being: Kafka—reader of etymologies—knew what depth of unbeing underlies this phrase.[53] Hence, Simon Sandbank's good surmise proves too hopeful—namely, that after every possible interpretation of the figure of the transmogrified Gregor Samsa has been set up and then knocked down as hermeneutically useless, what truly remains is "the insect."[54] The difficulty is that we never have more nor less than an uncanny sort of vermin—a figurative "construction"—along with other constructions "whitely merging in a corner" (DI 311). The insect itself, having no physical model, "cannot," as Kafka wrote to Kurt Wolff, "be depicted" (L 115). Another gain: the patient description by David Luke and Jürg Schubiger of Gregor's tergiversating rhetoric gives interpretation a starting point in the evasions of everyday figures of speech.[55]

But the greatest value of the successive application of rhetorical

52. Friedrich Beißner, *Der Erzähler Franz Kafka* (Stuttgart: Kohlhammer, 1952); Walser, *Beschreibung einer Form;* Ingeborg Henel, "Die Deutbarkeit von Kafkas Werken," *Zeitschrift für deutsche Philologie* 86, no. 2: 250–66; Rudolph Binion, "What *The Metamorphosis* Means," *Symposium* 15 (Fall 1961): 214–20.

53. Max Brod, *Franz Kafka: A Biography,* trans. G. Humphreys Roberts (New York: Schocken, 1947), p. 134; Pongs, "Franz Kafka—'Die Verwandlung,'" pp. 162–85; Weinberg, *Kafkas Dichtungen,* pp. 235–317.

54. Simon Sandbank, "Surprise Techniques in Kafka's Aphorisms," *Orbis Litterarum* 25 (1970): 261–74.

55. F. D. Luke, "The Metamorphosis," *Modern Language Review* 46 (1951): 232–45, reprinted in Flores and Swander, *Franz Kafka Today,* pp. 25–43; Schubiger, *Franz Kafka.*

criticism to *The Metamorphosis* has been, I think, that it has defined the levels of possible interpretations. "An interpretation is privileged," writes Heinrich Rombach, "if it enlarges the foundation of other interpretations—hence, interprets them."[56] It is not enough to note that *The Metamorphosis* invites a wide variety of disparate interpretations or that interpretations coexisting in semantic indifference constitute a structural feature of Kafka's work. Critics have begun to identify the kinds of interpretations that *The Metamorphosis* can attract; they have begun to evaluate these kinds and to grasp the extent to which Kafka's stories themselves instantiate the principles on which Kafka interpretations are based. These stories exist as the adventurous combat of types of interpretation of their own action, types that would determine the nature and direction of Kafka's future work. Kafka's stories dramatize the principles authorizing kinds of interpretation and hence kinds of consciousness that the literary act has of itself. Martin Greenberg's readings of "The Judgment" and *The Metamorphosis* have given a powerful impetus to the critical project of seeing in the stories a conflict of theories about writing.[57]

It appears that interpretations of *The Metamorphosis* can be provisionally divided into the symbolic and the allegorical. The nuclear fable of all symbolic readings goes somewhat as follows. Despite his transformation, Gregor Samsa remains an intact if humiliated moral personality. He is fundamentally the homeless man, the outcast social man; his life is empty of meaningful work, friendship, sexual love, family loyalty. He does not become a riddle as a result of his transformation. The reader can correlate that transformation with naturalistic intentions and empirical effects—with intentions such as resentment and laceration, familiar from the popular philosophy of our time (Freudianism); and with effects such as dependency and sickness, which we recognize from our own bodily experience. We therefore say that Gregor's outcast state is symbolic of the estrangement that the empirical person sooner or later comes to feel—the humiliated self-consciousness that perpetuates its estrangement in an ignorant and guilty way.

Symbolic readings agree in viewing Gregor's sorrow as the sorrow of a defeat in experience. At this level of interpretation it is an indif-

56. Heinrich Rombach, *Strukturontologie* (Freiburg im Bresgau: Alber, 1971), p. 139.
57. Greenberg, *The Terror of Art*, pp. 69–91.

ferent matter whether his defeat is seen essentially as a failure in his work life (Helmut Richter, Walter Sokel);[58] as a failure in intra-familial integration (psychologists Hellmuth Kaiser and Peter Dow Webster);[59] or as the failure of personal sufficiency (according to the standards of a *Bildungs*-philosophy exacting full self-realization through experience). What is important in the symbolic reading is that Gregor's predicament is in principle remediable. Thus, while *The Metamorphosis* describes a man whose experience has been deficient, it is not finally a descriptive work; its thrust is prescriptive. Read symbolically, the work asks us to complete it by supplying Gregor's deficient experience with a compensatory fullness; indeed, it gives us hints of this fullness. For example, Gregor's metamorphosis, which condemns him to fawn and to scuttle, to play the slave and the robot, is merely an extended metaphor of his deformed work life; his pro-letarianization and his political impotence within a pseudopatriarchal structure depict a work life as it must not be. The sense of the story then, according to Helmut Richter, is its implicit prophecy of an economic alternative.[60] And indeed, a hint of this reformation is given in the more or less happy renewal of the family's work life.

Another reading at this symbolic level is the psychological. When Gregor becomes a cockroach, he simply realizes in a vivid way the intentions that define him within a schizophrenic family situation. He punishes the family with his odium and punishes himself by assuming a cripple's or pariah's existence. He is punished by his sick body and by his dependency but achieves the covert, doubly aggressive expressiveness of the tyrant invalid and the family idiot. Yet bodily and psychological restoration is forecast in the moment of painlessness and translucency that Gregor achieves at his death . . . and so on.

The gist of all symbolic readings is most clearly present in early psychoanalytical readings, which fill in the literary text as analysis fills in the oral report of a dream, as if both texts were essentially nonliteral communications, full of gaps and ellipses. (This is the procedure of Hellmuth Kaiser and Peter Dow Webster.)[61] The supplemented text, like the once deciphered dream, projects a desirable

---

58. Richter, *Franz Kafka*, pp. 112–19; Sokel, "Kafka's 'Metamorphosis,'" 203–14.

59. Kaiser, "Franz Kafkas Inferno"; and Peter Dow Webster, "Franz Kafka's 'Metamorphosis' as Death and Resurrection Fantasy," *American Imago* 16 (Winter 1959): 349–65.

60. Richter, *Franz Kafka*.

61. Kaiser, "Franz Kafkas Inferno"; Webster, "Franz Kafka's 'Metamorphosis.'"

fullness of worldly experience; as the transcript of desires, it prescribes paths to gratification.

In sum, the symbolic reading asserts (1) the continuity of the empirical personality of Gregor Samsa with the monstrous vermin; (2) the meaningfulness of the metamorphosis in terms of intentions and effects taken from ordinary experience; (3) the deficiency and remediability of the experience with which *The Metamorphosis* is correlated; (4) the prescriptive and prophetic bearing of the work, hinted at in Gregor's and the family's end: at his death Gregor is a *schöne Seele,* a refined soul, and the family is restored to health and hope.

The allegorical reading opposes the symbolic reading in every detail. It takes literally the metamorphosis, the radical disjunction separating Gregor Samsa from the vermin. It considers the work as literally constituting an uncanny, unsettled existence. Hence, it reads the vermin's consciousness of his sister's violin playing, through which he senses the way to an unknown nourishment, not as compensation for his existence but rather as an ineluctable condition of it. Finally, his situation is not seen as a defective or any other kind of empirical situation: it cannot be grasped through familiar experience.

Mainly because this reading stresses the absolute disparity between the former Gregor Samsa and his new situation, his unbeing, it can be called allegorical according to Walter Benjamin's understanding of allegory as the nonpresence—that is to say, the nonnaturalistically experienceable character—of what is signified.[62]

What insatiableness, then, is allegorized in *The Metamorphosis?* What desire is alluded to in the metamorphosis of a man into an *Ungeziefer,* an unbeing? It is, first of all, Kafka's intention to exist as literature, to write fiction; for this intention to write—to paraphrase R. G. Collingwood—is realized only insofar as it both lives in the historical process and knows itself as so living.[63] In this story, writing reproduces itself, in the mode of allegory, as metamorphosis, literality, death, play, and reduction—the whole in a negative and embattled form.

The degree of Kafka's commitment to writing, to what he called *Schriftstellersein,* cannot be exaggerated, and his work necessarily re-

62. "Allegory. . . means precisely the non-existence of what it represents" (Walter Benjamin, *The Origin of German Tragic Drama,* trans. John Osborne [London: New Left Books], p. 233).

63. R. G. Collingwood, *The Idea of History* (New York: Oxford University Press, 1956), pp. 226–27.

flects the intensity of this commitment. But writing held different meanings for him at different times of his life; on no account should one overlook the historicity of Kafka's work as a reflection of the project of writing. This history nevertheless has a basic direction. Kafka came to realize more and more sharply the impoverishment, reduction, and shortcoming that writing entails.[64]

The decisive turn away from a eudemonic conception of writing occurs with the composition, in 1912, of "The Judgment." This work stands besides *The Metamorphosis* in the special intimacy of act and interpretation. "The Judgment" simply happens to Kafka; it is a kind of breakthrough, which he describes in his diaries in an ecstatic and confused way—in language that is violently figurative and also hermetically abstruse. The story cries out for clearer interpretation.

This is what it receives in *The Metamorphosis,* whose hero *is* "The Judgment," the insight liberated in that story: that Kafka must not betray his writing either by marrying or by supposing that his father is the source and goal of his art. This judgment metamorphoses Kafka's existence into *Schriftstellersein* in the mode of allegory—the mode that definitively detaches the particular entity from the plenum of which it dreams, whether this plenitude be conceived as an expansive state of mind, interpersonal recognition, or metaphysical truth. After "The Judgment," when Kafka writes, when he "descends to the dark powers," he takes up a position outside the house of life (L 333).

Kafka's radically figurative way of expressing the separation of literature from life is to declare literary existence outside of death. In his diaries Kafka wrote about the death scenes in his work: "But for me, who believe that I shall be able to lie contentedly on my deathbed, such scenes are secretly a game" (DII 102). This playfulness is present in *The Metamorphosis* in the profusion of its imagery of art and play and in the distance between the ghostly, smiling narrator and his monster. This distance reveals Kafka as always a little ahead of his subject; fundamentally, he is the narrator of the story who survives the death of his hero; he can be this narrator because he has already had the experience of death, existing now in the most radical estrangement from life. This is the point at which the play begins, and it is a play necessarily full of sorrow.

The sorrow belongs to the being who is literature, who is caught

64. And it has another basic direction—"the second helix"—which is discussed in Chapter Five.

up in an exemplary way in the passage from particularity to generality and as a consequence must suffer death after death without end.
The emblem of literature in its desire for generality and its condemnation to particularity is, in a certain sense, its literality—its need to
spell and be spelled out.[65] Literality is the main bearing of Kafka's
point of view throughout his fiction: you have never seen the like
before, so you must read what is written. Readers of *The Metamorphosis* are so thoroughly immersed in the perspective of the vermin that they can understand his world only word by word, and
always for the first time; the reader is metamorphosed into this text.

Kafka's crucial insight is the root separateness of literature and life:
"The only separation that can be made, the separation from the
homeland, has already taken place." He stresses the resistance of literature to the project of a life conceived as *Bildung*, as an extensive
totality of experience: "Nothing has changed; there, we are what we
were here" (L 204). This vision is dramatized in *The Metamorphosis* in
the vermin's gradual reduction and impoverishment, his loss of sensation and loss of locomotion. Kafka's art of constituting realities
stripped bare bespeaks a movement of the mind that proceeds by
reduction to radical immanence. Examples abound: in *Amerika*, the
subject Karl Rossman is reduced to bare existence in Brunelda's bedroom; in *The Castle* the object of experience, the village world, is
blanketed by snow, reduced to the bare *factum brutum* of a material
world.

Kafka's fiction now can be viewed as a contest between essentially

65. Mark Anderson writes informatively about "the complex and ambiguous status of the Latin term 'littera,' which in its singular form means 'letter' (of the alphabet)
and in the plural, 'litterae,' signifies . . . written document and literature. . . . Moreover, 'littera' is the origin for both 'literal' and 'literary,' which are often used as
opposites of one another. 'Literal' refers to strict, material, 'plain' meaning (as in 'the
letter of the law'), opposed to figurative, symbolic, or allegorical meaning. Yet the
figurative, or the figure, constitutes precisely the domain of literature, of the literary. . . . [Meanwhile] these coincidences are far from arbitrary, for precisely the
ambivalence of the 'littera,' its hovering between the material signs of the alphabet and
their figurative use, between 'litteralis' and 'litterarius,' is what makes writing possible" ("Kafka's Unsigned Letters: A Reinterpretation of the Correspondence with
Milena," *Modern Language Notes* 98 [April 1983]: 386). Anderson articulates the paradox that Tzvetan Todorov identifies apropos of Kafka: it is "the paradox all reflection
upon literature must confront: a verbal formula concerning literature always betrays
the nature of literature, because literature is itself paradoxical, constituted of words
but signifying more than the words, at once verbal and transverbal" (*The Fantastic*, p.
156).

symbolic and essentially allegorical interpretations of its own action. At every point the symbolic interpretation bespeaks the contrary of the allegorical: it invests the self with continuity, meaningfulness, expansiveness, and the prospect of reconciliation. The constitution of tragic, allegorical consciousness in *The Metamorphosis* includes the representation of symbolic consciousness. This occurs whenever the vermin asserts his identity with Gregor Samsa and tries to restore his old situation within the family and again whenever his reflections appear to justify the metamorphosis as punishment. That the symbolic mode is a seduction and an error emerges through the vermin's attempts to speak in metaphorical language. Kafka's aversion to noncitational metaphor is constant, but in the few places in *The Metamorphosis* where this language occurs, the reader patently finds himself inside a deluded consciousness. The vermin's attempt to come to terms with his experience through metaphor inspires derision, as when he likens his rivals to harem women or sees the office manager turn on the stairs, seeking transcendental deliverance.[66]

It cannot be this creature's fate to know a symbolic unity with his world. The prospect of redemption at the end of *The Metamorphosis* is a grotesque delusion: Gregor—we read—"thought back on his family with deep emotion and love" (M 54). To Kafka, immersion in the will of the family invariably means extinction in the state of greatest error: this is the case of Georg Bendemann at the close of "The Judgment."

The vermin is most an opaque bug, least the lucid beetle of "Wedding Preparations," whenever he uses his position in order to gain an expansive unity within the world. The music that summons him would provide him, he thinks, with an "unknown *nourishment*" (M 49; my italics), even though it cannot mean anything to him in terms of his former experience. To turn that experience to account, to go after the playing as if it were the player, would be to use literature as Kafka describes it in his most deluded work, "Letter to His Father"—

66. A field of worldly objects incandescent with significance would be a mere middle ground of Kafka's art. Symbol used firmly, to accomplish sense—a heightened moment of the perception of similitude—subverts Kafka's scheme, which is founded at all points on the struggle between symbol and allegory. It could be said of all Kafka's symbolic figures—metaphors and similes—what Proust said of Flaubert's, that there is hardly a beautiful metaphor to be found in his entire *oeuvre*. Here are Kafka's figures of similitude: "yellow enough to be thrown away," salesmen "like harem women," "like a dog."

it would be to bemoan in writing what he wished to bemoan on his father's breast. The vermin is the bloodsucking louse to which Kafka compares himself in his struggle with his father only when he attempts to deny his separateness, to deny his character as an allegorical figure.

In Kafka's letters to Felice Bauer written during the composition of *The Metamorphosis*, he noted that the story was bearable on account of its "sweet pages." When he read the story aloud to friends, they all laughed. These remarks can only refer to the narrator's playful relation to his protagonist, a distance that means not detachment but being ahead of the hero in the sense of knowing his errors. "A good thought," wrote Kafka, "the writer of epic knows everything."[67] All Gregor's errors come under the head of action in the symbolic mode—the mode that asserts the continuity of consciousness and being.

The priority of literalness and play over meaning in the story is the statement of the priority for Kafka of literature as allegory over literature as symbol, but this priority is one that has to be perpetually reasserted. It requires a corresponding priority of interpretative modes. Yet to find Kafka's stories essentially constituted by the combat of interpretative modes—one of which, the allegorical, has priority—is not to declare him ambivalent or indecipherable. The allegorical stands to the symbolic in Kafka not in ambivalent relation but in the relation of priority.[68]

67. "Gutes Wort: Der Epiker weiss alles"; quoted in Jürgen Kobs, *Kafka: Untersuchungen zu Bewußtsein und Sprache seiner Gestalten,* ed. Ursula Brech (Bad Homburg: Athenäum, 1970), p. 537.

68. In "The Deletions from Kafka's Novels," *Monatshefte* 68 (Winter 1976): 365–72, Clayton Koelb discusses the longest of the deleted passages from *The Trial,* which follows the discussion between Joseph K. and the chaplain. The passage turns on terms referring to light and darkness. "The action described by the excised material is symbolic in this vein: the chaplain leads K. from a place of total darkness (the cathedral proper) into a place of partial darkness (the sacristy), just as his parable of the Law had led K. from total ignorance to partial ignorance. And just as K. is not much enlightened by the story or its interpretations, so he is not much aided by the extremely dim light of the sacristy" (p. 371). But Kafka deleted this passage. "Almost all of this is removed in the revision. . . . The trip to the sacristy is eliminated entirely along with its very clear (one might even say obvious) symbolism" (p. 372). Following Koelb, I understand the deletion as dictated by Kafka's reluctance to have a narrator—one more fully in control of the scene than K.—urge on "truths" in the symbolic mode. For Koelb, such a deletion is made in conformity with a "deliberate 'principle of increasing ambiguity.'" I suggest a different intent, aiming to heighten the sense of the infirmity of symbolic representation.

Chapter Four

Metaphor and Chiasm

Reflecting on *The Metamorphosis,* Walter Sokel observed: "With this metamorphosis Kafka reverses the original act of metamorphosis carried out by thought when it forms metaphor; for metaphor is always 'metamorphosis.' Kafka transforms metaphor back into his fictional reality, and this counter-metamorphosis becomes the starting point of his tale."[1]

This comment was published in 1966.[2] In 1972, in their avant-garde work *Kafka: Toward a Minor Literature,* Gilles Deleuze and Felix Guattari wrote: "Kafka deliberately kills all metaphor. . . . Metamorphosis is the reverse of metaphor."[3]

Taken together, these two passages provoke some cogent questions. How shall we understand, for example, those famous literalizations of metaphor that shape the action of many of Kafka's stories— as "counter-metamorphosis" (Sokel) or "metamorphosis" (Deleuze and Guattari)? When metaphor is extended into Kafka's fiction, is it "transformed" (Sokel) or "killed" (Deleuze and Guattari)? Does metaphor itself chiefly involve an "act of metamorphosis carried out by thought" (Sokel) or a stabilizing act of thought establishing similarity

1. Walter Sokel, *Franz Kafka* (New York: Columbia University Press, 1966), p. 5.
2. I discuss this remark in Chapter Three.
3. Gilles Deleuze and Felix Guattari, *Kafka: Pour une litterature mineure* (Paris: Minuit, 1975), p. 40; trans. Dana Polan as *Kafka: Toward a Minor Literature* (Minneapolis: University of Minnesota Press, 1986).

90

("*ressemblance*," as Deleuze and Guattari go on to write)?[4] In this chapter, I mean to answer these questions and furthermore to suggest that Kafka's fascination with the trope of chiasm can be understood as an exigency of his meditations on metaphor.

Structuralist and poststructuralist criticism, with its interest in the logic of tropes, has chiefly concerned itself with metaphor.[5] The result has been to discredit the Aristotelian distinction between proper (or literal) and derived (or figurative) meaning. Instead, criticism dwells on the fact that the meaning of metaphors is indefinitely contextual. The distinction between metaphorical and literal meaning arises not from the figure itself but from its association with distinctive contexts. As Gerhard Kurz writes: "Metaphorical meaning is produced from the understanding of its entire context, which determines the possibilities of the meaning realized. Metaphorical meaning is, therefore, less a result than an act, a constructive production of meaning accomplished *via* a dominant meaning, a movement from . . . to."[6] Whatever stability individual metaphors might come to possess results from a tacit convention—a contractual, otherwise nonnatural exclusion of aspects of the literal (or dominant) from the figurative, which forces the metaphor to perform unequivocally.[7] When Kafka writes, for example, of "everything that holds us to life," saying that "even in flying away it illumines us . . . with its human light" (DI 28), we are required for intelligibility's sake to

4. Ibid.

5. See Jonathan Culler, *The Pursuit of Signs: Semiotics, Literature, Deconstruction* (Ithaca: Cornell University Press, 1981), p. 188; and Anselm Haverkamp, "Einleitung in die Theorie der Metapher," in *Theorie der Metapher*, ed. Anselm Haverkamp (Darmstadt: Wissenschaftliche Buchgesellschaft, 1983).

6. Gerhard Kurz, *Metapher, Allegorie, Symbol* (Göttingen: Vandenhoeck & Ruprecht, 1982), pp. 17-18. Fritz Mauthner wrote: "What really matters, what really has meaning, is not the image a word or sentence conjures up, but the action that it suggests or commands, warns from or prohibits" (quoted in Allan Janik and Stephen Toulmin, *Wittgenstein's Vienna* [New York: Simon & Schuster, 1973], pp. 127-28).

7. A rhetorical way of putting this is to say that every metaphor that works does so via a socially constrained *metonymization:* that is, the specification of those features, and only those, of the tenor and vehicle that may take part. This point bursts a priori any attempt to discriminate rigorously between metaphor and metonymy. Thus *Der Prozeß* (*The Trial*) proposes two different interpretations, one selecting a structure that resembles metaphor, the other a structure that resembles metonymy—interpretations that are hard to decide between. *Der Prozeß* can be taken as the metaphor of a legal contestation within agencies of the self (there is something to be done about this) or as the inevitable drift of bodily decay (nothing can be done).

exclude from the metaphor of "human light" a great many attributes of the human—those, for example, that define man as the animal who laughs, who smokes, who strolls, and so on.

Walter Sokel's comment about the "metamorphosis" that metaphor "always is" therefore broaches a fine enigma, to which Kafka is attentive. Metaphor, on (Kafka's) reflection, originates not as the finite metamorphosis of one image into another; such images function, instead, through association with contexts themselves threaded through by metaphor in a series without origin. Consider, from "Description of a Struggle," this conversation between narrator and supplicant:

> Don't you feel that it's this very feverishness which is preventing you from being properly satisfied with the genuine [*wahrhaftigen*] names of things, and that now, in your frantic haste, you're just pelting them with any old [*zufällige*] names? You can't do it fast enough. But hardly have you run away from them when you've forgotten the names you gave them. The poplar in the fields, which you've called the "Tower of Babel" because you didn't want to know it was a poplar, sways again without a name, so you have to call it "Noah in his cups." [DS 60]

The supplicant's metaphors seem randomly associated, held together only by a common flight from lexical meaning. He must continue to replace them because they fail to function *for him*. I stress "for him": as Mark Anderson has shown (and as Kafka surely realized), these metaphors are not entirely arbitrary; they do function as soon as they are situated in the context of progenitive patriarchy.[8] Metaphors trace crossings of fields in principle infinite; they mean something after their fields have been surveyed and demarcations instituted.[9] The "self-evident" "poplar" stands in one such field. For the supplicant, an anxious forgetfulness appears to erase all awareness of site—of what his metaphor replaces as well as what borders it.

8. Mark Anderson, "Kafka and the Place of the Proper Name," *Journal of the Kafka Society of America* 9, nos. 1/2 (1985): 9–14.

9. Cf. the title of Henry Sussman's study, *Franz Kafka: Geometrician of Metaphor* (Madison, Wis.: Coda Press, 1979). In some ways the thrust of my analyses follows his but diverges chiefly as a result, I think, of the different ways we construe "metaphor." Sussman, for whom the term means self-disrupting literary figuration, gives it a wider governance than I. My sense of Kafka's "metaphor" is a figure of resemblance exploded by another's will to difference, by a movement irreducibly rhetorical *and* existential. See my preface to this book.

The contractual (or, as it is also called, "interactional") fixing of meaning conceals the intrinsically metamorphic character of metaphor, which of its own accord tends to a zero-point of indistinction between tenor and vehicle. The urgency of social constraint becomes all the more evident when one realizes, on a moment's reflection, that all words function to a greater or lesser extent as metaphors. Fritz Mauthner, whom Kafka read, noted in *Beiträge zu einer Kritik der Sprache* (Toward a critique of language): "The two or the hundred 'meanings' [*Bedeutungen*] of a word or a concept are only so many metaphors or images, and as we no longer know the *ur*-meaning of any word, since the first etymology infinitely precedes our knowledge of it, no word ever has any but metaphorical meanings."[10] In meaning the same thing, each word performs only aspects of the virtually infinite other experiences of that word—the word being, as Nietzsche wrote, a "semiotically concentrated process," a sedimented history of its uses.[11] Words act as semiotic memorials to a history of usages held to be similar; words fold together implications made cognate by human wills.

Hence, it is not only to remarkable figures of speech singled out as metaphors that full constraints of context apply. So-called literal meaning is itself only the reminiscence of another previous reduction of metaphorical to literal meaning, the chief difference between a literal word and a metaphor being that the literal word conceals the memory of the will that confined its meaning to one field.

Among certain words not called metaphors, the dangerous openness besetting all words becomes especially apparent—these are homonyms. Richard Rand identifies the "disruptive force" hiding in this figure:

> Neo-classical theories of language could be said to recognize that words do not behave as "proper and immediate" and "unequivocal" signs. They seem to acknowledge that a given word can refer to many meanings, and many meanings to a given word, and that the choice of words is an intricate passage between the two, a translation that is never really self-effacing. But they recognize this fact by wishfully asserting its opposite. . . . It is only in the process of allowing for

10. Fritz Mauthner, *Beiträge zu einer Kritik der Sprache*, 3d ed. (Leipzig: Felix Meiner, 1923), 2:451.

11. Friedrich Nietzsche, "On the Genealogy of Morals," in *Basic Writings of Nietzsche*, ed. and trans. Walter Kaufmann (New York: Modern Library, 1966), p. 516.

certain "exceptions" that the theories begin to account for the facts of language: . . . a word may have more than one meaning, in which case the word is called a "homonym."[12]

Where there is homonymy, there is the proven disparity between the sign and any one substantial meaning it might be supposed to contain. For modern semanticists homonymies are "invalids" giving rise to "pathological conflicts"; Kafka gives gainful employment to these martyrs of reason.[13] Thus his title *Das Schloß* means *The Castle* but also "the lock" and is related to various verbs expressing the idea of closure, of walled-aroundness;[14] its hero the *Landvermesser* is a "country surveyor" and, furthermore, "a materialist 'mis-measurer'"[15] but also—by suggestion—"a hubristic lout." *Der Prozeß* means *The Trial* but also "the process" (of tubercular decay and of evasive misreading, among others). And "Rose," in "A Country Doctor," is at once a maid and a wound. A boundless duplicitousness of meaning informs such homonymic fictions: which is the literal and which the metaphorical meaning of such key words? It is impossible to answer this question, which is more nearly a state of affairs exercising the will to cognitive power in (fictive) reader or hearer. One meaning more nearly resembles what he or she wants it to mean or must want it to mean.[16]

The fact is itself suggestive that this knowledge has always been so long delayed: every metaphor is a homonym with respect to its literal and its figurative senses; all words are homonymic with themselves; and therefore all words are intrinsically unfusable metaphors.[17] The same signifier *Ungeziefer,* "vermin," means a kind of louse and a kind of human being; the phrase *am eigenen Leibe* means "on one's own

12. Richard Rand, "Geraldine," in *Untying the Text: A Post-Structuralist Reader*, ed. Robert Young (Boston: Routledge & Kegan Paul, 1981), p. 296.

13. Ibid., p. 298.

14. Marthe Robert, *Franz Kafka's Loneliness*, trans. Ralph Manheim (London: Faber & Faber, 1982), p. 156.

15. I owe this expression to Geoffrey Waite.

16. Readers bring to each word of the fiction a semantic prejudgment with which the meaning of the word is forced to correspond. Does this mean that they possess the meaning in advance of the word? That is most unlikely, since the prejudgment will be instantly adjusted by context.

17. To make this point, as Marthe Robert remarks, Kafka "condenses in his own images a maximum of meanings associated not by a logical tie but by pure contiguity" (*Franz Kafka's Loneliness*, p. 234).

body" and also "at first hand." What, therefore, does "vermin" mean, and what exactly is a "body"? How we read depends on the pre-judgment that governs the conformity we seek and find, depends on the semantic warp (the "metaphor") we introduce into the present field.

Kafka perceives that the apparent harmlessness of metaphors in common usage conceals the struggle of wills to make words mean one thing rather than another. In organizing stories around the effort to interpret image-words and concept-words advantageously, in making culpability and even death the cost of failure in this effort, Kafka dramatizes the severity of the struggle. The fictional enactment of metaphor discloses vividly not some primary sense of *les mots de la tribu* ("literalization") but rather the instability, the tendency to metamorphosis, in the basic metaphors by which human beings live. The imposition of meaning naturally involves force. We could think of the prison chaplain's insistence against Joseph K.'s will that "right" is only a metaphor of "necessity." "A Hunger Artist" ("Ein Hungerkünstler") exists as an unstable struggle between the reading of the story that asserts that hungering is an art (stress on *Künstler*) with that which makes art only the subterfuge of hunger (stress on *Hunger*).[18] This struggle rages in the hero: he is the arena of contesting interpretations of the metaphor, influenced by past and present spectators.

"The Judgment" repays close reading in this respect. It seems reasonable to read the title "Das Urteil"—the "sentence"—as a metaphor of the outcome of a trial of the son by the father. (The sentence is actually only a piece of the total controlling metaphor of the trial, *Gerichtsverfahrung*.)

The appositeness of the central metaphor is obvious. At first Georg comes to his father to tell him that he has decided to "report" (*anzeigen*) to his friend the news of his engagement. *Anzeige* is a juridical term meaning "denunciation" or "summons" and can therefore suggest Georg's self-incrimination. Georg then goes on to say literally to his father that he means only to tell him this fact ("Das wollte ich Dir sagen"). The father, however, construes the telling as requiring a judgment, and Georg, in lingering, appears to consent to this view. What is astonishing about the story is that the judgment the

18. Martin Greenberg, *The Terror of Art: Kafka and Modern Literature* (New York: Basic Books, 1968), p. 122.

father delivers mounts in severity to a death sentence. The sense of the encounter between son and father emerges as the son's search for exculpation by law and his readiness to accept this exculpation even at the cost of death.

However, for this metaphorical reading to work—to be consistent—a number of important implications of the story have to be curtailed. What remains hidden is the vital factor of metamorphosis within the metaphor. "Das Urteil" is after all not only part of the metaphor of a trial at law. Its sense within logic is that of a logical judgment, a proposition, a *Satz*; hence it is also part of a process of reasoning. The basic situation that the metaphor of a *raisonnement* returns to is not a litigation but rather Georg's attempt to think out by himself a solution to the tension in his life between the claims of eros and the claims of renunciation, between earthly love and another sort of commitment—a bizarre asceticism represented in the story by the Russian friend. The outcome of such a reflection would be an *Urteil* only in the sense of a *Satz*. Indeed, Georg's conclusion is simply the proposition that he shall write his friend.

The term *das Urteil,* however, has another sense, that of an opinion, a judgment (as a judgment of taste). Here it designates a paternal judgment a good deal less severe than a death sentence. As the outcome of an interpersonal exchange cooperatively evolving a moral position, it stands in as a metonymy of a "consultation," which suggests a more nearly normal state of affairs, a typical form of the father-son relation in its sanity.

The story "Das Urteil" may now be grasped as a loose frame containing at least these three basic situations. The title connotes a metaphor of different types of the personal and interpersonal situation of son and father—essentially involving (1) personal reflection, (2) interpersonal judgment, and (3) litigation, with a life-and-death stake at issue. The phrase *das Urteil* therefore conjures not a metaphor but the range of tension, play, and metamorphosis within several ways of reading the metaphor. Indeed the question of just what basic situation is going to be connoted by the metaphor makes up the contest and the goal of the story; the contest between son and father is one aiming to make metaphorical language mean one thing rather than another. The outcome is the son's death by drowning. The father has compelled the son to read his judgment as a condemnation of the only-apparent harmlessness of an initially posed process of reasoning-about-the-self.[19]

The presence of at least three different tenors within the vehicle of the metaphor "the judgment" dramatizes the metaphor's openness to interpretation. This instability exists, of course, even within metaphors that at first glance connote only a single frame.

"The Judgment" is all in all remarkable in Kafka's *oeuvre* for the extent to which it is informed by metaphor. It is about the way the metaphor of judgment is read, but more, it is an enactment of the stakes in the judging of metaphors as such. It does more than dramatize the decision taken by the Bendemanns about what sense of the metaphor of judgment shall prevail. It also designs their rhetoric and their strategies of power on the very epistemological model of metaphor, with the result that it will make sense to see father and son as seeking to destroy one another by literalizing the open figure that the other is (see Chapter Seven). The entire story is an object lesson in the pervasiveness of metaphor—especially in its power to institute energetic and possibly "constructive destruction" (DF 103).

To read Walter Sokel's formulation as I propose is to understand that the "'metamorphosis' [which metaphor always is]" is more than the bold and unusual linkage of perceived images; it is more than the overwhelming of one image by another, the literal by the figurative, which Kafka's stories then break down through "counter-metamorphosis" back into their "literal"—that is, sensory—perceptible components (traveling salesman/crawling insect). Kafka's tampering with metaphor aims to do more than release the dangerous pungency of particular literalizations. Indeed, such literalizations are what his stories do not ever bring about. Metamorphosis persists after the metaphor has been "transformed back into fictional reality." Kafka's fictions provoke ongoing metamorphosis, which exposes, dismantles, and hence destroys metaphor. Literalization is only a regulative idea within Kafka's critique of metaphorical reason.

19. A sort of metaphor lurks within much, if not all, metonymy as well. "Hands" is an effective synecdoche for "able-bodied seamen" because it exhibits through resemblance that feature of the vehicle—"hands *at work*"—which is normally intended. Hence the conventionality of the factor sustaining the trope by which "hands" stands for "men" is almost invisible: "hands" *resemble* men at work. The same is true of sails for ships, the sword for military might, etc.

A number of commentators have stressed a sort of final intensity and beauty with which Kafka sets forth his knowledge of the intrinsic openness of metaphor (and his revulsion at clichéd metaphor, metaphor as unitary meaning) by pointing to aphorisms in the series "Reflections on Sin, Pain, Hope, and the True Way" which "allusively" suppress the tenor entirely. "Like a path in autumn: scarcely has it been swept clear when it is once more covered with dead leaves" (DF 36). Such figures have the feel of metaphor but are radically indeterminate.

How then have I answered the questions about metaphor posed at the outset?

The so-called literalizations of metaphor found in Kafka's stories do not properly constitute instances either of "counter-metamorphosis" or "metamorphosis." They are fictional enactments of the capacity for metamorphosis already resident in metaphor—its indwelling flux, mingling properties of tenor and vehicle. Kafka's stories reveal the uncanny and energetic possibility of metamorphosis present in all figures. Metaphor is a metamorphically charged, upheaval-laden conjunction of images or concepts. As intelligible figure, as working meaning, metaphor involves an always social, conventional definition of, first, those aspects of the tenor that may be conserved in the vehicle and, second, those that must be excluded when not to do so would produce, in light of the social contract, monstrosity and nonsense. To state Walter Sokel's point strongly, Kafka's transformation of metaphor "back into" fiction focuses and brings to light (does not counter or reverse) the unstable play of tenor and vehicle in metaphor—and finally, indeed, in all language having metaphor as substrate.

Furthermore, the metaphors extended into Kafka's fiction are more nearly "transformed" than "killed," because what comes to light is precisely the bizarre life of the metaphor. What is transformed is only the restrictive social constraint on how the metaphor is to be read.

Metaphor is produced by thought neither exclusively in an "act of metamorphosis" nor in a stabilizing effort to establish resemblance. The intentionality governing the production of metaphor varies— from the desire to stabilize (by using clichés) to the desire to produce upheavals of meaning (by connecting the most unheard-of images). But quite apart from the intention of the speaker, every metaphor as such—whether banal or obscure—is informed by the possibility for infinite metamorphosis of the relation between tenor and vehicle.

Such considerations, I hasten to say, are at this stage hardly startling. Reviewing them, however, may make it possible to move on securely to the main point of this chapter: a discussion of another and vital kind of figure of thought in Kafka—chiasm.

"Chiasmus," according to *Webster's Third New International Dictionary,* is "the inversion of the order of syntactical elements in the second of two juxtaposed and syntactically parallel phrases or clauses." It has the logical pattern of repeating the elements of a series in inverse order. According to Wahrig's German dictionary, the chiasm causes "pairs of . . . concepts to confront one another in cross-over fashion."[20] The introduction of *concepts* takes us closer to the power of chiastic figuration in Kafka.

The kind of chiasm that recurs in Kafka with particular significance fuses both definitions above: it is a chiastic parallelism of concepts. Kafka exhibits his construction of a chiasm in the diary entry for January 16, 1922, on "assaulting the last earthly frontier":

> There are doubtless several reasons for the wild tempo of the inner process; the most obvious one is introspection, which will suffer no idea to sink tranquilly to rest but must pursue [*emporjagen*] each one into consciousness, only itself to become an idea, in turn to be pursued [*weitergejagt*] by renewed introspection. . . .
>
> This pursuit [*Jagen*], originating in the midst of men, carries one in a direction away from them. The solitude that for the most part has been forced on me, in part voluntarily sought by me—but what was this if not compulsion too?—is now losing all its ambiguity and approaches its denouement. Where is it leading? The strongest likelihood is, that it may lead to madness; there is nothing more to say, the pursuit [*Jagd*] goes right through me and rends me asunder. Or I can—can I?—manage to keep my feet somewhat and be carried along in the wild pursuit [*Jagd*]. Where, then, shall I be brought? "Pursuit" [*Jagd*], indeed, is only a metaphor. I can also say, "assault on the last earthly frontier," an assault, moreover, launched from below, from mankind, and since this too is a metaphor, I can replace it by the metaphor of an assault from above, aimed at me from above.
>
> All such writing is an assault on the frontiers. [DII 202]

20. "*Chiasmus*: kreuzweise Gegenüberstellung von Gegensatzpaaren oder gleichen Begriffen" (*Wahrig: Deutsches Wörterbuch* [Gütersloh: Bertelsmann, 1974], p. 807).

I call attention, in a preparatory way, to two features of chiasm: first, its difference from metaphor even as it appears as an extreme possibility of metaphor; second, its suitability to Kafka as a figure of thought in allowing him to disclose what is in play but suppressed in the ordinary constitution of self-understanding: namely, the case in which the word or concept is dominant and visible—the intention, however, hidden.

In this diary entry Kafka distinguishes between two trains of figurative logic. The first is a progressive elaboration of metaphor in which both vehicle and tenor are internally divided into contesting elements. The basic situation is introspection, involving a viewer and a viewed. This situation is represented as a pursuit—more expressively, as a chase or a hunt, the hunter being in pursuit of the trophy. But this figure is a metaphor; it may be varied as another metaphor of assault, indeed, as an "assault on the last earthly frontier." The logic of this development is provided by the dual structure of the act of introspection or writing. The act of assault, like the act of hunting, invokes an assailant and an obstacle.

These metaphors may look simple, and they can be read and assimilated rapidly, but of course they repay a more devoted reading. They should not after all merely reproduce—and hence produce complacency about—the structure and content of writing and introspection. For example, what exactly about the act of thinking or writing indeed resembles tracking-down—or should it be sticking and killing? What in the fate of the introspected or written image prompts the analogy of killed game? Is the impaled thought also "eaten," "assimilated"? Further, what is the meaning of the impulse (more aggressive than athletic? vice versa?) that inspires the thinker's or writer's "assault"? If there is this much violence in writing, can writing be truthful; can it preserve the integrity of the written thing?

The formulating and answering of such questions implies, of course, a to-and-fro movement between tenor and vehicle: we achieve stable meaning only by arresting this movement, which has a sort of chiastic character as, first, features of the tenor are allowed to project and fix obvious correspondences in the vehicle: for example, the introspector is keen-eyed and quiet in the way the hunter is. But then, in reading on more provocatively, we reverse the dominance of assumed features of the tenor—of the act of introspection—and allow the vehicle to precede it. Here the implications of piercing and killing illuminate areas more nearly hidden in the tenor: writing on life is a kind of killing of life ("we murder to dissect"). The mind moves from tenor to vehicle and then in reverse order, interminably: the movement is chiastic.

The passage from the metaphor, from writing as hunt to writing as assault, furthermore diagrams the movement we earlier called "metamorphosis." Kafka produces a second metaphor, but the second metaphor is not radically new: it only brings out a more nearly hidden implication in the first by a more nearly strenuous exercise of interpretation. Is chase (*Jagd*) to be nonviolent pursuit? Then authority goes more to the thing pursued, and there is in this movement a movement of emulation of the pursued by the pursuer. Or is pursuit to be violent hunting? Then authority would go to the hunter, who means to kill the thing hunted down. Then pursuit is more nearly assault. It is by no means a trivial struggle of interpretations within the poet, as to the meaning and authority of poetry, whether he stresses in the poetic pursuit the element of emulation or the element of assault.

We should, however, reserve the designation of chiasm, as Kafka does, for a tropic transformation involving reversal of terms within the vehicle (and not just in the movement back and forth between vehicle and tenor). Here, starting with the metaphor for writing of an assault on the frontier, we produce chiastically another metaphor for writing: writing is an assault upon the writer by the frontier. The relation of this new metaphor to the old is different from that between two consecutive readings of the same metaphor. It is more severely metamorphic in reversing priority and direction within the whole structure of relations governing vehicle and tenor. If in the first metaphor the writer/assailant attempted to imagine/pursue/hunt/assault the frontier, here the frontier imagines/pursues/hunts/assaults the writer/assailant. But observe that the difference is not only one of rank and direction. In order to render the chiasm intelligible, we must radically revise our understanding of the meaning of the second, the "objective" component within the initial metaphor—bring to it a meaning that in ordinary experience lies only at its farthest limits, almost unthinkable. We must conceive of "the frontier" as itself an agent of will, consciousness, and aggression.

This act of interpretation, however, is not single, does not stop with an uncanny reading of the objective term. It initiates a potentially endless series of interpretations by returning to the first pair of terms—the writer as the assailant of the frontier—and forcing its reinterpretation: What is to be understood now by an assault on a frontier that is itself capable of assault upon the assailant? Clearly, the character of the frontier in the first metaphor has to be revised (again, in a way that could not have been achieved by even the most imaginative reading of the metaphor): the writer too must be rethought as capable of initiating such an assault. The chiasm sets in motion a spiral of interpretation of increasing complexity. This movement is not just "aporetic," however; it does not lead to an interpretation suspended in doubt between ostensible antitheses. It is a movement that has to be gone through, taken to the limit in a maximum of imaginative interpretation—a process that takes place in time and therefore has the character of lived experience.

I stress at once the virtual interminability of the reading of the chiasm in Kafka and the real historical character of every reading that goes—if not the entire "distance"—then some measure of the distance by a movement continually reinforcing the scope of the two metaphors.

My second point can only be suggested at the conclusion of this short chapter. Kafka has an affinity for chiastic form, which emerges through the content of his chiasmi. The metaphor, for Kafka, typically represents an inner, a human, attribute or significance in its likeness to an outer or worldly thing. It is this typical feature of metaphor that inspires his aversion to the trope, since "the inner world can . . . not be described" (DF 65); metaphorical language functions to reify, as in the spurious *Vergleiche* ("comparisons" but also perhaps "deals") that represent sensuously the "spiritual" world. What Kafka can allow is a demonstration of the untruth of the untrue, the emptying of authority from the speciously plausible: this is achieved when the plausible but untrue metaphor is chiastically reversed. Kafka will write, "A cage went in search of a bird" (DF 36). He thus undoes the privileged status of the bird as an emblem of *Geist,* of spirituality, by assigning the attributes of willing and questing to the thing, the cage. This procedure is overt both in the form and the argument of the aphorism "In the struggle between yourself and the world second the world"

(DF 39). The court that in *The Trial* is summoned by the individual's guilt, the doctor who in "A Country Doctor" is put into the sickbed with his patient, are usurpatory chiasmi, reversing the relation of spiritual authority to the objects in its sway.[21]

Here we open up to a major intention of Kafka's work—one that has been stated succinctly by Karel Kosík:

> The everyday world that we know is not the known and recognized world. So that it can be *presented* in its reality, it must be stripped of its intimately fetishized familiarity and revealed in its alienated brutality. . . . For man to see the truth of his alienated everyday life . . . he must do "violence" to it. In what sort of society and in what kind of world must men "become" lice, dogs, and apes so that their true character can be adequately expressed? In what "violent" metaphors and allegories must man . . . be *presented*, so that . . . [men] can *see* their own faces and *recognize* their own world?[22]

Wilhelm Emrich importantly includes—under the head of the fetishized, familiar "pseudo-concrete"—human inwardness itself. Kafka, he writes, "represents individual inwardness, indeed what is 'authentically' innermost in man [*das eigene Innere, das 'eigentlich' Innerlichste*] in the form of alien and terrifying things or creatures that break into life. . . . Since the self is not an 'individual' [*eigen*], understood 'inwardness' ['*Inneres*'], it has to assume the form of something exterior, strange—but of something strange that breaks through the laws of the . . . empirical world."[23]

Such representations have a necessarily chiastic structure. In ordinary human beings we have this situation: conscious/unconscious—the conscious on the surface, the unconscious hidden; the conscious chiefly the reservoir of concepts, hence word-presentations; the unconscious the reservoir of "things," thing-presentations. The visible manifestation of the unconscious involves a chiastic reversal of this situation. We now have the thing—"the monster"—visible, on the

21. Marthe Robert derives the source of "Investigations of a Dog" from the chiastic inversion of the abominable metaphor "the Jew is a dog," which Kafka heard from his own father (*Franz Kafka's Loneliness*, p. 15).

22. Quoted in Alexej Kusák, "On the Marxist Interpretation of Franz Kafka," in *Franz Kafka: An Anthology of Marxist Criticism*, ed. and trans. Kenneth Hughes (Hanover, N.H.: University Press of New England, 1981), p. 100.

23. Wilhelm Emrich, *Franz Kafka* (Frankfurt am Main: Athenäum, 1965), pp. 120–21.

surface; and the meaning of the thing, the word for it, hidden. The monster and the persons who attend it struggle vainly to find this word.

The absence of univocal meaning in the thing-presentation is an aspect of its modality of unconsciousness that survives even its manifestation. Other features underscore its sheerly alien character (to consciousness). In the fact that it cannot be brought under a generic category (*Gattung*), it quite literally cannot mate (*sich gatten*): hence the sterility of Odradek, in "The Cares of a Family Man"; of Gregor Samsa; and of the cat-lamb figure of "A Cross Breed" ("Eine Kreuzung": *Kreuzung* connotes the very word "chiasm").

The application to metaphor of a chiastic logic makes explicit its unstable, reversible, usurpatory character. Metaphors that normally define the "higher" attributes of humans in terms of worldly things are properly the least stable of all, because they are least true. They are false because whatever of the spirit is named in them is named in the language of the world, which speaks of property and possession; hence it is its lie. What can be named is only the spirit's deformation. Such metaphors are, furthermore, false because humanity is not one "higher" thing but a division and a struggle between the higher and the lower. The higher is alienated in the lower. Hence the more truthful metaphor (such as the hunt, or pursuit: *Jagd*) identifies human self-division in an aggressive tonality.

Such metaphors are apt for chiastic reversal. Reversal makes the point that the higher term of the division has an only specious authority. The chiasm brings this speciousness to light by making dominant the "lower" term: the worldly, sensuous, "factical" side for which Kafka sometimes reserves the word "filth" and which Freud terms "the dross of phenomenal reality," situating it within the unconscious.[24] Kafka's monstrous heroes are representations of the unconscious obtained by chiastic reversals of the normal metaphor of man, which empowers self-consciousness.

Kafka's understanding and revision of the tropes of metaphor and chiasm are hardly a matter of mere rhetoric. They are consistent with an ontological insight into the dereliction, the untruthful character, of ordinary consciousness, whose prejudices in its own favor require abrupt reversal.

24. Quoted in Theodor W. Adorno, "Aufzeichnungen zu Kafka," in *Prismen: Kulturkritik und Gesellschaft* (Frankfurt am Main: Suhrkamp, 1955), p. 311.

Chapter Five

Kafka's Double Helix

Kafka's development is a double helix if "helix" can suggest a certain turning, with many hesitations and returns, farther and farther away from a virtual origin. Kafka's *first* helix is a turn from the natural certainty of the body and the senses, from the opinion that a truthful life can be lived as an extensive manifold of experience, to which the body is fitted as an agent of perception and appropriation. "If until now," writes the narrator of "'You,' I Said . . . ," "if until now our whole person had been oriented upon the work of our hands, upon that which was seen by our eyes, heard by our ears, upon the steps made by our feet, now we suddenly turn ourselves entirely in the opposite direction [into an element wholly opposed, *ins Entgegengesetzte*], like a weather vane in the mountains" (DI 26; Ta 21).[1]

This turning may be considered an originary assertion of literature, determining the basic directions of the life that Kafka was to call "authorial being [*Schriftstellersein*]" (L 333) and that from the beginning he associated with an "atrophying" of the bodily life. "When it became clear in my organism that writing was the most productive direction for my being to take, everything rushed in that direction and left empty all those abilities which were directed toward the joys of sex, eating, drinking, philosophical reflection and above all music. I atrophied in all those directions. . . . Naturally, I did not find this

1. See Chapter One, pp. 19–20.

purpose independently and consciously, it found itself" (DI 211). Both passages—the first in its image of the inanimate weather vane—assert the nonconscious, nonself-determined character of this turn from the body; it is inscribed in Kafka's being.[2]

In the "Letter to his Father," Kafka also directly addresses his destiny as a writer. "My writing was all about you; all I did there, after all, was to bemoan what I could not bemoan upon your breast. It was an intentionally long-drawn-out leave-taking from you, yet, although it was brought about by force on your part, it did take its course in the direction determined by me" (DF 177).[3] This passage, like the one above, registers a moment of violence at the origin of writing. But the difference between them is so crucial that this likeness serves chiefly to profile their disparity. The origin of writing is now not something like the wind (pneuma, divine afflatus) that blows the weather vane around, nor is it writing itself; it is Hermann Kafka. It is not writing that gives the organism its direction but the paternal organism that gives writing its initial direction.

Yet it is hard to believe that Kafka thought this second story of the origin of writing a better one. He did not think that his writing was his father's tool (though he feared this belief, and "The Judgment" records the intensity of his struggle to repudiate it).[4] Nor did Kafka regularly think that he had marked out the direction of his writing by acts of his own intending.[5] The account given in the "Letter" does not

---

2. According to Kafka, his stories are very little mediated by conscious intentional acts; the desideratum is to "experience a story within yourself from its beginning. . . . [You] want to be pursued by it and have time for it, therefore are pursued by it and of your own volition run before it wherever it may thrust and wherever you may lure it" (DI 61). Cf. Hartmut Binder, "Kafka's Schaffensprozess," *Euphorion* 70, no. 2 (1976): 129–74. Kafka was obviously unable to cede initiative to either pole entirely, however. "Far from being a comfort to him, his inescapable consciousness of creative powers was frightening because it seemed, on the one hand, as though he could extract from himself anything he wanted, and on the other hand as though he couldn't control the forces he called up" (Ronald Hayman, *A Biography of Kafka* [London: Weidenfeld & Nicolson, 1981], p. 106).

3. See Chapter Three, n. 41.

4. See the discussion of "The Judgment," Chapters Two and Four.

5. Looking back ruefully, on October 17, 1921, Kafka wrote: "There may be a purpose lurking behind the fact that I never learned anything useful and—the two are connected—have allowed myself to become a physical wreck. I did not want to be distracted, did not want to be distracted by the pleasures life has to give a useful and healthy man. As if illness and despair were not just as much of a distraction!" And further, "It is astounding how I have systematically destroyed myself in the course of

so much support his view of the writing destiny as it does the view he held of the writing of the "Letter": namely, that it was full of "lawyer's tricks" (LM 79). It is a text arising from the inferior order of "motivation," which Kafka defines as flight from the knowledge that self-knowledge, as the knowledge of good and evil, is already given along with the Fall—as flight into the belief that self-knowledge is something still to be achieved by a struggle resembling litigation. Motivations are the agents of the delusion that a truthful life can be founded on knowledge that still has to be acquired.

Kafka's turn to writing is in its beginnings an auspicious one. The sacrifice of the joys of sex, eating, and drinking appears to be repaid in richer coin in such early works as "The Judgment" and "The Stoker," though it is probably better to view them as urgent assertions of Kafka's need to affirm an economy of sacrifice in the face of the seductive alternative offered by Felice Bauer: the promise, namely, of a writing naturalistically at home, of domestic elation. From 1912 on, however, Kafka's confessional writings reveal more and more his uncertainty and indeed horror of an authorial fate that requires a continual emptying out of the abilities of the body. "The strength I can muster for that portrayal ['of my dreamlike inner life'] is not to be counted on" (DII 77). The strength that writing gives is not freely accessible, even to the self that has renounced everything for it:

> Writing denies itself to me [renounces me, *versagt sich mir*]. Hence plan for autobiographical investigations. Not biography but investigation and detection of the smallest possible component parts. Out of these I will then construct myself, as one whose house is unsafe wants to build a safe one next to it, if possible out of the material of the old one. What is bad, admittedly, is if in the midst of building, his strength gives out and now, instead of one house, unsafe but yet complete, he has one half-destroyed and one half-finished house, that is to say, nothing. What follows is madness, that is to say, something like a Cossack dance between the two houses, whereby the Cossack goes on scraping and throwing aside the earth with the heels of his boots until his grave is dug out under him. [DF 350; H 388]

---

the years, it was like a slowly widening breach in a dam, a purposeful action." But note how Kafka continues, detaching the intender of this purpose from himself: "The spirit that brought it about must now be celebrating triumphs; why doesn't it let me take part in them? But perhaps it hasn't yet achieved its purpose and can therefore think of nothing else" (DII 194).

If it is not he who writes but writing that writes, then writing can choose him as well as abandon him. How then could writing ever fail to inspire anxiety?

Kafka's existence as a writer now becomes "only barely possible in the broil of earthly life. . . . What right have I to be alarmed when the house suddenly collapses. After all, I know what preceded the collapse. Did I not emigrate and leave the house to all the evil powers?" (L 334–35). The directions of the life of writing become crazed—a mad "hesitation before birth" (DII 210), "a buzzing about . . . one's own form" (L 334), a perpetual "marching double-time in place" (DI 157). "The clocks are not in unison; the inner one runs crazily on at a devilish or demoniac or in any case inhuman pace, the outer one limps along at its usual speed. What else can happen but that the two worlds split apart, and they do split apart, or at least clash in a fearful manner" (DII 202). The writing destiny is purely and simply the "fear [that] keeps [him] from sleeping" (L 333–34).

By sober reckoning in daylight, however (some five months earlier) writing figures in only tenth place as one of the many projects that Kafka was unable to complete, following "piano, violin, languages, Germanics, anti-Zionism, Zionism, Hebrew, gardening, [and] carpentering" (DII 209). Writing's loss of authority, as Maurice Blanchot suggests, is linked to Kafka's shift to a religious perspective, to a religion in which writing is not the privileged form of "prayer."[6] Kafka is now bent on a salvation in "this other world" which excludes an idolatry of fictive images. In 1903 he had written: "God doesn't want me to write, but I—I must" (L 10). Toward the end of Kafka's life, according to Blanchot, God still does not want him to write, and he no longer has to write.

A turn of perspective, then, marks Kafka's being and writing,

6. Maurice Blanchot, "The Diaries: The Exigency of the Work of Art," trans. Lyall H. Powers, in *Franz Kafka Today*, ed. Angel Flores and Homer Swander (Madison: University of Wisconsin Press, 1964), pp. 195–220. A letter of Kafka's to Max Brod confirms Blanchot's sense of the negative connotation that writing had for Kafka at times toward the end of his life: "I'm not writing. What's more, my will is not directed toward writing" (L 153); or from the *Diaries*: "Undeniably, there is a certain joy in being able calmly to write down: 'Suffocation is inconceivably horrible.' Of course it is inconceivable—that is why I have written nothing down" (DII 201); or again, "There is in writing a perhaps dangerous . . . comfort" (DII 212), since "What *is* literature? Where does it come from? What use is it?" (DF 246).

especially after 1917.[7] This turning produces Kafka's *second* helix. The kind of reflection informing it, however, is better not described as "religious." It is certainly not religious in the sense of allowing Kafka to "live, at least here on earth, quietly, as with God, in unity, without contradiction . . ." (PP 119). It might be religious in the sense of widening his struggle from the order of unhappy reflection and its goad, the "crowd of devils" (PP 119), toward a figure of totality, a term of widest alterity. This term has authority: it can be acknowledged, borne witness to, or realized in struggle; and it is desirable that this be done. Kafka calls this other term "life's splendor" (DII 195). His enterprise is exemplary in the sense that it considers the individual an instantiation of a wider life.

Kafka's career now appears in its essential directions as an always involved *double* helix. The first is renunciatory: "The desire to renounce the greatest human happiness for the sake of writing keeps cutting every muscle in my body" (LF 315). The second is exemplary: "If there is a higher power that wishes to use me, or does use me, then I am at its mercy, if no more than as a well-prepared instrument; if not, I am nothing, and will suddenly be abandoned in a dreadful void" (LF 21). In the first instance, to be nothing is to be good for writing; in the second, it is to be good for nothing. Everything there was to sacrifice has been sacrificed: there is no more bodily life to burn. No further reward can be won by the calculus of renunciation, for it is a finally mercantile quid pro quo. If there was a time when everything Kafka wrote already had perfection—"When I arbitrarily write a single sentence, for instance, 'He looked out of the window,' it already has perfection" (DI 45)—now he need only look out the window and *he* has perfection. That is to say, precisely to the same degree that what he wrote was also radically imperfect, being a "communication" of the truth and hence a lie, so too what he now is is radically imperfect, being the imperfection of the creature. But this is the imperfection of a creature who knows his divided identity and who lives this truth; as a writer and as one who in all other ways testifies to it, he is, could be, an exemplary witness bearer.

7. "Between [August 10 and September 15, 1917] the following occurred: the first medical confirmation was made of Kafka's tuberculosis, [and] he again decided to break off his engagement to F" (Max Brod in DII 322). The time following is marked by Kafka's reading of Kierkegaard and his renewed interest in Judaism.

The first helix, then, is a spiral of reflection that advances at the cost of the natural life of the body, a movement that may not always issue into writing but conduces to writing (at least one sort of writing arises as the inscription of the "law" directly into resisting flesh). This spiral, however, can also become a cage, to be endured chiefly as a hindrance (GW 264). Kafka imagined in his journal that one could "choke to death on oneself. If the pressure of introspection were to diminish, or close off entirely, the opening through which one flows forth into the world" (DII 223). The second movement, the "exemplary," arises at a point past the point where writing begins, past the point of the maximum solitude of thought, isolation from the body, and the frenzied vanity of self-reflection. It advances to another place at which introspection and the body offer themselves as the field of determination in which Being—"the indestructible, . . . common to all" (DF 42)—acquires a historical existence. Kafka dignifies his suffering as martyrdom and exemplification: the writer "is the scapegoat of mankind. He makes it possible for men to enjoy sin without guilt, almost without guilt" (L 335). His humiliation is perfect; his suffering is no longer the sacrifice of his personal self for the sake of his "abilities" but testimony to the realization of a common being.

How compelling is the evidence of such a second turn in Kafka's life and work? The evidence I have adduced so far comes without its full context. Affirmative and edifying propositions are frequently or almost always hedged by Kafka, speculated into a doubt. The basic thrust of this doubt is supplied by the first helix: the career of writing includes the surmise that it is "diabolic" (L 334), a "contriving of artificial substitutes" (DII 207). When Kafka affirms, he necessarily affirms through an act of writing that pushes toward recognition of its own falsity: "Truth is indivisible, hence it cannot recognize itself; anyone who wants to recognize it has to be a lie" (DF 43). Despite the continual thrust of the first helix toward doubt of whatever can be said, however, Kafka's writing, especially in the later years, conveys a different ethos. The second helix produces whole orders of affirmation, one of which enlarges his self, even as the agent of introspection, and declares the work of self-consciousness valuable and productive. The self is dignified—and not only, as in the first turn, as the writing self; in the second helix the self is dignified on the strength of its care for its own being, however "alien" (DF 92) that being may be (*fremd, die Fremde, die du bist*: H 110).

The second kind of affirmation declares Kafka's writing to be essentially founded on and able to represent the human *world*—this world—the world of society, the world of other persons. The third dignifies as generally truthful the enterprise of his *thought*, especially as it is not self-interested and involves suffering and exertion.

To the first point about the self, Kafka wrote:

> I feel too tightly constricted in everything that signifies Myself; even the eternity that I am is too tight for me. But if, for instance, I read a good book, say an account of travels, it rouses me, satisfies me, suffices me. Proofs that previously I did not include this book in my eternity, or had not pushed on far enough ahead to have an intuitive glimpse of the eternity that necessarily includes this book as well.— From a certain stage of knowledge [*Erkenntnis*] on, weariness, insufficiency, constriction, self-contempt must all vanish: namely at the point where I have the stength to recognize as my own nature what previously was something alien to myself that refreshed me, satisfied, liberated and exalted me. [DF 91–92][8]

The effort of recognition is a mandate—consistent and durable:

> I should welcome eternity, and when I do find it I am sad. I should feel myself perfect by virtue of eternity—and feel myself depressed?
>
> You say: I should—feel. In saying this do you express a commandment that is within yourself?
>
> That is what I mean. . . . I believe . . . it is a continual commandment. [DF 92][9]

The commandment is likely to produce the spinning of the first helix—of anxious self-reflection. "This pursuit [of every idea by introspection]," writes Kafka, "originating in the midst of men, carries one in a direction away from them. . . . The pursuit goes right through me and rends me asunder." But this passage continues with a hope and a surmise.

> Or I can—can I? manage to keep my feet somewhat and be carried along in the wild pursuit. Where, then, shall I be brought? "Pursuit," indeed, is only a metaphor. I can also say, "assault on the last earthly frontier," an assault, moreover, launched from below, from mankind,

8. This passage does not make a complete statement; it is part of a longer dialectical aphorism that proceeds to jeopardize the authority of this extract.

9. Earlier German editions of this passage write "oneness," *Einigkeit*, for "eternity," *Ewigkeit* (H 110). Caution!

and since this too is a metaphor, I can replace it by the metaphor of an assault from above, aimed at me from above.

All such writing is an assault on the frontiers; if Zionism had not intervened, it might easily have developed into a new secret doctrine, a Kabbalah. [DII 202–3]

The Kabbalah is truthful writing.[10]

This diary passage vividly reveals the ethos of the second helix. It is striking in the way it connects "introspection," the "I," and the act of writing as aspects of a single being. By contrast, it was characteristic of Kafka's confessional writings in thrall to the first helix to distinguish these three categories severely and to consider "introspection" and the empirical "I" as defective forms of writing.

The second type of evidence affirms the responsiveness of Kafka's art and thought to the life of his epoch. "The question of conscience [consciousness, Bewußtsein] is a social imposition" (GW 273; B 285).[11] Kafka made this famous claim: "I have vigorously absorbed the negative element of the age in which I live, an age that is, of course, very close to me, which I have no right ever to fight against, but as it were a right to represent" (DF 99).[12] In "Josephine The Singer" the song of the artist is "a characteristic expression of our life . . . some approximation to our usual customary piping. . . . [Her] piping, which rises up where everyone else is pledged to silence, comes almost like a message from the whole people to each individual; Josephine's thin piping amidst grave decisions is almost like our people's precarious existence amidst the tumult of a hostile world" (S 361, 364, 367).

"Investigations of a Dog" also contains this social imperative:

10. In support of Kafka's belief that his writing represented the beginning of a new Kabbalah, there is this fact, discovered by Malcolm Pasley: At one point in the manuscript of *The Castle,* Kafka divided a line into groups of ten letters by inserting slashes: "*Dich Klamm r/ufen lassen / und zum vier/ten Mal nich/t mehr und ni/emals*" (Have Klamm c/all you and f/or the fourt/h time no lon/ger and neve/r). Pasley comments: "These mysterious signs are apparently neither logical nor rhythmic articulations of the text. It seems rather as if the writer meant to auscultate his text for esoteric meanings. . . . As a hesitant mystic, who characterized writing as a 'form of prayer,' Kafka was inclined to believe in a sort of secret authenticity of the original script" ("Zu Kafkas Interpunktion," *Euphorion* 75, no. 4 [1981]: 490).

11. Cf. Nietzsche: "Consciousness does not really belong to man's individual existence but rather to his social or herd nature" (*The Gay Science,* ed. and trans. Walter Kaufmann [New York: Random House, 1974], p. 299).

12. The corresponding proposition on the *first* helix: "Marriage is the representative of life, with which you are meant to come to terms" (DF 98).

"Only with the assistance of the whole dog world could I begin to understand my own questions" (S 289).[13] For further claims of this kind—for example, that "during the rest of his life Kafka tied himself ever more firmly to the Jewish community" and shared with Tolstoy the knowledge that "through the community the individual can feel himself sustained precisely at the deepest level of the individual self"—the reader can consult Max Brod's apologetic work *Franz Kafkas Glauben and Lehre* (beliefs and doctrine).[14]

Finally, the ethos of the second helix affirms Kafka's thought as exemplary. It is no longer a "whirring" or an eternal "hesitation." Kafka sees and thinks under a general mandate: "Anyone who cannot come to terms with his life while he is alive needs one hand to ward off a little his despair over his fate—he has little success in this—but with his other hand he can note down what he sees among the ruins, for he sees different (and more) things than do the others" (DII 196).

Kafka said to Gustav Janouch: "The poet has the task of leading the isolated mortal being into the infinite life, the contingent into the lawful. He has a prophetic task" (J 172). His "prophetic" power is born of his ontological distinction: "He does not live for the sake of his personal life; he does not think for the sake of his personal thoughts. It seems to him that he lives and thinks under the compulsion of a family, which, it is true, is itself superabundant in life and thought, but for which he constitutes, in obedience to some law unknown to him, a formal necessity. Because of this unknown family and this unknown law he cannot be exempted" (GW 269).[15] The

13. The dog, according to Marthe Robert, is Kafka's "authorized spokesman," a plain persona of Kafka, esp. in his relation to the Jewish community (*Franz Kafka's Loneliness*, trans. Ralph Manheim [London: Faber & Faber, 1982], p. 14).

14. Max Brod, *Franz Kafkas Glauben und Lehre* (Winterthur: Mondial Verlag, 1948), p. 41.

15. In his diaries Kafka quoted with approval a formulation from Wilhelm Dilthey's *Das Erlebnis und die Dichtung* (Experience and poetry), probably from 2d ed. (Leipzig: B. G. Tuebner, 1907), p. 55. Referring to the character of Tellheim in Lessing's *Minna von Barnhelm*, Dilthey wrote: "He has—what only the creations of true poets possess—that spontaneous flexibility of the inner life which, as circumstances alter, continually surprises us by revealing entirely new facets of itself" (DII 12). The ideal, in Dilthey's view achievable, is of a subjective life no different in kind from a poetic creation, the product of writing. If Kafka maintained the distinction between a certain form of subjectivity and writing, he nonetheless held to an ideal of subjectivity against which the authenticity of literature could be tested. It is this subjectivity that is here affirmed. In two essays—"Kafka's Poetics of the Inner Self," *Modern Austrian Literature* 11 (1978): 37–55; and "Language and Truth in the Two

metaphor of a superabundant family suggests an authority more fundamental than "society."

The helix of affirmation will seem less like religion if we stress that it is informed by a certain knowledge: namely, knowledge of thought as such. The three types of experience identified by the helix correspond to aspects of the act of thought that Kafka now affirms. Kafka acknowledges, first, the act of self-consciousness. Next, he affirms the worldly reality of the content of consciousness. He can dispute its truth but not its indisputable "that-it-is": "It is enough that the arrows fit exactly in the wounds that they have made" (DII 206). Finally, Kafka affirms a third term founding the act of thought as the union of observer and object. It is not a term that consciousness can know: "The observer of the soul cannot penetrate into the soul, but there doubtless is a margin where he comes into contact with it. Recognition of this contact is the fact that even the soul does not know of itself. Hence it must remain unknown" (DF 80).[16] No thought knows the soul, yet every thought manifests the unknowable truth of the soul, for "there is nothing else apart from the soul" (DF 80). The epistemological terms "observer," "contents," "soul" suggest the existential categories self, world, and being-in-the-world.[17] Affirmed, they supply additional evidence of the second helix and its

---

Worlds of Franz Kafka," *German Quarterly* 52 (May 1979): 364–82—Walter Sokel distinguishes between two sorts of poetics in Kafka, based on two theories of language. One side of Kafka's aspiration—marking his "idea of 'truth' and language"— is the "communal, collective, and universalist aspect." This is different from the "inward and subjective" side. The first aspect has a "naturalist," the second a "Gnostic spiritualist" dimension ("Language and Truth," p. 374). The second tendency is more nearly realized—if only "allusively"—in the act of writing by an "inner self." One could indeed show how in Kafka's art and life these two dimensions insistently contest each other. I want to stress, however, that in the second helix, the distinction between the community and the truth of the inner world falls away. Both come under the head of a common life—"the splendor of life," "a family superabundant in the force of life and thought." At moments, Kafka claims, his art and life achieve a truthful immersion of individuality and subjectivity in this wider life.

16. Cf. "The unity of mankind . . . reveals itself to everyone, or seems to reveal itself, in the complete harmony, discernible time and again, between the development of mankind as a whole and of the individual man. Even in the most secret emotions of the individual" (DI 316–17).

17. A precise equivalent for "world" is Kafka's category "something alien [*ein Fremdes*]," and for "being-in-the-world," "my eternity [*meine Ewigkeit*]" (DF 91; H 110).

kinds of affirmation; each event of consciousness becomes the occasion of an indispensable witness-bearing.

In the second helix, consciousness is no longer present either in its airiness: as "human nature, essentially changeable, unstable as the dust [*Das menschliche Wesen, leichtfertig in seinem Grund, von der Natur des auffliegenden Staubes*]" (PP 26); or in its vanity: "It is vanity and sensuality which continually buzz about one's own or even another's form—and feast on him" (L 334); or in its lostness: "A cobweb come adrift; being free of tension [from jostling, *von Rüttelung*] is its supreme though not too frequent joy" (LF 531; BF 737). Instead, consciousness—"this inescapable duty to observe oneself" (DII 200)—flows from a commandment. What is required is authentic, has the character of an articulation of being:

> The strange, mysterious, perhaps dangerous, perhaps saving comfort that there is in writing: it is a leap out of murderers' row; it is a seeing of what is really taking place. This occurs by a higher type of observation, a higher, not a keener type, and the higher it is and the less within reach of the "row," the more independent it becomes, the more obedient to its own laws of motion, the more incalculable, the more joyful, the more ascendant its course. [DII 212]

*   *   *

The strongest evidence of the "exemplary" turn is Kafka's famous intimation of his work as a new Kabbalah. This claim, however, follows a passage that raises an equally famous problem. There Kafka wrote: "'Pursuit,' indeed, is only a metaphor. I can also say, 'assault on the last earthly frontier,' an assault, moreover, launched from below, from mankind, and since this too is a metaphor, I can replace it by the metaphor of an assault from above, aimed at me from above" (DII 202-3). In another place this very metaphor is defined not only as an option but, worse, as a pretense: "Self-forgetfulness and self-cancelling-out of art: what is an escape is pretended to be a stroll or even an attack" (DF 81). The letter passage could produce the view that Kafka's turn to an exemplary position does not correspond to anything real in his experience but is instead obtained as a linguistic effect of the rhetorical figure of chiasm.

If this were so, Kafka's aphorisms featuring reversals or turnabouts would give evidence not of the second helix but only of its speciousness. Such "evidence" could always be fabricated by a practiced rhetorical intelligence, by wit. Simply by reversing familiar propositions about the preeminent relation of "I" to what is "not I"—to a single worldly instance or to the "eternity that necessarily includes" that instance (DF 91)—Kafka could produce aphorisms favoring the perspective of a being essentially different from himself. Kafka's flair for the quick profit of rhetorical reversal might be identified in the aphorism "In the struggle between yourself and the world second the world" (DF 39). The act of seconding reverses the familiar primacy accorded to the term of the self, the world's governor and opponent, but only in a secondary—that is to say, detached or mimicking—fashion.

In order to clarify this question, consider an apparently simple chiasm. In "Reflections on Sin, Suffering, Hope, and the True Way," Kafka wrote, "A cage went in search of a bird" (DF 36). What does this aphorism mean? It looks elliptical, opaque, and abysmal; but thought moves irresistibly to understand it and does so by imagining it to be the chiastic inversion of a first proposition that Kafka never wrote: the sentence, "A bird went in search of a cage." This proposition does seem immediately clearer. A bird—with its connotations of fragility, homelessness, and flightiness, too—suggests the spirit that desperately craves an imprisoning system. A driven yet self-determining creature, fallen out with its own nature and tormented by the anxiety of an empty freedom, seeks the law of any constraint whatsoever.

The metaphor of such a bird might indeed fairly represent a certain view of Kafka, Kafka suffering the anguish of the first helix, cut off from a world of live purposes; and he did, of course, write phrases of a similarly helpless kind, even forecasting the failure of his cage to be a genuine prison: "He could have resigned himself to a prison. To end as a prisoner—that could be a life's ambition. But it was a barred cage he was in. Calmly and insolently, as if at home, the din of the world streamed out and in through the bars, the prisoner was really free, nothing that went on outside escaped him, he could simply have left the cage, the bars were yards apart, he was not even a prisoner" (GW 264). It is then by reversing this proposition, we say, that Kafka produced the aphorism he actually wrote: "A cage went in search of a bird."

This new sentence takes seriously the injunction to second the world in the struggle between you and the world by requiring you to make the project of the cage your own. Kafka dignifies the cage—the opposite, the adversary term—as agent and, so it would seem, eventual victor in this struggle. An imprisoning system itself seeks out the individual mind. The movements of the bird will not long be "determined [in their essential] directions" by itself (DF 177). "The hunting dogs are playing in the courtyard, but the hare will not escape them, no matter how fast it may be flying already through the woods" (GW 288). All the bird's movements, all the freedom it knows, are seen from another perspective as only flighty divagations from impending capture. The bird belongs to another's project: it is the cage that is determining.

Kafka's aphorism speaks as a voice from the cage. It joins the second helix by adopting the perspective of a fate wider than a subjectivity—encompassing, subordinating, and determining the self in its native vanity and flightiness. The perspective is consistent with the martyr's logic of the second helix: it stresses the cost to a self bent on the destiny of exemplification.

This interpretation aims to clarify the central question: How much of the truth recounted in this aphorism is owed to lived experience? Or is the worldly perspective of the cage produced by an only playful reversal of a wisdom sentence privileging the human subject? The reality of the entire second helix is at stake: is it in principle only a linguistic turn? The reading above seems to give solid results, based on Kafka's acquist of true experience. The aphorism is parsimoniously explained by the notion of the second helix, and it is confirmed by what Kafka otherwise wrote in his posthumously published notebooks. But perhaps this reading of the aphorism is just a lucky fit. Is the method by which it is obtained reliable? We must try above all to understand how we are reading the apparently simple chiasm produced by the aphorism of the bird and the cage.

Our reading followed the rule of symmetrical reversal: it assumed that a plain meaning could be recovered by "reversing back" a reversal. Perplexed by the bizarre freedom of a cage that went in search a bird, we went back in search of it along the path of the reversal of a sentence about the familiar freedom of a bird. We then reversed "forward" the aphorism we found there ("freedom seeks constraint") in order to discover the meaning ("constraint seeks freedom") that completes the new aphorism. This rule, however, by which Kafka's chiasms of rhetoric and thought are read as finite and recoverable, is in fact unequal to them. What does one actually know when one knows the truth normally asserted, that "a bird went in search of a cage"? A bird like this is no symbolic free agent. In choosing un-freedom, it is already unfree—its freedom is "thing"-like. What sort of "cage"-like bird seeks out a cage?[18] The apparently simple figure is actually an unintelligible, probably a perverse metaphor. It exhibits its own reversal even before it has been chiastically reversed. The "straightforward" reading of this aphorism offered above was entirely ideological.

No chiasm of this metaphorical type can be understood by a logic of symmetry. Every such chiasm starts out by requiring that the second sentence be read in light of the first; otherwise the second sentence would not appear to have been obtained by chiastic reversal. Into the object-term ("bird") of the second half of the chiasm must be inserted the meaning of the same term ("bird") as it is defined, as subject, in the first half: namely, in relation to its object-term. The subject "bird" means "the desire for a cage," and when it is inserted into the second half, the second half reads, "A cage went in search of a bird that desires a cage." With what result for interpretation?[19]

18. This discussion is confirmed by Rudolf Kreis in *Die doppelte Rede des Franz Kafka: Eine textlinguistische Analyse* (Paderborn: Schöningh, 1976). Kreis stresses that the aphorism constructs a pair of unstable metaphors interminably active in producing new relations. "By acquiring legs" and to this extent approximating the bird, the cage is metamorphosed into a divided being. This is true, too, of the bird as soon as the reader has applied to the aphorism the rule of chiastic reversal. Once upon a time a bird went in search of a cage; but then, too, the bird—unfree and thinglike—split into a duplicitous being whose identity is now inexhaustibly involved with the cage. The bird becomes a "cage-bird." Kreis concludes: "Kafka's epistemological intention is to articulate the aphorism in the sense of its reversibility as a chain or series [produced by] the always generative relation of cage-bird-cage" (p. 51).

19. Two aspects of this procedure call for some explanation. First, the definition of the bird as "the *desire* for a cage" substitutes a metaphorical for the literally correct formulation "the *search* for a cage." To make an only literal substitution of the meaning of a term in the first half of the chiasm for the "same" term in the second is of course to restrict considerably the free play in the chiasm. The proposition "A cage went in search of the search for a cage" invites much less interpretation—in seeming more nearly tautological—than the proposition, "A cage went in search of the desire for a cage." But Kafka's chiasmi are aphoristic and not logical models of symmetrical reversal. A procedure more faithful to Kafka's actual practice would propose as the

How solipsistic an adversary! (one might conclude). This cage or caging principle is playing a game with a beaten opponent, one that is already playing its game. What sort of *fin de siècle* cage is this, at what low ebb of vitality? There is no genuine otherness to the object of its pursuit.

If this is what "cage" means, we are now eager to find out for a second time what the first part of the chiasm means.[20] It means, after further substitution, that a bird went in search of a cage that must search outside itself for the desire for itself. Does this proposition shelter in the term "cage" the Hegelian critique of the master, and

---

ground of the aphorism, from which the aphorism could be generated via chiastic reversal, a proposition employing not identical but rather "foreign, analogous terms," thus illustrating the slippage, the "glidingly paradoxical" character of Kafka's apparently logical sequences (see Gerhard Neumann, "Umkehrung und Ablenkung: Franz Kafkas 'Gleitendes Paradox,'" in *Franz Kafka,* ed. Heinz Politzer [Darmstadt: Wissenschaftliche Buchgesellschaft, 1973]). Kafka's aphorisms call for figurative interpretation, and even the more nearly tautological instance discussed above provokes an endless movement of interpretation. To write "the desire for a cage" for "the search for a cage" is only to dramatize an interpretative event that occurs even when the substituted terms are kept more nearly uniform. A second point: it is of course an arbitrary procedure to begin the interpretation of this chiasm by inserting into its second half the definition of the object-term "bird" obtained from relations in the first half. Equally, one could begin interpreting the chiasm by inserting into the second half the definition of the term "cage," also obtained from relations in the first half: i.e., "cage" or "the object of a bird's desire." The aphorism now reads, "The object of a bird's desire went in search of a bird." This sense of the aphorism opens up another field of meanings, bearing on the tyranny of desire, the value of *Gelassenheit,* the apothegm "He who seeks does not find, but he who does not seek will be found" (DF 80), and much more. This field also belongs constitutively to the aphorism. My concern is not so much to say which way the aphorism goes but to stress the richness, the many paths, of the field of possibilities that the aphorism opens up.

20. A final point about the method of this interpretation. I am attempting to find out what Kafka's "original" aphorism looks like after A[2] (the cage in the second half of the chiasm that went in search of a bird) has been substituted "back" for A[1] (the cage in the first half of the chiasmus that the bird sought). I am not offering an argument claiming that such a movement of substitution *has* to take place. In one sense, of course, the move is not permissible: the very difference between A[2] and A[1] could establish the impossibility of back substitution, since the first half of the chiasm is after all about A[1] and not A[2]. This objection makes logical sense but not existential, historical, or rhetorical sense. For it is impossible to stop the movement of interpretation that arises when A[2] is imagined to mean essentially what A[1] has been discovered to mean. That is because they are metaphors of one another. The chiasm simultaneously establishes a difference and then takes the difference away through a pointed play of resemblances.

does Kafka now invert Hegel by criticizing the slave?[21] "Freedom and bondage," wrote Kafka, "are in their essential meaning one . . . [but] not in the sense that the slave does not lose his freedom, hence in a certain respect is more free than the free man" (DF 94). In what sense, then, is the bondsman freer? Certainly Kafka's figurative slave in the bird/cage aphorism is not a real master acknowledging its own death; it is a slave that sought its spiritual advantage precisely vis-à-vis the master who desired its desire. The implication arises that there is another kind of master who does not so desire.

As we now read "forward" for a second time the aphorism of the second half, we grasp, therefore, that the cage in question, in the struggle to become the master that it is not, had to go in search of a slave in order to inculcate in it once and for all the truth that it is a master indifferent to the slave's consciousness of it as one that desires another's desire. The master sought a slave no longer conscious of its, the master's, flawed essence. But to be such a slave would then be to be more nearly a master, in the sense of being entirely at home in the simplicity of one's condition.

We therefore return to reread—for a final time—the first half of the aphorism. Such a slave indeed needed to search for the consciousness of abjection, for the genuine encagement of self-consciousness. What, then, does the aphorism that Kafka actually wrote tell us so far? The cage that went in search of a bird to encage would find in that bird no simple prey, would find in it both Prometheus and his eagle. But what about the desire of the cage to be master, to be Zeus? Here we could read, with profit, Kafka's parable "Prometheus" and be forced to think past Zeus and Prometheus to the "inexplicable" mountain, to the legend itself, and then beyond.[22] But what this reference assures

21. "The master is . . . a being-for-self which is for itself only through an other." G. W. F. Hegel, *The Phenomenology of Mind,* trans. J. B. Baillie (New York: Harper & Row, 1967), p. 239; cf. pp. 228–40.

22. The being who sought outside itself for the desire for itself could conjure an Otto Weininger–like negative figure of "woman." What implication does this reading have for its chiastic reversal: namely, the aphorism that Kafka actually wrote? The object of the cage's pursuit becomes "man," but then, if we return to the first half of the aphorism, it appears that man, an alleged wholeness of desire, desires encaging. A *soi-disant* wholeness of being equally implies imprisonment in its own essence. It is not the bird that is free; the cage is freer. The cage that seeks the bird brings the bird its own genuine "birdlike" power of flight. The cage is a benevolent objectivity. But how could such objectivity come to have volition and desire? This must be thought out, perhaps indeed by returning to what amounts to Kafka's critique of Hegel on Stoicism (pp. 157–57 below).

us of is that the "substratum of truth [*Wahrheitsgrund*]," (GW 252; B 99) lying beyond and beneath the legend is not the Absolute but rather something inexplicable.

If this reading, in a Hegelian ideolect that Kafka sometimes plainly assumes, is not misguided, how does it help to answer the question at hand, which concerns the experienced character—the more-than-verbal origin—of Kafka's aphorism "A cage went in search of a bird"?[23] Aside from its conceptual results, the reading makes a general point. As an interpretation proceeding via reversal, it never lands on a primary sense: it does not land at all. It prowls and whirs among the unstable, self-metamorphosing metaphors of a birdlike cage and a cagelike bird—terms that have already implicitly incorporated their opposite—in principle forever. These terms, being in the end formal fictions, metamorphosed metaphors, or simply monsters, do not permit of final reference to any such thing as "a wide alterity," a decisive turn to another life. They have the inexhaustible significance of rhetorical fictions; the reversals they engender simply jostle about the interpreter's conceptual associations.[24]

Such a movement is therefore not only or finally one of chiastic reversal but one of recursion to a third term: to the boundless field of incessant metaphorical exchange. This is the true and altogether unsettling order affirmed by the chiasm.[25] Thus the strict opposition of

23. See Chapter Four.

24. For another example of a recursive chiasm composed entirely by Kafka, see the text beginning "The animal wrests the whip from its master and whips itself in order to become master" (DF 37, 323). I discuss this aphorism in Chapter Six.

25. To generate new propositions by recursion means to determine the new term, the next term in the sequence, by one or more of the preceding terms. Douglas Hofstader gives this example of "recursion in language": "the phrase ['x'] must be analyzed to refer back to the previous question" (*Gödel, Escher, Bach: An Eternal Golden Braid* [New York: Random House, 1979], p. 588). Furthermore, works are recursive in a sense "not in common usage" when *figure* (the concluding half of the chiasm) and *ground* (the first half of the chiasm) cannot be distinguished (p. 70). My discussion of the recursive field of Kafka's chiasms in this and the following two paragraphs was anticipated by Gerhard Neumann's essay "Umkehrung and Ablenkung." It grieves me that I first read this work only while I was making last-minute revisions to this chapter. Neumann describes Kafka's paradoxes as composed of "deviations from normal understanding, from normal expectations as to thought and image, from normal logical procedure; shifts follow, but these can never be linked together as [instances of] blatant contradiction. . . . The process of unification never leads to a conclusive synthesis but continues on in an apparently endless series" (pp. 468, 474). In other words, the epistemological structure that I am here digging out of Kafka's chiasms is a subclass of what Neumann describes as Kafka's paradoxical

an initial judgment to its reversal is subverted by a term that turns out to be the condition of the impossibility of finite chiastic reversal. In such rhetorical instances, therefore, what is true is neither the assertion achieved by reversal which privileges the Other nor the "normal" wisdom-sentence which privileges the self but rather the principle of recursion, admitting a potentially infinite series of reversals.

This, then, is the final form of the argument that would disallow Kafka's claims to found authentically his self, the contents of his consciousness, and his thought. Such terms as subject and Other, it appears, are not sufficiently self-identical to have even minimal stability. The field of their union, which Kafka earlier called the "soul," cannot be articulated either by logic or experience. Such a soul is at

---

thought as such. Neumann adduces for his purposes a great many of the texts of Kafka that I also cite, and he too links decisively the categories of the "sliding paradox," suffering, and death. Yet Neumann addresses, strictly speaking, not structures of recursion but rather a kind of progressive variation and evasion in Kafka's thought, the outcome of which is the same as recursion but whose vector is different from that of reversal. We disagree, furthermore, in the matter of whether such structures are Hegelian and recoverable (as I believe) or are more radically agnostic. To the difficult question about the relation of the field of the sliding paradox to what Kafka called "real life" (DF 381), Neumann gives varying answers. Of the "process of unification" cited above, he concludes (I think somewhat prematurely) that it "continues until something leaps forth, which Kafka, without any consistency adducible from the movement of his thought, calls 'genuine life'" (p. 474). This equation, according to Neumann, is actually refuted by the aphorism in which this phrase appears. "What emerges from this labyrinth of thought," he writes, "is the movement of having gone astray into 'this region,' into which a way has evidently led but from which, however, none points back into life. The 'way' of this thought, which was supposed to have led into 'genuine life,' misses its goal. It leads into a zone of 'error'" (p. 475). But Neumann argues differently at the end of his essay: "Kafka himself was convinced that for him there had to be a place and a standpoint which he might reach by shaking off traditional habits of thought and imagery, a region where thinking was no longer a structure of rules by means of which something outside it could be captured but rather where thought and life became identical" (p. 508). Since Kafka declared that the relation of art and life was a variable one, Neumann's second position, in my view, is the one more nearly faithful to Kafka's intention. Neumann's first position is not, strictly speaking, intelligible, even when it is put forward by Kafka as part of a long and complex aphorism: this is the view that Kafka's text ends in a place from which there is not path back to life. In order for Kafka (and us, his readers) to have come to such a place, we must have been borne along by a wide cooperative intelligibility from which we have never taken leave, even when we think we have landed in the "unintelligible." On this point, see Martin Heidegger, who in *Being and Time* (trans. John MacQuarrie and Edward Robinson [New York: Harper & Row, 1962], p. 204) argues for the impossibility of an unintelligible utterance, of one that would not be part of human existence as an "articulation of intelligibility."

best a rhetorical energy reversing the wisdom of ordinary distinctions and propositions based on the self/other opposition. Kafka's chiasms create nothing more than the momentary illusion of a mind siding with genuine life, the indestructible event of being, the "higher power" that speaks through the whole human world.

Kafka's recursive logic reveals that apparently opposed terms are not stable terms but rather unstable metaphors of one another. His aphorisms generate as a third term a free play between given metaphors which accommodates new metaphors at the same time that it robs each of determinate meaning. This third term, therefore, could not refer to the condition of the soul as any sort of *being*-in-the-world.[26] "Then what kind of surplus is it?" (DII 184). It is a vertiginous spiral of indetermination, a no-man's land between the self and being—writing: "the Wilderness" (DII 195).

*   *   *

An interesting, a compelling—a deconstructive—view, perhaps, yet it is the view I have meant all along to oppose in arguing for the reality of the second helix in Kafka's thought that goes beyond a prowling and whirring among metaphors. Kafka's work offers a system of affirmations arising from a movement which, in the extremity of Heidegger's formulation, begets "[an]other [mode] of thinking that abandons subjectivity," in which "every kind of anthropology and all subjectivity of man as subject . . . is left behind."[27]

What sort of evidence could be adduced to confirm so large a claim? Two kinds suggest themselves. The first consists of conclusions themselves drawn from the analysis of Kafka's chiastic aphorisms; the second is based on Kafka's explicit statements on the question.

My counterargument proceeds as follows. The recursive movement produced by the aphorisms discussed above involves specific terms with specific content, logically and temporally determined by their relation and recurrence within the aphorism and historically determined by their place within an act of reading. As a consequence, the constitutive power of such terms as "cage," "world," and "master" is not nullified because the primacy of one such term A^2—A^2

26. See p. 114 above.
27. Martin Heidegger, "On the Essence of Truth," in *Martin Heidegger, Basic Writings,* ed. David Farrell Krell (New York: Harper & Row, 1977), p. 141.

123

being dominant over the term B^2 ("bird," "you," and "enslaved animal") in the second half of the chiasm—is undercut by chiastic "back-reversal," whence it is subsumed by the term A^1 from the first half of the chiasm—a term inferior to B^1. The principle of reversibility which would annihilate meaning would require that every attribute of A^2, the chiastic namesake of A^1, be contained by A^1. But what A^1 will always fail to contain is the temporal being-ahead of A^2. Attempting to subsume the attributes of A^2 under A^1 can never bring about their equivalence. Kafka's chiasms recursively redouble the attributes of a term only nominally; what the second term returns to is the same in name only. When terms recur chiastically, they also reintroduce a difference, consisting of the attributes they have acquired by virtue of their passage through the chiasm—attributes that may seem invisible but can be inked in again by thought.

These changes arise from the fact that the place of these terms within the intitial opposition was only virtual and transitory—in other words, from the fact that their initial opposition has been historically reversed. The original character of terms resurfaces, as a sort of memory, through the new character they acquire in the reverse position, whence they are once again reversed. But this reading cannot conclude with just any assertion as to the value or priority of terms. To read recursively is to acquire the historical experience of the residue of meaning that these terms leave along the track of their sublation.

By continuous chiastic reversal, the definitions of A^2 and B^2 are therefore enlarged, not canceled. They are enlarged in a direction productive of meanings for the reader who is determined to pursue them.

This point is quickly conveyed by an aphorism whose basic form is chiastic:

> "It is not a bleak wall, it is the very sweetest life that has been compressed into a wall, raisins upon raisins."—"I don't believe it."—"Taste it." —"I cannot raise my hand for unbelief."—"I shall put the grape into your mouth."—"I cannot taste it for unbelief."—"Then sink into the ground!"— "Did I not say that faced with the barrenness of this wall one must sink into the ground?" [DF 297]

The question at issue is this: Does the "voice" concluding the aphorism, unlike that of the second speaker, succeed in annihilating the wall built of sweetest raisins pressed together? Not at all. The aphorism inculpates the flimsy logic that is built on ostensible identities, for the "barrenness" of the wall at the end of the proposition is not the same as its empty "bleakness" at the beginning. The speaker who has the last word in the explicit text and appears to be speaking on behalf of death does not have the last word in the implicit text, which speaks to the reader on behalf of another truth. This is the truth of being, which the aphorism proposes as the building-labor of explication—a wall of truth, made up of sweetest explications of the aphorism pressed together.

Consider, too, the series of explicit reversals—remarkable for their clarity and mordancy—from "The Burrow":

> And it is not only by external enemies that I am threatened. There are also enemies in the bowels of the earth. I have never seen them, but legend tells of them and I firmly believe in them. They are creatures of the inner earth; not even legend can describe them. Their very victims can scarcely have seen them; they come, you hear the scratching of their claws just under you in the ground, which is their element, and already you are lost. Here it is of no avail to console yourself with the thought that you are in your own house; far rather are you in theirs. [S 326]

At the end of the passage the victimized speaker has been turned into an enemy (of his enemy) and "inside" has been defined in the radical sense as "below." The passage could appear by recursion to annihilate the opposition between the categories of victim/enemy, inside/outside, legend/knowledge, destroying the specificity of self-identical terms—destroying precisely the specificity guaranteed by that opposition. But this is an anxious conclusion. One is enjoined to think patiently the exact sort of sameness and difference that inhabits not just any two terms, but these: victim and enemy, inside and outside, knowledge and legend, as they are constituted by the passage at the end. It will be very interesting to do so.

In the matter of the allegedly self-deconstructing character of these texts, consider, finally, that in those we have so far looked at, the hermeneutic field of recursive substitutions was provoked in the reader; it was not explicitly enacted or discussed in the aphorism. Many of Kafka's aphorisms, however, plainly depict the experience of recursion for a consciousness. For example: "I can swim like the others, only I have a better memory than the others, I have not forgotten my former inability to swim. But since I have not forgotten it, my ability to swim is of no avail and I cannot swim after all" (DF 297). Here the ordinary empirical opposition of the inability to swim versus the ability to swim is subverted by the term of memory, of human temporality, that prevents the direct passage of priority from the former term (the inability to swim) to its opposite (the ability to swim). The progression from one concept to the other is obstructed by the historicity of these concepts for the author—their place within a personal history. Their embeddedness in a historical consciousness prevents them from being singled out and assigned strictly opposite values.

But is it not therefore plain that the third term grounding these reversals and functioning as their basis is the individual historical consciousness? One could, of course, reason skeptically against this view, noting that the very possibility of such a thing as an individual historical consciousness presupposes the self-identity of its constituent terms, all consciousness being consciousness . . . of *something*. And in this aphorism the meaning of the term "ability to swim" has evidently changed, at the end, from its meaning at the outset. It has become an allegorical figure taking on the full life principally denied to the "I" because of the preponderance in it of a negative inwardness.[28] The aphorism might thereby put into jeopardy the notion of an individual history and appear to generate the same mutations as the cage/bird aphorism: the terms of the opposition are unstably metaphorized.

The reality that aphorism asserts, however, is of the memory of experience and the experience of memory—one that cannot be so swiftly effaced. The vector of its explicit truth is the existential field of memory, of temporality, of individual human history. It is

28. Cf. the conclusion of "First Sorrow": "And so [the manager] succeeded in reassuring the trapeze artist, little by little. . . . But he himself was far from reassured. . . . Once such ideas began to torment [the artist], would they ever quite leave his alone? Would they not rather increase in urgency? Would they not threaten his very existence? And indeed the manager believed he could see, during the apparently peaceful sleep which had succeeded the fit of tears, the first furrows of care engraving themselves upon the trapeze artist's smooth, childlike forehead" (S 448).

not just rhetorical wit that brings about the play of the unstable metaphors of historical consciousness. If the aphorism threatens the category of memory by undermining the putative consistency of the objects of experience on which it depends, nonetheless, in the matter of stability and instability, the difference between the thing and the aberration from the thing is variable. "It is comforting to reflect," wrote Kafka, "that the disproportion of things in the world seems to be only arithmetical [the disproportion in the world appears mercifully to be only quantitative, *Das Mißverhältnis der Welt scheint tröstlicherweise nur ein zahlenmäßiges zu sein*]" (DF 38; H 43). Where the reality of a self is concerned, "degrees of evidentness" (as for Nietzsche) count. The experience of memory is inspired, Kafka implies, by a will to truth: "In an autobiography one cannot avoid writing 'often' where truth would require that 'once' be written" (DI 212). However disjointed the constitutive strata of remembered objects, memory moves across only certain of these strata and in a certain unshakable order; the signature of the remembered object varies, yet is read. The swimmer's aphorism submits the logical category of recursion to the existential category of the individual interpreter's history.

We read the specific terms and relations in Kafka's aphorisms with a logic urged by experience and thereby constitute new experience. Such experience tacitly owes its consistency to the experience of the author. The metaphors of the aphorism and their reversal have a power to bring about an interpersonal coherence on the basis of "the power of life" (DI 309).

Kafka's chiasms produce not tautologies and negations but mobile and differentiated identities, prompting an endless yet directed meditation. Within it, the asserted primacy of what is Other to introspection cannot be canceled out and it cannot be forgotten. The "higher power," to which there is no access except through a specific experience of what seems alien to the self, might itself be retraced in the movement of thought forced by the chiasm in recursive motion. The claim to the value of the world precisely at its last frontier of strangeness, as something with which thought could still virtually coincide, recurs in Kafka as a strong theory; and each subsequent turn of the second helix, even when it reverses this privilege, builds on the lived experience of the previous affirmation. The crucial moment asserts that a truthful consciousness is founded in the life of the world. "Life is denial, and therefore denial [is] affirmation" (GW 274). Kafka affirms "the strengthening power which that spectacle [—'the tremendous complex'—] gives *by contrast*" (GW 285; my italics). That power runs through the force field of the chiasm. Importantly, with the word "power" Kafka names both the splendid Other (the "power of life") and the consciousness that arises by contrast with—in recursion from—it.

I have drawn these emphases inductively from an interpretation of Kafka's aphorisms. Kafka himself, however, on rereading the rhetoric of his diaries, had occasion to describe the turn from subjectivity as the experience of a reversal. "Every remark by someone else, every chance look throws everything in me over on the other side, even what has been forgotten, even what is entirely insignificant. I am more uncertain than I ever was, I feel only the power of life" (DI 309). We note the negative experience of fragility but also the countering gain of an experience—of "the power of life." This formula could and does forecast a repeated and then solicited mode of being, "a merciful surplus of strength" (DII 184) capable of generating further reversals in consciousness: "a whole orchestration of changes on my theme" (DII 184). Such reversals in turn produce additional recursive goals while encouraging their pursuit, a solicitation of turnabouts and detours on behalf of a wider life. Thus Kafka attributes to even the "furtive answer" the energy to pursue its question on the least promising routes: "A veering round. Peering, timid, hopeful, the answer prowls round the question, desperately looking into its impenetrable face, following it along the most senseless paths, that is, along the paths leading as far as possible away from the answer" (DF 42).

Reversal is so much Kafka's recurrent signature that it is sadly perfect that his diary should conclude with such a movement. "Every word, twisted in the hands of the spirits—this twist of the hand is their characteristic gesture—becomes a spear turned against the speaker. Most especially a remark like this one. And so ad infinitum" (DII 232–33). The lustrous anguish of this sentence might be supposed to undercut every attempt to recover a speaker's meaning, who cannot stop reversing by rhetorical and intellectual energy the direction of the "word" uttered. But look again: reversal is the work of "the spirits." And this is how the diary entry, the last Kafka wrote, ends: "The only consolation would be: it happens whether you like or no. And what you like is of infinitesimally little help. More than consolation is: You too have weapons" (DII 233). What can this weapon be other than Kafka's word on behalf of meditated life?

Discoveries impose themselves on the finder. The writing self gives away its wonted primacy to an Other—a "higher power"—though it does not establish the latter's privilege by means of a single affirmation. The asymmetrical chiasm, which the Other explicitly completes, engenders successive reversals of its primacy in a movement that does not annihilate it but rather analyzes it *andeutungsweise*, by allusion, into the "tremendous complex" of its virtual representations (H 45; DF 40).

The reader lives Kafka's aphorisms as a consecutive movement of thought. Each moment of the attempt to grasp it has a finite historical character. This movement cannot be known from the perspective of the self named at the outset in the aphorism, which the valorization of the Other sublates. It can be known only from a standpoint more advanced, one that is achieved at the "end" of each recursive meditation—an end that is always, in fact, a necessarily premature breaking-off of reflection. Because this movement, being incomplete, implies its recurrence, the aphorism can be grasped fully only in the future perfect tense—as the history of its reversals recollected from a standpoint far advanced.

Though it is thinkable that the writer can have produced the metaphor of a term surpassing the subject by a blind leap of linguistic wit, the metaphor provokes a historical experience—that of an act of understanding having a finite, prospective-retrospective character. *But this experience of thought cannot be denied to Kafka*, especially since Kafka did not deny it to himself when he attributed to the furtive answer the energy to pursue its question on the most violently escapist routes. The aphorism is the product of this energy, set down as the memorial—as the exemplary and typical station—of its recollection. Like the tropes of a brother poet, Claude Vigée, creating in exile the literature of a small nation, the aphorisms are "symptomatic figures, but the symptoms are true, for they disclose reality. They seem exaggerated, because they are almost parabolic, being verbal images. Yet they are true."[29]

The logic of Kafka's rhetorical reversals is endlessly recursive; but its movement is articulated by the experienced reality that the terms of the recursion produce in reader and writer. Such recursiveness is itself conditioned by Kafka's turn to a perspective in which the subject is historically and metaphysically determined. The moment of elected objectification prompts a movement that can strike Kafka as the incising of a track toward life that *is* life. As he noted apropos of "Intuition and Experience [*Intuition und Erlebnis*]," "if 'experience' is rest in the Absolute, 'intuition' can only be the long way round, through the world, to the Absolute. After all, everything wants to get to the goal, and there is only one goal. Of course, the compromise might be possible in that the splitting up is only in time, that is to say, a splitting up such that, although it exists in every moment, it actually does not occur at all" (DF 97; H 116). The ground of this infinite metaphoricity, this endless splitting and joining of intuitions, is precisely not the world as the "fallen" world but rather as "life's splendor" (DII 195). In this formula we encounter again, as at the conclusion of "The Judgment,"[30] the fusion of a rhetorical and a vital category.

The illumination of recursive thought can be consoling and indeed more than a consolation: it can be a sort of grace, a "merciful surplus of strength [*Überschuß der Kräfte*]" (DII 184; Ta 531). This is the grace that fits aphoristic thought and writing to the passions of an "objective" self, generates a complex of perceptible figures (Kafka wrote "audible" figures) that is "not a lie" (DII 184). It is a moment of Kafka's Kantianism—of the Third Critique and the Reflection 1820a: "Beautiful things indicate that man is at home in the world [*in die Welt passe*] and that his very view of things is attuned to the laws of his perception."[31] The movement of recursive thought in Kafka, like

29. "Das sind natürlich symptomatische Bilder, aber die Symptome sind wahr. Sie enthüllen eine Wirklichkeit. Sie scheinen übertrieben, weil sie fast parabolisch sind, Sprachbilder. Aber es ist auch so" (Claude Vigée, *Heimat des Hauches: Gedichte und Gespräche* [Bühl-Moos: Elster, 1985], p. 138).

30. We will encounter again this infinite consternating metaphoricity at the close of Flaubert's *Sentimental Education* (see Chapter Seven).

31. Quoted and discussed in Walter Biemel, *Die Bedeutung von Kants Begründung der Ästhetik für die Philosophie der Kunst* (Cologne: Kölner Universitäts-Verlag, 1959), p. 127.

Kant's aesthetic play, can confirm as bliss the fit of aphorism and intuition. The chiastic aphorism that dignifies an Other even through recursive modification thus illustrates an exemplary turn belonging to Kafka's life, though it is clearest at the end of his life.

Importantly, *this turn belongs to his death.* Kafka's affirmation of an encompassing Other in a recursive rhetoric responds to an emergency, to the growing autonomy of a being that was "in" Kafka and will now determine him utterly: his death.[32] The first attestation by a physician of Kafka's fatal tuberculosis occurred between August 10 and September 15, 1917 (DII 322). Soon thereafter he began writing the series of aphorisms that Max Brod entitled "Reflections on Sin, Suffering, Hope, and the True Way," from which most of our chiasms have been taken. In one of these we read: "Death is in front of us, rather as on the schoolroom wall there is a reproduction of Alexander's Battle. The thing is to darken, or even indeed to blot out, the picture in this one life of ours through our actions" (DF 44). But now death is in front of us differently than is a picture.

This aphorism exhibits the chiastic movement of thought which, provoked by the coming event of death, lays down the following mandate, which I supply: "It is the task of my writing in the time which I wrest from death so to illuminate or clarify the picture of death that it becomes more than a picture." Or, in the words of Zarathustra (as he pursues beauty), the task is "to perish so that a picture may not remain a mere picture."[33] The heightened consciousness of death gives a different direction to the activity of thought. It aims to restore the painting to the crude original whose sense is killing—or something more.

Now certainly Kafka's writing self had long been in league with death. We have noted insistently Kafka's prescient diary entry written early in the year of his literary breakthrough, the composition of "The Judgment":

> When it became clear in my organism that writing was the most productive direction for my being to take, everything rushed in that direc-

32. Gerhard Kurz writes cogently of the centrality for Kafka of the consciousness of death; see *Traum-Schrecken: Kafkas literarische Existenzanalyse* (Stuttgart: Metzler, 1980).

33. *The Portable Nietzsche,* ed. and trans. Walter Kaufmann (New York: Viking, 1954), p. 235.

tion and left empty all those abilities which were directed toward the joys of sex, eating, drinking, philosophical reflection and above all music. I atrophied in all those directions. This was necessary because the totality of my strengths was so slight that only collectively could they even halfway serve the purpose of writing. Naturally, I did not find this purpose independently and consciously, it found itself. [DI 211]

Kafka could claim a spiritual distinction in the constant impoverishment of his own biological ground for the sake of literature. But now the self is directly confronted by its adversary—or indeed its liberator, and it will not do for it to hide from it by masking it "through our actions."

In the course of painting out the intrusions on the painting of death, Kafka, not surprisingly, also turns his brush around. For on the one hand, we see his readiness to die; on the other, death remains the last thing the writer Kafka ever wants. The many positive expressions in Kafka's notebooks and diaries of a desire to die—the assertion that it is "a first sign of nascent knowledge" (GW 280); his judiciously phrased astonishment on recognizing his decision to go systematically to rack and ruin (DII 195)—are the jubilating subterfuges of a self exhausted by the harsh demands of writing. Kafka's glorying in death masks the knowledge that his disappointed, defeated body cannot resist it anyway. For death is terrifying and meaningless: "To die would mean nothing else than to surrender a nothing to the nothing, but that would be impossible to conceive, for how could a person, even only as a nothing, consciously surrender himself to the nothing, and not merely to an empty nothing but rather to a roaring nothing whose nothingness consists only in its incomprehensibility" (DI 316).

True, Kafka claims that for the writer of fictions, death is "secretly a game" and that "in the death enacted, [he] rejoice[s] in [his] own death." But the condition of his rejoicing is that the death he enacts be someone else's and that the artist survive to "display [his] art" in the "lament . . . [that] dies beautifully and purely away" (DII 102). Real death for the writer is actually superfluous; the writer is already dead, "dead . . . in his own lifetime" (DII 196). But for the writer no less than for the empirical person, it is terrifying: the writer "has not yet lived, [whence] he has a terrible fear of dying" (L 334). The only death the writer wants is the imaginary completeness of writing "into the depths of the paper [all his anxiety], just as it comes out of . . . [his] depths" (DI 173).

Kafka's real death, "[un]ransomed by writing" (L 334), heightens a mode of being and thinking that I have called the recursive logic of the chiasm. In confronting its death, the self confronts an Other in itself—detached, implacable, possibly annihilating—its adversary . . . or indeed its liberator.

Kafka conceives of this encounter at once as an idea and as a staged rhetorical enactment. Within it the self survives, through its sublation, as a memory having the one function: to mark, as a negative surmise, the desire for a difference, staying the terrible possibility that the Other is only death, a boisterous nothing, a power of extinction. The scene of the rhetorical encounter can, in both senses of the word, *contain* the self and its death. The dying self acknowledges its dependency on an encompassing Other and also the commandment to participate thinkingly in it—"life's splendor," "a family . . . superabundant in life and thought" (GW 269). But the splendid family is also a "family animal" that includes among its members the will to destroy every individual being (L 294). The consciousness of death requires that Kafka at once affirm and resist the priority of the being for which the self is witness. The contemplation of the whole of life identifies the fatality that breaks it up but in breaking it up could lead to it.

Kafka's impending death gives urgency and distinction to the logic of recursion, which is the rhetorical enactment of being–toward–death. We have been asking throughout: Where does this recursive movement of thought lead? What value does it have? Has it a referent? Is the referent itself that being, that splendor, identified as the major term of the chiasm?

In casting the recursive movement as a kind of being–toward–death, these questions regain their original importance. Where does dying lead? What value does it have? Is its source and goal the being valorized in the prime chiasmus of self-surrender? The question of recursiveness becomes the question of death, and the question of the value and goal of the recursive movement becomes the question of the value and goal of death. The recursiveness of chiastic rhetoric not only thinks the relation of death and being, it enacts it. In so doing, it belongs to the rhetoric of invocation: "It is entirely conceivable that life's splendor forever lies in wait about each one of us in all its fullness, but veiled from view, deep down, invisible, far off. It *is* there, though, not hostile, not reluctant, not deaf. If you summon it by the right word, by its right name, it will come" (DII 195). Does the chiastic rhetoric of death lead on to a sort of being, so that all of Kafka's truth is a desire for death, and all Kafka's writing temporization?[34] Or is death, like writing, only endless "errancy," as in the fate of that other hunter (of images), the hunter Gracchus? Kafka noted, "The cruelty of death lies in the fact that it brings the real sorrow of the end, but not the end. . . . The lamentation around the deathbed is actually the lamentation over the fact that here no dying in the true sense has taken place" (DF 101). The experience of recursive thinking—there is no other way—might bring Kafka closer to the experience of his real death while still in this world. It is a tracking of death.

And yet the image of the track says too little: the movement of thought that draws this track is generative—inscription, signature, and womb (see Chapter One). The movement of the thinking subject articulates a world of inner perception, which has figuratively absorbed the perceptible world. Thought populates the difference between the self and being with an inexhaustible fullness of worldly images: the world is endurable a second time.[35] Kafka calls for such a positive inclusion of the world in recommending "a living magic or a destruction of the world that is not destructive but constructive" (DF 103). Only in the perspective of the chiastic reflection on death does the world become lucid and live. The way that leads to and from the fascination of death reproduces as metaphorical images the world of experience.

Now I sum up. Kafka's affirmation of being involves a restless movement of recursive logic which, as it proceeds, reverses even the judgment that submits the self to an Other or makes the writing destiny valuable only as it is illustrative. This movement advances to profile a third term alluding to the impossibility that the self could establish the primacy of an encompassing "eternity" by means of any

34. Kurz, *Traum-Schrecken*.

35. Cf. Paul Valéry: "The psychic world is composed of metaphors taken from the perceptible world" ("Introduction to the Method of Leonardo da Vinci," in *Paul Valéry: An Anthology,* ed. James Lawler [Princeton, N.J.: Princeton University Press, 1977], p. 14).

single positing act. The third term thus defers—but does not destroy—the affirmation. Such alluding expresses the working of death in life, which articulates by unsettling but does not shatter the whole. The formal equivalent of the writer's real death would be the chiasm that came to a close, but Kafka's chiasms do not close; they are informed by the mercy of an endless recursiveness—an eternal dying-in-life perhaps toward life. Such a movement is as much of death as Kafka the writer wants: it is the darkness that breaks up and brings into reflection the splendor of life.

The recursive turn obliquely empowers the dying self, which is to say, the self as it affirms (chiastically) the primacy of the Other on the self's own terms and therefore not finally against itself. "He has found Archimedes' fulcrum, but he has turned it to account against himself, clearly he was permitted to find it only on this condition" (DF 378). Yet Kafka does not finally use the Archimedean point of chiastic reversal against himself. The experience of death unsettles but resituates Kafka's personal "fate as a writer." The turn to alterity, to another universality, furthers the task of thinking this fate without end. A universality engenders a movement of thought that is positive, says Kafka, because it is the action of a dying self: "Suffering is the positive element in this world, indeed it is the only link between this world and the positive" (DF 90). But even this formulation translates suffering into the enterprise of founding "*this world*" (my italics).[36] Kafka perceives that for the self affirming "the splendor of life" the range of its action as it goes on dying is infinitely wide.

*　*　*

The possibility of experiencing truth—as we find it in Kafka—makes literary criticism possible. What, after all, are our literary criticism and literary theory thinking about, when they think eternally the problem of "representation," if not the relation of writing and truth? This thought becomes vacuous when it does no more than repeat the a priori difference between writing and truth, the a priori

---

36. For a discussion of Kafka's "suffering" in relation to other questions of rhetoric, chiefly of narrative perspective—a discussion that follows logically at this stage—see "The Author Survives on the Margin of His Breaks: Kafka's Narrative Perspective," in my *Fate of the Self: German Writers and French Theory* (New York: Columbia University Press, 1986).

difference within truth and within writing, and the difference between these differences. No one on earth lives the active knowledge of this difference; hence the difference is not a priori. Criticism, like the individual life, strives to recover, from the disproportion that "mercifully seems only quantitative," the truth in the verbal illusion. For there is not one universal rhetoric but *two* things, "only two things: Truth and lies" (DF 83).[37]

37. Manfred Frank and Gerhard Kurz, in *"Ordo Inversus"*: *Geist und Zeichen* (Heidelberg: Carl Winter Universitätsverlag, 1977), pp. 75–92, address the same issue but come to the opposite conclusion. They argue the irremediable negativity of the category of knowledge in Kafka. One sense of knowledge—as unknowable authentic "being" or "inner world"—is what human beings always already possess, but this knowledge cannot be stated positively; whenever stated, it is a lie. It can be freed only through the conscious negation of the lie. But it is not true—as I have attempted to show—that Kafka holds all notations equally to be lies. Neither is it true that genuine knowledge is freed by a negation which, in the study of Frank and Kurz, appears to be a (logical) procedure consisting of one stage. The truth of the aphorism occurs in and through multiple recursions, a movement that is historical in character and tends to recollect judgments that speak of the authority of a term opposite to the individual consciousness. In this statement of the goal—the freeing of knowledge—we agree, but we differ in the way. The "reversal of a reversal" (their phrase) does not return immediately to a positive, to the positive impossibility of truth. It returns rather to unstable metaphors of the positive, a field in which life and thought are ineluctably bound together and hence in principle true.

PART II

Kafka's Context

Chapter Six

Kafka, Nietzsche, and the Question of Literary History

The fascination of Nietzsche and Kafka is the fascination of what's difficult, a difficulty bound to increase when the question is posed of the historical relation of Nietzsche and Kafka. The question is made additionally difficult by the resistance of each to literary-historical recovery. Both Kafka, explicitly, and Nietzsche, through a reading of him by Paul de Man, assert the impossibility of any literary history that could include them.[1] This chapter explores the reason for their resistance, chiefly in order to see whether it can be reversed.

Both Nietzsche and Kafka deny the possibility of literary history by denying some of the fundamental relations assumed to constitute literary history. I am thinking, first, of their common critique of the concept of antithesis and the overcoming of antithesis, whose most inclusive rhetorical counterpart is the metaphor. This figure of thought and rhetoric informs literary history by "bridging" (as Hans Robert Jauss says) the individual literary work and its historical moment.[2] The second object of Nietzsche's and Kafka's critique is the concept of finite reversal, whose rhetorical counterpart is the sym-

1. Paul de Man, "Genesis and Genealogy (Nietzsche)," in *Allegories of Reading: Figural Language in Rousseau, Nietzsche, Rilke and Proust* (New Haven, Conn.: Yale University Press, 1979), pp. 79–102 (hereafter cited in this chapter as AR).

2. Hans Robert Jauss, *Towards an Aesthetics of Reception,* trans. Timothy Bahti (Minneapolis: University of Minnesota Press, 1982), p. 45, writes as an archetypical literary historian when he declares that "the gap between literature and history, between aesthetic and historical knowledge, *can be bridged* if literary history . . . discov-

metrical chiasm. Finite reversal is also involved in the moment of antithesis and its overcoming: it describes, for example, two authors held together and "embedded [at different places] in the historical process"[3] precisely by the figure of opposition or difference between them. A second writer is said to reverse absolutely the hierarchy of values or rhetorical strategies of the earlier writer—for example, Kafka reverses Goethe in the view of a historian like Wilhelm Emrich—and such reversals are used to emplot a literary historical narrative. But this use depends on the stability of the moment of chiastic reversal. If this moment cannot in fact be held firm, then it in turn will reverse the force of one writer's precedence or authority over the other, making the question of their difference one of incessant reciprocal usurpation, turning a figure of opposition into one of asymmetrical chiasm with unsettling effect.

Both Nietzsche and Kafka criticize the concept of finite reversal, yet Kafka's critique has implications so different from those of Nietzsche's that his position on reversal might itself constitute a finite reversal of Nietzsche's. Literary history could then take its bearings from the different views of Nietzsche and Kafka implied by the types of reversal enacted in their texts. But what the historian chooses to make of the reversal in their views of reversal will still depend on whether he or she adopts Nietzsche's view or Kafka's. And so, it would seem, the direction of such a literary history could be indefinitely modified, until it too had once again been reversed.

*　　*　　*

What is involved in the writing of a literary history that Nietzsche and Kafka should so oppose it? Literary history treats literary works in their irreducible connection with real things that are said to be accessible from outside the work. Let us call these real things, taken together, "the world of the historian's concern," as they converge on

---

ers . . . the socially formative function that belongs to [literature]" (my italics). Fredric Jameson also notes: "One of the ways one can begin to historicize is by making ['mythical binary oppositions or antitheses']—provided one gets rid of them later" ("Overview," in *Rewriting Literary History*, ed. Tak-Wai Wong and M.A. Abbas [Hong Kong: Hong Kong University Press, 1984], p. 343).

3. René Wellek and Austin Warren speak of "system[s] of norms embedded in the historical process," in "Literary History," in their *Theory of Literature*, 3d ed. (New York: Harcourt, Brace & World, 1956), p. 265 (hereafter cited in this chapter as TL).

the historical moment of the work in question. This world I call the referent; and in so doing, I assign the world the primacy, because referent means "the first term in a proposition to which succeeding terms relate."[4] The force of this primacy consists in the power of the referent to penetrate, saturate, coincide with, master, and contain the text of style.

The referent world may be the empirical life of authors, chiefly material (as their socioeconomic base) or interpersonal (their erotic objects) or else intellectual (such as a text they have read, of which conceptual reminiscences survive in the author's work: *Tristram Shandy* in Nietzsche's *Human, All-too-Human;* or *The Sentimental Education* in Kafka's "Wedding Preparations in the Country"; or, indeed, Nietzsche's *On the Genealogy of Morals* in Kafka's "Eight Octavo Notebooks" [DF 50–135]). Further, the referent may be the political life of the epoch, which in German literary histories of the nineteenth century expresses an ideal. (For Karl Rosenkranz, for example, this ideal is "the emergent self-consciousness of spirit that knows its own freedom"; for Georg Gottfried Gervinus, it is the *Grundidee*, the foundational idea of national political progress.[5] That is one literary history which would not include Kafka and Nietzsche!) The referent may further be the work's bearing on the future as, for example, what Jauss calls literature's "socially formative function";[6] or on the past, as when foregrounded linguistic elements are reified as conventional norms or when parts of an earlier work are used as connectors, because that work is considered to belong unproblematically to the canon, quite apart from whether, say, Nietzsche and Kafka made knowing use of it. Thus, portions of Friedrich Schlegel, whom Nietzsche probably did not read, are said to anticipate *Beyond Good and Evil,* and anticipations of Kafka's "A Country Doctor" are found in William Blake's "O rose, thou art sick!" Finally, the referent could be, à la Louis Althusser and Fredric Jameson, a historical structure immanent only in its effects or, à la Michel Foucault, the way in

4. *Random House Dictionary of the English Language* (1987).
5. This sentence is indebted to Michael Batts (University of Vancouver), "Historical Perspective in German Histories of Literature" (paper delivered at 16th Congress, International Federation for Modern Languages and Literatures, Budapest, August 1984).
6. See n. 2 above.

which the discourse of literature—including the discourse of literary historiography—is "circulated" and "owned."[7]

If, however, we define literary-historical writing so broadly, would there then be any kind of writing about literature that is not literary history writing and would not appeal to the referent? Here one could invoke various types of literary interpretation that pro-grammatically disavow referentiality: formalisms, which in principle produce meanings strictly immanent to the work; and avant-garde structuralism, which describes sign patterns within works as corre-sponding in an only arbitrary manner to meanings that are themselves the signs of other signs.[8] Finally, there is the discourse posing to literary history-writing its most forceful challenge—"deconstruc-tion"—which interrupts the structuralist patterning of textual and cultural signs by discovering so-called aporias, moments of absolute indetermination, producing a void of reference and equally, a bad infinity of virtual reference.[9] The challenge to literary history occurs when a kind of difference is posited between style and referent that introduces a perpetual delay or deferral of any coincidence of textual

7. Louis Althusser et al., *Reading Capital,* trans. Ben Brewster (London: New Left Books, 1970), especially pp. 182–93; Fredric Jameson, *The Political Unconscious: Narra-tive as a Socially Symbolic Act* (Ithaca: Cornell University Press, 1981), pp. 23–58; and Michel Foucault, *Language, Counter-Memory, Practice,* ed. and trans. D. F. Bouchard (Ithaca: Cornell University Press, 1977), p. 138.

8. "The signified is . . . *always already in the position of the signifier*" (Jacques Der-rida, *Of Grammatology,* trans. Gayatri Chakravorty Spivak [Baltimore, Md.: Johns Hopkins University Press, 1976], p. 73).

9. Werner Hamacher restates these distinctions in the course of advancing positive claims for deconstruction in a methodological preface that I quote (in translation and with the publisher's permission) at some length: "Among the generally respected basic theorems of the hedonistic as well as of the critical reading of literary texts is the claim that they are the verbal representations of realities. As regards the kind of consensus that this theorem enjoys, it remains unimportant whether one understands by 'reality' social *or* individual experience or whether one understands by 'representa-tion' a specific form of imitation [*Nachbildung*], construction, *or* expression. The bene-fit of transparency to which this proposition owes its attractiveness is obtained at the high cost of a hermeneutical consequence impossible not to draw from it. This propo-sition disposes over texts as empirical objects, which, by means of a more or less mechanical reduction, are then retranslated into corresponding meanings. And so under the dictates of this proposition, literary-critical/historical research is obliged to understand its task as the systematic restitution of those realities to which literary texts themselves are supposed to correspond; of the means of representation that are em-ployed to achieve correspondence with such realities; and the transformations that experience undergoes in the course of its literary articulation. It is in only mild mitigation of the claims advanced by such an understanding of literature and its

understanding and historical moment—in short, eschews the model of antithesis whose implicit teleology is of antithesis bridged and overcome.[10]

* * *

reading that literary texts are valued as the experience of reality sui generis. For as problematic as the theorem of reductiveness becomes when literary works themselves are granted an ultimate authority and a unique reality, it nonetheless remains impossible to overlook the fact that this maximal thesis as to the real character of literature— in flight from a poorly understood tension between experience and its representation—brings about a no less impoverished equivalence between them both. If the earnest attempt to relate literature as a representation to a reality—even a reality itself conceived as already literarily preformed—frees itself from the scandalous stumbling block that literature turns into via a social-historical, psychological, and anthropological reduction to empirical data while falling with fatal certainty into the trap of empiricism or historicism, so the hypostasis of the literary text as irreducibly unique liberates it from the requirements of intelligibility. If the concept of representation is in the one case the license of passing from it to something of which it is supposed to be the representation, then in the other case, in which it appears to be purified into the self-representation of a reality, that license is the prohibition against passing over to that representation from any reality other than its own. In both cases, the text is explicated according to the standard of an economy of meaningfulness, by means of which either the stability of the represented (whether state-of-consciousness, affect, or historical fact) or the representation itself *as* representation (whether creative process, self-sufficient structure, or immanent play of reference) is supposed to be grounded. In both cases, which arise as contrary consequences from the common maxim that literature is representation, a possibility, however, is overlooked for the sake of guaranteeing theory's craving for security: namely, that it is precisely not the task of literature to fulfill the concept of representation but rather, through a particular form of linguistic praxis, to put into question—and with no less 'objective' rigor than a theoretical treatise—literary structure and its implications. To the extent that literary history/criticism is concerned with *not* being a priori inadequate to the texts it chooses as its object by submitting them to linguistic-theoretical and aesthetic conventions and with *not* applying to them standards whose validity is contested by the texts themselves, then openness toward this at first only logical possibility must be taken up into the heuristic principles of its procedure. This is not to say that literature then becomes a type of linguistic praxis *toto coelo* different from representation, but rather that—especially in the case of a series of its outstanding texts—it could put into question the methodological premises of literary history/criticism and furthermore those of philosophical aesthetics, rather than fitting into them without reservation. Where it does so, literature is no longer merely the object of literary history/criticism but, *ordo inverso*, an object of criticism by literature" ("Das Beben der Darstellung," in *Positionen der Literaturwissenschaft: Acht Modellanalysen am Beispiel von Kleists "Das Erdbeben in Chile"* ed. David E. Wellbery [Munich: Beck, 1985], pp. 149–50). Hamacher argues that formalism, to the extent that it is intelligible, is a type of representationalism and hence does not constitute a threat to literary history of the same trenchancy as poststructuralism. See n. 10 below.

10. Not all literary *interpretation* is so deliberately antihistorical as the kinds of formalism I have mentioned; other types of interpretation plainly extrinsic or mimetic

Graf . . . defends the literary historians, who bring us
the "day's residue," as it were. Sadger's question as to
how one can explain the poet's psyche from his works,
which are distorted, is settled by the answer that science
is not meant to explain anything but rather to give
descriptions which leave no gaps.

Minutes, Meeting 33, Psychoanalytical Society, 1907

The task of defining literary history in a sufficiently distinctive way
becomes on reflection curiously difficult; for, as its degree of defini-

---

in bias can be said to produce literary historical miniatures. Indeed, very few formalist
interpreters would deny the historical reference in their narratives in the sense of the
political power at work in their own critical rhetoric, and so writing's *delay* (as
between style and referent) seems always susceptible to *relay*, to reference. Converse-
ly, not all kinds of literary history writing are (in principle) so deliberately antiformal-
ist: a literary history might proceed immanently with respect to works of art, texts of
style. Wellek and Warren agonize over this point. Their concern is to conceptualize a
literary history that will not reify the literary phenomenon as an empirical fact and
submit it to the power of sequences elaborated by "political, social, artistic and intellectual" historians. Therefore, they write, "our starting point must be the development of literature as literature. . . . [The] history [of a period] can be written only
with reference to a scheme of values [that] has to be abstracted from history itself. . . .
A period is not a type or class but a time section defined by a system of norms
embedded in the historical process and irremovable from it" (TL 264–65). But this
distinction is unclear. First problem: to what extent can "a scheme of values" be
abstracted from "the historical process" and yet be exhibited as embedded in it and
irremovable from it? Abstraction requires the mediation by concepts extrinsic to the
matrix, the bed. Second, what precisely constitutes the bed? The answer for Wellek
and Warren is individual literary works, but how does a group of works constitute a
"historical process"? In this instance the historical process could refer only to the
concrete differences between one work and another, but to identify differences does
not constitute a process, which requires a theory of change, and this motive will not
be found inside literary works. Later, in discussing the Russian formalist's historical
venture of explaining changes in convention, Wellek and Warren write: "Why this
change of convention has come about at a particular moment is a historical problem
insoluble in general terms. . . . Literary change is a complex process, partly internal
. . . but also partly external, *caused by social, intellectual and all other cultural changes*"
(TL 266; my italics). We have returned to a poetics essentially shared by Gustave
Lanson and, let us say, Ernst Robert Curtius and Rudolf Unger and Erich Auerbach.
See in this connection Paul de Man's "Modern Poetics," in *The Princeton Encyclopedia
of Poetry and Poetics* (Princeton, N.J.: Princeton University Press, 1972), pp. 518–20:
"Social, intellectual and political history play a large part" in the works of Lanson; and
like him, the German authors mentioned above "all start from the literary work as an
unquestionable empirical fact."

tion increases vis-à-vis literary interpretation, so does its vulnerability to the (Nietzschean) critique of antitheses. In *Beyond Good and Evil*, for example, Nietzsche attacks "the typical prejudgment and prejudice which give away the metaphysicians of all ages."[11] Metaphysicians oppose things with respect to their separate origins, these being—according to Nietzsche—one, "the lap of Being"; two, "this turmoil of delusion" (BW 200). Literary history would be subject to such a critique in appearing to claim an original foundation, an assured starting point, in the reality of the historical process. In this sense it is antithetical to formalist interpretation, which begins from an arbitrary place in a work avowedly fictive, nonempirical, and without self-identical being: "the literary work of art," for Wellek and Warren, is not "an empirical fact . . . neither real . . . nor mental" (TL 154, 156), and for Paul de Man, too, is "not a phenomenal event that can be granted any form of positive existence, whether as a fact of nature or as an act of the mind."[12] Nietzsche's doubt as to any certain "degree of apparentness" glooms the clarity with which the literary historian might view the ground of his discourse—the referent—and which now cannot be so readily extracted from turmoil, delusion, and error; and all literary history becomes a typifying of fictions by means of fictions (BW 236).

De Man's critique of Nietzsche's own literary historical practice in *The Birth of Tragedy* confirms this view. According to de Man, who writes in the allegedly deconstructive spirit of the later Nietzsche, the ground of literary history—the so-called realm of things, essences, and genetic totalities—is a delusion. Viewed in a suitably "ironic light," it dissolves into a world (in Nietzsche's terms, which I supply) "transitory, seductive, deceptive" (AR 100–102; BW 200). De Man links the seductiveness of Nietzsche's own literary-historical argument in *The Birth of Tragedy* to its many fictions, to its formal symmetries "easy enough to achieve in pictorial, musical or poetic fictions, but . . . never [able to] predict the occurrence of an historical event" (AR 84). Where in *The Birth of Tragedy* one might expect a referential discourse, a Dionysian discourse speaking of truth and falsity, we find instead a "theatrical fiction . . . compel[ling] the read-

11. *Basic Writings of Nietzsche,* ed. and trans. Walter Kaufmann (New York: Modern Library, 1966), p. 200 (hereafter cited in this chapter as BW).

12. Paul de Man, *Blindness and Insight: Essays in the Rhetoric of Contemporary Criticism,* rev. 2d ed. (Minneapolis: University of Minnesota Press, 1983), p. 107.

er to enter into an endless process of deconstruction" (AR 93, 99). Such an argument appears to destroy the possibility of literary history on the general grounds of the fictionality of the world—the main consequence being for de Man, who has learned from Nietzsche, that as the world and the text are both fictions, the ontological status of both remains suspended. Both fall away in their being to a vanishing point of indeterminable self-difference, which precludes firm reciprocal connections (AR 99).

Here, certainly, one might begin to dissociate this conclusion from Nietzsche's own, for Nietzsche's argument issues into a pragmatic revaluation of fictions according to their usefulness to life. The move cannot be made so rapidly, however. In *Beyond Good and Evil* we see Nietzsche confirming the view of an interminable suspension of meaning as between the text and the world of the author's lived experience. He does this by rejecting a counterargument to his previous critique of antithesis. The modern form of this counterargument would be as follows: There is a writing about the real—to which literary history belongs by virtue of the way it is founded. For one thing, it is founded differently from fiction in the sense of the wider generality, the collective nature, of its authorship or ownership, which includes its readership: that is, the collective manner in which it is produced and read. In literary history, as in epic narration but not as in modern prose (for Benjamin), many authors speak coherently through the nominal author as a chorus of voices responsive to the world.[13]

But at this point Nietzsche replies: "Why couldn't the world *that concerns us* be a fiction?" If so, then the world of the author's lived experience is itself a fiction, only a variation on the general thesis of the uncontrollable fictionality of the world—as indeed the author is himself or herself only a fiction. For "if somebody asked, 'but to a fiction there surely belongs an author?'—couldn't one answer simply:

13. "In epic a people are at rest after the day's work is done—harking, dreaming, and collecting. The novelist has departed from his people and its concerns. The birthplace of the novel is the solitude of the individual who cannot express in exemplary fashion his chiefest predilections, is himself without counsel and can counsel no one. To write a novel is to take to the extreme the representation of the incommensurable in human existence" (Walter Benjamin, "Krisis des Romans," in *Gesammelte Schriften: Kritiken und Rezensionen*, ed. Hella Tiedemann-Bartles [Frankfurt am Main: Suhrkamp, 1981], 3:230–31).

why? Doesn't this 'belongs' perhaps belong to the fiction, too?" (BW 237). It is, however, the author as a determinate spatial and temporal being who, for almost every literary historian, focuses—indeed, institutes—the connection between the fiction and the historical world; he or she is the way they belong together; he or she is "the true unit of literary history."[14] Hence, when Nietzsche denies the proprietary connection between the work and the author's lived experience of the world, announcing what today is called "the death of the author," he eliminates the chief referent in historical narrative.[15]

Nietzsche's critique of the author jeopardizes even an author viewed collectively or transpersonally, eliminating the possibility of a literary history of the kind foreseen by Foucault. Let us agree, à la Foucault, to stop asking of the literary work the "tiresome" question, what does the work "reveal of [the author's] most profound self?" and ask instead, "Who controls the discourse" of which the work is a node, a virtual focus of forces?[16] But then, by the factor of agency implied in the metaphor of the "who," we have again reintroduced a type of productive intention, however unconscious, to which the work refers. Thus Nietzsche's destruction of the link between work and author destroys the transpersonal literary history even of the kind implied in *The Birth of Tragedy*, where the "authors" are metaphysical agents—Apollo and Dionysus—and the self constituted by the work is not empirical but transcendental. Even the metaphysically authored tragedy "belongs to" Dionysus and Apollo: with the destruction of the idea of belonging, the idea of referent-as-cause is destroyed.

We must, however, look further on, past this point profiled by de Man, at which Nietzsche destroys the belonging relation between author and work. In a famous gesture—on the strength of his wonder

14. The quotation is from Robert Rehder, "Re-Thinking Literary History," in *The Teaching of Literature in ASAIHL Universities,* ed. Anthony Tatlow (Hong Kong: Hong Kong University Press, 1983), p. 20. I say that the author is the true unit of literary history for *almost* every historian, in order to make room for Heidegger, who in *Holzwege* and elsewhere, suggests a history of poetry that jumps over the empirical existence of poets and constitutes or connects to a history of Being.

15. "One should guard against confusion through psychological *contiguity* . . . a confusion to which an artist himself is only too prone: as if he himself were what he is able to represent, conceive, and express. The fact is that if he were it, he would not represent, conceive, and express it. . . . Whoever is completely and wholly an artist is to all eternity separated from the 'real,' the actual" (BW 537).

16. Foucault, *Language, Counter-Memory, Practice,* p. 138.

at what he is left with—and a bold surmise, Nietzsche makes a tool out of a fragment of the shattered fable of the true world and with it opens up a sphere of activity for the will. For if all so-called descriptions of the true world are themselves informed by "deception, selfishness, and lust," and to this extent are interpretive fictions, precisely therefore all forms of literary realism, including literary historical writing, are "insidiously related, tied to and involved with . . . seemingly opposite things"—that is to say, with the interpretation of fiction. The distinction between the two modes of writing is therefore itself only one of "degrees and many subtleties of gradation"; and these gradations, like those between the text of style and the historical moment, can be articulated or erased by a self in the sense that all interpretations are involved in a subduing of the phenomenon to purposes imposed by a will to power (BW 225, 513). "Like a sea of forces . . . [the will] returns from the play of contradictions to the joy of concord."[17] This description from *The Will to Power* is faithful to Nietzsche's own practice as a "historian" who in his cultural histories displays the willfulness and fictionality of his constructions: for example, in the capsule history of the pseudo-antitheses good/bad and good/evil in Section II of *The Genealogy of Morals* (BW 489–90). I would stress the word "narrator," however, over "historian," for Nietzsche substitutes for history writing a type of historicized allegory, a diachronic play of recurrent fictions of master and slave having heuristic force.

*   *   *

Kafka's critique of antithesis, of the antithetical logic of literary history, has more restrictive consequences. About "antitheses" Kafka wrote, "My repugnance for [them] is certain. . . . They make for thoroughness, fullness, completeness, but only like a figure on the 'wheel of life' [a toy with a revolving wheel]; we have chased our little idea around the circle. They [antitheses] are as undifferentiated as they are different" (DI 157). Kafka's repugnance for antitheses at once undifferentiated and different impugns the procedure of literary history, for the opposition that literary historical language will go on

17. Friedrich Nietzsche, *The Will to Power,* trans. Walter Kaufmann and R. J. Hollingdale, ed. Walter Kaufmann (New York: Vintage, 1968), p. 550 (hereafter cited in this chapter as WP).

talking of is the (provisional) antithesis of style and referent, as to source and modality of evidence. It then proceeds to undifferentiate this antithesis, to show how every stylistic effect is actually the effect of a cause independent of style—a parent cause, which its effect resembles. By this logic (to give an example), one of Kafka's signatures—his "open metaphors"—might be historically explained . . . by aviation, via Filippo Marinetti's destruction of analogy: "Aviationary rapidity has multiplied our knowledge of the world: hence knowledge by means of analogy will be more and more natural. And so one must suppress the terms 'as [*wie*],' 'like [*gleich*],' 'just as [*ebenso wie*],' 'similarly [*ähnlich*].'"[18]

Kafka's resistance to literary history, however, is attached to a syncope of a more radical kind, one that differentiates absolutely. Unlike Nietzsche, Kafka asserts the absolute and unbridgeable distinction between what he calls in various ways the sensory and the allegorical worlds. And unlike Nietzsche, his attachment to the opposition of sense and spirit precisely involves holding on to the concept of property, of "belonging to." For Kafka, the concept of belonging to, in the relation of language and referent, is not a fiction; it is necessarily the case. It allows him to identify negatively the language of the referent, of history, and to devalue it: language, "corresponding as it does to the phenomenal world, . . . is concerned only with property and its relations." Only when language is used in an allusive or, as I understand the word, allegorical manner (*andeutungsweise*), and not in a metaphorical manner (*vergleichsweise*), can it identify things of the spirit (DF 40). Thus Kafka, according to Kafka, writes a kind of allegory without historical power, with the diachronic element entirely suppressed. "It is only our conception of time that makes us call the Last Judgment by this name. It is, in fact, a kind of court martial" (DF 38). The concept of belonging to, of referent and property, lends Kafka's perspective a stability that only further jeopardizes a history writing aspiring to be about the phenomenal world and literature. For the truth of literature lies outside the phenomenal world. Kafka's language gains the ascetic freedom of allegory by identifying the real concept of property—that is, of its

18. Filippo Marinetti, "Die futuristische Literatur: Technisches Manifest," *Der Sturm* 3 (October 1912): 194; quoted in Herbert Kraft, *Kunst und Wirklichkeit im Expressionismus* (Bebenhausen: Rotsch, 1972), p. 13.

own "belonging to the world"—as the obstacle to its writing immediately about true things.

Kafka rejects literary-historical writing on the ground that such
writing feeds the metaphor whose lie starves him—namely, that the
German word *Sein* (being) means "belonging to him," his property
(DF 39). This *Sein/sein* metaphor—the familial or genealogical metaphor—is the very figure that literary history writing employs in practice. The being of the literary work is identified with its descent from
a paternal referent as its proper source.

Finally, in a passage that plainly identifies the logic of literary history with genealogy, Kafka explicitly repudiates the literary historical
recovery of his works. In the series of aphorisms called "He," a pronoun I take to refer to the author, Kafka writes:

> All that he does seems to him, it is true, extraordinarily new, but also,
> because of the incredible spate of new things, extraordinarily ama-
> teurish, indeed scarcely tolerable, incapable of becoming history,
> breaking short the chain of the generations, cutting off for the first
> time at its most profound source the music of the world, which before
> him could at least be divined. Sometimes in his arrogance he has more
> anxiety for the world than for himself. [GW 263–64][19]

Kafka, "He," figures as the angel destructive of history, a producer of
things that cannot be drawn into the history of the world or the
progress of its generations. In his works, says Kafka, the music of the
world ceases to sound. Their music is not the music of the world,
their world is not the world, is not its echo or copy. Moreover, these

---

19. The apparent surprise at the outset of the passage is the link between work that
is original and work that is dilettantish: i.e., that appeals chiefly for the delight it
gives. The connection of bizarre originality and delight is actually, however, a recurrent one in Kafka, who in his famous letter to Max Brod of July 5, 1922, links the
writing destiny (*Schriftstellersein*) with a mania for pleasure (*Genußsucht*) and for this
reason damns it as "devil's work" (L 332–35). His works are outlandishly novel,
products of a bizarre and unfamiliar sexuality, so heavy with selfish delight that for
the historical medium ("the chain of generations") they are "insupportable"; they
cannot be borne. At times (in an associated prose poem) Kafka can reckon his life and
thought as actually constituting "a formal necessity . . . of a family superabundant in
life" (GW 269). Not here. These products sink through the familiar life of generations,
interrupting history, breaking off the music of the world. In sinking they return, as
"devilish," to their source: *nach unten,* "underground." See my "Kafka's Other Metamorphosis," in *Kafka and the Contemporary Critical Performance: Centenary Readings,* ed.
Alan Udoff (Bloomington: Indiana University Press, 1987).

works cannot be included within a family, are deeply unfamiliar; they cannot be grasped as the offspring of a parent and cannot themselves be expected to produce further offspring, literary families.

What features of Kafka's works, for being "extraordinarily new," so deeply resist historical recovery? Here one could return to de Man's essay on Nietzsche's *Birth of Tragedy*, which also stresses the resistance of literature to literary history. De Man's point is that the actual performance of Nietzsche's narration opposes any model of the dialectical production of meaning according to the figure of sublated antithesis. That is because, first, of the aphoristic character of individual sections and, second, of the fact—according to de Man—that a reading of *The Birth of Tragedy* must include the notes and jottings, the paralipomena, surrounding it. Nietzsche's "narrative continuous texts" depend for their meaning on "discontinuous aphoristic formulations" (AR 101). Following de Man's lead, we would be led to the impossibility in Kafka's fiction, too, of establishing the discursive wholeness of traditional narrative: namely, the distinctiveness of beginning and end, whole and part, cause and effect. Kafka's work eschews the operation of a genetic principle involving "subject, intent, negation, totalization, supported by underlying metaphysical categories of identity and presence" (AR 81).

Let us look, then, at the feature of Kafka's rhetoric potentially most obstructive of dialectic, the figure of reversal itself. I focus on a kind of chiasm that might be considered Kafka's signature. A typical Kafkan chiasm reads: "In the struggle between yourself and the world second the world" (DF 39). The aphorism seems at first glance to conclude decisively by reversing the priority of the self to the world; the self now stands in "second" position. The logic of this chiasm would then be progressive and final, the second half of the chiasm decisively reversing the sense of the first by reversing the relation of its terms. On this reading, the identity of the terms holds steady, and only their relation is reversed: he or she who once confronted the adversary now stands behind the same adversary, seconding that adversary.

But, of course, a moment's reflection shows that there is more motion in this chiasm than meets the eye. For if the term "you" means "duelist with the world," and if the terms in the second half of the chiasm are the same as the first, then the duelist seconding the world can second it only for the sake of the duel that he or she is obliged to win and thus only for his or her own party. The seconder comes first. A self consents to accept the primacy of the world on the self's own terms according to the eternally recursive logic of Romantic irony. Furthermore, if the duelist in question is also capable of being at once duelist and second, then from the start the world is capable of being seconded and hence is not adversary. The chiasm must be thought further along, as a result of the fact that the self included in it functions not to stabilize it, not to organize and master its sense, but to launch it through never-ending turns of spiraling reflection.

Here is another example of a Kafkan chiasm flung by the self within it along new turns of reflection. Kafka composed the following gnome within a gnome:

> On the handle of Balzac's walking-stick: I break all obstacles.
> On mine: All obstacles break me.
> The common factor is "all."
>
> (Auf Balzacs Spazierstockgriff: Ich breche alle Hindernisse.
> Auf meinem: Mich brechen alle Hindernisse.
> Gemeinsam ist das "alle.")
>
> [DF 250; H 281]

The pure chiastic form of this opposition would read: "I shatter all obstacles; / [axis of reversal] all obstacles shatter me [Ich breche alle Hindernisse. / Alle Hindernisse brechen mich]." Semantically, this version is the same as the one Kafka actually wrote: both assert the reversal of the relation of dominance between the self and the adversary world. What is important in Kafka's actual phrasing, however, is the slight deviation, engendering movement, between the paradigmatic meaning of the concluding sentence and the implication of its syntagmatic form. Here we have to consult the German text: "Ich breche alle Hindernisse. . . . Mich brechen alle Hindernisse." The allegedly broken self—called "me [mich]"—holds fast to the first position in the concluding clause, which is the position of the Balzacian self in the lead sentence. As a result, the impression is produced that the hand which inscribes the motto of its own impotence on the stick head intends to testify to a remainder of its own power—the power of authorship. It does so even when this remainder consists only of the ability to perceive and note down precisely the ruins that shore it up. This tenacious survival of a negative authority has, however, a chiefly dispersive effect. For if so little power—so merely feigned a power of breaking obstacles by inscription—attaches to the aphoristic inscription of being broken, and hence there is nothing at all victorious for either party in that acknowledgment, then the aphoristic formulation itself would as such be something broken. And therefore it would certainly not have been proved that "all obstacles break me." In the way the chiasm includes the authorial self, which strides about in the frame of the aphorism in "*my* walking stick," it acquires a virtual endlessness.

The point is confirmed, I believe, when we consider that the aphorism ends not with the concluding sentence of the chiasm but with a commentary on it. Kafka says about the relation between the lead and the concluding sentence, "The common factor is 'all.'" What is held in common, therefore, is neither the first term nor the second. Balzac's "I" is not like the "I" (literally, the *mich*) of Kafka. Of course this disparity comes as no great surprise, for the pronoun "I" in this text or any other has a chiefly deictic sense: it points back to the person or scriptor, or to an aspect of the person or scriptor. In the first instance it points back to the scriptor Balzac but only remotely to the person; in the second instance it points back to the scriptor Kafka as a live mask of the person Kafka, the creator of this entire language game. This explicit relation of pronoun to author confirms the idea that the apparently binary chiasm develops from the intervention of a third factor. Kafka's genuine wisdom: Always triangulate! Furthermore, neither is the second term of both parts of the chiasm, called "obstacles," shared throughout the chiasm; Kafka insists on a disparity between even those parts where two identical signifers (the term "obstacles") are found in the same syntagmatic position. This insistence on difference at any cost is compatible with the intention of each and every Kafkan chiasm: to set in motion behind the apparent constancy of its expression a movement of thought that spirals on through endless reversals.

But no reader can have the experience of endless reversals: infinity is counterfactual. What, then, practically speaking, determines the point at which this chiasm breaks off . . . into meaning? Is it just as K. thinks, in *The Castle*, apropos of the value of the texts that the messenger Barnabas delivers: "They themselves change in value perpetually, the reflections they give rise to are endless, and *chance* determines where one stops reflecting, and so even our estimate of them is a matter of chance" (C 216; my italics)?[20] To speak against this grim conclusion is another famous moment in Kafka's spiritual autobiography, which begins with exactly the opposite sense of the chiasm of self and world—the world as the self's "seconder":

> From a certain stage of knowledge [*Erkenntnis*] on, weariness, insufficiency, constriction, self-contempt must all vanish: namely at the point where I have the strength to recognize as my own nature what previously was something alien to myself that refreshed me, satisfied, liberated, and exalted me. [DF 91]

The aphorism does not close on this optimistic note of natural *Bildung*, however. It proceeds to put into question the very intelligibility, in Kafka's case, of the distinction between "self" and "other": Kafka may not allow "the otherness [*die Fremde*], which . . . [he] is, to cease to be other. To do this is to . . . refute himself" (DF 91–92). His difference from the world must be absolute. Chance, as we saw in the previous chapter, might produce a sensation of life force but not obviously a heightened sense of self: "Every remark by someone else, every chance look throws everything in me over on the other side, even what has been forgotten, even what is entirely insignificant. I am more uncertain than I ever was, I feel only the power of life" (DI 309).

The famous diary entry figuring as a sort of preface to all such reflections plainly identifies the chiastic logic of reversal and recursion:

> This pursuit . . . [by introspection of every idea] carries one in a direction away from . . . [mankind]. Or I can—can I?—manage to keep my feet somewhat and be carried along in the wild pursuit? Where, then, shall I be brought? "Pursuit," indeed, is only a metaphor. I can also say, "assault on the last earthly frontier," an assault, moreover, launched from below, from mankind, and since this too is a metaphor, I can replace it by the metaphor of an assault from above, aimed at me from above. [DII 202]

20. See my *Fate of the Self: German Writers and French Theory* (New York: Columbia University Press, 1986), p. 179.

This passage stresses the uncertainty of Kafkan metaphor before producing its chiasm by the arbitrary action of replacing the first metaphor by the second. This rhetorical technique of arbitrary substitution and reversal could make us consider as an only willful construction the recurrent metaphor of the duel in which the combatant seconds his worldly adversary. It could arise as a quasi-automatic reversal of a banal wisdom-sentence about a subjectivity: that is, in the struggle between yourself and the world, second yourself. It would therefore be hard to see how such rhetorical figures could be made to yield a body of meanings and positions referable to Kafka's historical moment.

And yet it is remarkable, as I have stressed, that the passage about Kafka's assault on the frontiers concludes with an extravagant claim to meaning. "All such writing [read, chiastic writing] is an assault on the frontiers; if Zionism had not intervened, it might easily have developed into a new secret doctrine, a Kabbalah." In the preceding chapter I read this claim as authorizing, precisely, the formation of a self: the passage as a whole connects "introspection," the "I," and the act of writing as aspects of a single being having the truth and prestige of Kabbalah. But now I must stress the usurpatory element, which in fact condemned this enterprise to uncertainty: "If Zionism had not intervened. . . ." And since Zionism had been around all during Kafka's life, it is impossible to discount the operation of chance in this intervention. Self-constitution in Kafka is a matter of chance and arises essentially to reiterate a defense against the surmise that the Other is only death and extinction.

I cite finally a Kafkan chiasm so Nietzschean in its style that it may be viewed as Kafka's definitive reversal of Nietzsche. It is the stunning aphorism "The animal wrests the whip from its master and whips itself in order to become master, not knowing that this is only a fantasy produced by a new knot in the master's whiplash" (DF 37, 323). On the face of it, this chiasm conforms to Nietzsche's analysis of the will to power: it is the master who engenders the fantastic consciousness of the enslaved animal. Such an analysis might be adequate if the concept of mastery exhibited in it were a simple one, but it is not. The aphorism presupposes a notion of genuine mastery, of which we actually know only this much: whatever its content might be, it can never have anything in common with the animal's fantasy, which is a blind reaction to the lash. But how can such a notion of mastery actually be conceived in its superiority to, and independence from, the fantasy of the animal? With what mastery does the aphorism demystify the mastery of which the animal dreams and keep him a servant who does not know what his master does?[21]

Nietzsche's myth differs importantly from Kafka's. The slave type achieves a real mastery in time; this victory is recounted in *On the Genealogy of Morals* by a narrator who writes with the authority of the slave grown entirely lucid. The concept of mastery evoked by the freedman-narrator in Nietzsche is supposed to be true—a strong fiction and not a compensatory fantasy.

But Kafka's aphorism offers no *concept* of mastery—a case, of course, that might be quite appropriate to Kafka's horror of all forms of mastery. "Among all writers," as Elias Canetti remarked, "Kafka is the greatest expert on power," yet this expertness arose from his rigorous adoption of the standpoint of the humbled, unmitigated by a leaguing identification with others humbled.[22] Kafka's aphorism on mastery actually produces a *reflection* on power, a reflection in principle infinite. This reflection arises from the absence of a standpoint from which the aphorism, which speaks of a triumphal use of power, is narrated. Nietzsche worked out the narrative standpoint of his aphorism in terms of a self bent on mastery. In Kafka's case, what survives the aphorism is chiefly a question: from what standpoint, with what knowledge, is this narrator speaking? Does writing such aphorisms itself amount to anything more than a new knot on the master's whiplash? If the lash can acquire a new knot, it can acquire one more knot and still others thereafter. Indeed, Kafka wrote in 1917, "The whips with which we lash each other have put forth many

21. John 15:9–17.

22. Elias Canetti, *Der andere Prozeß: Kafkas Briefe an Felice* (Munich: Hanser, 1969), p. 76. "There is something deeply exciting about this stubborn attempt of someone who was helpless, to exclude himself from power in any form" (p. 75). Canetti's penetrating study of Hitler identifies the slavery of the being who strives at all points to "outdo [*übertreffen*]" his fellows: "Each enterprise of his and even his deepest wishes are dictated by a compulsion to outdo: One may go so far as to say that he is a *slave of outdoing*. But he is by no means alone in that. If we had to sum up the essence of our society in a single feature, we could simply point out: the compulsion to outdo" (Elias Canetti, *The Conscience of Words*, trans. Joachim Neugroschel [London: André Deutsch, 1986], p. 70).

knots these five years" (DII 187). This means that if the time-honored ethical concept of mastery through self-flagellation is only a fantasy, then the demystifying critique of the concept may also be a fantasy. The idea that self-flagellation is not a genuine self-overcoming may itself be a new knot—the newest but not the last—on the master's, not the narrator's, whiplash. In this way the meaning of the aphorism that speaks of the continually increasing power of the master under-cuts itself: of the master, and whether he genuinely swings a whip, nothing is known. "We are permitted," Kafka wrote, "to crack that whip, the will, over us with our own hand" (DII 166)—but who or what gives this permission? The chiasm is constructed to be her-meneutically endless: the positions of master and whip, of animal and fantasy, replace one another chiastically, incessantly.[23]

The thrust in Nietzsche of the master-and-slave parable is realist and final. Nietzsche's version produces between the two positions "degrees and subtleties of gradation" of distinguishable power. It might be objected, of course, that Nietzsche's own constructions of power are, on scrutiny, as unsettling as Kafka's and that they too are chiasmi without conceptual or affective unity. Typically, the master who is defined by his pathos of distance from the slave is by the same token defined by the slave; at the very origin of his *Selbstgefühl,* his sense of self, is the feeling of his distance from an Other. Does not this play of reversals divide the legendary wholeness of the master?

There is another striking example of chiastic reversal in consecutive aphorisms from *Beyond Good and Evil.* Nietzsche defines the soul as "a social structure of the drives and affects" and then the body as a "social structure composed of many souls." The integration of this chiasm produces this conclusion: The soul is a social structure of the drives; these drives together constitute a body, which is a social struc-

23. Jacques Derrida writes of the procedure of deconstruction as follows: "To 'deconstruct' philosophy is thus to work through the structured genealogy of its concepts in the most scrupulous and immanent fashion, but at the same time to determine, from a certain external perspective that it cannot name or describe, what this history may have concealed or excluded, constituting itself as history through this repression in which it has a stake" (*Positions* [Paris: Minuit, 1972], pp. 15–16; quoted in Jonathan Culler, *On Deconstruction: Theory and Criticism after Structuralism* [Ithaca: Cornell University Press, 1982], p. 86). Kafka's aphorism enacts this procedure in exemplary fashion at the same time that it sets into sharper relief than does Derrida's statement the totally unsettling consequence of working through a genealogy of concepts from an "external perspective that it cannot name or describe."

ture of souls. Soul is a social structure of souls, body a social structure of drives. Each category is tautological, and they are held together only by a polemical and playful willfulness. Yet this reversal nonetheless forecasts the chiasm which, like a wreck at the bottom of the sea of Nietzsche's thought, casts its menacing shadow upward through the lighter waters: this is the chiasm of resentment. The strong man generates resentment in the weak, yet the resentment of the weak makes man an interesting and therefore a strong animal. How could one escape this reversal? Have we reached the point at which Nietzsche reverses position into Kafka's and there is no longer a distinction between them?

The difference is present in Nietzsche's unifying notion of self: "No 'substance,' rather something that in itself strives after greater strength, and that wants to 'preserve' itself only indirectly (it wants to surpass itself)" (WP 270). If Nietzsche is celebrated for having deconstructed the ego fiction, it is often overlooked that he is a great affirmer of the self. In *Zarathustra* it is "the creative self . . . which creates value and will"—that "granite of spiritual *fatum*, really 'deep down' at the bottom" of our being.[24] Nietzsche conceives a self that holds together, in a life-enhancing relation of distinction and priority, opposite implications of the chiasm as a figure of thought and will. What is immediately telling, too, is Nietzsche's acknowledgment of the real historical conjuncture that determines the interpretative activity of his self. For him the fate of the self means not its story but its integrity, in defiance of the painful dislocations following from the injuries he suffered in the Franco-Prussian War.

An exhilarating passage from *The Gay Science* suggests a comparison between Nietzsche's and Kafka's attitude toward the operation of chance in interpretation. Nietzsche celebrates a mood of coherence linking his writing and the world; it is one marked by an abundance of signs, all immediately significant. "Whatever it is, bad weather or good, the loss of a friend, sickness, slander, the failure of some letter to arrive, the spraining of an ankle, a glance into a shop, a counter-argument, the opening of a book, a dream, a fraud—either immediately or very soon after it proves to be something that "must

24. *The Portable Nietzsche,* ed. and trans. Walter Kaufmann (New York: Viking, 1954), p. 147; and BW 352.

not be missing"; it has a profound significance and use precisely for *us.*" The significance might best be understood as the expert, dexterous labor of an interpretative consciousness, but chance is also at work lightening the labor: "Indeed, now and then someone plays with us—good old chance; now and then chance guides our hand, and the wisest providence could not think up a more beautiful music than that which our foolish hand produces then."[25]

In Kafka's Castle-world the chance moment that breaks off interpretation is associated with an all-pervasive fatigue; in Nietzsche's Genoa, with "great health." The difference is produced in Nietzsche by a mastering self exterior to signs—an appropriator of them. Philosophers, he wrote, "lack that *impersonal* participation in a problem of knowledge; as they are through and through themselves a person, so too all their insights and knowledge grow together to become a person, to a living complex, whose individual parts depend on one another, interpenetrate, are nourished in common, which, as a whole, has a unique aura and a unique aroma. . . . If one stops them from building their own nest, they perish, like birds without shelter."[26]

We conclude, then, that Nietzsche produces chiastic structures as daring closure by acts of interpretation. The strong self arrests the recursive play within the figure. It follows, therefore, that chiastic aphorisms having the form of a struggle for authority between the self and the world must end without irony and with affirmation of the self. "This highest degree of self-possession deprives an individual of all particularities—except the very one of being master and center of himself." He is a "sort of system complete in itself, completing itself continually."[27] This point should be understood strongly: the self is

25. Friedrich Nietzsche, *The Gay Science,* ed. and trans. Walter Kaufmann (New York: Random House, 1974), pp. 223–24 (hereafter cited in this chapter as GS).

26. Friedrich Nietzsche, *Werke in drei Bänden,* ed. Karl Schlechta (Munich: Hanser, 1954–56), 1:943.

27. Ibid., 1:407. Cf. "Why I Am So Clever," in *Ecce Homo:* "Meanwhile the organizing 'idea' that is destined to rule keeps growing deep down—it begins to command; slowly it leads us *back* from side roads and wrong roads; it prepares *single* qualities and fitnesses that will one day prove to be indispensable as means toward a whole—one by one, it trains all *subservient* capacities before giving any hint of the dominant task, 'goal,' 'aim,' 'meaning'" (BW 710).

the being that lives beyond truth, beyond belief in one true historical meaning; the self lives as a maker of fictions from history for life.[28]

It follows further that the heuristic antithesis and finite chiasm of literary history writing are themselves fictions, although they permit coordination (narrative) within the universal field of fictions. Indeed it is impossible that these terms of style and referent, self and world, would not be "insidiously related, tied to, and involved" with each other (BW 200). Thus Nietzsche authorizes a literary history, with the provision that the family resemblance it produces between the fiction and the historical reality is itself a fiction. This is not finally literary *history*.

Kafka, on the other hand, maintains his repugnance for weak antitheses yet is captivated by the great antithesis of the sensory and allegorical worlds. Nietzsche's critique of antithesis is that it does not sufficiently respect the fact of intertwining; Kafka's horror of antithesis is that it does not sufficiently respect the fact of separation. Kafka disclaims the possibility of literary history through a consciousness fiercely divided between allegory and the language of the sensory world. This division is active in the perpetual undecidability of his aphorisms in the form of chiasmi. Kafka's "self," he stresses, is a precipitate of the acts of chance that break off interpretation, and hence it is not a self. "Self-control is something for which I do not strive. Self-control means wanting to be effective at some random [*zufälligen*] point in the infinite radiations of my spiritual existence" (DF 37; H 42). This view is consistent with another strong view of Kafka's, that his self is precipitated by the distractions of experience from his native desire to die.

Like K., Kafka the writer also accedes to chance, especially as it engenders breaks in the narrative perspective of his novels and stories.[29] There is a kind of self-construction in Kafka's accession—like K.'s—to chance, but it is unlike the dance of self and chance in Nietzsche. Kafka means to affirm his indifference to the concerns of a practical, world-mastering, empirical consciousness. His self is de-

28. "Nietzsche's purpose was to destroy belief in a historical past from which men might learn any single, substantial truth" (Hayden White, *Metahistory: The Historical Imagination in Nineteenth-Century Europe* [Baltimore, Md.: Johns Hopkins University Press, 1973], p. 332).

29. See my *Fate of the Self,* pp. 176–77.

fined not by particular interests but by its narrating attentiveness to the products of a dream play in which he is the dreamer. The self is precisely its lucid tolerance of whatever arises in the place where control, for the sake of mastery and reward, has been relinquished.[30] This view contrasts sharply with what we recall of Nietzsche's description of the self forming itself through acts of mastery. Kafka returns to the point of the nonsingle subject: "In one and the same human being there are cognitions [*Erkenntnisse*] that, however utterly dissimilar they are, yet have one and the same object, so that one can only conclude that there are different subjects in one and the same human being" (DF 42; H47).

The historian, of course, is not bound to the claims of Nietzsche and Kafka: What does he or she make of their difference? If the historian reads these two writers together in the manner of Kafka, then his or her view of their relation is one of interminable irony: the distinction between Nietzsche on self and fiction and Kafka on chance and truth is itself firm only as a matter of chance. On the one hand, there cannot be a literary history, because the difference between these two writers is undecidable by a self. On the other hand, the historian writing like Nietzsche could seize the power to arrest this irony. A strong mode of reading the difference between these writers would reverse the distinction that Kafka makes. We could dare to read Kafka's asserted love of the totality of the historical truth exactly in the manner of Nietzsche writing on "the historical sense." Here is Nietzsche:

> If one could *endure* . . . the losses, hopes, conquests, and the victories of humanity; if one could finally contain all this in one soul and crowd it into a single feeling—this would surely have to result in a happiness that humanity has not known so far: the happiness of a god full of power and love. [GS 268]

And here is a fuller statement of Kafka's experience of world encompassment:

> I feel too tightly constricted in everything that signifies Myself: even the eternity that I am is too tight for me. But if, for instance, I read a good book, say, an account of travels, it rouses me, satisfies me, suffices me. Proofs that previously I did not include this book in my

30. Ibid., p. 267.

eternity, or had not pushed on far enough ahead to have an intuitive glimpse of the eternity that necessarily includes this book as well.— From a certain stage of knowledge [*Erkenntnis*] on, weariness, insufficiency, constriction, self-contempt must all vanish: namely, at the point where I have the stength to recognize as my own nature what previously was something alien to myself that refreshed me, satisfied, liberated, and exalted me. [DF 91]

True, the passage, as I stressed earlier, is incomplete; it proceeds to disparage the weak Hegelian rigor of its terms and undercut its ambition. But this movement does not rule out a Kafkan hero who dares to substitute himself for chance, and Kafka has indeed illustrated such a figure in K. in *The Castle*.

Here is an example of K.'s daring. The relation of K. to the castle can figure as a form of truth-seeking. Entry into the castle is entry into the truth of things. In such a metaphor, the distinctive quality of interpersonal relations is carried over into the relation of knower and known: the known is figured as *acknowledging* the knower. Where there is truth, there is reciprocal recognition.

An early passage speaks this way of K.'s serious acceptance of the quest and struggle for admission to the castle: "So the Castle had recognized him as the Land Surveyor. That was unpropitious for him, on the one hand, for it meant that the Castle was well informed about him, had estimated all the probable chances, and was taking up the challenge with a smile" (C 12).

The metaphor restates the failure of knowledge in approximately these Faustian terms: All you know of the spiritual object is what you assume; it is not me. The truth condescends to be known not as it is in itself but in the manner appropriate to the human subject, a manner that does not jeopardize it. Truth can be known only as what it is not.

But this point, for Kafka, requires adjustment. The condescension of truth figures parabolically in *The Castle* as only one side of K.'s experience. "On the other hand," writes Kafka of the readiness of the Castle to take up the struggle, "it was quite propitious, for if his interpretation were right they had underestimated his strength, and he would have more freedom of action than he had dared to hope. And if they expected to cow him by their lofty superiority in recognizing him as Land Surveyor, they were mistaken; it made his skin prickle a little [he felt a slight shudder, *es überschauerte ihn leicht*], that was all" (C 12; R 484). There is a Promethean, an altogether usurpatory, feeling to such parables of selfhood in their very independence of Halakah.[31]

Here I am reading Kafka, through K., as himself daring, with a shudder, the defiant acts of arrest and comprehension that constitute a self. This is a Nietzschean Kafka. Equally, readers aware of the New Nietzsche, the "nomadic" Nietzsche of Deleuze and Foucault, will recall that a good case can be made for reading Nietzsche's self as "Kafkan": not as a maker of fictions but as itself a fiction, which would then have to be said to be constructed by chance. Such a self belongs, in Gottfried Benn's words, to Nietzsche's "astronomy"—the disruption of "chance, the uncaused event, the scattering of errors."[32] The self is not exterior to its fictions. Both Nietzsche and Kafka contain the possibility of reversal with respect to each other's position on reversal.

There would appear then to be no theory possible of a final reversal establishing a decisive difference between these writers that could not itself be reversed by each one's own theory of infinite reversibility. Nietzsche's self accommodates chance, Kafka's chance precipitates a self. A literary history including Nietzsche and Kafka halts before the interminable reversal, the unstable chiasm, indwelling their positions. This chiastic motion produces a vortex within the textual field where will and chance collide, spinning every sentence on its axis.[33] What is the empirical referent of the negativity of the pivot on which Nietzsche's and Kafka's parallels, to quote Kafka, "like a weather vane" thus turn round "entirely in the opposite direction [into an element wholly opposed, *ins Entgegengesetzte*]" (DI 26; T 21)? Where do we

31. This is what Walter Benjamin was the first, rightly, to perceive; it speaks on behalf of his own intellectual daring. See my essay (with Michael Jennings) "Walter Benjamin/Gershom Scholem *Briefwechsel, 1933–1940*," *Interpretation: A Journal of Political Philosophy* 12 (May, September 1984): 357–66.

32. Gottfried Benn, "Nietzsche nach fünfzig Jahren," in *Gesammelte Werke: Essays, Reden, Vortrage* (Stuttgart: Klett-Cotta, 1977), 1:490.

33. Cf. Paul de Man: "Chiasmus . . . can only come into being as the result of a void, of a lack that allows for the rotating motion of the polarities" (AR 49). In my essay "Kafka's Double Helix," *Literary Review* 26 (Summer 1983): 521–33, I point out the association of the pivot in Kafka's chiasmi not with "lack" but with the term of the "world" as the not-self and also with the term of death. But "the world" cannot have a finite historical referent; in such a referent the worldhood of the world remains invisible. The same philosophical difficulty attaches to a historical representation of death.

find in history the shaft on which that arrow turns, and how confine precisely the wound the arrow makes, so that with Kafka it might be "enough" to say, "the arrow . . . fit[s] exactly into it" (DII 206)? That spinning pivot—the wound it inflicts and the vertigo it induces—is the scandal and the provocation of literary history.

Chapter Seven

Consternation:
The Anthropological
Moment in Prose Fiction
(Cervantes, Flaubert, Kafka)

By the "anthropological moment" I mean the moment when one human being, to his or her consternation, perceives another as inhuman, while struggling to conclude that this strangeness is part of a design. The struggle aims to escape consternation—"a sudden, alarming amazement or dread that results in . . . paralyzing dismay."[1] In the anthropological moment the object that alarms and amazes is another human being. The subject suffering consternation seeks relief, even by violent means. If the meaningful design is grasped, relief from interpersonal pain comes with the "negative pleasure" of the sublime.[2] With the waning of the true sublime—"a moribund aesthetic"—the anthropological moment gains sway.[3]

Thus described, the anthropological moment corresponds to an

---

1. There is an oxymoron of senses of the word in its etymological history. The *Random House Dictionary of the English Language* (1967) gives the root *sterna,* which means "to make to shy or dodge." "Consternation" thus suggests a concentration of contrary movements whose issue is immobilization and a trace of this agitation. The second edition of the *Random House Dictionary* (1987) registers a different etymological surmise, linking "consternation" to *sternere,* to "strew," which also points, however, to the rigidity of *stratum,* "pavement." Though "sense development [is] uncertain," the opposed meanings of unsettling and hindering survive.

2. The phrase "negative pleasure" is from Immanuel Kant, *The Critique of Judgement,* trans. James Creed Meredith (Oxford: Clarendon, 1911), p. 91.

3. Thomas Weiskel, *The Romantic Sublime: Studies in the Structure and Psychology of Transcendence* (Baltimore, Md.: Johns Hopkins University Press, 1976), p. 6.

empirical moment in the practice of anthropology, which describes cultures remotest from the observer's own while struggling to produce a logic of this other humanity. The moment harbors the fundamental power of philosophical reflection; it breaks down the observer's idea of the human and makes a natural prejudgment a matter for wonder. According to Heidegger, this power should not be confused with what German authors call philosophical anthropology, which is supposed to make harmless the radical strangeness of human beings to one another and to themselves. It is too sociable a science. In his book on Kant, Heidegger terms philosophical anthropology "a reservoir of essential philosophical problems": that is, a place where these problems are stored in forms in which they have been settled for small stakes.[4] The movement of Heidegger's thought—the so-called *Kehre* or turning from the existential project of *Being and Time* to the fundamental ontology of the later work, to a thinking of being as language—is based on " [an]other [mode] of thinking that abandons subjectivity," in which "every kind of [philosophical] anthropology and all subjectivity of man as subject . . . [are] left behind."[5] I also point up a moment of "abandonment," when intersubjective dialogue in literature is left behind for a moment that contests the power of subjects to understand language, including literary language.

A genuine anthropology would be one in which hermeneutics and the impossibility of hermeneutics contend. The predicament of the consternated interpreter is schizophrenic. Derrida writes in a Heideggerean manner about Jean Laplanche's psychoanalytical study of Friedrich Hölderlin's poetry that the work affords "an exemplary access to the essence of schizophrenia in general: this essence of schizophrenia is not a psychological or anthropological fact available to the determined sciences called psychology or anthropology."[6] Lacanian psychoanalysis, which aims to be an *un*determined science, provokes between analyst and patient (as Stuart Schneiderman explains) this very schizophrenic consternation:

4. Martin Heidegger, *Kant and the Problem of Metaphysics*, trans. James S. Churchill (Bloomington: Indiana University Press, 1962), p. 219.

5. Martin Heidegger, "Letter on Humanism," in *Martin Heidegger, Basic Writings*, ed. David Farrell Krell (New York: Harper & Row, 1977), p. 207.

6. Jacques Derrida, "La parole soufflée," in *Writing and Difference*, trans. Alan Bass (Chicago: University of Chicago Press, 1977), p. 173.

Whereas normal conversation attempts to gain some sense of mutual understanding leading to communication, [Lacanian] psychoanalysis tries precisely to break down communication and whatever understanding the analysand has already arrived at. . . . Lacan, like most analysts, listened to something other than what was said; he listened as if the remarks that were about him were really addressed to someone else and as if the remarks of the analysand that were supposed to be about himself were really about another. . . . By acting much of the time as if he were a creature from another planet, even another galaxy, Lacan gave the impression that he was hearing something other than what you were saying.[7]

Lacan meant to induce consternation, the heightened negative of the anthropological moment, as a "scrupulously maintained, . . . fruitful, well-tuned discord."[8] If fruitful and well tuned, however, such discord must also include positive moments of apparently truthful interpretation—which is to say, moments of anthropological consternation that succeed in recovering a design.

It appears to be the privilege of literature—and specifically of prose fiction—to represent such moments of anthropological consternation in their fullest measure of negativity. Let us take the oblique path and consider some alternative genres: for instance, the written-up accounts of actual anthropological practice. Here the negative moment of consternation is the very condition of scientific anthropology, which tests itself on the radical otherness of the native respondent. But in the verbal records of such transactions, the rhetoric of consternation is necessarily suppressed in favor of agreement and accord—of science and information.[9] Also, something of the visual problematics

7. Stuart Schneiderman, *Jacques Lacan: The Death of an Intellectual Hero* (Cambridge, Mass.: Harvard University Press, 1983), p. 118.

8. Ibid., p. 119.

9. More and more often, the awareness endemic to literature, of the merely factitious status of represented persons and the only doubtful ability of literature to communicate a moment of calculable otherness at the order of representation, has come to the fore in anthropologists' accounts of other cultures. James Clifford, e.g., writes: "I think we are seeing signs that the privilege given to natural languages and, as it were, native cultures is dissolving. These objects and epistemological grounds are now appearing as constructs, achieved fictions, containing and domesticating heteroglossia" ("On Ethnographic Self-Fashioning," in *Reconstructing Individualism: Autonomy, Individuality, and the Self in Western Thought*, ed. Thomas C. Heller, Morton Sonda, and David E. Wellbery [Stanford, Calif.: Stanford University Press, 1986], p. 143).

of dialogue is necessarily left out of the protocol that follows, for in the instance of consternation, seeing is important as what is not believing, and believing is not seeing.

The same aptitude for the presentation of dialogue is rarely realized in lyric poetry, although this is the project that Nathaniel Tarn has been calling for.[10] Consternation might seem the appropriate appanage of history writing, but here too the problematics of the visible are given short shrift. Natalie Z. Davis, a historian who advised the filmmakers of *Le Retour de Martin Guerre*, noted: "In the film, I was a historian who wanted to make the past come alive in the details of experience, the historian who so much wants to be in the past that she pretends she's an anthropologist and is *observing* it" (my italics).[11] In one respect, of course, films are very apt for problematical representation: they can evoke a real and a phantasmal visibility, and so they can suggest a consternating visibility in excess of the facts and, equally, a consternating failure of the visible to manifest the facts. Paul Valéry wrote of the way "artists are useful: they preserve the subtlety and instability of sensory impressions. A modern artist has to exhaust two-thirds of his time trying to see what is visible—and above all, trying not to see what is invisible. Philosophers often pay a high price for striving to do the opposite."[12] In films the artist's task can become philosophical; films can dismiss the artist's alleged loyalty to the visible.

But in one important way films fall short. They have by and large failed to develop a code of metanarrative signals—a commentary twilighting the narrative all along the way—being chiefly dependent for commentary on the limited field of the voice-over or the image of its impersonator. This is impoverishing, because the fullest presentation of the anthropological moment requires the vital dimension of the conflict to be illuminated—namely, the *impensé,* the ideological factor informing the "positions" that seem to constitute the anthropological dispute but which, in the absence of the *impensé,* do so only trivially. Such positions are construed by observers only insofar as

10. In conversation with the author.
11. Natalie Z. Davis, cited in *New York Times*, November 13, 1983, sec. 11, p. 2.
12. Paul Valéry, "Introduction to the Method of Leonardo da Vinci," in *Paul Valéry: An Anthology*, ed. James Lawler (Princeton, N.J.: Princeton University Press, 1977), p. 50.

they can be attributed to the self-awareness of the dialogists. It needs to be shown, however, how in the anthropological moment the *codic immersion* of interrogators, of which they themselves are ignorant, precipitates their consternation or what the anthropologist E. Michel Mendelson calls "the role of the discourse in our understanding of the problems it conveys to us."[13] This code can be indicated by narrators, if only by the hinting of rhetorical gestures, although this does not protect them, either, from blindness to the conditions of their own mastery of that code.

In consternation the code of public behavior that sustains the moral unity of persons shatters. Such a moment has been described by Tony Tanner as a constitutive feature of the novel. His book *Adultery and the Novel* links the early novel to its responsiveness to types of social transgression, of which adultery is said to be the most drastically usurpatory, producing in its wake unintelligible characters.[14] In consternation the code shatters in a dialogical situation; here we can recall the aptitude of the novel for the expression of various dialogues: between character and character, narrator and character, narrator and narrator. Narrators can emphasize, over the heads of the dialogists, the wider code that explains their consternation—and implicates themselves. In Thomas Mann's *Doctor Faustus*, for example, Zeitblom finds consternating a moment in his biography of Adrian Leverkühn which requires him to report a dialogue of Leverkühn's, one that to Zeitblom's dismay Leverkühn himself does not find consternating. Zeitblom escapes his distress by surrendering the narrative to Leverkühn: "The biographical moment has come," writes Zeitblom. "And accordingly, I myself must cease to speak. . . . In this twenty-fifth chapter the reader hears Adrian's voice direct."

> But is it only his? This is a dialogue which lies before us. Another, quite another, quite frightfully other, is the principal speaker, and the writer, in his stone-floored living-room, only writes down what he

13. Letter to the author, May 11, 1980.
14. Tony Tanner, *Adultery in the Novel* (Baltimore, Md.: Johns Hopkins University Press, 1979). The speech of Shakespeare's Troilus comes to mind as an incomparably fierce instance: Troilus laments Cressida's adultery as jeopardizing the "rule in unity itself" (*Troilus and Cressida* 5.2). If this example diminishes, of course, the *novel*-specific character of the moment of consternation, it heightens its connection with adultery.

heard from that other. A dialogue? Is it really a dialogue? I should be mad to believe it. And therefore I cannot believe that in the depths of his soul Adrian himself considered to be actual that which he saw and heard—either while he heard and saw it or afterwards, when he put it on paper; notwithstanding the cynicisms with which his interlocutor sought to convince him of his objective presence. But if he was not there, that visitor—and I shudder at the admission which lies in the very words, seeming even conditionally and as possibility to entertain his actuality—then it is horrible to think that those cynicisms too, those jeerings and jugglings came out of the afflicted one's own soul.[15]

Zeitblom's way of sublimating a devilish dialogist is to deny that any such dialogue has taken place. The German word, meanwhile, for "jeerings and jugglings" is *Spiegelfechtereien*: hence, "joustings with a mirror image." In surmising that this meeting is a product of Adrian Leverkühn's mirror phase, Zeitblom hints at the inauthenticity of his own dialogue with Leverkühn throughout. Their dialogue can now be seen as controlled by Zeitblom, as an anthropological dialogue with a devil designed always to be kept within bounds of the "humanistic." The discourse of Zeitblom and Leverkühn itself belongs among the joustings of the mirror phase, and Zeitblom does not wish to know that Leverkühn comes out of the afflicted Zeitblom's soul.

I am concerned, then, with literary moments of staged interpersonal consternation and recovery or covering up. Prose fiction is distinctive for the abundance of such moments. And now a crucial point: the same anthropological moment can be found to inform the reading that such fiction provokes. Here I do not mean to advance the interpersonal model of reading as a dialogue between author and reader, which is a highly contestable form of reading, so much as to stress the omnipresent moment of defamiliarization. Fiction as such defamiliarizes; it means to astonish and unsettle every step of the way. For it necessarily unsettles conventional patterns of signs, especially by transforming the conventional relation of the literal to the figurative in ways bound to induce consternation.

This chapter treats such transformations as they occur in major fiction, in the dialogues between characters that unsettle them. This

15. Thomas Mann, *Doctor Faustus,* trans. H. T. Lowe-Porter (New York: Vintage, 1948), p. 221.

unsettling is communicated by a communication itself unsettling. The consternation of fictional characters amplifies its strangeness in the relation between text and reader, inflicting a kind of reading trauma defined by the issues under tension in the text. Such moments heighten the constitutive strangeness of fiction.

* * *

Before turning to examples from Cervantes, Flaubert, and Kafka, consider this model—built up chiefly from Hölderlin and Nietzsche—of what happens, or fails to happen, when there is consternation at the order of reading. The first point on this negative path: words that inspire understanding do not consternate. Understanding means the facility with which signs can be returned to a wide range of contexts and uses in which they have previously figured. Understanding proliferates doubles of the sign in question, which are or can be resituated. This is Nietzsche's idea when he defines key words, powerful concepts, as "process[es] . . . semiotically concentrated."[16] Understanding multiplies the sign, virtually remembering it in each moment of its semiotic history for me: every time I understand a word, I recapitulate a moment in what Lacan calls my "semantic evolution: this corresponds to the stock of words and acceptations of my own . . . vocabulary, as it does to my style of life and to my character."[17] My semantic evolution is involved in that of my group. Nietzsche writes of the communal abundance of meaning as "the ultimate result [of the development of this communicative function]: an excess of this strength and art of communication—as it were, a capacity that has gradually been accumulated and now waits for an heir who might squander it. (Those who are called artists are these heirs; so are orators, preachers, writers . . .)."[18] This is to catch the prolific hermeneutic or meaning-squandering function of literature.

This moment might, of course, itself induce a secondary consternation, the confusion of excessive significance, of too many doubles,

16. *Basic Writings of Nietzsche,* ed. and trans. Walter Kaufmann (New York: Modern Library, 1966), p. 516.
17. Jacques Lacan, "The Function of Language in Psychoanalysis," in Anthony Wilden, *The Language of the Self* (Baltimore, Md.: Johns Hopkins University Press, 1968), p. 21.
18. Friedrich Nietzsche, *The Gay Science,* trans. Walter Kaufmann (New York: Random House, 1974), p. 298.

too much metaphor, which Nietzsche contrasts with the strength of the Dionysian type. The "art of communication commanded in the highest degree by the Dionysian type [is] marked by the ease of metamorphosis; it is impossible for him to overlook any sign of an affect."[19] Such a Dionysian art might induce in the ordinary reader a cascade of affect-laden metaphorical displacements, an experience of meaning verging on consternation—but not principally negative: it suggests the category of "semantic saturation," that abundance of information which formalists call "beauty."[20] Its interpersonal analogue is the delirium—the lucky jousting in front of a mirror, *Spiegelfechterei*—of being-in-love, the bliss of perfect interpersonal recognition.

Nietzsche gives a semiotic account of being in love with the world as text.

> The involuntariness of image and metaphor is strangest of all: one no longer has any notion of what is an image or a metaphor: everything offers itself as the nearest, most obvious, simplest expression. It actually seems, to allude to something Zarathustra says, as if the things themselves approached and offered themselves as metaphors. ("Here all things come caressingly to your discourse and flatter you; for they want to ride on your back. On every metaphor you ride to every truth. . . . Here the words and word-shrines of all being open up before you; here all being wishes to become word, all becoming wishes to learn from you how to speak").[21]

For Nietzsche the world is a text—occasionally a good text—requiring interpretation. But seen with "great health," the world's signs are more than signs: they are vehicles of the things they name, that "ride upon their backs." The impulse of active interpretation is at low ebb. Things ride in on their own names. And these things too are metaphors; they and their meanings flow into the discourse of the

19. *The Portable Nietzsche*, ed. and trans. Walter Kaufman (New York: Viking, 1954), pp. 519–20.

20. A certain modern form of this beauty is described by Anthony L. Johnson as arising through "the 'profanation' of the signified, achieved by increasing its plasticity in the interests of the signifier's capacity for 'self-display' and inventiveness" ("Jakobsonian Theory and Literary Semiotics," *New Literary History* 14 [Autumn 1982]: 1).

21. *Basic Writings of Nietzsche*, pp. 756–57; *Portable Nietzsche*, pp. 295–96. This rhetoric of fulfilled knighthood, of the journey to the Grail, also suggests Don Quixote's wish-dream.

inspired reader. In love, the world's text approaches with the visibility of a loved body; and as around "the high body, beautiful, triumphant, refreshing, . . . everything becomes a mirror," all discourse then mirrors, like an aroused lover, the thing, book, or body it is given to understand.[22]

In consternation, the book yellows, the body fades—the mirror shatters. The world's signs become opaque: they do not produce mirrors for a doubling. They create no spectral doubles of themselves: they cannot produce metaphors.

Now if a sign can be imagined that cannot be carried over into any other context, it is absolutely literal: it is only the crack where a meaning is lacking, a place marker of the context that embeds its opacity and that can itself be seen as growingly reduced to opacity by this break in its texture.[23] Hence the consternation of reading an entirely foreign word and, equally, of registering in a book a "human being" (scare quotes) as monstrous. In Kafka's *Metamorphosis*, Gregor Samsa, the buglike victim, is called an *ungeheueres Ungeziefer* ("monstrous sort of vermin"). While he may be a monstrous human being, he is certainly the shadow of an outlandish pair of words, chiefly marked by their negative *un-, un-* sound and therefore having only *etymological* significance (they have no other clear-cut significance) as a creature unsuited to a household (*infamiliaris*) and unacceptable as a sacrifice (Middle High German, *ungezivere*).[24] Here I have reached for an etymological dictionary for relief from the consternation of a pair of (almost) literal signs. If Gregor is a human being, then he lives out his career entirely as this etymological designation, as household trash to be swept out. Kafka's theme is the effort by Gregor himself and his

---

22. *Portable Nietzsche*, p. 302. Evidently Nietzsche's rhetorical vision does not fail to promise a new Kabbalah of sorts, though even this real appropriation of metaphor would have to be classed by him as a fiction.

23. Cf. the observation by Friedrich Kittler: "The sigh 'oh [*ach*]' is the sign of that unique entity [the soul], which, if it were to mouth any other signifier—as signifiers exist only in the plural, any signifier whatsoever—would have to return immediately to its own sigh; for then it would have ceased to be soul, it would have become *words*, language [*Sprache*] instead" (*Aufschreibesysteme 1800 . 1900* [Munich: Fink, 1985], p. 11).

24. Hermann Pongs, "Franz Kafka—'Die Verwandlung': Zwischen West und Ost," in *Dichtung im gespaltenen Deutschland* (Stuttgart: Union, 1966), p. 264. See Chapter 3, pp. 57–58.

family to interpret other than by etymological approximation an unintelligible and continually changing body, to add to an obscure sign some other definite meaning. The mood of the story, as Kafka and Friedrich Beißner wrote, is horror, an exacerbated form of consternation before an irreducibly literal human being (M 187).

Yet the opaque sign can also arrest and fascinate. Schizophrenia, Laplanche suggests, is an arrest of the metaphorical function: all moments of experience fascinate and stun the schizophrenic equally. Hölderlin is an example. "Above all it is a matter of his hypersensibility," writes Laplanche, "the sustained and ravaging echo that prolongs the smallest experience of the least liveliness into long periods of depression or excitement; like an ultrafine crystal or a string drawn too taut, it finds itself in a sort of unstable equilibrium that inclines it to resonate endlessly, even to sounds that have nothing in common with it except for remote harmonics."[25]

What Hölderlin cannot do is relay the sign to a definite context: not to do so is to be wholly exposed to the moment; it is to be helpless in the sense that Freud gives to *Hilflosigkeit*—a breaking down of the barriers that protect the subject, with the effect of preventing him or her from producing an exact or applied reaction.[26] The consternating detail marks a weakness of ego defenses. Harold Searles observes: "Without the establishment of firm ego boundaries, a differentiation between metaphorical meanings and literal meanings cannot take place; [but] it would seem equally correct to say that metaphor, at least, could never develop if there had not once been a lack of such ego boundaries."[27] What is at stake is the facility of repeated genesis of a doubled consciousness that will not prove deranging. In W. Stählin's view (as discussed by Gerhard Kurz): "With metaphor we have a situation of *the consciousness of doubled meaning*. In intending an expression metaphorically, we intend a meaning that is supposed to arise out of the standard meaning without annihilating it. . . . We are conscious of the normal meaning and at the same time of its transfor-

25. Jean Laplanche, *Hölderlin et la question du père* (Paris: Presses Universitaires de France, 1961), p. 91.

26. Ibid., p. 93.

27. Harold F. Searles, "The Differentiation between Concrete and Metaphorical Thinking," in *Collected Papers on Schizophrenia and Related Subjects* (London, Hogarth: 1965), p. 583; quoted in Rolf Breuer, "Irony, Literature, and Schizophrenia," *New Literary History* 12 (Autumn 1980): 118.

mation into a new metaphorical meaning forced by the context or the situation."[28] With the lack of all ego boundaries, however, with the limitless expansion of the spaces between doubles of consciousness, meaning becomes interminably metaphorical and hence by the dialectic entirely literal. The sign that means everything in general means nothing in particular. Hölderlin gives his own troubled account of how things and signs could captivate him in their infinite and empty suggestiveness:

> I am not entitled to complain about Nature—which heightened my sense of the shortcomings of things [das Mangelhafte], in order to make me all the more intensely and joyously aware of what is excellent. Once I have arrived at the point of mastering the knack of feeling and seeing in things that fall short less the indefinite pain that they often cause me than precisely their special, momentary, particular lack, and thus also of recognizing their beauty, their characteristic good—once I have achieved this, then my spirit will become calmer and my activity make a steadier progress. For when we experience a lack only infinitely, then we are naturally inclined, too, to want to repair this lack infinitely, and then our strength often gets entangled in an indefinite, fruitless, exhausting struggle, because it does not know definitely where the lack is and how precisely to repair and supplement this lack.[29]

Hölderlin's exacerbated sense of lack, the failure of the energy of specification, is, for Lacan, the product of an unconscious that lacks a certain decisive regulatory function. "By means of the hole that [this absence] opens in the signified, [it] attracts the cascade of revisions of the signifier, whence proceeds the increasing disaster of the Imaginary."[30]

The moment in which the world grows increasingly literal is threatening and needs to be explained. Cervantes' Don Quixote, Flaubert's Sentimental Education, and Kafka's "The Judgment" describe different characters' responses to consternation. Don Quixote saves himself by enlarging his credulity, blaming magic, and sum-

28. Gerhard Kurz, Metapher, Allegorie, Symbol (Göttingen: Vandenhoeck & Ruprecht, 1982), pp. 17–18.
29. Friedrich Hölderlin, Sämtliche Werke, ed. Friedrich Beißner (Stuttgart: Kohlhammer, 1961), 6:326.
30. Jacques Lacan, writing on the Schreber case in La Psychanalyse 4 (1958): 44–45; quoted in Laplanche, Hölderlin, p. 46.

moning up religious patience: God will help His faithful knight. In *Sentimental Education*, Frédéric Moreau saves himself by constructing erogenous rhetorical fictions of selfhood; mastery of the Oedipus complex will save the consternated lover. In "The Judgment," Georg Bendemann consents to his own literalization and death; his hope lies in immersion in a sort of Dionysian capitalist flux, an urban rage of sex and commerce. In each case the anthropological moment shatters the reading relation: interpersonal distress in fiction is amplified into a reading trauma. Thereafter it is every hermeneut for her- or himself. Literature rewrites anthropology by suggesting that interpersonality is founded on the violent suppression of a more native unintelligibility. Interpersonality is the reward for the lost knowledge of the universal failure of reading.

* * *

"I can see nothing, Sancho," said Don Quixote, "but three village girls on three donkeys."
                    MIGUEL DE CERVANTES, *Don Quixote*

Chapter 10 of Part II (II. 10) of *Don Quixote,* in which Quixote first lays eyes on the pseudo–Dulcinea del Toboso, is told by two narrators. One narrator, conventionally called the Second Author, presents the "history" written by Cide Hamete Benengeli, who is a more obviously fictive narrator. The double frame increases the likelihood that the encounter has been thoroughly designed. The Second Author declares that he aims to present Don Quixote's behavior at a maximum of unbelievableness (which is to say, as inviting a maximum of consternation for the reader) and yet as true.

When the author of this great history [Cide Hamete Benengeli] comes to recount the contents of this chapter, he says that he would have liked

176

to pass it over in silence, through fear of disbelief. For Don Quixote's delusions here reach the greatest imaginable bounds and limits, and even exceed them, great as they are, by two bow-shots. But finally he wrote the deeds down, although with fear and misgivings, just as our knight performed them, without adding or subtracting one atom of truth from the history, or taking into account any accusations of lying that might be laid against him. And he was right, for truth, though it may run thin, never breaks, and always flows over the lie like oil over water.[31]

So the surface of the episode is true; we will find truth in its unction. We have only to distinguish its surface from its depth.

One such surface truth is plainly the truth of enchantment: enchanters, Don Quixote declares, have transformed Dulcinea "into a figure as low and ugly as that peasant girl's" (p. 531). The alibi of enchantment is the means by which Don Quixote sublimates his consternation, but this solution is only provisional.

There is another striking truth in the rhetorical surface of the episode, a conspicuous confusion of signifiers about hackneys and she-asses: a sublime horseplay. Don Quixote's consternation at Dulcinea's appearance generates a parallel disturbance and play of the letter.

"Your Worship," says Sancho Panza, "has nothing more to do than to spur Rocinante and go out into the open to see the lady Dulcinea del Toboso, who is coming to meet your worship with two of her damsels." Sancho proceeds to describe the coming of the princess in a rhetoric he has learned from Don Quixote. His encomium returns to a famous set speech by Don Quixote; in Sancho's words, "her maidens and she are one blaze of gold, all ropes of pearls, all diamonds, all rubies, all brocade of more than ten gold strands; their hair loose on their shoulders, like so many sunrays sporting in the wind and, what's more [we are alerted to a supplement], they are riding on three piebald nackneys [or cackneys], the finest to be seen." For *hacaneas* ("hackneys"), Sancho Panza has said *cananeas* ("nackneys" or "cackneys"). "Hackneys, you mean, Sancho," replies Don Quixote.

31. Miguel de Cervantes, *Don Quixote*, trans. Bernard Cohen (Harmondsworth: Penguin, 1950), p. 524. Page numbers given in the text refer to this edition.

"There is very little difference," answers Sancho, "between nackneys [or cackneys] and hackneys. But let them come on whatever they may, they are the bravest ladies you could wish for" (p. 528).[32]

Sancho Panza speaks many such catachreses, of course, which Don Quixote as often tries to correct;[33] but this one appears to have a special function. "Hackney" is a rich and aporetic word which—as the *Oxford English Dictionary* points out—"has engaged the most eminent etymologists" but whose "ulterior derivation is still unknown." It stands for high and low; it is at once "an ambling horse or mare especially for ladies to ride on—often white," and, from the fact that hackneys were hired out, "a prostitute."[34] It also came in Cervantes' time to designate a pen-for-hire; and in Sancho's citing the word from the world of Quixote's chivalric books, it calls attention to Sancho himself as a plagiarist to the second power.

Given at least this semantic field, it is a matter of no mean difficulty to decide what is achieved when *cananeas* replaces *hacaneas*. For Sancho himself there is "very little difference"; he is a systematic leveler of discursive differences. The word *cananeas* is rendered by English translators, with an eye to Cervantes' intent, as a degradation: it is not hard to hear it in "cackneys" or indeed in "nack-" (that

32. This passage, esp. as it involves the relation of the words *cananea* and *hacanaea*, is a familar topic for students of *Don Quixote*, as well as of Tirso de Molina's *El burlador de Sevilla*. Bruce Wardropper discusses the relation of these words in the course of distinguishing between the two works in their use of *cananea* ("Who Was Catalinón's Intercessor?" in *Estudios literarios de Hispanistas Norteamericanos dedicados a Helmut Hatzfeld con motivo de su 80 aniversario*, ed. Josep M. Sola-Solé, Alessandro Crisafulli, and Bruno Damiani [Barcelona: Hispam Colección, 1972], pp. 349–54). I am grateful to Alban Forcione for bringing this essay to my attention.

33. "The single most significant difference between Don Quijote and Sancho Panza: Don Quijote's speech acts continually reflect his will to structure, to provide definitive endings and dependable meanings to events in the world. Sancho, in contrast, presents a will to unstructure definitions and meanings. For Sancho, definitions and meanings are exorbitant desires, not implacable realities" (Ramon Salivar, *Figural Narrative: The Flowers of Fiction* [Princeton, N.J.: Princeton University Press, 1984], p. 40).

34. Leo Spitzer was the first to point out, apropos of the verbal play on *cananea* in *El burlador de Sevilla*, the connotation of *puta* in *hacanea* ("En lisant le *Burlador de Sevilla*," *Nouveau Monde* 36 [1935]: 281). Wardropper ("Who Was Catalinón's Intercessor?" p. 352) agrees that the "sexual implications of equitation are involved . . . even though English hackney did not acquire its meaning of 'prostitute' until long after (1679, *OED*) the word was appropriated by Spanish (1490, Corominas)."

is, "nag-") or "knock-neys."[35] But Hackney is also a place name,[36] and therefore in a number of coherent ways Sancho can have inserted into his word *cananeas* the place name Cana (in Galilee), the place of Christ's first miracle, his turning water into wedding wine. The water (of the lie) miraculously vanishes under the oil of truth, the wine of presence.

This, then, is Sancho's sublimated consciousness of the miracle he means to perform to provision a sort of wedding—of Don Quixote and Dulcinea del Toboso. Sancho Panza as a *figura Christi* could sound absurd, but hasn't he after all learned from Don Quixote, two chapters earlier, that "chivalry is a religion" (p. 520)? And that sublimation is everywhere explicitly at stake is borne out by Sancho's speech to the saddle-nosed country girl: "O Princess and world-famous lady of El Toboso! How is it that your magnanimous heart is not softened when you see the column and prop of knight errantry kneeling before your sublimated presence?" (p. 529). Sancho's language is capable of wide religious reference: he knows populist religious rhetoric. I hold that the miracle of Cana is a self-reflexive mark of Sancho's growing consciousness of his power to perform miracles with words.[37]

Another intertextual line of descent, however, needs to be brought into play. The word *cananeas* literally means "Canaanite women": it alludes in the plural to the woman of Canaan who besought Christ to drive out the devil from her daughter. Christ granted her prayer, and the woman of Canaan was blessed, as indeed her land had always been blessed. In this sense Sancho Panza salutes the peasant women as legendary survivals of the Promised Land, the land of milk and honey. Both these meanings work in the way that Cana works, but they

35. Miguel de Cervantes, *The Ingenious Gentleman Don Quixote de la Mancha,* trans. Samuel Putnam, 2 vols. (New York: Viking, 1949), 2:569.

36. It seems likely that Cervantes knew "Hackney" as a place name, since he might well have known that "Hackney" or "Hackeney" was an important family name in the Low Countries and the Rhineland. In the Alte Pinakothek in Munich, e.g., one can see a triptych painted by Joos van Cleve (1480-1540/41) for Saint Mary's Church in Cologne. The main panel depicts the death of Mary; the side panels portray the patrons—the brothers Georg and Nicasius Hackeney.

37. Wardropper ("Who Was Catalinón's Intercessor?") reserves the association of *cananea* with "lady of Cana" for *El burlador de Sevilla,* where it points to the Virgin, at whose behest Christ performed the miracle.

are special for arising from a signifier displaying itself as a citation, as I shall explain.

Older annotated editions of *Don Quixote* allege two main sources of Sancho's catachresis. The first is Alfonso Lopez Pinciano's *Filosofia poetica* (1596). In the course of cataloguing the principles of jokes, the author mentions "[sheer] ignorance," as for example "to say *cananea* instead of *hacanea*."[38] According to the implications of this commentary, Cervantes means Sancho to speak as a fool; Sancho is presented as someone than whom every reader is smarter. Every reader will know what Sancho doesn't know, namely that he is speaking in the very character of the fool. This is quite unconvincing.

Another commentary is more bemusing. It cites a passage from the play *Minerva Sacra* (1616), published a year after Cervantes' death, in which a clownish figure reports:

> Ya ha sabido, señor padre,
> Cómo entró su enquillotrençia
> De la Princessa en la Corte,
> Sobida en su *Cananea*.[39]

Following these implications, Sancho would presumably be speaking with the same intention as the zealous narrator in this play, who struggles to speak a chivalric idiom; Sancho, too, would mean to improve *hacanea* (already high and low) with his *cananea*. Does he succeed, then? If *cananea*, in the sense of a courtly language, is high—and high, too, for its biblical overtones; indeed, higher than "hackney"—it is also lower than "hackney" for simply being a crude neologism and, again, low (very low) for inverting the *hac* of *hacanea* to the diabolical syllable *ca*. According to this reading, Sancho has

38. Miguel de Cervantes, *El ingenioso hidalgo Don Quijote de la Mancha,* ed. Clemente Cortejón, 6 vols. (Madrid: V. Suarez, 1905–13), 4:166.

39. "You have already known, señor padre, how her *enquillotrençia* [a fancy nonce word] the Princess entered the Court mounted upon her *cananea*" (Miguel de Cervantes, *El ingenioso hidalgo Don Quijote de la Mancha*, ed. Francisco Rodriguez Marín, 7 vols. [Madrid: Tip. de la "Revista de archs., bibls., y museos," 1928], 4:210–11. The author of *Minerva Sacra*, Miguel Toledano, born twenty-three years after Cervantes, prints a sonnet of Cervantes as part of the dedication of his work to one Doña Alfonsa Gonzalez de Salazar. By thus saluting a relative of the wife of Cervantes, Toledano affirms the filiation of his work from *Don Quixote,* which he interprets from the special perspective of the cousin.

imposed a low/high category on a high/low category; and thus there is regenerated in a small philological compass some of the consternation that Don Quixote feels on encountering the enchanted Dulcinea.

I make this point strongly because Cervantes does: just after the pseudo-Dulcinea struggled to get free, "Sancho moved off and let her pass, delighted at having got well out of his fix. And no sooner did the girl who played the part of Dulcinea find herself free, than she prodded her nackney [or cackney, *cananea*] with the point of a stick she carried, and set off at a trot across the field" (p. 530). Now, it is the reader's turn to say: "*Hacanea*, you mean, Cervantes." The reader is speaking like Don Quixote but —if he or she has already read this novel—will know that a version of Sancho's answer is the best: not, perhaps, that "there is very little difference . . . between nackneys [or cackneys] and hackneys" but that the difference is impossible to specify. For, as Don Quixote says in II.32, in response to the related question of whether Dulcinea is or is not fantastic, "These are not matters whose verification can be carried out to the full" (p. 680).[40]

I cite these words proleptically, because one might be inclined to solve the enigma of *hacanea/cananea* by an appeal to the third term, the referent. What, after all, *is* the creature whose name they are all busily distorting? Evidently, both Quixote and Sancho must be mad, since the animal in question is neither a hackney nor a cackney; it is a she-ass. Don Quixote himself seems perfectly lucid on this point II.10) when, speaking of the malevolence of the enchanters who have transformed Dulcinea into a figure "as low and ugly as that peasant girl's," he adds, for proof: "And they have deprived her too of something most proper to great ladies, which is the sweet smell they have from always moving among ambergris and flowers. For I must tell you, Sancho, that when I went to help my Dulcinea on to her hackney—as you say it was, though it seemed a she-ass to me—I got such a whiff of raw garlic as stank me out and poisoned me to the heart" (p. 531).

The reality of Dulcinea as a great lady is confirmed by her differ-

---

40. In Wardropper's view ("Who Was Catalinón's Intercessor?" p. 350), it is not necessary to second-guess the narrator here; the meaning is plain. In saying *cananea*, "the narrator sides not with Don Quijote's point of view but with Sancho's, asserting that the girl is not a princess but a peasant": i.e., *cananea* means "not *hacanea*." But since when do peasants ride *cananeas*? What, indeed, are *cananeas*?

ence from the peasant girl, who is merely "playing a part" (p. 530). The precise measure of their difference, at this juncture, is proposed as the difference between a hackney and a she-ass; the identity of Dulcinea depends, therefore, on a secure identification of this animal as a she-ass. Once its identity has been established, the reader's consternation can be confined to a local misunderstanding and easily resolved. Sancho Panza, it follows, got the name of the animal wrong, although his intent to improve it is apparent from his magniloquence. And Cervantes, the author, merely cited Sancho Panza in order to emphasize the joke of a naive mistake. The reader's perplexity, which is a matter merely of names, not things, can then be dismissed.

But this name play can be contained only if the identity of the animal is actually established, and this depends in turn on the accuracy of Don Quixote's perception and the account of what he has seen. It is therefore of some importance that on closer inspection Don Quixote's claim turns out actually to be twice uncertain. Of course Sancho did not say the animal was a "hackney"; he said it was a "cackney," nor did Don Quixote ever see the she-ass as anything more than a semblance.

Regarding the question of the reality of Dulcinea and hence of Dulcinea's mount: In II.32, which speaks of the difficulty of verification, Quixote broods on the malign enchanters who have transformed Dulcinea "from beauty to ugliness, from angel to devil, from sweet smelling to pestiferous, from eloquent to rustic, from gentle to skittish, from light to darkness." These enchanters are "born into the world," he adds, "to obscure and obliterate the exploits of the good." We cannot trust Quixote on this point either, however: as the duchess observes, basing herself on the text of Quixote's adventures, "We gather . . . that your worship never saw the lady Dulcinea, and that this same lady does not exist on earth, but is a fantastic mistress, whom your worship engendered and bore in your mind, and painted with every grace and perfection you desired."

Now Quixote replies with some finality: "There is much to say on that score. . . . God knows whether Dulcinea exists on earth or no, or whether she is fantastic or not fantastic. These are not matters whose verification can be carried out to the full" (p. 680). The strict identification of the she-ass as she-ass would contribute to this verification, but it has been impossible to make.

God knows the difference . . . and not even his representative on earth, the author. Indeed, this point would have to be a foregone conclusion, since Cervantes told it to us from the start. "When Sancho got up to mount Dapple, he saw three peasant girls coming in his direction, riding on three young asses or fillies—*our author does not tell us which*—though it is more credible that they were she-asses, as these are the ordinary mounts of village women; *but as nothing much hangs on it, there is no reason to stop and clear up the point*" (p. 527; my italics). But whether or not anything much hangs on it is not so foregone a conclusion.

In its thrust this point heightens the difference between our tale (as told by its author, Cide Hamete Benengeli) and the tale of its telling (the Second Author's tale), which produces this comment on the insignificance of the missing detail. But just as the detached narrator-persona of Cervantes may declare that little hangs on Benengeli's failure to identify the animal on which the pseudo-Dulcinea rides, it becomes the reader's task to decide whether indeed anything much hangs on Cervantes' dismissal of this matter. And having done the reading work, the reader will not now believe it is trivial but will prowl between the lines of what the author plainly says, provisionally holding that only the first part of his proposition—that the author is unreliable—is reliable. Cervantes, it appears, has only pretended to ask for obedience, so rewarding is the refusal to obey him on this point. The outcome has been to focus a question of the greatest significance for the novel: namely, that of the reality of Dulcinea and the ordeal of verification. To enter into this sublime horseplay is to discover that there cannot be a covering up of differences that does not elsewhere force the question of differences and of their verification.

In resisting Cervantes the narrator, the reader does so on the strength of Don Quixote's surmise that authors—whether tellers or retellers—may indeed be enchanters, and so the reader's sanity is at stake. "In Part Two" (as Robert Alter notes), "when Don Quixote's ambition has precipitously caught up with him and he is pursued everywhere by the knowledge that he is already in a book, he begins to suspect that his chronicler may not be a sage after all but rather one of those willful sorcerers who are persecuting him."[41] Moreover,

41. Robert Alter, *Partial Magic* (Berkeley: University of California Press, 1973), p. 9.

adds Don Quixote to Sancho, "if the author of that history of my exploits, which they say is now in print, chanced to be some enchanter hostile to me, he has probably changed one thing into another, mingling a thousand lies with one truth" (p. 682).

The author Cervantes himself calls down this charge. Certainly he makes fiction very strange by complicating the narration exorbitantly, by producing within the book of the Second Author—the author's double—a stranger doubling whereby the teller of a tale becomes the figure telling the telling of the tale.[42] Cervantes actually appears to have Sancho Panza speak details of the novel *Don Quixote* in which he figures. Cervantes pretends that the scene of Don Quixote's encounter with the pseudo-Dulcinea is copied out of the text of Cide Hamete Benengeli, who does not say for certain whether the girls were mounted on fillies or young asses. Cervantes ventures the opinion "it is more credible that they were she-asses," a view with which Don Quixote finally agrees; he says at first, "I can see nothing but . . . three donkeys" but then concludes, "It seemed a she-ass to me." But for Sancho, right from the start, the beast in question is a nackney (or a cackney), and it is as this creature that Cervantes finally sends it trotting off across the field, quite as if he is now reading Sancho (who has a strong view of the identity of the animal), rather than Cide Hamete Benengeli and Don Quixote (who are not sure). The effect of this multiplication of perspectives, this virtual infinity of selves that read the selves that write, is that each must yield its authority to another, whose task is always to pronounce on its legitimacy. Such a multiplication of lawyers and judges cannot fail to engender consternation. Cervantes himself appears as the chronicler, the evil demiurge. His double narrative design has served not to seat authority and contain ambiguity but to disperse them additionally, with Sancho—the unseater, the carnivalesque uncrowner of authority par excellence—as his chosen instrument. But Sancho uncrowns Cervantes as well.

"The story is told," writes Geoffrey Waite, that Philip III peered out of the window in the Alcázar palace and, upon seeing below the then incredible sight of a man laughing, was heard to quip: 'Either the

---

42. *Don Quixote* is the story of its own recounting; according to Lukács, this shapes the form of the novel as such (*The Theory of the Novel*, trans. Anna Bostock [Cambridge, Mass.: MIT Press, 1977], p. 76).

man is mad, or he is reading *Don Quixote.*' "[43] Actually, it isn't necessary to make this choice, for if the man is reading *Don Quixote* well,
he will be as mad as Don Quixote. The work removes the distinction.
Don Quixote exists to make the reader mad—which is to say, to keep
the moment of consternation alive forever.

Not all readers of *Don Quixote*, of course, have been so inclined to
see its intricacy as consternating. Leo Spitzer takes what he calls
Cervantes' "linguistic perspectivism" all the way in the opposite direction, to arrive finally at Cervantes' "glorification of the artist."[44]
For Spitzer, the *artifex* is in effect a reflection of a God beyond mere
perspectivism. But this claim will seem dubious: a glorification of the
artist as consterator is all we are entitled to conclude, an enchanter
whose enchantments perplex.

Erich Auerbach, in *Mimesis*, acknowledges the character of *Don
Quixote* as enchantment—sunlit and pleasant; its "multiple, perspective, nonjudging, and even nonquestioning neutrality" is the mark of
an "unproblematic gaiety." Auerbach goes on to compare Cervantes'
approach with the

> neutral attitude which Gustave Flaubert strove so hard to attain and to
> which it is not unrelated. . . . Yet it is very different from it: Flaubert
> wanted to transform reality through style; transform it so that it would
> appear as God sees it, so that the divine order—insofar as it concerns
> the fragment of reality treated in a particular work—would perforce be
> incarnated in the author's tale. For Cervantes a good novel serves no
> other purpose than to afford refined recreation, *honesto entretenimien-
> to.*[45]

No one would dream of denying the difference between Cervantes
and Flaubert, but Cervantes' gaiety is not so uncritical and unproblematic that he could himself avoid getting lost in it—enchanter
but himself enchanted, enchained.

*   *   *

43. Geoffrey Waite, "Lenin in Las Meninas: An Essay in Historical-Materialist
Vision," *History and Theory: Studies in the Philosophy of History* 25, no. 3 (1986): 249–
50. The story returns to a citation from Léon Bonnat's preface to Aureliano de
Beruete, *Velázquez* [1898], trans. Hugh F. Poynter (London: Methuen, 1906), xxi.
44. Leo Spitzer, "Linguistic Perspectivism in the *Don Quijote*," in *Linguistics and
Literary History: Essays in Stylistics* (New York: Russell & Russell, 1962), p. 41.
45. Erich Auerbach, *Mimesis: The Representation of Reality in Western Literature,*
trans. Willard Trask (Princeton, N.J.: Princeton University Press, 1968), p. 357.

Erich Auerbach's view of Flaubert's project—to "transform reality through style . . . so that the divine order . . . would perforce be incarnated in the author's tale"—is a view with which Kafka might be said to have agreed when he gave the ending of *Sentimental Education* the scriptural validity of the fifth book of Moses (DII 196). Where are the signs of that divinity?

The final meeting in *Sentimental Education* between Frédéric and Madame Arnoux is unsettling through and through. In *Don Quixote* the disruption of the signifier *hacanea* occurs in speeches that frame the encounter between the lovers. In *Sentimental Education* the relation of word and meaning is disrupted throughout the lovers' meeting, which is framed with silence. The peak scene of consternation between Madame Arnoux and Frédéric produces Frédéric's silence and a sort of fatal reading silence following the last phrase "Et ce fut tout [And that was all]" (pp. 423, 416*).[46] The emptiness at the close repeats the blanks which, as Proust noted,[47] inform the three one-sentence paragraphs at the beginning of the episode:

> Il voyagea.
> Il connut la mélancholie des paquebots. . . .
> Il revint. [p. 419][48]

The blank at the close of the chapter is, however, a blank with a difference. If the first series marks *Frédéric*'s customary vacuousness and incoherence in pursuit of his desire, the second marks the disappearance of *Madame Arnoux* as a character in the novel and, more important, as the object of Frédéric's desire. In the course of the episode Frédéric actually emerges as a more and more realized figure. The movement by which he is detailed—inked in as an acting, desiring being—is crossed by a successive derealization of Madame Arnoux. By a precise use of signs she is whited out and then obliterated,

46. Gustave Flaubert, *L'education sentimentale,* ed. Edouard Maynial (Paris: Garnier, 1958). Page numbers cited in this text and notes refer to this edition; asterisked page numbers refer to the English translation: *Sentimental Education,* trans. Robert Baldick (Harmondsworth: Penguin, 1964).

47. Marcel Proust, "A propos du 'style' de Flaubert," *Nouvelle revue française,* January 1920.

48. "He travelled. He came to know the melancholy of the steamboat. . . . He returned" (p. 411*).

as if it were a matter of expunging a fantasy. Observe the imperson-
alizing nomination at the close. She has left Frédéric's room.

> Frédéric ouvrit sa fenêtre, *Madame Arnoux*, sur le trottoir, fit signe
> d'avancer à un fiacre qui passait. *Elle* monta dedans. La voiture
> disparut.
> Et *ce* fut tout. [p. 423; my italics][49]

Ce. What is this *ce?* Whose word is it? It is Frédéric's despair, and
the reader's.

The scene has begun with the blanks of Frédéric's fortieth year,
interrupted by Madame Arnoux's visit to his room. Thereupon they
walk together through the streets of Paris, speaking in the language of
romantic novels. When they return, Frédéric's glimpse of Madame
Arnoux's white hair strikes him "like a blow full in the chest" (p.
414*). He discharges his consternation in a spasm of tender speech,
then gets drunk on his compliments and believes what he says. The
sight of the tip of her boot "troubles" him. He embraces her, but she
pushes him off. He is again seized by wild desire and also revulsion
and then rejects her by turning away—an act she takes for delicacy.
They linger, she cuts off a lock of her white hair, and she leaves. "Et
ce fut tout."

In this agitated field I fix on two consternating moments: first,
Frédéric's sensation of a blow on the chest at the sight of Madame
Arnoux's white hair and his reaction, which is to speak in the rhetoric
of romance; next, his desire and revulsion following the sight of her
boot and the sense that she has come to offer herself. The feelings
enacted in these moments, however, are so deeply involved in rhetoric that one can grasp Frédéric's consternation only by understanding how his rhetoric functions to create, repress, and recreate desire.

Everything in this scene takes place in the unsettling mood produced by the confusion of the literal and metaphorical meanings of
words. At the outset of their meeting, as Madame Arnoux describes
her life in Brittany, she mentions her small house, where, she says, "I
go and sit . . . on a bench I call: 'le banc Frédéric'" (pp. 420, 413*).
This innocent metonymy (in which the name "Frédéric" appears to

---

49. "Frédéric opened his window. On the pavement Madame Arnoux beckoned to
a passing cab. She got in. The carriage diappeared. And that was all" (p. 416*).

represent the total experience of Madame Arnoux as she sits dreaming of her lover) looms as a bizarre metaphor in which the vehicle (Frédéric *as* bench) figures too large. Earlier, in Chapter Three, I cited Lacan's suggestive remark that "any conjunction of two signifiers would be equally sufficient to constitute a metaphor, except for the additional requirement of the greatest possible disparity of the images signified, needed for the production of the poetic spark, or in other words for there to be metaphoric creation."[50] Here, I am afraid, the point seems wrong. In Flaubert, the collision of disparate signified images stifles the poetic spark. Tenor is supposed to "devour" vehicle,[51] but the vehicle—or bench—proves undigestible.

On the other hand, if we have just now had a metonymy whose vehicle (the bench) turned deadly literal (in the sense of having a definite worldly reference), we soon after have, in a speech of Frédéric to Madame Arnoux, a literal word that turns infinitely metaphorical. It is the name "Marie," which has one and only one referent. "For me," says Frédéric, "your name contained all the delights of flesh and spirit, and I repeated it again and again, trying to kiss it with my lips. I imagined nothing beyond your name" (p. 414*).[52]

When this entire episode is enlarged to include earlier events in the novel, however, the notion of definite reference vanishes, so that it becomes impossible to distinguish literal from metaphorical meanings. Frédéric and Madame Arnoux are described as strolling through Paris. Although the streets are noisy, they walk undisturbed, as if "they had been walking together in the country, on a bed of dead leaves" (p. 413*).[53] These dead leaves refer the reader to Frédéric's early revery when, returning from his first meeting with Madame Arnoux, he observed, "She looked like the women in romantic novels" (p. 22*).[54] In such a mood, noting the hills beside the river, he

50. Jacques Lacan, "The Insistence of the Letter in the Unconscious," *Yale French Studies* 36/37 (October 1966): 125.
51. Maurice Merleau-Ponty, *Phenoménologie de la perception* (Paris: Gallimard, 1945), p. 213.
52. "Et les délices de la chair et de l'âme étaient contenues pour moi dans votre nom que je me répétais, en tâchant de le baiser sur mes lèvres. Je n'imaginais rien au delà" (p. 422).
53. "Comme ceux qui marchent ensemble dans la campagne, sur un lit de feuilles mortes" (pp. 420-21).
54. "Elle ressemblait aux femmes des livres romantiques" (p. 9).

has thought "what bliss it would be to climb up there beside her with his arm around her waist, listening to her voice and basking in the radiance of her eyes, while her dress swept the yellow leaves along the ground" (p. 21*).[55]

Years later, at their reunion, they come full novelistic circle. Because of this early fantasy of dry leaves, the simile at the close of the novel—"dead leaves"—loses all material reference and signals an at best very queer, only paper gain of true experience. The lovers' last walk, like the first walk with Madame Arnoux, which Frédéric fantasized, is composed of the leaves from novels (this one included). "Dead leaves" are thus leaves twice dead: when they were alive, they were already dead. The lovers walk on a bed of dead metaphors. This fact about style is interesting thematically, of course, since together they will go on speaking in such clichés; but the phrase is especially interesting as the signifier of another signifier within the novel. It is an internal citation of a figure ("yellow leaves") marked as itself returning to yet other novels. Hence, the figure at the close of this novel has a vast but only potential meaning, is itself neither literal nor metaphorical. This disconcerting fluidity of literal and metaphorical meaning signals a deeper, more pervasive uncertainty about the ceremony of reconciliation that Frédéric and Madame Arnoux enact.

Readers have traditionally been puzzled by the rhetoric that Frédéric and Madame Arnoux speak to each other, and this has led to contradictory accounts of the meaning of the scene. According to one reading, it amounts to a profanation, a degradation of their bond, because Frédéric flees his consternation by speaking specious Romantic language. According to another, the scene is a celebration of their bond, just because they do settle their consternation—even if bookishly—and are not destroyed by it. In instances of his dismay, let it be noted, Frédéric recovers "romantically." At the sight of Marie's white hair, he conceals his disappointment by speaking in the rhetoric of novels. Then, believing that she has come to offer herself and

---

55. The "thought" is in the *style indirect libre* (indirect free style): that is to say, it is not definitively attributed by the narrator to his character—Frédéric. It is stated as if it were a general proposition while actually showing Frédéric *believing* in the proposition as adequate to what he feels: "Quel bonheur de monter côte à côte, le bras autour de sa taille, pendant que sa robe balayerait les feuilles jaunies, en écoutant sa voix, sous le rayonnement de ses yeux!" (p. 7).

feeling desire, revulsion, and a sense of impending sacrilege, he acts out the behavior of a man (a certain kind of man) who has already made love: Frédéric "turned on his heel and started rolling a cigarette" (p. 415*).[56] This phrase also evokes the rhetoric of Romantic novels: it alludes to Rodolphe in *Madame Bovary*, who, after he has made love to Emma Bovary in the forest, puts a cigar in his mouth, then turns away to fix the bridle of his horse with a penknife.[57]

The "trouble" between Frédéric and Madame Arnoux is produced throughout the scene by a rhetoric suggestive of cheap novels—and yet this language is not steadily inferior to Flaubert's own lyric representation of intimate moments. It has the effect of producing an endless relaying, an echoing away of significance, as metaphors lose their way to an order of real things and finite meanings yet, as signs, fugitively evoke the contexts in which they have earlier appeared and which might never mean anything more than the words in a forgotten book, itself an echo.

But surely the scene is not all vanishing rhetoric; something is actually taking place, the acts of lovers who are experiencing real emotions. It is after all in an effort to master disturbing acts and feelings that they speak their phrases. And here the matter of Flaubert's rhetoric of acts—especially his choice of tense—is significant. The scene continues: "When they returned, Madame Arnoux took off her hat. The lamp . . . lit up her white hair. It was like a blow full in the chest" (p. 414*). These events are conveyed in the past historic (*rentrèrent, ôta, éclaira, fut*: p. 421), the tense of epic narration, the code of action; and it is to conceal his shock that Frédéric goes down on his knees and begins to murmur gorgeous platitudes in the imperfect, the tense of habitual behavior. As habituation calls attention to the consciousness registering this repetition—to an interposed consciousness—the imperfect tense produces the mood of inwardness. What triggers Frédéric's consternation in this scene, then, is an alarming image of Madame Arnoux coming at him from the

56. "Il tourna sur ses talons et se mit à faire une cigarette" (p. 423).

57. "Rodolphe, le cigar aux dents, raccommodait avec son canif une des deux brides cassée" (Gustave Flaubert, *Madame Bovary* [Paris: Aux Quais de Paris, 1958], p. 174; in English, *Madame Bovary*, ed. Paul de Man, trans. Elinor Aveling Marx and Paul de Man [New York: Norton, 1965], p. 116).

world. In response, Frédéric performs a balancing act to right the scene for his desire: he dyes her white hair purple by imagining her gloriously otherwise, in the imperfect.

The reader can sustain Frédéric's mood by reading the first sentence that follows his encomium as a reliable description of Madame Arnoux's feelings. "She rapturously accepted this adoration of the woman she had ceased to be [Elle acceptait avec ravissement ces adorations pour la femme qu'elle n'était plus]" (pp. 422, 414*). The sentence appears to further the coherence of the novel as a history. It indicates the real communication between the two lovers. Frédéric is startled by Madame Arnoux's abrupt action and, needing to dispel the shock, thinks better of her, whereupon his feelings pass back to her—a connection assured by the continuity of tense. The imperfect (of inwardness) through which Frédéric identifies his own feelings identifies those of Madame Arnoux. A text that in the imperfect bridges speaker and hearer appears to exemplify in principle the real continuity of inwardness and event—to enact the experience of persuasion.

This conclusion as to continuity, however, is overly optimistic. Only in a special and privative sense does the imperfect in the sentence about Madame Arnoux's feelings show solidarity with the preceding sentence, as we shall see.

According to one authority, Pierre Cogny, the coherence sustained by the imperfect of *acceptait* is only grammatical and anticipatory, dictated by the obligatory imperfect of the hypothetical *n'était plus*.[58] But the sentence is enigmatic in another way, being one of those sentences which, according to Roland Barthes, can be written but not read. The power of the passage depends on the effect of helpless immanence of the lovers within their world. But the feelings attributed to Madame Arnoux are not those that a living speaker could ever experience. Madame Arnoux cannot simultaneously experience rapture and the consciousness that she no longer exists as the being entitled to this rapture. Such a conjunction is possible only in a story that inserts directly into the consciousness of a rapturous feeling the undercutting presence-of-mind of another. Who then is finally feeling

58. Pierre Cogny, *L'education sentimentale de Flaubert: Le Monde en creux* (Paris: Larousse, 1975), p. 182.

rapture here; who is judging the ravishment as a delusion, and who is giving this account?[59]

If this sentence is not Madame Arnoux's, it can have been spoken for her by the author—but then it is too sneeringly brutal in punishing her for crude delusion. The indictment fits Frédéric better! In light of what follows, I read this presence-of-mind as Frédéric's. The *acceptais* in the imperfect merely extends into a new paragraph the field of the *style indirect libre* conveying Frédéric's desires, not the least of which is the desire to be master. The thought that his rhetoric is overpowering her intoxicates him. And in the following sentence he indeed rises "drunkenly" to consciousness of his mastery; it appears that only Frédéric's consciousness in the *style indirect libre* fabricates the continuity of the lovers' minds.[60]

And so, therefore, everything in this scene that follows on this moment can have been composed in the *style indirect libre* as a record of events *experienced by Frédéric*. The distinction between what can be done and what can only be said is in this way erased. It becomes impossible to distinguish the time of public action conveyed by the imperfect from the temporality of Frédéric's consciousness. Even more drastically, it becomes impossible to distinguish the sphere of epic objectivity articulated by the past historic from that of inner

59. I do not expect every reader to agree that Madame Arnoux cannot at the same time feel rapture and perceive that Frederic's adoration is intended for the woman she no longer is. It can be argued, as indeed Charles Bernheimer has done in a letter to me, March 21, 1986, that the sentence has eminent psychological plausibility. According to his reading, it is not necessary to assume in this sentence the presence of a second consciousness; rather, Madame Arnoux "knows on one level that her present appearance undercuts the romance of the past, and her ecstasy is produced precisely in a movement . . . away from the present moment. 'Her ecstasy' and 'no longer being' do not undercut each other, but the one explains the other. Ecstasy is denial of the body so as to recreate the pleasures in rhetoric." As interesting as this objection is, I find it quite inconsistent with the knowledge we obtain through Frédéric that Madame Arnoux has come to offer herself. By what means does she suppose the gift will prove acceptable—by virtue of the charm she possesses as the woman she formerly was?

60. Thinking of Frédéric as narrator invites one to consider him as a persona of the author. In this case the interpenetration is interesting and vivid. We read that Frédéric, growing drunk on his compliments, begins to believe what he is saying. This sentence, which represents the peak point of Frédéric's labor to escape his consternation, is an escape stage-managed by the author at the same time that it consternatingly indicts the author. The charge that Frédéric assumes mastery from credulousness induced by the toxin of rhetoric poisons the author, who is also drunk on words.

consciousness articulated by the imperfect.[61] For instance, the touch of the lovers' hands in the past historic brings about the first breakup of the imperfect; with the verb *se serrèrent* ("clasped") the text passes into the past historic. It would be tempting to read the disruption of the tense of inwardness as the overcoming of repression, the emergence of an active sexuality, and the turn to the epic world. But this moment is followed (in the same sentence) by a return of the imperfect, as the point of Madame Arnoux's boot is seen protruding from under her dress.

One could try to naturalize this perturbation as suggesting the conflict between Frédéric's perception of real acts and his continued effort to will them into a form shaped by erotic desire. But this—the critic's phantasm—is without surety. For there is no verb in any tense which could not stand for Frédéric's imaginary desire, no epic world that is assuredly anything more than an expression of Frédéric's imagination of the epic. At no point, it seems, has Frédéric definitively stopped writing the novel which, as we saw earlier in this novel, he had "started writing . . . [and in which] the hero was himself, the heroine Madame Arnoux" (p. 36*).[62] Nothing in the novel escapes the potential status of Frédéric's novelistic—and at moments dramatistic—report of the world; thinking of Arnoux's dying by an accidental gunshot wound, Frédéric sees a succession of pictures of domestic happiness, "brooding over this idea like a dramatist writing a play" (p. 314*). In earlier conversation with Madame Arnoux, Fré-

61. Two eminent examples of this confusion frame this speech. The first precedes it: "He regretted nothing [Il ne regretta rien]" (pp. 414*, 421); the second concludes the chapter: "And that was all [Et ce fut tout]" (pp. 416*, 423). There are no earlier examples in the novel of sentences in the past historic obviously written in the *style indirect libre*. This helps confirm the claim that in this chapter Flaubert chooses to annihilate the distinction between the epic order of the past historic and the internalizing order of the imperfect, relaying the perspective of effaced distinction back onto the previous chapters.

62. "Il se mit à écrire un roman. . . . Le héros, c'était lui-même; l'héroïne, Mme Arnoux" (p. 24). The initial setting of this novel is, to be sure, Venice; its working title is "Sylvio, the Fisherman's Son"; the heroine is Antonia; and the hero is presumably eponymous. Frédéric, we learn, stopped working on it, discouraged by "the echoes from other writers which he noticed in his novel [les réminiscences trop nombreuses dont il s'aperçut le découragèrent]" (pp. 36*, 25). Flaubert, of course, unlike Frédéric, never dropped *Sentimental Education*. He did not allow himself to be discouraged by the echoes in his novel . . . of Frédéric's own. Indeed, he took heart and profit from them, composing his novel precisely from their interference.

déric "extolled the great lovers of literature" before "beginning to be carried away by his own eloquence" (p. 201*). Whose consciousness does the last sentence belong to? Is it a part of Frédéric's panegyric to the great lovers of literature that they too were carried away by their own eloquence, and is the point that Frédéric now in his own view has become one of these lovers by virtue of his ability to be carried away by his own eloquence? The last sentence is novelistic, but who is thinking it? And because here as elsewhere Frédéric's consciousness is wholly in the service of his desire, everything reported by him responds to desire; everything could have the character of a phantasm. "Et ce fut tout." What then is this *ce?*

The *ce* refers to what has happened during the scene but also to what has not happened; it refers, by implication, to the education of Frédéric's desire as a matter of what has happened and what has failed to happen throughout the novel. But the dissolution of markers distinguishing the order of event from fantasy jeopardizes the distinction between Frédéric's merely phantasmal erotic life (linked with the imperfect) and a more or less active sexuality (linked with the past historic). The dissolution of all boundaries between inside and outside orders, the confounding of real and imaginary voices and acts, results in vague and dreamy inanition, taking on as it were the quality that Frédéric's highest stimulation takes. In this scene desire and revulsion, like the fear of incest, crown with a kind of orgasm of inaction the peak promise of sexual longing. With the gesture of lighting a cigarette, Frédéric assumes the after-signs of a venting of desire through the overwhelming consciousness of its actual impossibility. His act culminates a misfiring of the culmination which in this novel is said to be found only . . . in novels.

The celebration of blankness as the height of sexual excitement will go on to trigger the happy memory of the close of the novel—the memory of the bliss of impotence which overcame the young Frédéric at the bordello in Nogent. But even in noting this continuum, the reader is uncertain of the extent to which the novel remembers Frédéric's inaction at the brothel to be itself the product only of Frédéric's imaginative desire for maintaining purity. His peak perception of the impossibility of orgasm was perhaps only a wish-dream.

But surely something happens by the close of this scene, indeed happens brutally and thus serves to discriminate between action and fantasy: it is Madame Arnoux's gesture of cutting off with scissors a lock of her white hair. Following as it does Frédéric's recognition of the incest taboo, it has led commentators to read this moment as a plain exhibit of the infliction of Oedipal traumas. Much the most tactful commentator in this vein, Charles Bernheimer, brings together psychoanalytic experience and rhetoric under the head of the fetishism of clichés. The rhetorical code of the lovers, he writes, is a popularized version of the literary ideal of Platonic love:

> [This] allows Frédéric to reconstitute Madame Arnoux as a whole being, but one that is entirely abstract, an artificial creature of ready-made phrases. Here we are reminded of the etymology of the word "fetish" from the Latin *factitus*, made by art, which developed in Portuguese and Spanish into words designating precisely the work of imitation through signs. Frédéric does still refer to a more explicitly bodily fetish when, observing the point of Marie's *bottine* protruding a little from under her dress, he declares, "the sight of your foot disturbs me." . . . But by the very act of articulating his disturbance, Frédéric removes it from the silent dimension of subjective feeling and makes it part of a shared code of sublimating discourse. The code is a defense against the reality of perception: the shocking sight of Marie's white hair, and behind that, of the mother's castration.[63]

By brutally cutting off a lock of white hair, Madame Arnoux destroys the possibility of joining herself and the fetish, which is the condition of Frédéric's desire for her.

This reading is actually too optimistic. It subdivides the world of the novel into the "silent dimension of subjective feeling" and the "code of discourse": that is, Romantic rhetoric. Romantic rhetoric, however, constitutes more than one pole of a binary opposition: it triangulates this polarity, in the sense that no verbal representation in the novel escapes such rhetoric, and this in the precise sense that no sentence in the novel is proof against espousal by Flaubert in the name of Frédéric; nothing is proof, that is, against the operation of the *style indirect libre* that makes every description a report of Frédéric's consciousness of the described thing. No description of acts escapes contamination by the Romantic rhetoric of Frédéric's "subjectivity," and so even his "silent subjectivity" is a Romantic idea. There can be no

63. Charles Bernheimer, *Flaubert and Kafka: Studies in Psychopoetic Structure* (New Haven, Conn.: Yale University Press, 1982), p. 109.

passing out of the order of subjective silence into the order of the Romantic code, since as a state of mind given within this novel, subjective silence is already involved in the Romantic code. That is to say, it is represented through a narrative itself indefinitely mingled with Frédéric's own Romantic consciousness.

This consciousness, vast and anonymous, is the one true subject of the novel, the dreary agitated dream of life, correlative of "et ce fut tout."[64] This *ce,* this "that," takes up without distinction the lives of Frédéric and Madame Arnoux, the world of this book, the world. As the unconsummated union of prostration and flight, "that" *is* consternation.

Critics could believe that they had formulated an understanding of this scene in a language faithful to it. I have described how Frédéric's language, through the *style indirect libre,* functions not only to articulate the facts of desire but to create desire, even as it fades into silence. Frédéric completes his own language with silence—a mark, perhaps, of the awareness that his longing is only the rhetorical construction of desire, its facsimile. The critic's authoritative analysis will be true, itself least the product of rhetoric only, after it too has been silenced and banished into the past historic of someone else's narrative, when this essay figures as an event in someone else's story. And yet Flaubert reminds us that in all the tenses of narration, language can serve the rhetorical construction of desire, and we cannot say that even an imagined sobriety of the future will not itself be a product of another's rhetoric, of another's desire. This is a consternating state of affairs.

* * *

To survive after Flaubert, fiction could choose to display a violence of dramatic effects, woo a definiteness of acts, so as to escape a dreadful authorial freedom, a space of writing prone to the evasions of irony and the style of free indirect speech. In Kafka's story "The Judgment," free indirect speech continues as the main narrative device, but it also falls decisively away at the moment of violence, when an independent voice speaks from beyond the grave of the

64. "Tired out, full of contradictory desires, and no longer knowing what he wanted, he felt an infinite melancholy, a longing to die" (p. 209*).

figure who has maintained this perspective. Everything, however, including this voice, is unsettled in a particularly violent mode of the way in which the lovers' scene in Flaubert was unsettled: by a destabilization of metaphor.

In "The Judgment" Kafka radically metamorphoses metaphor. To read the story is to be caught in a whirligig of metaphor. The story consists of two parts and a brief coda or ejaculation, the orgasmic nature of which Kafka said he literally had in mind as he concluded the piece. The first part is about a son writing a letter on the subject of his engagement to a friend who lives in Russia; the second is a wild discourse between son and father, culminating in the father's sentencing his son to death. The son obeys. The coda reads, "At this moment an unending stream of traffic [or act of sexual intercourse] was just going over the bridge [In diesem Augenblick ging über die Brücke ein geradezu unendlicher Verkehr]" (S 88; E 68). All parts of the story involve metaphor; most important is the way in which Georg Bendemann and his father read metaphor and actually suit their actions to metaphors and metaphorical relations.

"The Judgment" is one of the few stories that Kafka attempted to explain, as follows:

> The friend is the link between father and son, he is their strongest common bond. Sitting alone at his window, Georg rummages voluptuously in this consciousness of what they have in common, believes he has his father within him and would be at peace with everything if it were not for a fleeting, sad thoughtfulness. In the course of the story the father . . . uses the common bond of the friend to set himself up as Georg's antagonist. . . . Georg is left with nothing. [DI 278]

The analysis is stated in a sort of structuralist idiom and prompts the translation of this interpersonal relation into a figure, into metaphor. The friend is that body of predicates "shared" by father and son, by tenor and vehicle; he enables the metaphor, first of father *as* son, then of son *as* father. Importantly, the story ends with the splitting apart of the metaphor: the father draws into himself all those qualities which when possessed by Georg were analogues of qualities of the father. Georg is reduced to the literal being of an incomparable self, a surd; like Gregor Samsa in *The Metamorphosis*, he is now as good as dead. The father, meanwhile, becomes at once himself and the figure of himself: he is his own metaphor, a thoroughly figurative being.

This tropic translation sounds farfetched but will perhaps sound less so if we read Kafka's second comment on the story. He writes to Felice Bauer:

> The story is full of abstractions, though they are not admitted. The friend is hardly a real person, perhaps he is more that which the father and Georg have in common. The story is perhaps a journey around father and son, and the changing figure of the friend is perhaps the perspectival change of the relations between father and son. [LF 267]

The "changing figure of the friend" is an index of the increasingly aberrant transfer of qualities from the son to the father, the outcome of which is to reify (literalize) the son and transfigure (metaphorize) the father. The father pronounces sentence as a godlike figure of authority. The son, reduced to unconscious being, is "driven" out of the room by the sole force of the father's sentence. The son has been emptied of all the human traits that he and his father have shared; those traits have gone over to the father, who in this way redoubles his being, has for an instant a quite literally superhuman, autonomous power as a metaphor which—normally for Kafka dependent on the world of extrinsic reference, the materiality of the vehicle—here draws that world wholly into itself.[65] The growing reification or literalization of the son and the growing transfiguration or meta-

65. The title of the story stuggests that the precise meaning of the friend, the body of attributes binding father and son, is judgment. And indeed the story produces at key junctures three different conceptions of judgment. At the outset the son, who thinks that he has the friend (of his father) entirely within himself, produces judgments in the neutral, epistemological sense of *Urteile* as descriptive propositions. The preferred form of his mastery is cognitive. The character of the opening encounter between father and son is defined by the father as another mode of judgment: as a taking of mutual counsel, as reciprocal interpretation. Once the encounter shifts into its wild adversary key and the son's consternation at the growing strength of his father increases, judgment turns into a verdict, a death sentence. The friend, the change of perspective on the relation between father and son, means the increasing investment of judgment with interpersonal performative force. This change is, as I have suggested, enacted as a semiotic process, as the theoretical drama of the increasing pull of tenor (father) upon vehicle (son) until meaning has wholly ingested its own metaphorical sign, which then leads a straitened existence within the living figure. See Chapter Four, pp. 95–97.

phorization of the father, empowering him absolutely, occurs in definite stages of their rhetorical drama. To the father's every figurative statement Georg responds with a crude literalizing, as if this could impose powerful constraints all in his favor on the necessarily figurative language of dialogue. Georg aims to deny his father the power to speak figuratively and to interpret his own speech through the figurative stock of language.[66] The path to mastery of the "human figure"—the story says—is to interpret the world by assuming all the world's perspectives. It is to put on the strength of understanding in the rapidity, coherence, and accuracy of metaphorical appropriation. This is the way to the fullest reproduction of the Real.[67]

The dialogue between Georg and his father is almost entirely a matter of rhetoric aimed antagonistically to elicit a reading from the other. To the extent that reading fiction constitutively involves decisions as to literal and metaphorical meanings, their dialogue amounts to a fiction of reading. More than *Don Quixote* or *Sentimental Education*, Kafka's story thematizes as well as inspires readerly consternation.

In "The Judgment" we are alerted to the struggle of wills by the son's effort to literalize his father's language, as if this were the way to reify, seize, and possess him. Theirs is the wild contest for the sole power to make metaphors. Says the father: "I've established a fine connection with your friend, and I have your customers here in my pocket." Thinks Georg, literalizing, "He has pockets even in his

66. "The metaphorical meaning must be defined not as an aspect of the syntactical-semantic unit of the sentence but rather as the aspect of an *utterance*. Only with an utterance do we have a communicative situation in which it can be decided whether an expression is meant metaphorically or not" (Kurz, *Metapher*, p. 13). Here Kurz defines a fundamental principle of the interactional theory of metaphor. In this light we can see that Kafka dramatizes this model in the privative mode of a refusal to admit metaphorical meaning.

67. There is, contrary to the received view, a good deal of this Hegelianism in Kafka, though "The Judgment" may be only a noble parody of the process. This appropriative Kafka is bent on the potency of the philosopher of *The Phenomenology of Mind* who has drawn into himself all his worldly semblances. Cf. the posthumously published fragment, discussed in Chapter Five and again in Chapter Six, on the recognition of one's "eternity." It is important to remember, meanwhile, that this long aphorism proceeds to put itself into question. Nonetheless, Kafka's aphorisms, in suspending terms, also proceed quite literally to "hang" their developed variations at a higher place on the whole helix of interpretative possibilities to which they give rise.

shirt!" and that with this comment "he [Georg] could make him [the father] an impossible figure for all the world" (S 16). At this moment Georg's literalizing project will be an open secret less to the English than to the German reader, who immediately picks up the unstressed metaphor: in German "the shirt without pockets" is a funeral shroud. Georg's remark is cruelly witty in a double register: he literalizes the pocket of "in my pocket" and the shirt of "the shirt without pockets." To this the father responds: "How you amused me today, coming to ask me if you should tell your friend about your engagement. . . . He knows everything a hundred times better than you do yourself." "Ten thousand times!" says Georg, taking the numerical point literally, so as "to make fun of his father, but in his very mouth the words turned into deadly earnest" (S 87).

Just a little before this scene, the struggle turned on a word, which like the "cackney" or "nackney" of Sancho Panza, is importantly self-reflexive. In "The Judgment" this is the act of "covering [zudecken] with a blanket." The father asks Georg twice: "Am I well covered up [bin ich gut zugedeckt]?" "Don't worry," says Georg, "you're well covered up." "No," cries the father, "you wanted to cover me up, I know, my young sprig, but I'm far from being covered up yet" (S 84; E 63). And here he seems to mean "I'm not dead and buried yet." The father is reading the word with elaborate figurative stress—which can and should include the secondary self-reflexive meanings of zudecken as "to cover" a subject (so thoroughly as to bury it), "to heap meanings of one sort or another on someone," as "to cover with reproaches," and finally, "to fit words to a meaning" with the negative implication of covering it up.[68] The father exults to think that Georg

68. Grimm illustrates the word zudecken with the phrase "a thought, a meaning, a truth is covered up (or closed off) by words [ein Gedanke, ein Sinn, eine Wahrheit wird durch Worte zugedeckt]" and further cites a phrase from Goethe: "the various kinds of interpretation . . . which are applied to the text, which are attributed, imputed or 'stuck on' to the text, with which it could be covered up (or closed off) [die verschiedenen Auslegungsarten . . . die man auf den Text anwenden, die man dem Text unterschieben, mit denen man ihn zudecken konnte]" (Deutsches Wörterbuch von Jacob Grimm und Wilhelm Grimm [Leipzig: Hirzil, 1954], 16:319). Gerhard Kurz has also noted the self-reflexive hermeneutic implications of the word zudecken as part of a discussion of overt and covert meanings in Kafka. "The texts themselves," he writes, "contain turns of phrase which provoke an allegorical reading, for example, 'That could obviously be meant only in a spiritual sense,' in 'The Great Wall of China' [GW 156]; 'The Hunger Artist' is a 'suffering martyr . . . although in quite another sense'

imagines he has identified him, read him exhaustively. To do so in this story means to take the figure literally; and here where the word *zudecken* has, to speak with Gilbert Ryle, the higher-order function of denoting reflexively the intention of the speaker, to take the figure literally means to make someone acquiesce in a literal reading of himself.[69] For whoever reads the metaphor literally, condemns it to the fatal solitude of a thing; and as whoever reads the metaphor literally, kills it, so also whoever as a metaphor is read literally, dies.

Georg makes the fatal mistake of attempting to read his father as a feeble, toothless old thing in soiled underwear. His "devilishness" is to refuse to the father a necessarily metaphorical existence, for the father cannot be defined as an assemblage (Heidegger's *Gestell*) of literal characteristics—the features of his old body. Georg, the literalist, is appropriately disarmed when the father issues him a death sentence: where it would serve him to let his father's language assume an only figurative resonance, he cannot; he is driven to his death by drowning, moist on his own petard. Interestingly, and inevitably, the father appears to die in the act of executing his son. He himself is executed by his fatal attraction to essence, to complete self-possession. Of course, as a father, he cannot exist without a son—just as, as an allegorical figure for metaphor, he cannot exist without a worldly vehicle. Kafka's phrase for essence is "independent activity ruled by its own law" (DII 201); this, he says plainly, is the condition not of metaphor but rather of the other term on which it always depends— the world. For this father, the son is his world. In compelling his son to read the son's own being literally, he reifies the other, annihilates the other save as an opaque sign; himself becomes pure figure, and— as in Kafka's parable on figures—"wins . . . but alas only figuratively" (PP 11). In reality, he loses. No more than he, readers cannot take a literal meaning from the story, not even a literal meaning about metaphor, without condemning the story, and themselves, to death.

[S 271]; there are 'various possibilities of interpretation' in 'The Problem of Our Laws' [S 437]; truths that are covered up [*zugedeckt*] and truths that are opened up [*aufgedeckt*], as the metaphorical play of 'cover up' [*zudecken*] and 'open up' [*aufdecken*] in 'The Judgment' suggests" (*Traum-Schrecken: Kafkas literarische Existenzanalyse* [Stuttgart: Metzler, 1980], p. 133).

69. Gilbert Ryle, *The Concept of Mind* (Chicago: University of Chicago Press, 1984), pp. 195–98.

Kafka appears to have inscribed fully into the consternation of characters that traumatic destabilization of reading—especially as it involves the interference of the literal and figurative meanings of metaphor—which seemed in Cervantes or Flaubert a narrative intrusion.

* * *

We have looked, then, at ways in which consternation passes over from scenes of interpersonal collision in prose fiction into the order of reading. The troubled encounter of fictive characters is doubled, complicated—its energy amplified—in the reader's consternation as reader. The anthropological moment in literature unrepresses reading. Anthropology might be said to be governed by conservative strategies for resisting the awareness that the other person is the Other of the Same, in the sense that it is the unconscious, the repressed Same of everyday discourse. In literary consternation naive readers are exposed. They are exposed to the fact of the merely contrived security of their ordinary understanding of linguistic figures.[70] Through literature they are reacquainted with the social force that incarcerates tropes in the prison library in which resigned readers of the everyday live out their sentence.

70. What happens in the genesis of monstrosity is a recalibration of the metaphorical possibilities of the literal. The moment is anthropological in the sense that it forecasts the constitution of each and every other human type. Nothing human is alien to me in the precise sense that I contain in the suppressed field of meaning and vision within metaphor (this occlusion produced by social constraint) every other human possibility. The unconscious is the discourse of the Other, in the strict sense of the unrealized possibilities of metaphor.

Chapter Eight

The Curtain Half Drawn: Prereading in Flaubert and Kafka

Finding is nothing. The difficulty is in acquiring what has been found.

PAUL VALÉRY, *The Evening with Monsieur Teste*

Trouve avant de chercher.

BASHO

Simply as readers, we are haunted by the ghost of what we have already read. We do not enter even once into the same river of signs, and sometimes a book grows turbulent from the confluence of ghosts. We could get lost in the disturbance when memories of what we have read usurp what we want to read for the first time.[1]

1. Here is Milan Kundera's account of a comparable phenomenon: "The bowler hat was a motif in the musical composition that was Sabina's life. It returned again and again, each time with a different meaning, and all the meanings flowed through the bowler hat like water through a riverbed. I might call it Heraclitus' ('You can't step twice into the same river') riverbed: the bowler hat was a bed through which each time Sabina saw another river flow, another *semantic river*: each time the same object would give rise to a new meaning, though all former meanings would resonate (like an echo, like a parade of echoes) together with the new one. Each new experience would resound, each time enriching the harmony." The harmony reappears as "the semantic susurrus of the river flowing through [the lovers]" (*The Unbearable Lightness of Being* [New York: Harper & Row, 1984], p. 88). This invocation of a harmony of ghostly and textual meaning gives rise to the suspicion that it is heard by the lovers or told by the narrator in bad faith.

This phenomenon, which I call prereading, heightens the flux of spectral associations accompanying every sentence that seems to offer only itself to be read. In prereading, we are so taken up with remembering passages newly invoked that the result may be a single impression—the sense that we never read for a first time. Such an experience of possession could make readers despair of reading, but despair is only optional. The phenomenon of prereading also creates a place for the new as what has already happened without our knowing that it has happened. Indeed, this could be a particular aim of the *novel*: to alert us explicitly and for the first time to the truth of prereading—displacing but not destroying the acquisition of knowledge from the future into an eternal present perfect: Become, as readers, what you have already read.

It can seem the goal of novelists to plot prereading in ever more refined and telling ways. Flaubert and Kafka are two who manipulate the time of reading with cunning and design. What they finally require is the understanding "You will not be able to read this novel for a first time." But prereading, for them, is also an opportunity for delaying the goal of acquisition.[2] They introduce into the turbulence of memories another turbulence—an anxious impression of something forgotten—so that, before we can say, "I already know what this is about," they make us say, "I have forgotten what."[3] In their novels Flaubert and Kafka so arrange the process of acquiring the preread that only a special vigilance will reveal the way it works. But in thus revealing by concealing prereading, they only make us marvel, after we have discovered it, at its universal operation.

2. *L'Education sentimentale* explicitly poses riddles throughout—some of which are solved and some of which remain unsolved. This leads Joelle Gleize to speak of the novel's "burlesque parody of delayed explanation" ("Le Défaut de ligne droit," *Littérature* 15 [1974]: 80). Similarly, Ruth V. Gross points out, in connection with Kafka's story "An Everyday Confusion," that a great many of Kafka's texts "toy with the reader's hermeneutic anticipations, allowing the hermeneutic code to function . . . in a particularly negative fashion." This code is braided with an unexpectedly rich "referential code," which Gross defines (following Roland Barthes) as consisting of "the already-written" and the "already-thought" ("Rich Text/Poor Text: A Kafkan Confusion," *PMLA* 95 [March 1980], 168-69).

3. Or, before we can say, "I already possess what is essential to make this scene work," they make us say, "I cannot find it." Valéry wrote, "A work of art should always teach us that we had not seen what we see" ("Introduction to the Method of Leonardo da Vinci," in *Paul Valéry: An Anthology*, ed. James Lawler [Princeton, N.J.: Princeton University Press, 1977], p. 50). Flaubert and Kafka play with this point and then reverse it. They teach us that we never see for a first time.

The penultimate scene of *Sentimental Education*—the visit of Madame Arnoux to Frédéric's room, their last encounter—illustrates how Flaubert deploys prereading.

> He was alone in his study when a woman came in. . . . In the twilight he could see nothing but her eyes under the black lace veil which masked her face.
> After placing *a little red velvet wallet* on the edge of the mantelpiece, she sat down. The two of them sat there, unable to speak [p. 412*; my italics]⁴

I shall be concentrating on this little red velvet wallet—on its past and also its projections into the future of this scene.

Frédéric breaks the silence by asking Madame Arnoux about her husband. Marie Arnoux's answer is immediately to speak about money. After leaving Paris she and her husband had settled in the depths of Brittany, where they could live cheaply and pay off their debts. Frédéric recalls the financial disaster that had overtaken them, and this reminds her of the reason for her visit. "Pointing to the little red wallet, which was covered with golden palms, she said, 'I embroidered that specially for you. It contains the money for which the land at Belleville was supposed to be the security'"(p. 412*).⁵

Thereupon, Madame Arnoux, after describing her house,

> started looking with greedy eyes at the furniture, the ornaments, and the pictures, in order to fix them in her memory. The portrait of the Marshal was half hidden by a curtain. But the golds and whites, standing out in the midst of the shadows, attracted her attention.
> "I know that woman, don't I?"
> "No, you can't!" said Frédéric. "It's an old Italian painting." [p. 413*]

This moment is broken off by the narrator, who speaks for Madame Arnoux in indirect discourse the sentence that Kafka treasured among all the sentences of Flaubert he knew: "Elle avoua qu'elle désirait faire

---

4. The French text used in this chapter is Gustave Flaubert, *L'education sentimentale*, ed. Edouard Maynial (Paris: Garnier, 1958), cited hereafter by page number; the English text, cited by asterisked page numbers, is *Sentimental Education*, trans. Robert Baldick (Harmondsworth: Penguin, 1964).

5. The land at Belleville refers to a farm that Frederic had sold, then lending the money to Monsieur Arnoux in an attempt to bail him out of trouble.

un tour à son bras, dans les rues [She confessed that she would like to go for a stroll through the streets on his arm]" (pp. 420, 413*).[6]

I call attention to the repetition and also to the intensification of the red velvet wallet as "the little red wallet, which was covered with golden palms." The "golden" palms might by themselves point ahead to the figure of the kept woman Rosanette Bron, called "the Marshal"—who can be bought for gold, whose name conjures a uniform with gold trim, and who in at least one striking scene has been linked with gold, especially by contrast with Madame Arnoux. During the wild night at the Alhambra, dancing in a whirl, the Marshal "nearly caught Frédéric with the tip of her golden spurs" (p. 134*). Thereafter, in bed, Frédéric hallucinated "two big dark eyes" before dreaming that "he was harnessed side by side with Arnoux in the shafts of a cab, and the Marshal, sitting astride him, was tearing his belly open with her golden spurs" (p. 134*). The connection is made explicit when Madame Arnoux's big, dark eyes catch sight of the Marshal's portrait half hidden by a curtain. "The golds and the whites" attract her attention and lead her to believe that she recognizes the subject. Frédéric fobs her off, but his denial (*Verneinung*)— that "it's an old Italian painting"—only confirms its identity. The reader remembers that Pellerin, the painter of the portrait, had chosen to paint Rosanette in the style of "a Titian, which would be set off with touches in the style of Veronese" (p. 154*).

---

6. "What a sentence!" wrote Kafka to his fiancée Felice Bauer, "What a construction!" (LF 157). Kafka so much admired Flaubert and especially *Sentimental Education* that in a childhood fantasy, which he described to Felice, he "dreamt of reading aloud to a large crowded hall (though equipped with somewhat greater strength of heart, voice and intellect than I had at the time) the whole of *Sentimental Education* at one sitting, for as many days and nights as it required, in French of course (oh dear, my accent!), and making the walls reverberate" (LF 86). This fantasy marks a rare and auspicious event in literary history. A writer (Flaubert) whom another writer (Kafka) consciously and explicitly admires actually supplies the fullest source of illumination of the latter's own literary practice. It is not, avowedly, an affair of imitation. "The hollow which the work of genius has burned into our surroundings is a good place into which to put one's little light. Therefore the inspiration that emanates from genius, the universal inspiration that doesn't only drive one to imitation" (DI 173). Kafka's main debt to Flaubert was for the narrative practice of the so-called *style indirect libre* (indirect free style). For a comprehensive treatment of the Flaubert-Kafka nexus, see Charles Bernheimer's *Flaubert and Kafka: Studies in Psychopoetic Structure* (New Haven, Conn.: Yale University Press, 1982); and also *Der junge Kafka*, ed. Gerhard Kurz (Frankfurt am Main: Suhrkamp, 1984).

It is notable that in two places in this passage Madame Arnoux herself prereads. Her plain purpose is to fix things in memory as if there were no previous memories of them, to make of this moment of reading the pure occasion of personal experience. But while meaning to fix the new for future remembering,[7] she is quickly arrested by an object already dimly remembered. A scene projected as the birth of the new becomes crucially a scene awakening ghosts of the past.

At this moment Madame Arnoux incorporates the figure of the reader of this novel. Flaubert stages the experience of prereading through her as the reader's alter ego, one who here only surmises that she has previously seen the subject of the painting. The reader, on the other hand, remembers exactly whose painting she fails to see. The consciousness of prereading is heightened as if for the feat of recollection that he or she will now be required to perform, for there is more historical irony in motion here than meets the eye put off from penetrating the scene by a half-drawn curtain. The curtain half conceals more than Pellerin's painting of Rosanette; it veils a prehistory of scrupulously incised signs, masking a revelation unspeakably (unseeably) harmful to Madame Arnoux, to Frédéric, and perhaps to the reader.[8] Frédéric's impulse to draw the curtain is prompted by horror.

The scene represents a virtual but uncompleted junction between Madame Arnoux and the Marshal, whose portrait she is in danger of seeing. Throughout the novel Madame Arnoux and the Marshal continually approach each in the imagination of the characters: they cohabit in the experience of Monsieur Arnoux, Frédéric, and, of course, each other. On two brief occasions they see each other face to face, and Frédéric sees them see each other: once in Arnoux's shop, toward the close of the novel; and once or possibly several times on

7. The temporality of this mental impulse informs the entire conversation that follows between Frédéric and Madame Arnoux. The verbal tense equivalent of this movement is the future perfect, which at one point surfaces explicitly and with particular force. After Frédéric has praised her for what she had made him feel in the past, Madame Arnoux says, "We shall have been well loved [Nous nous serons bien aimés]" (p. 421, mistranslated on p. 413* as "We have loved each other well"). With this she tips her hand—the "hand" of a type of perception that intends to become memory as swiftly as it can. It is the signature of their entire meeting, and here we see it signed at the outset.

8. I.e., if we did not hide from it in the knowledge that the scene contributes to a science (poetics) in which it is important to instantiate prereading.

the Champ de Mars. Frédéric has taken Rosanette to the races. "A hundred yards away, a lady appeared in a victoria. She leant out of the window, then drew back quickly; this happened several times, but Frédéric could not make out her face. A suspicion took hold of him: it seemed to him that it was Madame Arnoux. But that was impossible! Why should she have come?" (p. 206*) And then a little later, out of nowhere,

> the victoria reappeared; it was Madame Arnoux. She turned extraordinarily pale.
> "Give me some champagne!" said Rosanette.
> And, raising her glass . . . , she shouted:
> "Hi there! Here's a health to decent women, and my protector's wife!"
> There were roars of laughter all round her; the victoria disappeared. [Pp. 208-9*]

In the first scene discussed, Frédéric's dismay is plain in the irritated defensiveness of his language. In the second, in which the full reality of the horror is at hand, a muteness or emptiness, an effacement of Frédéric as receptor or second narrator, enacts his aversion. This mode of aversion again overwhelms the report of the second and final meeting of the two women. Frédéric and Madame Arnoux have once again met after their broken rendezvous.

> "What torments I have suffered! Don't you understand?" . . .
> A passionate sob shook her body. Her arms opened; and, standing up, they clasped each other in a long kiss.
> The floor creaked. A woman was beside them, Rosanette. Madame Arnoux had recognized her, and gazed at her with staring eyes, full of surprise and indignation. At last Rosanette said: . . .
> "So you're here, are you, darling?"
> This familiarity, in her presence, made Madame Arnoux blush, like a slap in the face. . . .
> Then the Marshal, who was looking idly round the room, said calmly:
> "Shall we go home? I've a cab outside."
> He pretended not to hear.
> "Come along, let's go!"
> "Why, yes!" said Madame Arnoux. "Now's your chance! Go! Go!"
> They went out. She leant over the banisters to have a last look at them; and a shrill, piercing laugh came down to them from the top of

the staircase. Frédéric pushed Rosanette into the cab, sat down opposite her, and did not utter a single word all the way home. [Pp. 353–55*]

These scenes are charged with a kind of horror for Frédéric, because in his imagination Madame Arnoux and Rosanette are rivals. But the horror is not intense; it is mitigated into a form of embarrassment, because while these scenes jeopardize Frédéric's possession of the women, they do not jeopardize his consciousness of their rank. Madame Arnoux's difference from and superiority to Rosanette survive: in the code of character, her delicacy and intensity of feeling contrast with Rosanette's shallow brashness through such signs as her veiled presence in the victoria, her blush at Rosanette's familiarity, and the force of her "shrill, piercing laugh," which registers in advance Frédéric's "humiliation and regret for a happiness he would [now] never know" (p. 355*).

Throughout the greatest part of the novel, until the end, Frédéric's sense of self is defined by a position which at each moment may be occupied by one or the other woman but not both. To substitute the one woman for the legitimate occupant of that position is to commit a kind of sacrilege, and this is what Frédéric does by inviting Rosanette on the first day of the Revolution of 1848 to sleep in the bedroom he has rented for Madame Arnoux. Rosanette duly sees Frédéric punished, "sobbing with his head buried in his pillow" (p. 283*).[9] The same point is made indirectly after Frédéric's brief fling, during which time both women are simultaneously present to him—one in actuality and one in memory—without their causing him the most obvious pain:

> The company of these two women made as it were two melodies in his life: the one playful, wild, amusing; the other grave and almost religious. And the two melodies, sounding at the same time, swelled continually and gradually intermingled; for, if Madame Arnoux merely brushed him with her finger, his desire immediately conjured up the image of the other woman, since in her case his hopes were less remote;

9. This point is not of course a new one, but it is essential to review it. It was made by Victor Brombert in *The Novels of Flaubert: A Study of Themes and Techniques* (Princeton, N.J.: Princeton University Press, 1965), pp. 127–40. My discussion of the "substantial" content of the concealed revelation in the half-hidden painting is in many places indebted to Brombert's chapter on *L'education sentimentale*.

while if, in Rosanette's company, his heart happened to be stirred, he promptly remembered his great love. [p. 149*]

Is this mingling painful? The account in the passage covers up Frédéric's pain by producing a "beautiful" musical simile. But it does not rule out a suspicion of its horror—a horror that becomes plain at the beginning of the next paragraph when the melodic mingling is reduced to a "confusion brought about by the similarity between the two establishments." The musicalizing of the two strains is furthermore cast in the *style indirect libre*, which allows us to hear Frédéric's own voice as dominant ("his heart happened to be stirred"; "his great love"). It is he, then, who supplies the optimistic analogue, and it is the more nearly authoritative narrator who thereafter steps outside Frédéric's perspective to define it as a confusion.[10] A genuine principle is affirmed through its violation: if the one woman is present, the other must be remote, so that the knowledge that the inferior is infringing on the place of the other can be denied. To hold them both present in the same position is insupportable; to see them both as chosen and to be forced to decide between them is horrible.

But even more horrible for Frédéric, it seems, would be to admit to knowing that no such tension exists; to be conscious of the fact that as between these women, the "sacred" (the bourgeois) and the "profane" (the easy), there might be no distinction; that it does not and would not matter who was chosen; that the tension, the excitement, between them was never more than a wish-dream or a frantic sur-

10. After writing these lines I came across Peter Brooks' discussion of this passage in his essay on *L'education sentimentale*, "Retrospective Lust, or Flaubert's Perversities," in *Reading for the Plot: Design and Intention in Narrative* (New York: Vintage, 1985), p. 190: "There is a kind of anti-principle of form at work in the novel: the principle of interference. Its theory is first explicitly offered when Frédéric finds himself dividing his life between sacred and profane love, as it were, paying court to both Mme Arnoux and Rosanette. . . . By couching the passage in terms of music, pre-eminently the artistic medium of passion and the apex of the Romantic hierarchy of the arts, Flaubert appears to promise some superior harmonic resolution of Frédéric's passional conundrum. But the start of the next paragraph characterizes the blending of the two melodies as 'this confusion,' and such clearly is the result." This conclusion is like my own. I shall disagree with Brooks, however, by identifying the logic of this and related passages not as an "anti-principle" but as a principle whose violation this passage recounts, a principle whose violation must not occur except at immense personal cost, and one that goes a long way toward establishing the meaning of the novel, where Brooks finds none.

mise. Frédéric weeps with sorrow that it is the Marshal and not Madame Arnoux who lies in his arms: he weeps for their difference. Afterward, in order to feel the passion he is simulating for Madame Dambreuse, he has to "summon up the image of Rosanette or Madame Arnoux" (p. 369*). There is no question that the reader is supposed to feel what Frédéric fails to—namely, the horror he represses when without qualms he substitutes Madame Dambreuse for Madame Arnoux, and Rosanette for Madame Arnoux—and furthermore to feel that this leveling of the difference that has keyed his life risks stultifying him irreparably.[11]

It is coherent within this account that Frédéric's simultaneous affair with Madame Dambreuse and Rosanette can be giddy and energizing when for a time it proceeds without an effective consciousness of Madame Arnoux. Frédéric's life here becomes a kind of loop-the-loop whose configuration resembles the fundamental figure of his life—the tension between the sacred and the profane lover—but is like a harmless, masterful fiction or replica of it.[12] It is organized around a pair of lovers who never come close to being (horribly) substituted for one another, because the difference between them is trivial from the start—trivial in the sense that it can be consciously articulated and mastered without pain. This triangle imitates the triangle organized by a "sacred" mediator, but it is in fact vacuous. Flaubert makes the point plain: "The more [Frédéric] deceived one of his mistresses, the more she loved him, as if the two women's passions stimulated one another and each woman, out of a sort of rivalry, were trying to make him forget the other" (p. 383*). In the same passage Flaubert makes equally clear the condition of the lucky delirium of an empty rivalry: the extinction from practical consciousness, through the motivation of the alibi, of the Third. "Soon his lies began to amuse him; he repeated to one the vow he had just made to the other; he sent them two similar bouquets, wrote to them both at

11. As between a *hacanea* and a *cananea*, says Sancho Panza, there is no (or little) difference. As between a possibly sacred animal (sacred as the beast of a sacred burden, the divine Dulcinea) and a profane one, is there, then, to be no difference—no difference between the steed of the divine Adamis of Gaul and Rocinante, and no difference between Marie (Arnoux) and Rosanette?

12. I take the figure of the loop-the-loop from Jean Laplanche's lustrous book *Hölderlin et la question du père* (Paris: Presses Universitaires de France, 1961), where it is applied to Hölderlin's relation with Suzette Gontard (Diotima).

the same time, then made comparisons between them; but there was a third woman who was always in his thoughts. The impossibility of possessing her served as a justification for his deceitful behavior, which sharpened his pleasure by providing constant variety" (p. 383*).

This situation is in principle unstable for the man whose vitality is a function of the difference between the women he cares for. And indeed the relation with Madame Dambreuse founders on a return to consciousness of the effaced figure of Madame Arnoux. For if it is true that the alibi of the "impossibility of possessing her" has extinguished practical consciousness of her,[13] then it follows that an awareness of her can be awakened only by a penetrating impingement of a sign from the outside. That impingement indeed comes, in the form of a "little casket with silver . . . clasps," which "Madame Dambreuse playfully describe[s] as an old tin can." It is one of Madame Arnoux's personal effects displayed for bidding at the auction that Frédéric and Madame Dambreuse attend,

> the casket [Frédéric] had seen at the first dinner-party in the Rue de Choiseul; afterwards it had passed to Rosanette before coming back to Madame Arnoux; his gaze had often fallen on it during their conversations; it was linked with his dearest memories, and his heart was melting with emotion when all of a sudden Madame Dambreuse said: "You know, I think I'll buy that." [p. 407*]

Frédéric fights off the moment in which Madame Dambreuse will usurp Madame Arnoux by absorbing into her the metonymical figure of her casket: "'There's nothing remarkable about it' [he says]. On the contrary, she thought it very pretty; and the crier was praising its delicate workmanship: 'A jewel of the Renaissance! Eight hundred francs, gentlemen!'" (p. 408). The scene has the pathos for Frédéric, the one tender onlooker, of, let us say, *The Roman Slave Market* of Jean Léon Gérôme.[14]

The monstrous conjunction of "a jewel of the Renaissance" and the

13. An alibi—because when has it ever before been possible for Frédéric to possess her? The issue is one of his having ceased to sustain against all obstacles the hope of possessing her.

14. See the analysis of this painting in Anne, Margaret, and Patrice Higonnet, "Facades: Walter Benjamin's Paris," *Critical Inquiry* 10 (March 1984): 406–7.

sum of money for which it is being prostituted now prereads the scene of Madame Arnoux's return to Frédéric, with her bag of money and his old "Italian" portrait. Between these two moments run all the futility and inanition of the years in the middle of Frédéric's life— years in which he did indeed have "other loves, but the ever-present memory of the first made them insipid" (p. 411*)[15]

At the end of the novel Frédéric is briefly restored to life by the reappearance of Madame Arnoux. But this reunion is threatened by Madame Arnoux's glance at the half-curtained Renaissance painting. Why? What horror is at stake in the revelation? That horror is, as it were, contained in the prehistory of the little silver box, with which, right from the start, Monsieur Arnoux has entangled the two women—his wife and his mistress. We can review its progress.

Frédéric catches sight of "a little box with silver clasps" (p. 56*) on the occasion of his very first visit to Madame Arnoux's quarters. He sees it among various "homely objects . . . lying about: a doll in the middle of the sofa, a fichu against the back of a chair, and on the worktable some knitting from which two ivory needles were hanging with their points downwards."[16] The narrator comments, "It was altogether a peaceful room, with an intimate yet innocent atmosphere." The conjunction of the box with an innocent and sanctioned sexuality is strengthened when Marie Arnoux goes "into her boudoir to fetch the little box with the silver clasps which [Frédéric] had noticed on the mantelpiece. It was a present from her husband, a piece of work of the Renaissance. Arnoux's friends complimented him, and his wife thanked him; he was touched, and suddenly kissed her in front of all the guests" (p. 59*).

When the box reappears, it is in a sharply changed scene of domestic laceration. Madame Arnoux and her husband have been quarreling about his having bought a cashmere shawl for his mistress—for Rosanette. Monsieur Arnoux denies the charge: "'In short, I tell you that you're wrong. Do you want me to give you my word of honor?' . . . She looked him straight in the eyes, without saying anything;

---

15. Insipid, we might add, and not acute or dangerous, because the hope of consummating this other love, or of any manner of drawing it near, is dead.

16. These chaste ivory needles preread contrastively the harlot Rosanette's gold spurs mentioned above. (I owe this observation to Anne Carson.)

then she stretched out her hand, took the silver casket which was on the mantelpiece, and held out an open bill to him" (p. 170*).

Frédéric, who watches the scene and sees Arnoux flush with guilt, is implicated in his guilt, for it is he who urged Arnoux to buy the present for Rosanette; he had taken Rosanette's side in order to ingratiate himself with her. And so when Frédéric, to console Madame Arnoux, says "You know that I don't share," he is simply lying. Rosanette is precisely the being whom he wishes to share with Monsieur Arnoux, if only by an eccentric path of desire to his wife, one that will bring him into intimacy with her by means of her conjunction with Rosanette in the life of Arnoux.[17] This tangled connection, meanwhile, of their sacred and profane desires, is imaged by the beautiful Renaissance casket prostituted to a trade in prostitutes. In this scene, too, the casket is preread by the earlier scene displaying Rosanette posing as a lady of Venice, according to a Renaissance conception of Pellerin's, which Frédéric is buying:[18] "On the carpeted balustrade there would be a silver dish . . . and a casket of old, yellowish ivory, overflowing with gold sequins;[19] some of these sequins would have fallen on the floor and lie scattered in a series of shining drops, so as to lead the eye towards the tip of her foot. . . . Taking a stool to do duty as the balustrade, [Pellerin] laid on it, by way of accessor[y] . . . a tin of sardines . . . and after scattering a dozen ten-centime pieces in front of Rosanette, he made her take up her pose" (p. 155*).

The next time the silver casket appears, it is fully depraved: in Rosanette's house it has become the tin (of sardines—the "tin can," in Madame Dambreuse's phrase). On his way out, after a futile exchange, Frédéric spies "on the table, between a bowl full of visiting-cards and an inkstand, . . . a chased silver casket. It was Madame

17. But this project is self-defeating, since to the extent that he succeeds in emulating Arnoux, Frédéric acquires in Madame Arnoux a woman scarcely distinct from Rosanette. Hence, Rosanette becomes for Frédéric an object of desire independent of Arnoux's desire for her and yet of a desire at no point original with him.

18. "Frédéric—probably because of some hidden resemblance between . . . [him and Arnoux]—felt a certain attraction towards him" (p. 176*).

19. "Ivory casket" and "silver dish" connote the sacred lover Madame Arnoux in a double register: "ivory casket" returns to her chaste ivory knitting needles; "silver dish" to her "silver casket." Each yields a synecdoche which, fused with its counterpart, reproduces the very silver casket.

214

Arnoux's! He felt deeply moved, and at the same time horrified, as if by sacrilege. He longed to touch it, to open it; but he was afraid of being seen, and he went away" (p. 259*). Whom is he afraid of being seen by? Evidently by Rosanette, who would witness the symbolic penetration; moreover, by touching the box, Frédéric would identify—in the language of desire—the literal body of Madame Arnoux. It is intolerable that both women should occupy the same position.

Afterward, when Arnoux is again straitened and no longer possesses Rosanette, the box finds its way home, stripped of its glamour. Hence it resurfaces at the auction, where it is bought by Madame Dambreuse as a thing "perhaps [good] for keeping love letters" (p. 408).

What I have chiefly wanted to stress is the cross-linkage between the two chains of images. The first is anchored in the little silver box, which sometimes has the aura of "the Renaissance" and of a licit (married) sexuality but also contains bills having the modern aura of illicit sexuality; finally, it acquires a sarcastic reminiscence of its sacred function as a container of love letters. This is the one chain; the other is anchored in the portrait of Rosanette. In its original conception it also frames a little box charged with the aura of "the Renaissance," spilling out its quantity of gold sequins represented by a dozen ten-centime pieces. A little like the famous plates in *Madame Bovary* depicting the glories of Mademoiselle de la Vallière, a mistress of Louis XIV—plates adored by the young Emma but into which the points of meat knives have scratched a different legend of greed—so these art objects of the Renaissance, in *Sentimental Education,* are scratched with the script of a cruder purpose. In their history they exhibit a steady decline from the values of the Renaissance, the work of art, and precious metal to anonymous modernity, careless sexuality, and coin. The little silver box, with its chain of predicates, passes from Madame Arnoux to Rosanette and then back to Madame Arnoux; by means of it Madame Arnoux is degraded, her difference from Rosanette is compromised. Consider now Rosanette's portrait and the ivory casket it is supposed to frame. Does the painting also threaten Madame Arnoux—and hence Frédéric's sanity? Can it be linked with her? In the closing scene Madame Arnoux stands in danger of seeing it, but what exactly would she see if she did see Rosanette rigged out as a lady of Venice?

It is precisely here that we are required to perform our feat of prereading, for the "original" of Pellerin's conception has changed— changed in a way that once startled Frédéric, too. One day following his successful duel with Monsieur Cisy, Frédéric,

> coming out of the reading-room, . . . caught sight of some people in front of a picture dealer's shop. They were looking at the portrait of a woman with these words underneath in black letters:
> "Mademoiselle Rose-Annette Bron, the property of Monsieur Frédéric Moreau of Nogent."
> It was her all right, or something like her, with her breasts bare, her hair down, and holding a *red velvet purse* in her hands, while a peacock poked its beak over her shoulder from behind, covering the wall with its great fan-like feathers. [Pp. 236–37; my italics]

This painting of the Marshal clutching a "red velvet purse" amid plumes—all in white and gold—is what Marie Arnoux, bringing Frédéric a "red velvet wallet" embroidered with golden palms, would see if he lifted the curtain: an intolerable semblance of herself.[20] What is kept from Madame Arnoux, what is half kept from Frédéric, is not kept from the reader, who discovers in this moment of prereading the horrible suggestion that inculpates all storied objects both inside and outside Flaubert's text: they are subject to a universal destiny of erosion, degradation, and disgrace. As the story of Mademoiselle de la Vallière, in *Madame Bovary* (painted on plates, to Emma's delight), glorifies "religion, the tendernesses of the heart, and the pomps of court"—thus leveling and mingling spirit, authority, and sexuality so that its legend of glory propped up by need already contains the legend of appetite in the "scratching of knives"—so too it is the fate

20. "Palms" makes a further cross-reference because in an early scene palms are associated with Madame Arnoux but in a way appropriate to Rosanette. After Frédéric has fallen in love with Madame Arnoux, he is flung into an erotic wish-dream by "the sight of a palm-tree" in the Jardin des Plantes: "They travelled together on the backs of dromedaries, under the awnings of elephants. . . . At other times he dreamt of her in yellow silk trousers on the cushions of a harem. . . . [But] as for trying to make her his mistress, he was sure that any such attempt would be futile" (p. 78*). Immediately after the report of this fantasy, Deslauriers brings Frédéric to the Alhambra, a dance hall, where he meets and is captivated by Rosanette. Thereafter, in the crucial scene in which Frédéric discovers Madame Arnoux's silver casket at Rosanette's, he finds Rosanette lying in "white cashmere trousers . . . languid . . . and motionless on the divan. . . . She leant her head on his shoulder, with the provocative expression of a slave girl" (pp. 257-59*).

of art, power, and eroticism in *Sentimental Education* to contain its own degradation.[21] Frédéric's half consciousness of Madame Arnoux's degradation can be grasped thus: the romantic object, Frédéric's pole star, upon its appearance is already "scratched" by his awareness of its potential contamination by the half-curtained portrait. Like the auratic, the storied silver box stuffed with a bill, like her red velvet purse stuffed with coin, the substance of Madame Arnoux is itself virtually corrupt. Such figures of corruption are grotesque, derisory, *kitschig*: their beauty is only specious; their contents are objects of need and are fungible. One expects of the storied object that it will be valued and kept in the possession of its owner, that it will have the aura of its creator and confer something of this aura on its possessor. *Sentimental Education* horrifies by presenting storied objects as objects of exchange and as already containing the marks of their abuse. This is the insight from which Frédéric means to shelter Madame Arnoux at a moment of greatest "meaning," shelter himself and any reader who does not at all points preread the novel. It is a moment that cannot even be bypassed except as an avoidance of prereading.

The figure of the half-drawn curtain protects Rosanette's portrait from being read by Madame Arnoux; reading is half curtained in Flaubert. That is to say, the force and promise of what one has already read in the novel, preparing one's way into later scenes, is made only half plain. This veiling movement is in Flaubert's case part of a system that includes as its dominant syntactical feature "veiled discourse."[22] We could recall now, for example, how deliberately

21. Gustave Flaubert, *Madame Bovary,* ed. Paul de Man, trans. Elinor Aveling and Paul de Man (New York: Norton, 1965), 25.

22. "Veiled discourse" is a translation of Hugo Friedrich's phrase *verschleierte Rede,* with which, in his study of the French novel, *Die Klassiker des französischen Romans* (Leipzig: Bibliographisches Institut, 1939), he characterizes Flaubert's distinctive narrative technique as one of theatrical impersonation. The source of the characters' gestures is concealed. (I was alerted to this expression by Brombert's treatment of the *style indirect libre* in *The Novels of Flaubert,* 169–73.) There are many aspects to this haunting phenomenon of merged narration. Are such sentences *spoken* by characters in their own language to represent or express their states of mind, or are they *written* by the author on the characters' behalf? This state of affairs also constitutes a kind of irony. Sentences having to do with Frédéric's inner life, sentences that only he is entitled to speak, are spoken for him by the narrator but in a manner of disowning his own authority. "He regretted nothing"; "his former sufferings were redeemed" (p.

inexplicit is the hint at the beginning of the novel which makes intelligible the crucial scene concluding it—the evocation of the brothel at Nogent: "Venus, queen of the skies, your servant! But Poverty is the mother of Continence, and heaven knows we've been slandered enough about that!" (p. 30).[23] And, similarly, there is the veiling of the narrator's judgment of the lovers throughout their final reunion.[24]

414*)—these phrases invoke a speaker different from Frédéric, but do not identify the speaker as their author. They quote without attribution. Of course, if they were truly anonymous in the most radical sense, we could not identify them as quotations. In so identifying a statement, we say it has already been spoken or written by someone. Who? We may not be sure, but we have an idea: it is something we have read before in a book—and spoken there by someone *better* than Frédéric. Jonathan Culler's *Flaubert: The Uses of Uncertainty* (Ithaca: Cornell University Press, 1974) makes a number of valuable contributions to this difficulty; see esp. pp. 112–14, 185–207.

23. In the memory of the brothel at Nogent the positive possibilities of sacred and profane love are mingled. The alibi of this "happy memory" is the sanctification of a first state of sexual indifference before love and sensuality, before the Madame Arnoux- and Rosanette-possibilities of experience have become separate. Frédéric conjures a utopia of leveled difference which in empirical fact amounts to the "confusion" of his mature project. The brothel is an economic utopia, generating from the complete fungibility of its objects an aura of the sacred untouchable individual; there Buridan's ass is ennobled as a knight of resignation.

24. In an unpublished essay on "patterns of desire in *Sentimental Education*," Harold Collins of Princeton University calls attention to another veiled form of Rosanette's presence in this final scene, one that requires an equally acute effort of prereading: "When Frédéric asks Madame Arnoux how she first discovered his love for her, she replies: 'It was one evening when you kissed my wrist between my glove and my sleeve. I said to myself: "Why he loves me . . . he loves me"' [p. 414*]. This is a memory of an event not present in the text. Instead, Flaubert gives the reader another memory in place of Madame Arnoux's. In the description of Frédéric and Rosanette at the horse races, we read that 'keeping hold of her wrist, he pressed his lips to it, between the glove and the sleeve' [p. 205*]." Collins's point is that Flaubert plots a movement of duplication internal to Madame Arnoux's identity, hollows out her distinction as the "sacred lover," whether Frédéric or the reader likes it or not. Collins emphasizes Flaubert's (not Frédéric's) demonstration of the divided and disjunct character of Madame Arnoux. Madame Arnoux is constituted as Frédéric's "center" in such a way as to make the factitiousness of the construction utterly apparent. Apropos of the passage in which images of Madame Arnoux mingle for Frédéric with those of Rosanette like two melodies (p. 149*), Collins observes, "The women in the novel become interchangeable in ways that subvert the most obvious polarity of Madame Arnoux as an ideal and the others as degraded substitutes. . . . We can only ask, what signifies what, who stands in for whom?" Collins also refers to the moment when Frédéric makes use of "his old love. He told [Madame Dambreuse] about all the emotions which Madame Arnoux had once aroused in him—his yearnings, his fears, his dreams—as if she had inspired them" (p. 361*). Collins adds, "We are jarred by

Flaubert wishes to half-hide the knowledge that were Madame
Arnoux to see Rosanette's portrait, she would see her double. Frédéric would see these women—and we too would see them, for the
last time, at the end of Frédéric's life—face to face, identical. This is
too dangerous: it is the novel's principle that these women must not
be seen beside each other, *inside* each other, and equivalent. And
Flaubert, it seems, must himself shelter from the too vaunting and
visible yoking of the sacred and the profane. That we know this (or
think we know this) is tribute to his art of evoking the consequences
of what we have once read.

But we are not to forget that as Madame Arnoux's double, the
reader, for all the superiority of his or her memory, is nonetheless
implicated in her degradation. For just as the romantic figure, on
entering the scene, is already "scratched" by the corrupt semblances
of her which her past throws up, so too each reader, in prereading,
shares her fate: each has already read the present text; each is its ghost.
The reader cannot become the word that offers itself to be read as an
original word; prereading, he or she lags behind its freshness. The
reader judges it, hence is judged by it, and hence is condemned as a
semblance.

* * *

And for the sake of greater discretion they even referred
to . . . Frédéric as K.
GUSTAVE FLAUBERT, *Sentimental Education*

---

the reversal of polarities. Madame Arnoux becomes yet another non-privileged signifier, a token by which Frédéric can denote for his own convenience a condition of
desire." Collins adduces, finally, other moments suggesting the only fragmented and
substitutive character of Madame Arnoux. This point is indisputable; my focus, however, has been on Frédéric's unsteady effort to avoid this knowledge. Consider the
specific instance Collins mentions of pre-reading required of the reader in the last
scene. Unlike the one I have been elaborating, there is no uptake shown on Frédéric's
part. It is important that he is kept out of knowledge of the duplication. I am concerned with a moment in which Frédéric is fully aware of a duplication about to be
enacted and struggles to avert it. This moment is part of a sequence of similar
moments.

The reader's act of bringing prereading to light, which is chiefly inductive and implicit in Flaubert, is explicit in Kafka. Flaubert's reader could value his discovery of prereading mainly as the reward of diligent memory work. In Kafka the phenomenon is written into *The Trial* with blindingly clear evidence, for the novel *begins* with a moment of prereading. That it does so, however, can come to light fully only for the reader who has afterward been alerted to it, who has read on, prereading in turn a later scene. I refer to chapter 9, the scene of Joseph K.'s discussion with the prison chaplain, which contains K.'s defense of "personal experiences."

The opening exchange in the cathedral between the chaplain and K. turns on K.'s behavior during the year of his trial. The chaplain tells K. that he fears his case "will end badly" and asks him what step he proposes to take in the matter (T 264).

> "I'm going to get more help," said K., looking up again to see how the priest took his statement. . . . "You cast about too much for outside help," said the priest disapprovingly, "especially from women. Don't you see that this isn't the right kind of help?" . . . There was no longer even a murky daylight; black night had set in. All the stained glass in the great cathedral could not illumine the darkness of the wall with one solitary glimmer of light. . . . "Are you very angry with me?" asked K. of the priest. "It may be that you don't know the nature of the Court you are serving." He got no answer. "*These are only my personal experiences*," said K. There was still no answer from above. "I wasn't trying to insult you," said K. And at that the priest shrieked from the pulpit, "Can't you see one pace before you?" It was an angry cry, but at the same time sounded like the unwary shriek of one who sees another fall and is startled out of his senses." [T 265–66; my italics]

The chaplain makes a key distinction between the light produced by "personal experiences" and the light that would be necessary to illuminate at least one step of K.'s way. For the chaplain—in the words of a great aesthetician, Oscar Wilde—"personal experience is a most vicious and limited circle,"[25] despite the fact that it is exactly what all men or, better, "all guilty men" invoke. But how reliable is any such distinction produced by an official of the court? It does seem

25. "The Decay of Lying," in *Oscar Wilde: Selected Writings* (London: Oxford University Press, 1961), p. 26.

very reliable in this scene, where the imagery of darkness and blindness evokes a low point in K.'s mastery of his situation.[26] The balance of authority between K. and the court here shifts decisively in favor of the court. Nothing about the chaplain's response suggests that he is vicious or benighted, and the weight of the accusation of ignorance falls on K.'s appeal to his personal experiences, just as if the narrator had insisted on making the point directly.

And indeed the chaplain's accusation has a good deal of plausibility. From the beginning K. has determined on conducting his case in the light—for him the unaccustomed light—of personal experiences. The decision actually seems to be made for him with the authority of a directly intervening narrator. This occurs early in the novel, during the scene of K.'s arrest. In a flash of clarity, K. poses the essential questions pertaining to his arrest: "Who could these men be? What were they talking about? What authority could they represent?" And then the narrator begins to involve himself in K.'s situation in a way that jeopardizes his own critical distance, saying directly of K.: "He had always been inclined to take things easily, to believe in the worst only when the worst happened, to take no care for the morrow even when the outlook was threatening."

The text continues in its more dominant mode of *erlebte Rede*, of "veiled discourse," except for a second decisive interpolation on the part of the narrator (which I italicize):

> But that struck him as not being the right policy here. . . . There was a slight risk that later on his friends might possibly say he could not take a joke, but he had in mind—*though it was not usual with him to learn from experience*—several occasions . . . when against all his friends' advice he had behaved with deliberate recklessness and without the slightest regard for possible consequences, and had had in the end to pay dearly for it. That must not happen again, at least not this time; if this was a comedy he would insist on playing it to the end. [T 7–8]

K. is determined to approach his predicament with the wisdom drawn from personal experience—one that tells him, namely, that

26. In a recent essay Walter Sokel also assigns plain authority to the prison chaplain on the basis of what seems his superior understanding of the parable of "The Man from the Country" ("The Trial," in *Deutsche Romane des 20. Jahrhunderts: Neue Interpretationen*, ed. Michael Lützeler [Königstein: Athenäum, 1983], 112).

even if this is a legal comedy, he will play his part in it. Indeed, he never steps out of his role, and his comedic vision survives until the moment before his death. Observing the warders of the court who have come to stab him, he asks: "'So you are meant for me?' The gentlemen bowed, each indicating the other with the hand that held the top hat. . . . 'Tenth-rate old actors they send for me,' said K. to himself" (T 280).

The interpretative decision that K. makes on the strength of personal experiences proves fatal.[27] He is led to read his situation as a "case," as a trial by civil authority, to which he brings conventional expectations: that in being apprehended he will have been arrested and in being arrested he will be detained; that his arrest is based on a specific charge and that the charge, being plausible, constitutes grounds for arrest; that the verdict will conform with the sense of the charge, and so forth. For in a state governed by law—as personal experience attests—what other than a comedic fiction is a trial in which none of these conventions holds?[28]

Once K. begins to reason this way, however, he is lost. The project of maintaining and demanding from a court confirmation of innocence of a charge that is never specified is a manifest impossibility; grasped as a court case, his *Prozeß* is bound to fail. In adapting his predicament to personal experience, he only confirms the chaplain's point: in a case in which "the proceedings gradually merge into the verdict," the manner in which the accused conducts his case determines its outcome (T 264).

Another way of putting K.'s situation is to say that he is determined to read his *Prozeß*—a word that means "trial" but also means a "process" of whatever sort—through the common metaphor of a

27. A "comedy" in K.'s everyday understanding isn't fiction—this is the point—hasn't the integrity of fiction; it's a philistine's view of the fictive.

28. One of the passages that Kafka deleted from the final text of *The Trial* describes Joseph K. seeing a policeman on the way to his execution and whispering into the ear of one of his executioners: "The state is offering to come to my assistance. . . . What if I transferred the trial into the domain where the writ of the state law runs?" (T 325). As Clayton Koelb points out, the passage introduces a sharp distinction between the Law and the law ("The Deletions from Kafka's Novels," *Monatshefte* 68 (Winter 1976): 370–71). I find in Kafka's decision to delete this passage evidence of the importance for him of merging the two orders in the consciousness of Joseph K.

civil trial. This is what personal experience drives him to, though this model of understanding will destroy him.[29]

What, then, is the alternative? How could K. conduct his case otherwise? The alternative lies in his overcoming this dominant, persuasive metaphor furnished by personal experience; the liberating perspective lies, like the reader's own hope for enlightenment, in interpreting his process with the seized freshness of a literal reading, one genuinely faithful to the details conveyed by the narrator. But then, of course, there would have to be such a thing as a state of affairs different from K.'s own prejudgment of it. Events would have to stand out for a moment and assume the character of an objectlike text existing apart from the expectations of the interpreter. How could K. or the reader see the object radiantly and see it whole? The object would have to have a beginning, would have to be presented for at least an instant as what it truly is. There would have to be a beginning to K.'s ordeal, a moment when it is his alone and before it has become the "personal" but in fact vulgar and anonymous vehicle of conventional understanding: namely, a case which, even as an infelicitous case, falls under the jurisdiction of civil law. His ordeal would have to have a beginning before it has been preread.

But this is precisely what the novel is determined to prevent. Consider the famous opening sentence of *The Trial*: "Someone must have traduced Joseph K., for without having done anything wrong he was arrested one fine morning." The narrative begins not with the first event of the plot but with a first interpretation of the event; the interpretation of the arrest as part of a conventional trial provoked by K.'s defamation *is* the beginning. The novel is ahead of its own plot in the radical sense that Joseph K.'s manner of continually prereading the events of his trial is itself preread by the narrator. And even if,

29. The point is entirely consistent with Kafka's scathing criticism of the attempt to found personal existence on an understanding of "the fall of man" which has to be acquired by personal experience. This, for Kafka, is the false way entirely, for the knowledge of good and evil is already given to us. Knowledge is not the point; what we lack is the strength to do good. The pursuit of a heightened consciousness of good and evil, the effort to elaborate the moral consciousness, is a pure evasion of what is already known. The product of the evasion that is at one with the heightened consciousness of good and evil and whose special arm is reasoning, Kafka calls "motivations." See Chapter Four.

thereafter, Kafka at times breaks up the one perspective in which reader, narrator, and Joseph K. appear to be immersed—creating by these breaks the illusion that K.'s is a potentially corrigible, only one-sided, and merely particular or personal perspective—we see that from the outset, in the crucial matter of the kind of process that this is, there is to be no other perspective.[30]

K.'s own interpretation has been preread by the narrator. It is forced on him, as it is forced on the reader, before the process begins, as an inescapably self-evident mode of understanding. Impersonating the incontrovertible voice of personal, of worldly experience, the narrator erects legal thinking as the only legitimate sort of interpretation. He connects an arrest with a charge, as its condition, and defines an arrest in the absence of a charge, according to the logic of civil law, as a comedy parasitic on the norm, which, as a result, has—like himself—been "traduced." He utters all this in a matter-of-fact tone impossible to resist, because it is at the beginning and we are disarmed. And yet it would have to be resisted, it seems, for life depends on being not so disarmed and on thinking this beginning event differently. K. has grounds enough to approach or leave his case differently, since his arrest is basically peculiar and hence not an arrest.[31] To seize these grounds would be to liberate the perspective of a

30. This point should make plain the difficulty of deciding whether or not to adhere to the redoubtable critical figure of Kafka's *Einsinnigkeit* (monopolized perspective). This position holds that Kafka's narrative mode is "congruent," that many of Kafka's novels and stories are wholly "without narrator"—which is to say, they hide the function guaranteeing the difference between the information possessed by the central figure and the information required to shape the presentation of that central figure (and his or her information). In fact, however, breaks can always be found in Kafka's so-called perspective of narrative congruence. So much for strict *Einsinnigkeit*. The right term would be *Zweisinnigkeit* (divided perspective), as has recently been proposed by Sokel ("The Trial," p. 110). On the other hand, in *The Trial* both narrative tracks issue from the depot of the metaphor of a civil trial. The function of the two-tracked perspective is only to maintain a formal, vindictive, and equally arbitrary counterpoint to Joseph K.'s strategies of affirming his innocence: the narrator wants him to confess his guilt. But he too is unable to identify the offense of which K. is guilty; he too is constrained by the metaphor of the trial by civil law. The only possibility of enriching his perspective is, I propose, to read it "allegorically" (*andeutungsweise*), as pointing beyond the contrary assertion of guilt by a guilty narration to an act of verbal composition. Hence it refers us to a being who, unlike Joseph K., writes.

31. What, e.g., does it mean to have been arrested and yet to be free to come and go as one pleases?

literalism unconstrained by previous personal experiences of law and legal metaphor. But by defining the arrest as only the miscarriage of a civil arrest, the narrator defeats this liberation in advance.

The structure of prereading in *The Trial* differs from what we have seen in Flaubert in its degree of evidentness. In Kafka the circle of signifying moments, which turns on K.'s "personal experiences," is not only realized explicitly by the detective reader, is not only realized implicitly by the actors in the text—like Madame Arnoux in *Sentimental Education*—but is also identified by the actors in the text. They act out their knowledge of it, indeed, immediately after the opening in the exchange between K. and the warder in the traveler's suit, who is called Franz (!).

> K.: Who are you?
> FRANZ: Did you ring?
> K: Anna is to bring me my breakfast.
> FRANZ: He says Anna is to bring him his breakfast. [T 4]

Then, in the perspective of Joseph K., the narrator remarks: "The strange man could not have learned anything from [this sentence] that he did not already know" (for "have learned," Kafka writes, literally, "have experienced [*erfahren*]"; R 259). The effect of this comment is to undermine from the start the value of experience, which is here said to have the cognitive authority only of what is already known— indeed, to have cognitive authority at all only as the repetition of a previous moment, only insofar as it is preknown. Quite consistently, when the warders (Franz included) speak of the dwindling value of the personal property of the accused (deposited at the depot) as a truth "confirmed by experience [*erfahrungsgemäß*]," K. pays "hardly any attention to this advice" (T 6; R 261). Thereafter, quite inconsistently, K. resolves to learn *from experience* to play along with the arrest. He will be reproved for this by the chaplain, and both he and the reader will have reason by the end to doubt the promise made early by the deluded warder Willem, that K. will learn from "experience [*erfahren*] everything" pertaining to the proceedings (T 6; R 260).

Prereading, as a term demystifying "experience," is vivid all throughout *The Trial*, in the passages quoted thereafter in the prejudgments made by K. on his own arrest and trial. It is performed essentially by the plot, which is prejudgment itself, in the sense that "the world [of experience] in Kafka's text is seen as the result of the thought process peculiar to the perspectival figure, the hero Joseph K."[32] More radically, as we have seen, it structures the narration, being incorporated directly in the narrator's prejudicial surmise, which precedes the *mise en scène*. These are the senses in which pre-reading in *The Trial* is explicit—though it is fully explicit only for readers who know that what they are looking for is what they have already read, and that therefore, in the spirit of Kafka's aphorism, they are in a certain sense "found." For "he who seeks does not find, but he who does not seek will be found" (DF 80).

*   *   *

The ways in which novels of Flaubert and Kafka elaborate prereading together illustrate a growing tendency of the modern philosophical novel. The plot of *Sentimental Education* is anticipated by moments of prereading that invite excavation and exposure; by virtue of this obligatory salvaging work, the plot becomes implicitly and in part the struggle of reading for the half curtained plot.[33] The reader is

32. Theo Elm, "Der Prozeß," in *Das Werk und seine Wirkung,* vol. 2 of *Kafka-Handbuch,* ed. Hartmut Binder (Stuttgart: Alfred Kröner, 1979), p. 435. In "Kafka's Rhetorical Moment," *PMLA* 98, no. 1 (1983), Clayton Koelb shows how a similar temporal structure informs the very language of K.'s arrest. What effectively justifies the arrest for K., for the complicit narrator, and for the unwary reader is an appeal to an anonymous personal experience, which endows the moment with anterior reference. Koelb writes: "The first K. hears of [his arrest] is from one of the 'warders' who appear in his room: 'Sie dürfen nicht weggehen, Sie sind ja verhaftet'" ['You can't go out, you are arrested'] (p. 38). The *ja* is very odd and in fact dysfunctional if it is supposed to strengthen the performative effect of the utterance. In fact, it appeals to and ascertains a prior state of affairs. Thereafter, the inspector appears in turn to appeal to the warder's statement in saying, "You're under arrest, that's correct, that's all I know." Koelb adds: "It would seem therefore that the Inspector is assuming that K. is already under arrest. But that, of course, is what the warder also apparently assumed. Who has arrested K.?" (p. 39). The answer is that K. (and the narrator) have. K. (and the narrator) have bought into K.'s arrest on the strength of personal experience, and Kafka the narrator does everything at once to reveal and conceal this truth.

33. In *Reading for the Plot,* Brooks is concerned to stress that *Sentimental Education* is without plot and that the reading it defines is of a new type that must endure the absence of plot, albeit with the residual consciousness (from Balzac) of what the missing plot must be. While Brooks's argument is cogent, I am more concerned to stress the equally important promise of a particular meaning adumbrated in this novel: namely, the threat to meaning of a leveling of difference between sacred and profane lovers.

charged with the task of constituting the novel's design. In Kafka the function of the preread is more overt, though it is not necessarily easier to grasp. Here the novel's plot is not in question: the plot is itself the repetition and proved ubiquity of prereading. On axes drawn between Flaubert and Kafka showing the increased explicitness of prereading, especially as it enters the narrative mechanism itself, one could begin to redescribe such modern philosophical novels as Rainer Maria Rilke's *Notebooks of Malte Laurids Brigge,* André Gide's *Counterfeiters,* and William Faulkner's *Absalom, Absalom!* Each arises as a model type within the development of prereading, whose counterpart in the human sciences is the elaboration of the hermeneutic circle of interpretation.

Chapter Nine

The Trial/"In The Penal Colony": The Rigors of Writing

In discussing *The Trial*, I interpreted Joseph K.'s trial by a negative route. I identified his reading of the trial as based on a defective metaphor, the impoverishing everyday equivalent of a trial by a civil court of law. Sooner or later the question must arise, what beyond the intention of condemning the poor and anonymous character of the personal experiences of Joseph K. can have prompted Kafka to arrange his trial? Is it to prove the now familiar thesis that truth cannot be described but only its inverse—namely, error, and indeed someone else's error?[1] More directly, what truth for Kafka—exceeding, as it must, the truth of personal experiences—shelters in this work?

Kafka suggests in theory and practice that all thinking irresistibly inclines to take place in metaphors. The corollary question is, therefore, within what metaphor has Kafka arraigned the anonymous and escapist metaphor that Joseph K. has found for his trial? Since no such single, explicitly figured statement appears to organize *The Trial* as a whole, we must look for an answer in the strictest possible analogue to the text, in the spirit of Hölderlin's description of the "tragic poem" as a carrying over of the author's inwardness into a foreign,

---

1. E.g., Gerhard Kurz, paraphrasing Kafka, writes "Thinking and speaking . . . are [as such] untruth" (*Traum-Schrecken: Kafkas literarische Existenzanalyse* [Stuttgart: Metzler, 1980], p. 195). Kurz then proceeds to nuance this position.

analogous material.[2] And here we will be well served to reflect on that dimension of Kafka's being to which he never gave a personal origin, attributing it to a sheerly unknowable other source—that dimension he called *Schriftstellersein,* "being as a writer." How could Kafka's meditation on questions of guilt and innocence fail to involve writing? Equally, how could his continual meditation on writing by writing fail to involve questions of guilt and innocence—indeed, to the point where the very project of writing *The Trial* would founder under their weight?

To answer these questions, we shall have to take an indirect route, via a story that culminates in the scene of writing in Kafka's "In the Penal Colony." For although it is often noted that Kafka wrote "In the Penal Colony" while writing *The Trial*, it is insufficiently appreciated that this story is about Kafka's writing *The Trial*.[3] "In the Penal Colony" enters the process of writing *The Trial* as its reflection, producing a perspective different from the one in which the novel was being composed, so as to alter the thrust of its composition, which was heading aground. Kafka strove to shake the novel free from the apathy that was choking it.

This history begins on July 23, 1914, when Kafka's engagement to Felice Bauer was broken off in Berlin at the hotel Askanischer Hof at what he called the hotel "tribunal" (*Gerichtshof*). It provoked a crisis described in a diary entry of July 28 in rare italic: "*I am more and more unable to think, to observe, to determine the truth of things, to remember, to speak, to share an experience. I am turning to stone—this is the truth* [*that is something I must register, das muß ich feststellen*]. . . . If I can't take refuge in some sort of work [in a project, *in einer Arbeit*], I am lost" (DII 68; Ta 411).

Kafka was roused from immobility by an event no less momentous than the outbreak of World War I. "General mobilization," he wrote in his diary July 31. As a result of the conscription of his brother-in-law, Kafka was obliged to move out of his parents' apartment to

2. Friedrich Hölderlin, *Sämtliche Werke* (Stuttgart: Kohlhammer, 1961), 4:150.

3. Mark Anderson's unpublished essay "The Ornaments of Writing: Kafka's 'In der Strafkolonie'" is an important exception. It too shows that the story "refers to the writing of two earlier Kafkan texts: 'Das Urteil' . . . and *Der Prozeß*." Only after writing this chapter did I remember that I had read Anderson's essay in 1984. On rereading it, I see that I must be indebted to it for a major subliminal impulse.

make room for his sister and "receive the reward for living alone. But it is hardly a reward; living alone ends only with punishment." His interpretation of his situation, from the ordinary standpoint tactless and even presumptuous, is from the writer's standpoint entirely rigorous: "As a consequence," he declared, "I am little affected by all the misery"—that is, by everyone else's misery—"and am firmer in my resolve than ever. . . . I will write in spite of everything, absolutely; it is my struggle for self-preservation" (DII 75).

The attitude recorded in this second diary entry is quite remarkable. Three days earlier, Kafka had written in his journal that he was desperately seeking refuge. Now, he has evidently intuited enough of The Trial for him to be able once again "to think, to observe, to determine the truth of things" with a vengeance. So we could in our minds rewrite the earlier entry: "I am turning (not to stone but) to script; that is a truth I must register . . . and I can."[4]

Kafka continued to work on The Trial—and to work well on it— for a couple of months.[5] On August 15 he noted: "I have been writing these past few days, may it continue. . . . [I] have the feeling that *my monotonous, empty, mad bachelor's life has some justification*" (DII 79; my italics). This passage makes an important distinction: the stake for Kafka in writing The Trial is far greater than refuge from his empirical miseries; it is a matter of "justification," of calling forth "the freedom that perhaps awaits me" (DII 92). The distinction is of the kind that he will introduce, three years later, apropos of his story "A Country Doctor": "I can still have passing satisfaction from [such]

4. Kafka's diary entry for July 29, 1914—two days earlier—alludes explicitly to The Trial in describing one "Joseph K., the son of a rich merchant," who has been "reproached" by his father "for his dissipated life" (DII 71).

5. My narrative of these events follows the same trajectory as does that of Jens Kruse in his suggestive essay "Lukács' Theorie des Romans und Kafkas *In der Strafkolonie*: Eine Konstellation im Jahre 1914," *German Studies Review* 10 (May 1987): 237–53. But from this juncture on, our readings diverge. For Kruse, The Trial and "In the Penal Colony" articulate the alienation produced in Kafka by the terrible political events of 1914. I stress how, *according to Kafka*, just the opposite is true: these horrors are entirely contingent with respect to the project of The Trial. What "In the Penal Colony" means to identify and exorcise is *this very view* that makes of contingently inflicted traumas the genuine concern of writing. Kruse, too, cites the diary passage in which Kafka compares the invasive, corrosive effect of his thoughts during the war to that of his thoughts about his fiancée in former times. But Kruse fails to note what Kafka has said about his preoccupation with such events: they *cannot* serve as explanations of his apathy—the apathy that arrests the writing of The Trial.

230

works. . . . But happiness only if I can raise the world into the pure, the true, and the immutable" (DII 187). Kafka's happiness in 1914 depended on his continuing to write *The Trial*—which means, practically speaking, proceeding to condemn Joseph K.

His elation was short lived. Later in August and throughout September, Kafka's writing jammed, a difficulty he blamed on reasons where he could find them: first, the "inhibiting effect of . . . [his] way of life"—that is, his "monotonous, empty, mad, bachelor's life" (even in writing *The Trial,* he was too much like Joseph K.); then he offered, as a surmise, his "sorrow over the Austrian defeats and . . . [his] anxiety for the future." But he swiftly repudiated these explanations for a deeper constraint, the last boundary: "apathy, . . . coldness of heart, that forever comes back and forever has to be put down again" (DII 98, 92). Thereafter, Kafka registered that Felice too was "probably . . . interfering" (DII 93); finally, he blamed anonymous "small obstacles" that he could not "push past"—concluding, though, that he was again "toying with thoughts of F" (DII 95).

One could think of these obstacles as shadows of the war and Felice cast upon the rigorous dullness of his inner life, but perhaps they are, after all, too small a hindrance. A correct interpretation depends on how one reads Kafka's statement "I am little affected by all the misery," together with his putting Felice and the war in place of his native apathy as causes of his standstill. If Kafka's first claim to hardness is true, then the second group of motives read like ordinary excuses. Their deliberate understatement, however, emphasizes the very apathy they mean to hide: the "small obstacles" are *Verneinungen*—psychoanalytic disclaimers—too important to be left out of account.[6] On this view, one of the benefits of Kafka's continuing to write *The Trial* would be to reestablish his indifference to Felice and to the war on the basis of a higher fate, a scriptive suspension of the ethical (and not on a damnable absence of feeling); it would define his *Trial* project as going beyond rehabilitation of the author, which would have ceased to be a stake. Not to go on writing would therefore be a disaster. Kafka's literature stands exposed as pretense only,

6. On *Verneinungen*, cf. this passage from *The Trial*: "After a while she [Leni] asked: 'Have you got a sweetheart?' 'No,' said K. 'Oh, yes, you have,' she said. 'Well, yes, I have,' said K. 'Just imagine it, I have denied her existence and yet I am actually carrying her photograph in my pocket'" (T 136).

the mask of a natural poverty of feeling—a way of "acting out . . . [his] inherent baseness before the eyes of the world without forfeiting its love" (LF 545). His aim could never have been redemption but only the vanity of deceiving the human tribunal.

However Kafka himself understood this constellation of fates, affects, and excuses, it amounted to an appalling burden. And so, at the beginning of October 1914, he sought a change by taking a week's leave from the office in order to "push the novel on" (DII 92). But, typically, time free from the office proved useless to his plan. With the prospect of justification fading, Kafka asked for a second week's leave, during which he wrote, in three nights or fewer, "In the Penal Colony."[7]

This conjuncture is crucial. It determined the special way in which "In the Penal Colony" relates, first, to the law administered by a world at war and, second, to the disturbing involvement of women in the process of justification. Military—that is to say, peremptory— justice and a seductive woman tormented Kafka *as the author of The Trial*. What they meant for him, at once contingently interfering with his novel and fundamentally supplying its themes, became clear to Kafka only in works other than *The Trial*. This is what he noted, I believe, when he wrote in his diary, on the point of beginning "In the

7. According to Malcolm Pasley and Klaus Wagenbach, "In the Penal Colony" was written between October 4 and 18, 1914 (SE 398). Hartmut Binder tries to fix the date of the conception of the story by identifying the event that allegedly provoked it: on October 15, 1914, Kafka received a letter from Grete Bloch, Felice's friend, which once again opened up the possibility of an engagement to Felice. Binder comments: "Kafka, 'creative only in self- torment' [DII 116; cf. LF 314: 'What is stopping me can hardly be said to be the facts; it is . . . a desire and a command to torment myself for some higher purpose'], was assailed by destructive fantasies of punishment, in which he executed himself with torture machines, especially when the relation to women, ergo, to the representatives of life [cf. DF 109: 'The world—F. is its representative— and my ego are tearing my body apart in a conflict that there is no resolving'; and LF 303: 'You alone create my only valid connection with people'], personified in him the claims of society, which, on account of his inner resistance to marriage, evoked guilt feelings" (*Kafka-Kommentar zu sämtlichen Erzählungen* [Munich: Winkler, 1975], p. 174). Furthermore, according to Binder's dating of the chapters of *The Trial* in his *Kafka-Kommentar zu den Romanen, Rezensionen, Aphorismen und zum Brief an den Vater* (Munich: Winkler, 1976), pp. 218–61, it would have been just after completing "In the Penal Colony" that Kafka composed the chapters of *The Trial* often referred to as "the second phase" and thus described by Ritchie Robertson: "In the second phase the Court has withdrawn; K. no longer deals directly with its representatives, but with intermediaries like the Advocate and Titorelli, and is aware of the Court only as a vast, shadowy, inaccessible organization" (*Kafka: Judaism, Politics, and Literature* [Oxford: Clarendon, 1985], p. 10). K. is guilty and decisively doomed.

Penal Colony": "Two weeks of good work [though hardly at all on *The Trial*]; full insight into my situation occasionally" (DII 93).

To try to understand how martial law and a woman interfere with Kafka's writing *The Trial* (or, granting equally his denials, how they only seem to interfere with his writing), we could reach for the handy scourge of guilt by association. *The Trial* is and was for Kafka the story of a culprit. "Rossmann [the hero of *Amerika*] and [Joseph] K. [are] . . . the innocent and the guilty, [though] both [are] executed . . . in the end" (DII 132). Now for a story to be written about a culprit, there must be, somewhere—in the jury box containing Kafka the person, Kafka the author, and Kafka the narrator of *The Trial*— one dispassionate juror. The distance from which the story of a guilty protagonist can be written must also be a place of calm or at least of some theory, in the (Heideggerian) sense of "letting [something] . . . come toward us in a tranquil tarrying alongside."[8] Some persona of Kafka must be detached enough to tell the story of a condemned man unlike himself—a distinction borne out in *The Trial*, when the accused Joseph K., after determining to write an exhaustive autobiography, does not (or cannot). His story has to be told by another—the author—by someone not sunk to the same depth in guilt, someone who, unlike "an accused person . . . , was [not] himself implicated and [did not have] . . . all sorts of worries to distract him" (T 146).[9] Typically, during this period Kafka could succeed in writing "The Village Schoolteacher" with the right degree of calm, because he grasped that while of course his guilt was beyond question, "it [was] . . . not so great as Father pictures it" (DII 102).

The hypothesis about the jamming of Kafka's work on *The Trial* by the burden of empirical worries and distractions claims that the burden is unbearably increased by the high specific density of the guilt impacted in them. Kafka accused himself of damnable selfishness—in his words, "nothing but pettiness, indecision, envy, and hatred" (DII 77).[10] He is a shirker both as a fiancé and as a prospective infantryman: in either case, he cannot bring himself to volunteer.

8. Martin Heidegger, *Being and Time*, trans. John Macquarrie and Edward Robinson (New York; Harper & Row, 1962), p. 177.

9. "If I were another person observing myself and the course of my life, I should be compelled to say that it must all end unavailingly, be consumed in incessant doubt, creative only in its self-torment" (DII 116).

10. Kafka identifies these emotions as aimed "against those who are fighting and whom I passionately wish everything evil" (DII 77).

These accusations were actually bitter enough to inspire a plan of suicide, which he confided to his diary (DII 93). "The thoughts provoked in me by the war," he earlier wrote, "resemble my old worries over Felice in the tormenting way in which they devour me from every direction." Without distance from them, Kafka could only sink into the ground: "I can't endure worry, and perhaps have been created expressly in order to die of it" (DII 92). He cannot contemplate his engagement and the war, both of which he is guilty of evading, and also judge innocently, with detachment, another's evasions—which is to say, write *The Trial*. Thus far, perhaps, common sense.

Yet it is necessary to insist on the occult topography of Kafka's despair: particular accusations weigh so heavily only *because* they invade the writing of *The Trial*, which has to arise from a different source. Incalculably graver, therefore, are the "apathy" and "coldness of heart" that arise from this very source and are the real causes of the standstill of his novel. This picture of causes undermines the theory that interpersonal crises have brought about his despair. Kafka's moods—"this fate [that] pursues" him (DII 98) and not his ethical experience—accuse him of shirking his fundamental nature. Like the anxieties of "The Burrow" dweller, his are "in their destructive effects . . . perhaps much the same as the anxieties that existence in the outer world gives rise to," but they are "different from ordinary ones, prouder, richer in content" (S 339).

It was in such anxiety that Kafka began writing "In the Penal Colony." The intention of the story was to channel a path for *The Trial*. Kafka submitted himself to the harrow *of* "In the Penal Colony," which, like the harrow *in* "In the Penal Colony," was designed to open textlike wounds and to keep them always "clear [legible, *klar*]" (S 147; E 209). The stakes involved in this venture were, of course, enormous; *The Trial* was intended as a work of justification.[11] If Kafka's aim in writing "In the Penal Colony" was to lighten his guilt by discovering its nature, we should expect to find in the story encouraging scenes and arguments. And indeed the story reveals its interest in mitigation early on, "owing to," as Malcolm

11. That Kafka would think of one writing project as the means of opening a way to another certainly has a precedent: his intention in beginning his diary in 1910 was to free an impulse to write fiction which had gone underground.

Pasley says directly, "the presence of the traveler as an independent witness."[12] From the outset, the traveler registers indifference, disbelief, revulsion at the procedure he is witnessing.

"In the Penal Colony" appears to dramatize this crucial point: the claim that a man or woman can have knowledge of his or her guilt is to be doubted. The explorer, from whose perspective almost all the events of "In the Penal Colony" are narrated, disagrees with the officer in charge of the execution, who is full of conviction. For the officer, "guilt is always undeniable" (S 145); this view, for the explorer, is absolutely wrong. He thinks, rather, that it is "the injustice of the procedure and the inhumanity of the execution [that are] . . . undeniable" (S 151). "In the Penal Colony" casts doubt on the fact of anyone's guilt and hence on the efficacy of punishment for redemption. It does so radically for Kafka the author: it breaks up a paralyzing belief in the machinery of exculpation, and to this extent the story is redemptive.

Thus "In the Penal Colony" turns *The Trial* around. For there, Joseph K. begs the priest to tell him how any man can be called guilty: "We are all simply human beings here," he expostulates, "one as much as the other." "That is true," says the priest, "but that is how all guilty men talk" (T 264). Moreover, Kafka has arranged things so that the priest, rather than Joseph K., must be believed. The cathedral scene in which K. offers up this surmise is so packed with symbols of his benightedness, and the priest is so consistent in rebutting him, that K.'s position seems untenable. His imminent punishment is not to be doubted. But that, of course, is not the entire story; the auspicious truth that Joseph K. cannot embody is revealed in another work.

"In the Penal Colony" systematically offers counterexamples to the claims made by the court. In centering on the traveler, the story rejects any proposition in the form "X. is guilty." "Guilty" means guilty *of* some offense; that offense must collide at a legible point with a law, whose violation is identified in the verdict. But at two crucial places in the story, the officer in charge of the execution asks the traveler to read the text of the victim's sentence. The traveler stares at it, perplexed. The point is that the commandment cannot be read: it cannot be translated from an inspection of signs. The officer insists

12. Malcolm Pasley, "In the Penal Colony," in *The Kafka Debate: New Perspectives for Our Time,* ed. Angel Flores (New York: Gordian Press, 1977), p. 298.

that the commandment can be read both in the ordinary way and also in a deeper way: (1) he can read it immediately, but (2) the script of the sentence can be deciphered by the living body—literally, by the "wounds"—of the tortured culprit on the bed of the execution machine. The condemned prisoner reads with his body in a state of heightened awareness the words inscribed in the flesh.[13]

Now this is not an unfamiliar claim: Joseph K., for one, gets to hear it. The prospect of physical transparency—the body tortured into a fullness of receptive intelligence—fits very well into that codex of rumor which makes up the law of the court. "You'll come up against it yet [*Sie werden es zu fühlen bekommen*]" (T 10; R 263), warns the warder—inevitably—as the prison chaplain explains, for the verdict merges with the proceedings: that is, with the feelings and conduct of the accused throughout them (T 264). The verdict coincides with the prisoner's experience of his ordeal. And indeed, the outcome for Joseph K., who has evidently conducted his trial badly—obtusely, faintheartedly—is to be stabbed to death "like a dog," an unteachable dog. This conclusion, in which Joseph K. himself produces the likeness of "the dog" and does so in his dying moment, appears to prove the rule: the accused's conduct of his trial corresponds with the verdict, and the shame is immense.[14] A corollary would be that the priest—rigorous expositor of the law—having lived an unmystified life, dies an exemplary death.

But look, again, at "In the Penal Colony" in this respect: consider the outcome for the officer, the apparently faithful administrator of the Old Law, of his submitting to legal execution. His death is not exemplary; he is not illuminated. He carries over into death the same look of conviction he wore throughout his life but nothing more. And not unlike the accused Joseph K., his fate is to be stabbed with cold metal—an iron spike is driven into his forehead. The fate in

13. In a wicked way, Kafka's tormented prisoner responds to Goethe's invocation of a fullness of experienced life: every object—every stab of the needle—opens up in the victim a new organ of perception. Goethe remarked, "Man knows himself only in so far as he knows the world, which he becomes aware of only in himself and himself only in it. Every new object, rightly contemplated, opens up a new organ [of awareness] in us" ("Bedeutende Fördernis durch ein einziges geistreiches Wort," *Goethes Werke* [Hamburg: Christian Wegner, 1960], 13:38).

14. Even at his death, Joseph K. produces another blind analogy. Is the shame that is supposed to survive him the shame of his simile?

death of an upholder of the law, in "In the Penal Colony," is the fate of the guilty one in *The Trial*: he is struck down.[15] "In the Penal Colony" asks the questions: Who shall keep the keepers of the law? What man or woman among us is any more guilty than any other? And it asks them both as rhetorical questions and as literal questions having the answer "No one." In the meantime we note that the ignoramuses—the condemned soldier and the explorer, the unlettered one and the lettered one who cannot read the text of the law— go free. "In the Penal Colony" frees Kafka, too, for the worthy task of condemning Joseph K. We must see what really for.

*   *   *

In the penultimate chapter of *The Trial*, the scene in the cathedral, the prison chaplain reproves Joseph K. "You cast about too much for outside help," he declares, "especially from women." Joseph K. resists this accusation. He sets about defending the influence of women accomplices in his case. "If I could move some women I know to join forces in working for me, I couldn't help winning through. Especially before this court, which consists almost entirely of skirt-chasers." What the priest does next is warn Joseph K. that he is furious with him; K.'s mood is doubled by the growing oppressiveness of the scene, the murkiness of the air: "Black night had set in" (T 265). Everything in the moment suggests K. at a point of greatest benightedness, and in his next words the cause becomes clear. "It may be," he says, "that you don't know the nature of the Court you are serving"; in the silence that follows, he adds: "These are only my personal experiences." An instant later the priest shrieks from his pulpit: "Can't you see one pace before you?" The narrator, who does not sound like Joseph K., remarks: "It was an angry cry, but at the same time sounded like the unwary shriek of one who sees another fall and is startled out of his senses" (T 265–66).

The moment has the quality of a revelation, in the spirit of Heideg-

15. I allude to the phrase with which Kafka describes the fate of Karl Rossmann (the hero of *Amerika*) and of Joseph K: both are "executed without distinction in the end," writes Kafka, adding of Rossmann (the innocent), "with a gentler hand, more pushed aside than struck down." Kafka's readers must be warned against the diaries in English translation, which say that it is "the guilty one," Joseph K., who is "more pushed aside than struck down" (DII 132).

ger's aperçu that "poetic discourse" can disclose the existential possibilities of moods.[16] Joseph K. has asserted that he, unlike the priest, knows the nature of the court and that he knows it on the basis of personal experiences. The priest's response is to indict this position of blindness and error so dense and heavy as literally to drag the speaker down to his fall.

The revelation comes well prepared. From the outset the novel conceives of Joseph K.'s trial by the court as the issue of his acknowledging the question of its nature and authority. "What authority," he asks of the men who come to arrest him, "could they represent?" (T 7). But K.'s summation in the cathedral is the yield of a year's evasion of the force of this great question, which has its provisional answer in an earlier scene: "This legal action was nothing more than a business deal" (T 159). K.'s evasion of the question in the cathedral is further clarified by his moods immediately preceding and following.

At the beginning of his exchange with the chaplain, Joseph K. repeats what he has often thought before: "I am not guilty . . . it's a mistake" (T 264). This is a position that Joseph K. can maintain only in defiance of reason. "You are held to be guilty," the priest has said—for the court is drawn by the guilt of those it arrests. Joseph K. can maintain his innocence vis-à-vis the law of the court only by believing that in arresting him the court has made a mistake. But what does K. know of the nature of the court which could allow for a mistake of this sort? We have seen that he will try to authorize his judgment of its (derelict) character by an appeal to his own experiences. But the chaplain has already preempted this argument, for to Joseph K.'s claim of innocence on the grounds that no one man is any more guilty than another, the priest retorts: "That is true, but that's how all guilty men talk" (T 264). This is to say that the perception of the nature of the court which accuses it of dereliction cannot be well founded on personal experiences, since the personal experiences of the defendant are distorted, circumscribed, and obscured precisely by the terms of the charge he cannot endure. (This misshaping burden might be called his "guilt.") Joseph K. is inculpated by his very impatience to find himself innocent;[17] it prevents him from taking on

16. Heidegger, *Being and Time*, p. 205.

17. Franz: "He admits he doesn't know the law and yet he claims he's innocent" (T 10).

the question: What, apart from my need to find myself innocent, is the nature and authority of the court that has arrested me?

Since personal experiences end precisely where what one is afraid of begins and hence cannot survey what one is guilty of, they are very likely able to offer only the worst road to this reflection. It is therefore impossible that Joseph K. can produce a saving insight. He will not broach the possibility of his guilt; he will not follow the track of an equivocation that must affirm—as the claim of innocence must deny—an "arrest," the sense of which is to be seized by the question of the nature and authority of the law.[18] But at what level does this question of authority most concern Kafka?

When one speaks of the ministry that held Kafka on trial and in thrall, it becomes necessary to speak of literature. It is impossible to overestimate the intensity with which Kafka felt its claim or the force he spent inquiring into its nature. Now the relation to literature of the categories of the law, of being on trial, and of guilt has often been noted apropos of *The Trial* but almost entirely through the dim binoculars of Kafka's relation with Felice Bauer. Stated plainly, Kafka puts a guilty persona of himself on trial for having decided against marriage and for that bachelorhood in which he could apply himself to literature. In a letter to Felice sent a few weeks after he had begun composing the novel, Kafka indeed wrote: "You see, you were not only the greatest friend, but at the same time the greatest enemy, of my work, at least from the point of view of my work. Thus, though fundamentally it loved you beyond measure, equally it had to resist you with all its might for the sake of self-preservation" (LF 437).

But Kafka's letters to Felice from the very outset emphasized the fullness of the hopes he attached to literature. He values it as a literally constitutive function of his identity. "My mode of life," he wrote, "is devised solely for writing" (LF 21). "When not writing, I feel myself being pushed out of life by unyielding hands" (LF 116). "My attitude to my writing . . . is unchangeable; it is a part of my nature" (LF 279). "Not a bent for writing, my dearest Felice, not a bent, but my

18. The attitude that Kafka appears to solicit from Joseph K. is alertness to the possibility of his guilt. This means the possibility of a guilt that one might pronounce in words that conjure the longed-for assimilation of adversative authority. One takes on the burden of an arrest by an unknown, invisible authority as if it were one's own desire. And thus one asks the question of the meaning of this other law with all possible ardor, an attentiveness that turns one's whole life into a question.

entire self" (LF 309). Indeed, his "whole being," as he wrote to Felice's father in 1913, was "directed toward literature; I have followed this direction unswervingly . . . , and the moment I abandon it I cease to live. Everything I am, and am not, is a result. . . . It is the earthly reflection of a higher necessity" (LF 313). To marry would be to deflect his rigor, to squander his intensity. Kafka broke off his engagement with Felice on the strength of a decision he had been contemplating for a year, yet in the bachelorhood that enveloped him, as we have seen, he could not write.

He was mortified by this state of affairs. Breaking with Felice, he was guilty of abandoning the woman whom he made fascinating. Literature could appear as the one possible agency of his exculpation; he needed to go on inquiring into the nature of the justifying authority—his writing—at the same time that literature remained hidden, absconded. What judgment was contained in the fact that it would not come? His broken engagement made acute the question of the authority of literature—an authority possibly dubious in itself, a mere formality, or one that he was guilty of evading. But his broken engagement did not raise the question for the first time or in its most rigorous form.

The intensity of Kafka's relation to literature produced the redemptive expectations of *The Trial* apart from Kafka's relation to his fiancée. Toward the end of his life, he described to Max Brod "his bizarre kind of writing, the only goal of which is his own salvation or damnation" (L 347). Yet in a stunning phrase written when he was only twenty, Kafka made the same claim while suggesting the impertinence of it: "God doesn't want me to write, but I—I must" (L 10). These propositions taken together constitute a space outside God's order, in which safety is gained by taking obscure, even "devilish" risks. Kafka prowls about on a proving ground for justification according to a law unknown or of his own devising—but not wholeheartedly enough.

This state of affairs is actually represented in *The Trial*. The connection between Kafka the writer and the writing commandment that held him in thrall is systematically paralleled by the bond between Joseph K. and the law. In a diary entry for 1910, Kafka wrote: "How do I excuse my not yet having written anything today? In no way [*mit nichts*] . . . . I have continually an invocation in my ear: 'Were you to come, invisible judgment [*Gericht*]!'" (DI 36, Ta 31). Between 1910 and 1914 the claim of the court sounded more and more definitively. In 1913 Kafka described himself as a man "chained to invisible literature by invisible chains [who] . . . screams when approached because, so he claims, someone is touching those chains" (LF 308). This could make us think of a scene in *The Trial* in which an accused gentleman in the law offices screams when Joseph K. touches his arm "quite loosely"; the usher explains: "Most of these accused men are so sensitive" (T 81).

The period preceding the writing of *The Trial* was increasingly full of Kafka's expressions of his shortcomings vis-à-vis his writing. He was thirty on June 3, 1913; on November 18 of that year he wrote: "How many doubts have I meanwhile had about my writing" (DI 308). On March 9, 1914, several months before the "tribunal" in the hotel, he noted: "I have written nothing for a year" (DII 25); on April 8, 1914: "Yesterday incapable of writing even one word. Today no better. Who will save me? And the turmoil in me, deep down, scarcely visible" (DII 31). Kafka's thirtieth year, like Joseph K.'s, stood in a steadily disintegrating relation to the law (of writing) at the same time that the law required a fuller and fuller devotion. Kafka protested that his own powers were as such too fragile. He made the point with great power in a diary entry for August 6, 1914, in the middle of the composition of *The Trial*:

> What will be my fate as a writer is very simple. My talent for portraying my dreamlike inner life has thrust all other matters into the background; my life has dwindled dreadfully, nor will it cease to dwindle. Nothing else will ever satisfy me. But the strength I can muster for that portrayal is not to be counted upon: perhaps it has already vanished forever, perhaps it will come back to me again, although the circumstances of my life don't favor its return. Thus I waver, continually fly to the summit of the mountain, but then fall back in a moment. Others waver too, but in lower regions, with greater strength; if they are in danger of falling, they are caught up by the kinsman who walks beside them for that very purpose. But I waver on the heights; it is not death, alas, but the eternal torments of dying. [DII 77]

Literature, like the court, is the grim ministry requiring the sacrifice not only of sexual love but of everything else that might be called lived experience—a sacrifice that Kafka certainly had not yet made.

To judge from his moods, Kafka's relation to writing is guilty, and it seems to be intrinsically guilty. As long as he lives, he cannot be equal to his fate as a writer. This is the logical content of the mood of cold apathy that comes again and again to arrest *The Trial*. His guilt toward writing can be seen as a whole constellation of guilts whose outline can be drawn. Kafka's confessional writings modulate the guilt of writing in terms of (1) *any* writing he could produce[19] but also (2) his failure to produce *any* writing at all. A sort of surplus guilt, more nearly remediable, arises from the improper connection of writing and worldly experience. Kafka is guilty as a writer because (3) his work aspires to a vindication of his personal experience and (4) in this way becomes a surrogate for the shortcomings of experience. It is thus a writing that is bent on rehabilitation and, hence, redemptive in an only trivial way—the Freudian way of providing substitutive gratification. It is a writing whose purpose he has posed in advance and from which he can discover nothing except this purpose. This will not do. If a single one of Kafka's formulations on this matter can serve, it is this letter to Felice:

> Writing means revealing oneself to excess; that utmost of self-revelation and surrender, in which a human being, when involved with others, would feel he was losing himself, and from which, therefore, he will always shrink as long as he is in his right mind—for everyone wants to live as long as he is alive—even that degree of self–revelation and surrender is not enough for writing. [LF 156]

Yet in 1912 Kafka was able to say of the quality of his surrender:

> I have never been the sort of person who carried something out at all costs. . . . What I have written was written in a lukewarm bath. I have not experienced the eternal hell of real writers. [L 82]

What is certain is that the relations with others constituting ethical experience cannot supply writing with a model for its own discipline. The view that writing aims at the exculpation of the authorial personality is therefore perverse. The "lukewarm bath" images an unsavory confusion of two orders that belong apart, according to a hierarchy:

19. "Writing itself often leads to false formulations. Sentences have their own force of gravity from which one cannot escape" (LF 389).

the degree of Kafka's belonging to writing stands above interpersonal relations "real" or internalized. The lukewarmness in the question of the law (of writing) that Kafka registers in himself is what he will find in Joseph K.: lukewarmness in the question of the law. In tracing Joseph K.'s bad faith, Kafka enacts his own captivation by the law (of writing) and his inadequacy before it.

If we consider Kafka the writer's relation to the law of writing as systematically guilty, we will wonder what good it could do him to continue to write *The Trial*. How could the literary condemnation of a persona vindicate its author? If Kafka's act of writing—including the very act of writing "In the Penal Colony"—was itself guilty, how could his writing acquire the authority to free him from guilt? And yet how, except by writing, could the answer be determined? Writing "In the Penal Colony," Kafka responded to the offer of redemption on conditions of the greatest risk. In the story the guilty writer puts the guilty writer on trial.

A glimmer of a solution to these difficulties arises from a lately refined scrutiny of one aspect of "In the Penal Colony." It is the link between the self-destructive machine administering martial law and the law of that writing that holds Kafka in thrall.[20] For the essence of the machinery of justice in "In the Penal Colony" is a writing instrument, which writes the victim's sentence into his living body.[21] The allegory of the writing machine is clarified by the logic of the execu-

20. "As it systematizes in an image the whole first phase of Kafka's mature writing, the penal apparatus is also a metaphoric description of this writing itself." This insight is Walter Sokel's, in *Franz Kafka* (New York: Columbia University Press, 1966). p. 26. I diverge a little in my view of what kind of writing this is. Anderson, in "The Ornaments of Writing," p. 14, goes on to note: "Kafka's 'Strafkolonie' takes the equation of self and literature literally: . . . the decorated body of the condemned man is also Kafka's own body turned into the substance of his art. The process of inscription in this text describes the writing of [the] . . . earlier text. Pain, pleasure, redemption all derive from the ornaments of writing."

21. Kruse discusses this point as part of his argument associating the world views of "In the Penal Colony" and Lukács's *Theory of the Novel*: both works depict the dissolution of an order of things hale and synchronic into a modernity fragmented and diachronic, marked by the chase of events after one another in time. Kruse's evidence: in the beginning, under the Old Commandant, the moments of the administration of justice are simultaneous: the offense is plain; its guilt cries out for all to hear; offense, indictment, condemnation, and sentencing are simultaneous. Diachrony is introduced into law only as a means of translating into a form apprehensible to the culprit the sentence of the Old Commandant, which appears to be a kind of image apprehended whole in an instant of time ("Lukács' *Theorie des Romans*," pp. 248–49).

tion—a scriptive logic, a type of storytelling and storyreading. In an explicit manner, the application of the punishment has the character of a read tale, with its retarding tropes, peripety, discovery, and definitive ending.[22] "In The Penal Colony" is haunted by a consciousness of the act of writing—or, more precisely, of reading writing—as corporal punishment.[23] The execution of a sentence as a kind of performance of narrative parallels the execution of a sentence via the act of writing *The Trial*: like the officer, Kafka too has undertaken to compose (*The Trial*) for the sake of his redemption.[24]

Is it entirely clear, however, that the self-destruction of a legal procedure, which so much resembles Kafka's trial by writing, is auspicious? After all, the collapse of this figure of writing as corrective punishment would also tend to collapse the association of law with the process of writing—hence, strip writing altogether of its redemptive claim. Kafka's last defense therefore runs as follows: Only if writing can be associated with an altogether different procedure can there be redemption in it. In this light, we may read "In the Penal Colony" as identifying, destroying, and hence exorcising a definition of writing that would destroy Kafka as it destroys itself. The story dramatizes an image of what must not be the case if Kafka is to survive: namely, the association of writing with the Old Law. "In the Penal Colony" aims to *rewrite writing* in inverse order, so that writing might constitute the promise of a redemption.

Only at this point does the story confront us with its fundamental question: What is the principle of the writing fatally associated with martial law? What degrades such writing to corporal punishment without redemption? It is, I propose, the belief that the accused's fate, his personal *fatum*, might be communicated to him by an act of writing authentic by virtue of its fidelity to the victim's ethical experi-

22. Ibid., p. 248.

23. For a discussion of the torture instrument as a machine inflicting reading, see Clayton Koelb's essay "*In der Strafkolonie*: Kafka and the Scene of Reading," *German Quarterly* 55 (1982): 511–25.

24. I cited above the passage from the diaries in which Kafka describes the agony of his "talent for portraying [in *The Trial* his] . . . dreamlike inner life." Mark Anderson brilliantly connects the conclusion, which speaks of the "eternal process of dying," with the "image of the not yet dead officer [of 'In the Penal Colony'], suspended in the grip of the writing machine." Here Kafka draws "a self-portrait of his then stalled work on *Der Prozeß*, that is, in his ardently desired but failed attempt to achieve redemption through writing" ("The Ornaments of Writing," pp. 20-21).

ence—a moment of communication which, furthermore, amounts to his final experience. In this view, the trajectory of the sentencing needles is perfect insofar as they follow the tracks that the experience of others has already inscribed in the victim's body. The orgasmic character of the illumination identifies a commonplace about reading: "By a kind of Platonic recollection," as Vincent Descombes puts it, "the text with which we fall in love will be the one wherein what we know already can be learned and relearned."[25] "In the Penal Colony" derides this view: if the prisoner were to find bliss in recognizing that "Honor your superiors" expresses the core of his ethical being, it would be over his dead body. He is being murdered for the crime of having failed to salute a closed door behind which his ethical superior is asleep. For Kafka the writer, the belief that writing redeems insofar as it produces moral illuminations of experience is a belief to be resisted.

That is the point of his continuing to write *The Trial*, the sense of his decision: "I will not give up. . . . I've summoned up my last resources to this end. I made the remark that 'I don't avoid people in order to live quietly, but rather in order to be able to die quietly.' Now I will defend myself" (DII 73). But what is at stake in his final defense by writing goes beyond reproducing and justifying his lived experience. This is the insight that Kafka will have to affirm continually. In choosing to execute Joseph K., he does so on the grounds of an offense for which he, the writer, does not intend to be liable. It is not to be doubted: K.'s guilt in *The Trial* turns essentially on his attachment to his personal experience. From the outset, he has determined to fight his accusers with the wisdom drawn from personal experience, and this decision destroys his case in advance.

From his conversation with the painter Titorelli, K. learns that according to the Law the innocent shall be acquitted, even though, says Titorelli, he has "'never encountered one case of definite acquittal.' 'Not one case of acquittal, then,' said K., as if he were speaking to himself and his hopes, 'but that merely confirms the opinion that I have already formed of this Court. It is a pointless institution from any point of view. A single executioner could do all that is needed.' 'You mustn't generalize,' said the painter in displeasure: 'I have only

25. Vincent Descombes, *Modern French Philosophy* (Cambridge: Cambridge University Press, 1980), p. 4.

quoted *my own experience. . . .*' '*That's quite enough,*' said K. . . . He had no time now to inquire into the truth of all the painter said" (T 192–93; my italics).

In the cathedral scene the prison chaplain judges K.'s attachment to personal experience as the meaning of his fall. The perception making up the solid content of "In the Penal Colony" is the impossibility that writing could be faithful to ethical experience and, being read, could make up the content of a final ethical experience. This truth emphasizes the particular ground of Joseph K.'s offense in *The Trial*: his invocation of lived experience to supply a plan of exculpation. In destroying this model figure of attachment to experience, Kafka means to dissolve one more little obstacle to the freedom that perhaps awaits him (DII 92).[26] This insight clears a space in which he can advance in writing *The Trial*. He has, for a time, the reason and the power to execute K.—a power that comes from having dared to write "In the Penal Colony," from having put on trial in the figure of the officer not a persona of his empirical personality but of the author who is condemning an empirical personality to foreordained destruction. "Someone must have been telling lies about Joseph K." Indeed someone has been: it is the author, writing out of an assumed moral superiority to his double.

The purpose of bringing *The Trial* to an end, therefore, is to annihilate Joseph K. and the officer as embodiments of this error. In claiming to read off their fate in advance from the script of personal experience, they display the same obtuseness that avenged itself on Kafka in the form of cold apathy—the result of composing *The Trial* in the locus of his interpersonal concerns, aiming to vindicate his ethical personality by arranging in advance its judicial murder. The execution of Joseph K. is only the most complete reckoning with the suspicion that *The Trial* was begun in reaction to the interference of a woman and the war. Kafka finally condemns the recourse to empirical explanations of apathy as its solvent.

26. The stakes supporting this gesture are particularly high, as is suggested by a fact about the manuscript of *Der Prozeß* pointed out by Erich Heller: on the last page, on which Joseph K. is executed, Kafka writes, not "K." but "I" (BF 642). See John Winkelman, "Felice Bauer and *The Trial*," in Flores, *The Kafka Debate*, pp. 311–34. The conclusion of *The Trial* therefore has the logic of the conclusion of the diary entry beginning "'You,' I Said" (DI 28–29), discussed in Chapter One; the narrator survives in executing a character about whom there must be no doubt that it is a persona, a deadly possibility of himself.

The basic stake in Kafka's writing exceeds the destruction of error: simply put, it is ecstasy. Writing, Kafka enacts his craving for a final word—as a being that craves a final breath, craves the ecstasy beyond which there need be no more breathing: "There is no having, only a being, only a state of being that craves the last breath, craves suffocation" (DF 37). Such writing has little to do with moral reflection drawn from an "inner world" of lived experience. Kafka distinguishes between the being that craves the last breath, being perfect, and the self in splinters that chokes on itself: "How would it be," Kafka would write, "if one were to choke to death *on oneself.* If the pressure of introspection were to diminish, or close off entirely, the opening through which one flows forth into the world" (DII 223; my italics).[27] The risk of not writing ecstatically is—quite literally— choking, not bursting out; for the goal is "not shaking off the self, but consuming the self" (DF 87). These sentences were written toward the end of Kafka's life, but early in his diary, too, Kafka recorded his desire "to write all my anxiety entirely out of me, write it into the depths of the paper just as it comes out of the depths of me, or write it in such a way that I can draw what I have written into me completely" (DI 173). The movement of this desire is for an opening, a widening, of his straitened being and an inhalation of what he has written like breath—the breath of freedom that recreates being.

If such writing leaves him, he cannot breathe at all. "In the Penal Colony" opens toward ecstatic writing because it is not about experience but about writing: it is a taking of metaphysical breath in annihilating the seductive proposition that there could exist a kind of writing that would be faithful to experience and would vindicate the sufferer by being finally expressive of his experience. *This postulate is always to be doubted.* The author cannot be indicted; he goes free to write as long as he writes otherwise than the officer, the sentencing machine with women's handkerchiefs tucked into its military collar.

That such insight appears to be winnable only through writing helps to specify the difference between Kafka and Joseph K. Unlike

27. When Kafka seeks to curb in his fiancée the taste for self-improvement that has led her to read the work of Herbert Eulenberg, he attacks that prose as "breathless and unclean" (LF 129). In a striking number of scenes in *The Trial*, unbearable oppression is conveyed by airlessness. See Elias Canetti, *Der andere Prozeß: Kafkas Briefe an Felice* (Munich: Hanser, 1969), p. 33.

the author of *The Trial*, Joseph K. does not write a line in self-discovery: "How dreary such a task would be" (T 161). The totality of the act of writing in *The Trial* is displaced from K. onto the adversary party and devalued, for writing appears as an indecipherable or obscene screed, a shabby appurtenance of his tormentors. "The word as warder [*Scherge*]," wrote Jakob van Hoddis, "or language as the bureaucracy of the soul"; *The Trial* shows this as the deficient case.[28] Furthermore, there is a kind of logic in K.'s not writing that follows from his decision to grasp his case within the frame of a trial by civil law—more precisely, as an only comic variant of a true case at law: the script is not one to which he has to contribute, for he has found himself innocent in advance, the victim of judicial error. The constraints of comedy that bind Joseph K. are only apparently innocent: genuine innocence, for Kafka, would lie in perfect surrender to the iron points of fiction: "It is enough that the arrows fit exactly in the wounds that they have made" (DII 206).

K.'s unregeneracy goes on increasing precisely at the point where Kafka completed "In the Penal Colony" and took up writing *The Trial*. K. grows more and more obtuse, riper for punishment, hence menaced; he seems less and less like the narrator, the conveyer of the menace. The impression of their difference is marked by K.'s collapse into Leni's webbed hands and quite particularly by K.'s amazing disclaimer in "The Lawyer" episode, even though "the thought of his case never left him now," that "if he were to achieve anything, it was essential that he should banish from his mind once and for all the idea of possible guilt" (T 142, 158–59). Hence this second, important distinction: Joseph K., who is guilty of having acceded to his arrest yet of having evaded the question of its authority, will not acknowledge a guilty conscience. As a persona of Kafka, K. can be conceived as conscienceless because of his very rejection and devaluation of writing. But the terms of conscience and writing are precisely constitutive of Kafka. Accused before his law, Kafka writes and judges his own productions. Because he abides and makes generative his anxiety, he is able in this novel to evoke an ecstatic relation to the law: it is in seizing and plunging the knife into your own body when you

---

28. Jakob van Hoddis, "Von Mir und von Ich," *Prosastücke 1907–1913: Dichtungen und Briefe*, ed. Regina Nörtermann (Zurich: Arche, 1987), p. 66. My thanks to Peter Musolf for bringing these words to my attention.

have grasped that it is not your adversary's but your own. "More than consolation," wrote Kafka at the end, is "You too have weapons" (DII 233). "Mount your attacker's horse and ride it yourself" (DII 224). The foretaste of that ride is in Joseph K.'s dream, but Kafka had to delete it from *The Trial*, for K. does not deserve it:

> How easy it was to outwit the Court! [K. dreams.] Titorelli . . . seized hold of . . . [him] and started to run, pulling K. after him. In the twinkling of an eye they were in the Law Courts and flying along the stairs, upward and downward too, without the slightest effort, gliding along as easily as a buoyant craft through water. And at the very moment when K. looked down at his feet and came to the conclusion that this lovely motion had no connection with the humdrum life he had led until now—at that very moment over his bent head the transformation occurred. The light which until then had been behind them changed and suddenly flowed in a blinding stream toward them. K. looked up, Titorelli nodded assent and turned him round. He was in the corridor of the Law Courts again, but everything was quieter and simpler [*ruhiger und einfacher*] and there were no conspicuous details. [T 309; R 459]

In a late aphorism Kafka gives this moment a background at once archaic and apocryphal but assuredly literary: " 'But then he returned to his work just as though nothing had happened.' This is a remark that we are familiar with from a vague abundance of old stories, although perhaps it does not occur in any of them" (DF 48). Kafka (as Ritchie Robertson suggests) might have known this Hasidic saying about the world redeemed: "Alles wird sein wie hier—nur ein ganz klein wenig anders [Everything will be as it is here—only a very little bit different]."[29] Such is the reward of writing well.

29. My conclusion is much indebted to Robertson's *Kafka*, pp. 119–20, which stresses both the deleted chapter from *The Trial* and Kafka's aphorism about "old stories." Robertson also supplies from Walter Benjamin's *Schriften* (ed. T. W. and Gretel Adorno [Frankfurt am Main: Suhrkamp, 1955] 2:97) the Hasidic saying but not the context of writing to which, I believe, K.'s proposed transformation alludes (p. 120). It is characteristic of Kafka to think of the "other world" as different from "this world" not by the addition of something new but by the intensification of something already at hand: "What in this world is called suffering in another world, unchanged and only liberated from its opposite, is bliss" (DF 46). "Nothing," he wrote, "has changed; there, we are what we were here" (L 204). See Chapter Three, p. 87.

Chapter Ten

Kafka as Expressionist

It is just such hermeneutic trials that involve us when we ask the question of the place of a writer in a literary movement. Suppose we consider Kafka an essential and powerful Expressionist author. Have we, in saying this, asserted anything more than a tautology? Have we said anything other than that Kafka has covertly supplied our definition of Expressionism?[1] That he could do so, of course, is made fairly explicit in the preceding chapters. A definition of Expressionism that excluded Kafka's distinctive features would be severely privative.[2]

1. "Kafka's literature of existence—in an of course incomparable way—is part of the Expressionist literature of existence. As literature in Kafka speaks of border skirmishes between life and death, Expressionist literature speaks of existential border situations—of anxiety, the experience of death, guilt, and suffering. Its recurrent metaphorical paradigms are already familiar from Kafka: homelessness, the loss of orientation, impotence, 'thrownness,' exposure, vulnerability, anxiety, madness, sickness, imprisonment, alienation. All are metaphors of Gnostic origin. They define Expressionist literature as a literature of the existential experience of alienation. They too speak of the 'dream terrors' of existence" (Gerhard Kurz, *Traum-Schrecken: Kafkas literarische Existenzanalyse* [Stuttgart: Metzler, 1980], p. 150). It is telling that Kurz shows up the lurking danger of tautology in the course of resisting it: Kafka belongs to Expressionism at the same time that he is "incomparably" different.

2. This question has been posed in quite specific terms by Paul Raabe in "Franz Kafka und der Expressionismus," reprinted in *Franz Kafka*, ed. Heinz Politzer (Darmstadt: Wissenschaftliche Buchgesellschaft, 1973), pp. 386–405. Raabe argues that Kafka is not Expressionist; he does so in opposing Walter Sokel's claim that Kafka's works during the period of 1912–17 are "classical Expressionist." ("Der Expressionist Franz Kafka: Zur 80. Wiederkehr seines Geburtstags an 3. Juni 1963,"

"Categories of people," writes Ian Hacking, "come into existence at the same time as kinds of people come into being to fit those categories, and there is a two-way interaction between these processes." Hence, history writing (such as Foucault's) can be understood as "stories about the connection between certain kinds of description coming into being or going out of existence, and certain kinds of people coming into being or going out of existence."[3] These remarks ought to illuminate the question we are considering: To what extent should Kafka be understood as having created tautologically his reception as an Expressionist? Or is there a phenomenon "Expressionism" to which Kafka may (or may not) be annexed without altering its identity? Hacking's comment suggests that neither question is quite the right one. Kafka helps create the description of a literary movement that ran its course during Kafka's lifetime, and the movement thereupon reshapes him and his work to come under its category. But a point needs to be added: the movement defines him otherwise, unexpectedly. To treat Kafka as Expressionist is to be willing to give him back features belonging constitutively to Expressionism and different from those he lends to it.

And he then gives more back to the description, and it gives still more back to him, until this "two-way interaction" achieves a certain equilibrium for a generation of interpreters. Defining the relationship of a writer to a literary movement is very much a matter of devising a metaphor that has the power to reshape its once proper meaning.

Kafka is fruitfully considered an essential and powerful Expressionist writer. To explain why, I shall take a long way round. I am prepossessed in favor of this idea, rapt as I am by the memory of an event that took place in the fall of 1958—one of the last public events in the history of German Expressionism. Its venue was the West Side apartment of Walter Sokel, who, having recently finished writing a

---

Forum [Vienna] 10:289). Raabe's essay, however, unduly emphasizes the tellingly negative detail with a sort of casual positivism: Kafka hated noise; how inappropriate, therefore, to attach him to the clamoring of the Expressionists. Kurz notes that for Kafka's contemporaries, certainly, his connection with Expressionism was beyond question; Kurz cites the obituary of Marie Puymanova, who eulogized Kafka as "an Austrian Expressionist" (*Traum-Schrecken*, p. 218).

3. The quotations from Ian Hacking are found in Peter Barham, "Two Ronnies," a review of R. D. Laing's *Wisdom, Madness, and Folly: The Making of a Psychiatrist* in *London Review of Books*, July 4, 1985, p. 12.

book on Expressionist literature,[4] celebrated the occasion by inviting the most important of living and available German Expressionist writers.[5] This was Richard Huelsenbeck, who, along with Hugo Ball, Klabund, and Tristan Tzara, founded the German section of the Dadaist interlude of Expressionism in Zurich in 1916; some forty years later, he was practicing as a psychiatrist on Park Avenue.[6] Together with a few other acquaintances, Huelsenbeck heard a reading of poems by Reinhard Paul Becker, later a professor of German literature at New York University. I quote, in translation, one of the poems that Paul Becker read on that occasion.

Synchronization

On an evening in November Twentyseven,
    as a woman somewhere in Berlin
    draped a fluffy furpiece over her arm,
    as a girl in Munich pushed down
    the latest in cloches over her short black bob,
    and Josephine Baker in her dressing room
    stepped into the banana apron for her number,
on this foggynovembernight
a simple man in love with his wife
and blissful returned from a walk.

And on the same yellow evening,
    while four Brownshirts beat a Red to death
    in a dark street in the Rhineland,
    while Al Capone in Chicago
    dreamt of burying a friend,
    and the hot Jupiter lamps were finally extinguished
    over the Leda-face of Garbo,
on the same evening this simple man
took off his collar and stud in front of the mirror
and put it carefully down in place.

4. Walter Sokel, *The Writer in Extremis: Expressionism in Twentieth-Century Literature* (Stanford, Calif.: Stanford University Press, 1959).

5. He could very nearly have invited Alfred Ehrenstein, the dramatist, who had seemed to have disappeared. While Sokel was composing the pages devoted to Ehrenstein in *Writer in Extremis*, the writer, unbeknownst to him, lay dying of cancer in a dismal room *across the street*. By 1958 Ehrenstein was dead.

6. In 1918, Dadaism, still under the leadership of Huelsenbeck, had been transplanted to Berlin, where it began to acquire a Left social-reformist character. Cf. Roy F. Allen, *Literary Life in German Expressionism and the Berlin Circles* (Ann Arbor, Mich.: UMI Research Press, 1983), p. 39.

And a little later that evening,
    as the couples danced the Charleston again
    only a few weeks after Rilke's death,
    at the moment that the aged Dada
    in a bar poured absinthe in his ear
    to stupefy himself and wept and wept,
    because his life was so red and dead and bled,
    the man and the woman went to bed
and lay listening to all that time
and grasped each other anxiously.

Then for a second the earth stood still:
    Charlie Chaplin stopped, motionless, somewhere
    An automobile braked to a screeching stop,
    The girl in Munich looked mistily into the void,
    Josephine Baker waited, tan and enchanted,
    Garbo knowingly shut her eyes,
    And Dada cocked his head, and listened to the stillness:
The man had fled time into the woman,
I sprang between them onto the halted globe
and whirled along, around this time and death.[7]

Asked for a comment, in the ensuing quietness, Richard Huelsenbeck, the Dada, observed: "His parents would be so proud."

*   *   *

Some exact chronology is required to explain Huelsenbeck's remark. Counting back thirty years from the time of this writing, Huelsenbeck heard Reinhard Paul Becker read a poem celebrating his own conception, some thirty years earlier, in "November Twentyseven." Rilke died in December 1926, hence somewhat earlier than the "few weeks" before November Twentyseven which Becker's poem gives as Rilke's death date. An explanation for this poetic license? It contributes to the myth many poets construct, that the new poet begins just where the overpowering master has left off. As if to have been conceived during the great precursor's lifetime would be to be conceived by him, be the slave of his myth, be forever after spoken by him—but as if, too, to wait too long to be conceived and thus claim succession to the crown of poetic authority were to allow a

---

7. Reinhard Paul Becker, *Veränderungen auf eine Briefstelle und andere Gedichte* (Wiesbaden: Limes, 1960), pp. 36–37 (© by Limes Verlag Niedermayer & Schlüter GmbH München; printed here by permission).

dangerous interval in which a rival and usurper could intrude. Rilke died in 1926, Kafka in 1924; between these dates, by general consent, lies the death day of Expressionism—by which is meant the German aspect of an upheaval in art and literature particularly visible in the years between 1910 and 1925.

Becker's poem, residually Expressionist in mood,[8] actually evokes the margin of *post*-Expressionism. A glance at the poem focuses, through its specific differences, some of the things that therefore do belong to Expressionism. Huelsenbeck's comment picks up the benevolent relation in this poem between the generations. The speaker blesses his father (speaks of his father as *selig*, as blessed or blissful), but Expressionist literature profiles the furious rivalry of the lamed or held-back son and the unnaturally potent father. Anxiety in Expressionist literature is all on the side of the son and his shameful dream of usurpation; the father is an intact, indivisible force. But in "Synchronization," anxiety is all on the side of the married couple. And though the narrator leaps onto a world of "time and death," still the world has stopped where he stands to let him on; and in that leap there is a more willing consent, a yea-saying to destiny, than is found among such father-hating Expressionists as Arnolt Bronnen, the author of *Parricide*, and Walter Hasenclever, author of *Son*. For the Expressionists, says James Rolleston, time "is a paralyzed apocalypse, . . . the suddenly spatial vision of temporality as a completed entity."[9]

"Synchronization" literally acknowledges the passing of Dada in the figure of "the aged Dada," a burnt-out case, and to a certain extent explains its passing. The old Expressionist is excluded from the poem's permissive attitude to a new culture of film and spectacle, in which Greta Garbo and Charlie Chaplin and Josephine Baker and the Charleston can seem genuine sources of beauty, freedom, and grace.[10] This development marks an age in which Dada (and, by

8. Becker's poem is dedicated to George Grosz, the Berlin Expressionist painter and caricaturist of the main (and crudest) social types of Wilhelmine Germany. In 1958 Grosz was living in ill health on Long Island; in 1959 he returned to Berlin. Three decades later, his work as a diarist and poet is being studied with great interest.

9. James Rolleston, *Narratives of Ecstasy: The Romantic Temporality in Modern German Poetry* (Detroit, Mich.: Wayne State University Press, 1987), p. 19.

10. Kafka allegedly said to Gustav Janouch: "Chaplin is a technician. . . . As a dental technician makes false teeth, so he manufactures aids to the imagination. That's what his films are. That's what films in general are" (J 159).

substitution, Expressionism) has lost its iconoclastic purpose. The new popular culture confuses the parties of the older cultural war.

At the outset of the period 1910–25, there was, first of all, no popular culture of film and technically-produced spectacle from which poets and writers could borrow images to articulate their main brief: their defiance of middle-high culture, the prop of a prosperous, tasteless, power-serving middle class. The Expressionist enemy was the stereotypical culture of *Bildung*—of alleged self-actualization through renunciation of personal values, an ethos perceived by its critics to be all in the service of a state, the alibi of an educational system aiming to manufacture functionaries. Expressionists viewed it as a sort of spilt religion, a prose of empty edification leading to national service, a world view propagated in the gymnasia for the type whom Dostoevsky once excoriated as "our romantics": "Their characteristic is . . . to give way, to yield, from policy; never to lose sight of a useful practical object, to keep their eye on that object through all the enthusiasms and volumes of lyrical poems, and at the same time to preserve 'the good and the beautiful' inviolate within them."[11] The Expressionist target (on the level of the superstructure) was a middle-high culture adorning the national obeisance to authority; the Expressionist writer aimed to shock out of their wits the consumers of an art of uplift, half-in-love-with-death.[12]

After Heine and the 1840s, there had never again been in Germany

11. Fyodor Dostoevsky, *Notes from Underground,* in *Three Short Novels of Dostoevsky,* ed. Avrahm Yarmolinsky, trans. Constance Garnett (New York: Doubleday, 1960), p. 219. The Expressionists, who read Dostoevsky and Nietzsche continually, would remember Nietzsche's jibes against Schiller—"the moral trumpeter of Säckingen," "the 'noble' Schiller, who lambasted the ears of the Germans with big words" ("The Case of Wagner," in *Basic Writings of Nietzsche,* ed. and trans. Walter Kaufmann [New York: The Modern Library, 1966], p. 617). On the Expressionist reception of Nietzsche generally, see Geoffrey Waite, *Nietzsche/Hölderlin: A Politics of Appropriation* (Gainesville: Florida State University Press, forthcoming). Preparing the way for Heinrich Mann's portrait of Professor *Unrat* ("Garbage," also "Non-Minister") were sentiments such as these, in a distich by Richard Dehmel: "But the kitchen odor of Goethe and Schiller sticks / Clinging in nose and mouth, my brains steam classically" (quoted with other examples in Hansjörg Schneider, *Jakob van Hoddis: Ein Beitrag zur Erforschung des Expressionismus* [Bern: Francke, 1967], p. 27).

12. Carl Sternheim's target: "'the heroic life of the bourgeoisie—*bürgerliches Heldenleben,*' a life . . . of surpassing vulgarity, crass scramble for status, and suicidal rush into a great war. 'After us, collapse!' exclaims one of Sternheim's characters in a play he wrote in the last year of peace. 'We are ripe'" (Peter Gay, *Weimar Culture: The Outsider as Insider* [New York: Harper & Row, 1970], p. 5).

an audience able to take in and value innovative lyric poetry.[13] Cultural experience, or what the eighteenth century took seriously under the heading of taste, was a shibboleth, less than a memory. Classical Weimar culture, as it survived into the nineteenth century, was not the element of new personal experience, potentially receptive to new poetry.[14] Indeed, it could be wondered where this training by experience was to be found. Nietzsche noted:

> The abundance of disparate impressions greater than ever:—cosmopolitanism. . . . The tempo of these influxes a *prestissimo*. Impressions wipe one another out; one instinctively resists taking anything in, accepting anything deeply, "digesting" anything. . . . A sort of adaptation to being overwhelmed by impressions sets in: man forgets how to act; he can only still react to stimuli from the outside. He spends his power partly in assimilation, partly in defense, partly in response. Basic weakening of spontaneity.[15]

Urban life as a whole inspired a self-protective blunting of sensibility for survival; even adventurous strolling was not the medium for a training of taste, where experience could consist only in shocklike *Erlebnisse* ("the content of the hour").[16] The Expressionist attacked the middle-high culture parasitically at home in the middle-class living room while outside shocks were instantly muted, by the assaulted sensibility, into dullness. With respect to the content of the new popular culture, Expressionist writing does not take direct aim at it, but neither, certainly, does it speak in its name.

Expressionist writers, Kafka included, were interested, of course, in the movies. In fact, there is an Expressionist cinema, but it is certainly not the source in turn of popular and creatively engaging

---

13. Walter Benjamin, "On Some Motifs in Baudelaire," in *Illuminations*, trans. Harry Zohn (New York: Harcourt Brace & World, 1968), p. 158.

14. Cf. Wilhelm Dilthey, in *Die Einbildungskraft des Dichters: Bausteine für eine Poetik* (The poetic imagination: contributions to a poetics): "It [is] all over for the principles of that poetics which once upon a time in idyllic Weimar had been debated by Schiller, Goethe, and Humboldt" (*Gesammelte Schriften* [Leipzig: Teubner; Göttingen: Vandenhoeck & Ruprecht, 1914–77], 6:104.

15. Friedrich Nietzsche, *Werke in drei Bänden,* ed. Karl Schlechta (Munich: Hanser, 1954–56), 3:628. I am grateful to Professor Richard Murphy for bringing this passage to my attention.

16. Benjamin, "On Some Motifs in Baudelaire," p. 165.

figures of beauty, freedom, or grace.[17] It is no accident that what some consider the only popular Expressionist film—*The Cabinet of Doctor Caligari* (1920)—is told by an idiot.[18] Expressionist writers showed sporadic concern that commercial low-culture movies would ruin the sensibilities of an audience potentially receptive to artistic innovation. In 1920, for example, Carlo Mierendorff declared: "People live only on pictures: the pleasures of the illustrated papers, the rhapsodies of endless movie dramas."[19]

But Mierendorff's complaint is made on behalf not so much of artistic culture as of a revitalized popular speech. Thereafter, one witnesses a growing enfeeblement of the authority of middle-high culture, even in the absence of Expressionist critique, and the rapid assimilation of superior innovative art of whatever kind to pop culture. This is the fate of the work of art in the age of its mechanical reproducibility—by no means merely derided by Walter Benjamin, who celebrated the promise in toys, detective-novels, and technically produced images of all kinds. The great critics of cultural debasement are then Georg Lukács and Theodor Adorno—not to overlook Gustav Janouch's mythical Kafka, for whom the images of photographs and films are lies. The same objection might be found in Kafka's stories themselves, in his preference as storyteller for the forms of an older popular culture: the trapeze artist, the circus rider, the hunger artist. Some readers even detect in "Josephine the Singer or the

17. Some examples of Expressionist cinema are *The Cabinet of Dr. Caligari, Nosferatu, The Golem*. I exempt *Doctor Mabuse*. If this film contains, perhaps, an image of beauty and charm in the Folies Bergères queen who loves Dr. Mabuse despite his hypnotic powers, this image becomes swiftly diluted in a medium of silly tastelessness far ahead of its time. The not-so-canny police chief, e.g., is called "De Witt." *Dr. Mabuse* is "something like a serial posing as a mystery play. . . . Fritz Lang is also responsible for 'Metropolis,' but that's another story" (*New York Times*, August 27, 1927, p. 1).

18. The film's asylum director declares, "Now I can heal him: he believes I am Caligari." What popularity the film had was very likely due to this significant perversion of the nonconformist intention of the original script. Thus Siegfried Kracauer, *From Caligari to Hitler: A Psychological History of the German Film* (Princeton, N.J.: Princeton University Press, 1947), pp. 66-67. Even so—according to Kracauer—*Caligari* remained "too high-brow to become popular in Germany" (p. 77). This was the fate, generally speaking, of the style and pathos of Expressionism.

19. Quoted in *Expressionismus: Manifeste und Dokumente zur deutschen Literatur 1910–1920*, ed. Thomas Anz and Michael Stark (Stuttgart: Metzler, 1982), p. 601.

Mouse People" an excoriation of the beginning of a popular culture bent on entertainment and implying the actual death of art;[20] Kafka's story was finished in 1924. That Josephine the singer whom in 1927 Paul Becker's poem praises is indeed more buoyant and confident.

The Expressionist response to modern communication was rather one of intense curiosity with regard to technique and somewhere in this the hope of a vehicle of messianic change: "Our task," wrote Ivan Goll, "is to compress our deepest experience [*Erlebnis*] into telegrams—still better, in stenographic form."[21] Expressionist writers were captivated by the communicative possibilities of the movies: Alfred Döblin's aesthetics of prose is based on the goal, literally, of a movie style (*Kinostil*); he wants a prose with images as piercing and compact as screen images swiftly scanned. Movie style is of course what is still Expressionist in Paul Becker's poem, whose metaphor of synchronization comes from film technique—but with this crucial difference: he takes a formal aspect from the *talkies*, which is exemplary for bringing about its own sort of marriage.[22] The first commercial film to synchronize picture and sound, *The Jazz Singer*, was in fact shown on October 6, 1927, scant weeks before November Twentyseven. The conception day of Paul Becker's poetic persona was thus a triumph of synchronization: the poet arrives to voice the arrested gestures of a pantheon of screen idols.[23] But the demise of

20. E.g., Wolf Kittler, "Der Turmbau zu Babel, das Schweigen der Sirenen und das tierische Pfeifen: Über das Reden, das Schweigen, die Stimme und die Schrift in vier Texten von Kafka" (doctoral diss., Erlangen, 1978), p. 124.

21. Ivan Goll, "Das Wort an sich: Versuch einer neuen Poetik," *Die neue Rundschau* 32 (October 1921): 1083; quoted in Anz and Stark, *Expressionismus*, p. 615. For a good discussion of megalomania and typewriters around 1900, see Friedrich A. Kittler, *Aufschreibesysteme 1800 . 1900* (Munich: Fink, 1985). Gilles Deleuze, in his *Movement-Image*, trans. Hugh Tomlinson and Barbara Habberjam (Minneapolis: University of Minnesota Press, 1986), p. 127, attaches primarily to Kafka the distinction between technology that serves communication by mastering space and time (the railroad, the airplane, the steamship) and technology that interrupts and damages communication (mail, telephone, telegraph); Kafka perceives that these devices—like ghosts—drink the sense out of what is sent before it arrives.

22. Synchronization brings about the correct coordination of picture and sound track; they are "'combined' on a single strip of film to provide a married print" ("Synchronization," in *The Focal Encyclopaedia of Film and Television Techniques*, ed. Raymond Spottiswoode [New York: Hastings House, 1969], p. 803).

23. Early talkies certainly sealed the end of the Expressionist film, with its use of interesting camera angles. In talkies the movement of the camera was restricted by the requirement that actors speak into planted microphones. The stylized sets and decor

the silent film (which, as Adorno has noted, almost coincided with Kafka's death in 1924), marked the demise of the Expressionist interest in cinema.

This new accent—Becker's valorization of the image content of talkies—can be profiled swiftly through a contrary example, the poem "Kinematograph" (movie projector), written in 1911 by the arch-Expressionist poet Jakob van Hoddis.

Movie Projector

The theater darkens; racing past we see
The Ganges-palms, temples, and Brahma.
A silent, throbbing family drama,
With sophisticates, ball, and masquerades.

Revolvers are drawn. Jealousies are rife.
Smart Aleck's in a duel, head- and heedless.
Now we see, all rucksack, pack, and goiter,
The Alpine dweller on her steep and rocky fortress.

Her path inclines abruptly, past a rooky wood.
It twists and threateningly ascends
The slanted cliffwall; the view into the valley
Is livened up with cows and fields of barley.

And in the darkened space—right in my face—
It flashes in. Horribly. Frame by frame.
The End. Arc lights are sizzling with fire.
We drag ourselves outside—yawning, horny.[24]

Film gives van Hoddis his serial, staccato, paratactic form; as for filmic content—its sense, as somatic reception and as meaning—it is at once all jarring flashes and flabby banalities, like everyday language "slack to the bursting point."[25]

---

of Expressionism became to some extent determined by their usefulness in concealing mikes: of course, large vases and umbrella stands were ideal. The birth of synchronization meant that the camera, after its Expressionist interlude, would be once again enchained.

24. Jakob van Hoddis, pseudonym of Hugo Davidsohn, *Weltende: Gesammelte Dichtungen*, ed. Paul Pörtner (Zürich: 1958), p. 38 (my translation).

25. The phrase is Theodor Adorno's, used to describe the consciousness depicted by Kafka. See his "Notes on Kafka," in *Prisms*, trans. Samuel and Shierry Weber (London: Spearman, 1967), p. 252.

In his conversations with Janouch, Kafka said something like what this poem says: "I am an Eye-Man. But the cinema disturbs one's vision. The speed of the movements and the rapid change of images force men to look continually from one to another. Sight does not master the pictures, it is the pictures which master one's sight. They flood one's consciousness" (J 160).[26]

Kafka's remark does not tell the whole story of his relation or, in general, of the Expressionist relation to those communicative (or jamming) techniques we link with pop culture, movies and newspapers in particular. This relation is a three-part movement of assault, working-through (by the abstraction and manipulation of formal features of the trauma), and cathartic rejection of their impact—as if to mime the mechanism were also to double, to alienate, and thus to annihilate this initial threatening strangeness.[27] "With parataxis, *Reihungsstil* [serial style], and nominative style, Expressionist authors thematize the experience of incoherence in reality and language—though contemporary critics failed to grasp the epistemological and linguistic aspects of this gesture."[28] Add: its depth-psychological dimension. Let us look again at the author of "Movie Projector."

Jakob van Hoddis was the pseudonym of Hans Davidsohn, a young Jewish poet from Berlin, who was afterward to suffer from a predicament diagnosed as schizophrenia. To Hoddis more than to any individual goes the distinction of having fired the pistol shot that started off the urban Expressionist lyric. His inaugural poem, called "The End of the World," appeared in the Berlin journal *Der Demokrat*

26. An early indication of Kafka's keen awareness of movies is his draft conception of the fiancée of Georg Bendemann, the hero of "The Judgment." She was to be the daughter of a movie theater owner (*Kinematographenbesitzer*—literally, the owner of a movie projector). This is found in the original manuscript of "The Judgment"; see Gerhard Neumann, *Franz Kafka, Das Urteil: Text, Materialien, Kommentar* (Munich: Hanser, 1981), p. 34. The point becomes particularly interesting if we construe the fiancée, Frieda Brandenfeld, as the figure of a full and exhilarated life of freedom outside the sphere of family influence. For a penetrating analysis of Kafka's mixed relation to images as such, see Gerhard Neumann's "Umkehrung und Ablenkung: Franz Kafkas 'Gleitendes Paradox,'" in Politzer, *Franz Kafka*, pp. 499-509.

27. "Kafka's sensitivity to noise is like an alarm that registers extra, not yet articulated dangers. One can escape them by shunning noise like the plague—there is already enough to shun in the familiar dangers, whose well-coordinated attacks Kafka resists by naming them" (Elias Canetti, *Der andere Prozea: Kafkas Briefe an Felice* [Munich: Hanser, 1969], p. 29).

28. Comment quoted by Anz and Stark, editors of *Expressionismus*, p. 602.

in early 1911. "My gifts as a poet," wrote Johannes Becher, "are simply not equal to conjuring up the impact of that poem. . . . These two stanzas—eight lines!—seemed to turn us into different human beings, lifted us out of a world of middle-class drear, which we despised but did not know how to shake off."[29] "The effect of this poem," conclude Silvio Vietta and Hans-Georg Kemper, "already implies the attitude toward art characteristic of the Expressionist generation of artists; they see their project as the fundamental metamorphosis of man through art"[30]—a task requiring the preparatory project of clearing a space for this transformation: hence, "The End of the World."

The End of the World

The hat flies off the citizen's pointed head.
All zones of air resound, as if with screaming.
Roofingmen fall off and break in half.
And on the coast, you read, the tide is rising.

The storm is there, and savage oceans skip
Upon the land to squash thick dams to bits.
Almost everyone is plagued by sniffles.
Railroad trains are falling off the bridges.[31]

What was felt as revolutionary in the poem is, of course, the impudent (or scant) linkage between these images, which illustrates *Reihungsstil* and anticipates the Dadaist ideal of *das simultanistische Gedicht*. "Simultanistic poetry," wrote Richard Huelsenbeck, "teaches the meaning of hurling all things together pell-mell: as Mr. Schulze reads, the Balkans train crosses the bridge at Nisch, and a pig screams in the cellar of Nuttke the slaughterer."[32] Hoddis's apocalypse is there, not only in the content of the images but above all in the crazy

29. Johannes R. Becher, "On Jakob van Hoddis," *The Era of German Expressionism*, ed. Paul Raabe, trans. J. M. Ritchie (Woodstock, N.Y.: Overlook, 1974), p. 44 (translation modified).

30. Silvio Vietta and Hans-Georg Kempner, *Expressionismus* (Munich: Wilhelm Fink, 1975), p. 30. I am indebted to this study for many of the perspectives informing my discussion of Expressionist poetry in the context of contemporary films and newspapers.

31. Hoddis, *Weltende*, p. 28 (my translation). With "citizen" I translate *Bürger*, which means, more literally, "bourgeois."

32. Richard Huelsenbeck, "Dadaistisches Manifest," in *Dada Almanach*, ed. Richard Huelsenbeck (Berlin: Erich Reiss, 1920), p. 39; reprinted in Anz and Stark, *Expressionismus*, p. 76.

mixing of levels—of high and low pathos—in the scrambling of the emotional register that arranges our average view of the world. This technique will recur as a signature of Expressionism: sharply condensed images in frightening association; the arbitrary dismemberment of familiar argument or situation; effects of disparity just held together by rigorous metrics or a uniformly reckless or scathing attitude. In "The End of the World" every line except the sixth introduces a new subject. Catastrophes do not cohere. The poem requires a "reading," as Vietta observes, like the one suited for linotype catastrophes in the newspaper at the breakfast table—or of course, on the newsreel.[33]

To bring this to a point: Hoddis, composing the key poem of the Expressionist movement, "The End of the World," was operating his kinematograph, his movie projector. The form is unmistakable, drawn from the urban culture that invents mechanical techniques, produces and instantly blunts shocks, and sells tickets to the easily comprehensible image. His poem manipulates these elements with a kind of contempt.

Kafka, who is the superior of Hoddis even in miming movie techniques, gives us similar examples of these tactics in the stories composed at the end of 1912 and constituting *his* breakthrough: "The Judgment" and *The Metamorphosis*. In "The Judgment" the father comes into being through a random series of metamorphoses; these changes are not motivated. At first the son is strong enough to carry his father to bed in his arms. Kafka notes that "while Georg took the few steps toward the bed, the old man on his breast was toying with his watch chain." In the middle of domestic apocalypse, as Oedipal fantasies are eventuating, at *the end of the world* . . . of family, the victim temporizes and trifles—"plagued," as it were, "by sniffles." But Kafka's father is the irrepressibly Expressionist father, the hard underbelly of the citizen with the pointed head. In "The Judgment" the father connives with his own metamorphosis. As the son carries him off to bed, the father is already renewing himself: the son is soon reduced to observing the old man "[fling] off the blankets with a strength that sent them all flying and sprang erect in bed." Georg gapes and shrinks into a corner. "Balancing himself by only one hand which lightly touches the ceiling, the father leant forward and then in

33. Vietta and Kemper, *Expressionismus,* p. 31.

a loud voice cried, 'Take note: I sentence you now to death by drowning'." An old baby in soiled underwear has risen up a giant, radiant with insight, an avenging god! Metamorphosis! George is driven out of the room. The event is described as an apparently coherent series.

> Out of the front door he rushed, across the roadway, driven toward the water. Already he was grasping at the railings as a starving man clutches food . . . . He spied between the railings a motor-bus coming which would easily cover the noise of his fall, called in a low voice: "Dear parents, I have always loved you, all the same," and let himself drop.
> At this moment an unending stream of traffic was just going over the bridge. [S 87–88]

One can recall "railroad trains are falling off the bridges." The direction of the apocalypse has been reversed; the technique is the same. Kafka has composed a slightly more articulated "throbbing family drama" around Hoddis's lines: "Almost everyone is plagued by sniffles. / Railroad trains are falling off the bridges." Trying to motivate the denouement of "The Judgment" is not much easier than supplying epic connections for "The End of the World." What is important is that Kafka invites us to produce these connections but in fact has only flung into our face the images of the movie or the dream.

"Kafka does not make a radical departure from the traditional formal laws of thought," writes Gerhard Neumann. "He does not destroy either the semantic, grammatical, or syntactic structure of his texts (as Expressionist writers tried to do)."[34] Neumann allows us to see the point that must be held firm if Kafka is to be distinguished from the Expressionists; more important, he specifies the issue that puts their difference into question. This is the intactness of the so-called semantic structure of the text, which, in the case of "The Judgment," remains highly questionable.[35]

The Metamorphosis, of course, is marked by an even more sharply serial conjunction of images. They are related only by contiguity—by

34. Gerhard Neumann, who is essentially writing about Kafka's "thought stories," continues, "[Kafka's] concern is much different: with extreme meticulousness he pursues conventional thought processes in order to arrive at the point where they collapse" ("Umkehrung und Ablenkung," p. 486).
35. Consult Chapter Two, where I have explored this point in relation to the mixing of the literal and figurative levels of metaphor.

temporal succession or by spatial side-by-sideness—related in a visual grammar, so to speak, independent of the factor of resemblance and hence at odds with the semantic aspect. Such relations based on contiguity and not on resemblance are metonymic. A prime example, of course, is the metamorphosed hero of this story, who is unlike anything else having visual existence inside or outside the story. Strictly speaking, he is not *a* metonymy but *the* metonymic, the radical factor of dissimilarity engendering a necessarily serial relation between himself and others. To the extent that he penetrates the domestic world, he engenders disparity. Gregor is finally at home in his surroundings only after they have been emptied of any suggestion of the objects to which he was attached in his human past. He is at home only when he inhabits a cave, to whose smooth walls he is able to cling by dint of the glue that he himself exudes. No food appeals to him; he cannot make out the shapes outside his window; he cannot detect that his body has accumulated a fur of dust balls and scraps of rotting food. He is—such as he is—a monster, bringing about the loss of all relations to things and others by resemblance. When Kafka's publisher wrote to him about an illustrated title page for *Metamorphosis*, Kafka wrote back: "It struck me that [the] illustrator might want to draw the insect itself. Not that, please not that! . . . The insect itself cannot be depicted" (L 114–15). Kafka's objection was based precisely on the fact that to do so would be to represent the metamorphosed creature as a stable image—as self-identical. But the point is that this monster must be radically un-self-identical, a being suffering the maximum of self-dissociation. Any image of him, radically disparate as it must be from any image in his environment, produces the incorrect image of a being identical with itself. Taking the monstrous noun into which Gregor Samsa has been transformed as the subject of a clause, it is impossible to imagine the conjunction linking this clause to any other clause; the text in which he figures is radically paratactic, if not indeed an anacoluthon.

Meanwhile, as this apocalyptic metamorphosis slumbers in the Samsa back room, urban life goes on: the father declines a beer; the sister sends into Gregor's room a plate of stale white sauce; the cleaning woman slams the front door too loud for anybody's satisfaction. But this life is monstrously fragmented whenever Gregor enters the scene. And finally, in the matter of disparity, there is no consciousness within the story equal to this event—certainly not Gregor's and not even the narrator's. We pick up the latter's presence from sly hints along the way, as when the text notes—soon after Gregor's discovery of his metamorphosis—that upon imagining his father's and his sister's surprise on being summoned to help him out of bed, he, Gregor, "could not repress a smile" (M 9). The smile of a monstrous vermin? Carsten Schlingmann calls it "the strangest smile in the history of literature."[36] It is, let us note, a smile not on Gregor's face but on the face of the narrator, and on ours, the readers with whom he is in collusion. This is the familiar ironic or feelingless or slightly contemptuous attitude of the Expressionist narrator toward the ghastly disparity of the scene he relates: I am thinking, now, of the morgue poetry of Gottfried Benn. There is no attempt made to figure forth in the Expressionist narrative a superior metonymy: that is, a symbol—a part of the whole which is a reflector of the whole. The narrator has a certain remote superiority, but it is not based on understanding.

The foregoing then, are some of the formal features of Expressionist narrative, and my starting point was to say that many of them are suggested or reinforced by movie techniques. To conclude this point: *The Metamorphosis* gives us an exemplary literary representation of the *zoom-in*. Here is Gregor just entering the family living room for the first time after his metamorphosis.

> Now Gregor did not enter the room after all, but leaned against the inside of the firmly bolted wing of the door, so that only half his body was visible and his head above it, cocked to one side and peeping out at the others. In the meantime it had grown much lighter; across the street one could see clearly a section of the endless, grayish-black building opposite—it was a hospital—with its regular windows starkly piercing the façade; the rain was still coming down, but only in large, separately visible drops that were also pelting the ground literally one at a time. [M 15]

* * *

I mentioned newspapers. My thesis about movies and newspapers is the following: These media are symbols of the rapid, assaulting,

---

36. Carsten Schlingmann, "Die Verwandlung—Eine Interpretation," in *Interpretationen zu Franz Kafka: Das Urteil, Die Verwandlung, Ein Landarzt, Kleine Prosastücke* (Munich: Oldenbourg, 1968), p. 93.

mechanical spirit and tempo of city life. They symbolize modern power; it is no accident that in "The Judgment" the mark of the (apparently) wasted, abandoned power of the father is the superannuated newspaper he reads. When, standing high on his bed, he upbraids and then condemns his son to death, he accompanies these verbal gestures with the physical one of throwing at Georg "a newspaper sheet which he had somehow taken to bed with him. An old newspaper, with a name entirely unknown to Georg" (S 87). "Do you think I read my [old] newspapers?" cries the father to Georg, with sinister emphasis. To throw away an old newspaper (to perform a double negative) is to indicate the return to power.

The link of newspaper to power, meanwhile, is even plainer in *The Metamorphosis*. In Chapter Three we saw that it was a rule of this story world: the person in power at any moment reads or manipulates the newspaper. Gregor has clipped the love object that hangs on his wall from an illustrated newspaper. It is a sorry comment on his loss of power and identity within the family that it is on newspaper that his first meal of garbage is served; the father, meanwhile, downcast for a while, fails to read the newspaper aloud to the family. When the boarders come to dominate the family, it is they who ostentatiously read the newspaper at the dinner table. The newspaper represents an order of efficient language from which Gregor is excluded.

In another perspective we could say that he who does not have the newspaper *is* the newspaper; he who does not have the phallus is the phallus. Which is nothing good. Gregor is the newspaper in the sense that he is an absolute *novum*; his metamorphosis has the force of news, a startling, fragmented report of the not-experienced, (un)communicable to the others as shock, horror, and fascination yet a sign without meaning, without tradition, without coherence, and so forth.

In his essay "On Some Motifs in Baudelaire," Walter Benjamin describes the newspaper as the symbol and agency of disintegrating experience. Referring to the phenomenon of involuntary memory in Proust, he writes:

> It is a matter of chance . . . whether an individual can take hold of his experience. It is by no means inevitable to be dependent on chance in this matter. Man's inner concerns do not have their [merely] issueless private character by nature. They do so only when he is increasingly unable to assimilate the data of the world around him by means of

experience. Newspapers constitute one of the many kinds of evidence of such an inability. If it were the intention of the press to have the reader assimilate information as part of his own experience, it would not achieve its purpose. In fact its intention is just the opposite, and it is achieved: to isolate events from the realm in which they could affect the experience of the reader. The principles of journalistic information (freshness of news, brevity, comprehensibility, and above all lack of connection between individual news items) contribute as much to this as does page make-up and the paper's style. (Karl Kraus never tired of showing how the linguistic usage of newspapers paralyzed the imagination of their readers.) Information remains isolated from experience in another way: information does not enter "tradition." Newspapers appear in large editions, and few readers can boast of any information which another reader may require from him. Historically the various modes of communication have competed with one another. The replacement of the older narration by information, of information by sensation, reflects the increasing atrophy of experience.[37]

Thus Benjamin. Of course the newspaper had not always been an instrument furthering personal disintegration and depoliticization. It once functioned as a medium of bourgeois emancipation, a product of the trading cities, instrumental in a class struggle against clerical and state interests.[38] In the eighteenth century the press was the political preceptor of the bourgeoisie, furthering rational communication and undermining the dogmas of the dominant class. The early bourgeois press struggled tirelessly against censorship; Christoph Wieland, Kant, and Jean Paul wrote strenuously on its behalf.

The crucial distinction about the late nineteenth-century newspaper is that it became an organ of a bourgeoisie that had ceased to be a revolutionary class and sought conformity with and protection from the state. Here we point to the phenomenon—so retarded in Germany—of the development of large-scale capitalist enterprises.

The twentieth century newspaper, the modern newspaper, is altogether different, being based on the instantaneous communication of novelties and requiring machines for rapid printing—machines that in turn need to be run as often as possible in order to offset enormous printing costs. German publishers began to bring out several different newspapers at various times of the day. "At a certain moment in this

37. Benjamin, "On Some Motifs in Baudelaire," pp. 160–61.
38. Jürgen Habermas, *Strukturwandel der Öffentlichkeit: Untersuchungen zu einer Kategorie der bürgerlichen Gesellschaft* (Neuwied: Luchterhand, 1962).

development," comments Peter de Mendelssohn, "it is no longer the product that needs the machine but the machine that needs the product."[39] This is the sort of autonomy of mechanical production that Georg Kaiser pillories in his two-part play, *Gas*. In 1914 the daily *Berliner Illustrierte*—having abandoned the principle of subscription and addressing itself to a mass public milling about on the streets each with a penny or two to spend—began printing more than a million copies a day. Newspapers needing new customers every day turned to sensational headlines, shocking pictures, accounts of freaks and of new inventions. One issue of the *Berliner Illustrierte* pertinently featured "the automobile as hearse: a new mode of burial." A good deal of this violence informs, willy nilly, even Kafka's style. Kafka was acutely conscious of the tempo of Berlin: from 1912 on and for some eight years of his life, he corresponded daily with his fiancée in Berlin, a secretary with ad hoc procurist authority for the Carl Lindberg Company, one of Europe's leading innovators and suppliers of machines for remote and rapid communciation: namely, the "parlograph," the dictaphone. Kafka's consciousness of his Felice was from the start a consciousness of Berlin: in conceiving a family name in "The Judgment" for the fiancée of his poetic double Georg Bendemann, Kafka wrote "Brandenburg," then "Brandenfeld," and afterward noted the influence on his choice of the "memory of the Mark (i.e., the county Brandenburg)" and "Berlin." After visiting Felice in Berlin in 1914, Kafka contemplated moving there, and in his diary he stated the connection explicitly: "Perhaps I love . . . [Berlin] because of Felice and because of the aura of thoughts that surrounds her" (DII 27). In 1914 he visited Berlin three more times;[40] and during the last year of his life, the only extended period in which he lived apart from his family, he stayed in Berlin, where he wanted to be.

The Metamorphosis begins: "When Gregor Samsa woke up one morning from unsettling dreams, he found himself changed in his bed into a monstrous vermin" (M 3). The story "A Fratricide" begins: "The evidence shows that this is how the murder was committed" (S 402); toward the end it contains these lines: "'Wese!' shrieked

39. Peter de Mendelssohn, *Zeitungsstadt Berlin: Menschen und Mächte in der Geschichte der deutschen Presse* (Berlin: Ullstein, 1959), p. 95; quoted in Vietta and Kemper, *Expressionismus*, p. 119 (my discussion of the newspaper is indebted to pp. 118–19).

40. He made the first of these visits in order to establish an understanding that he and Felice were engaged; the second, to celebrate their engagement officially; and the third, to break it off.

Schmar, standing on tiptoe, his arm outstretched, the knife sharply lowered, 'Wese! You will never see Julia again!' And right into the throat and left into the throat and a third time deep into the belly stabbed Schmar's knife. Water rats, slit open, give out such a sound as came from Wese" (S 403). *The Trial* ends thus: "But the hands of one of the partners were already at K.'s throat, while the other thrust the knife deep into his heart and turned it there twice. With failing eyes K. could still see the two of them immediately before him, cheek leaning against cheek, watching the final act. 'Like a dog!' he said; it was as if the shame of it must outlive him" (T 286). We can add to this shock list the mechanical frenzy of the communications systems of the urban Hotel Occidental in *Amerika* and the torture machine of "In the Penal Colony."

The imagination of this great poet, whose refinement and intensity are not in question, cannot escape the need, if his life is to take place, of repeating and therefore numbing or exorcising the horrors conveyed to him by urban newspapers. Even if Kafka's imagination of atrocity was fed more by the daily reports of industrial mutilation that crossed his desk than the horrors communicated in the *Prager Tagblatt*, which he nonetheless read, he would have found newspaper imagery and form salient in the work of the poets and playwrights of Berlin. "And on the coasts," one reads, "the tide is rising."

Reinhard Sorge's play *Der Bettler* (The beggar) stages this café scene:

> *2nd person, reading aloud from the paper:* Get this, earthquake in Central America.
>
> *Voices:* Hey: how many died?
>
> *2nd person, reading aloud:* Five thousand.
>
> *3rd person, listening:* Puh![41]

Being blasé leads not to wanting to stay blasé but to craving sensations of heightened intensity. The campaign of Expressionist writing is unsettled by the paradox of a public consciousness that needs to be destroyed by means that pander to it, and this awareness marks it importantly. If the so-called New Romantics (including the George-circle) turned away from this public with disgust, rejecting it as a

41. Reinhard Sorge, *Der Bettler: Eine dramatische Sendung* (Berlin: Fischer, 1912), p. 19.

potential basis for modern literature, the Expressionists sought in it a wide responsiveness. To this Kafka is only occasionally an exception; we recall his admitted "craving" (*Gier*) to have his book *Meditation* published (L 85). Expressionist writers were not concerned simply with depicting an alienated and deformed humanity in need of renewal. These writers were concerned that their appeal be heard, and so the new literature would have to compete with the new mass media shaping consciousness. The urban bohemia itself became a sort of stock exchange on which the most sensational literary developments were bought and sold (and this includes the Bohemia of Prague, too). Alfred Richard Meyer recalls Berlin:

> It is impossible to imagine our excitement in the evening, when at the Café des Westens or sitting out on the street in front of Gerold's, at the Gedächtniskirche, we waited for *Sturm* or *Aktion*. Who was in, who out? The stock market reports were not interesting. We ourselves were the quotations. Who was this new star? Alfred Lichtenstein-Wilmersdorf. And his poem called "The Dawn." Would it surpass van Hoddis' "End of the World"?[42]

I have emphasized in Expressionist writing the parodic relation of indebtedness and critique to the techniques of the mass media, these media being symbols of the abrupt, mechanical tempo of everyday life which must be expelled for the sake of a human time, the time of renovation. Imitation as part of a movement of expulsion is not mere naming and miming. Works containing the violence of everyday life mean to contain it by strict form. Georg Heym's poem "Der Gott der Stadt" conveys *Erschütterungen* (shatterings) in rhymed pentameter. Georg Trakl's imagist diction—associative, only loosely connected, indefinite—takes shape around symbolic extensions of Christian images like shepherd, dove, and cross.[43] Kafka imposes strict form

---

42. In *Expressionismus: Aufzeichnungen und Erinnerungen der Zeitgenossen,* ed. Paul Raabe (Olten: Walter, 1965), p. 55; quoted in Vietta and Kemper, *Expressionismus,* pp. 121–22.

43. See Raymond Furness, *The Twentieth Century, 1890–1945: The Literary History of Germany* (London: Croom Helm, 1978), 8:145–46. Of interest to my argument about the centrality to Expressionism of Kafka's experiments with metaphor is Furness' stress on what is "crucial to Trakl"—namely, metaphor detached from a context that could function as its tenor, and hence "autotelic." For Furness, "the most distinctive use of independent metaphor at this time, however, is found in the work of Kafka" (p. 147).

through so-called monopolized perspective: fictional action is narrated in the early stories almost exclusively from the perspective of the suffering hero. And Kafka concentrates action into gesture—leading Adorno to characterize his novels as "the last of the dwindling liaison texts to silent movies; the ambiguity of the gesture lies between sinking into muteness (with the destruction of language) and rising out of it in music."[44]

This mimetic relation to the mass media suggests the fear of ever more fragmented perception, social and familial conflict, and self-dissociation—and the craving, too, for a new start as abrupt and as violent as the mechanical fury already in motion. Of these factors, however, none is entirely peculiar to German Expressionism, and all are present to some degree in post-Romantic literary movements. In fact, by viewing Expressionism as a response, however many-sided, to the Industrial Revolution in Germany, we identify it not as an essentially modern act but as a belated German response to an event that had already occurred in radical form in France and England. We then find the mood of Expressionist poems just as vivid, say, in *The Prelude*:

> Oh, blank confusion! and a type not false
> Of what the mighty city is itself
> To all except a straggler here and there,
> To the whole swarm of its inhabitants;
> An undistinguishable world to men,
> The slaves unrespited of low pursuits,
> Living amid the same perpetual flow
> Of trivial objects, melted and reduced
> To one identity, by differences
> That have no law, no meaning, and no end;
> Oppression under which even highest minds
> Must labor, whence the strongest are not free.[45]

Wordsworth gives an account of London at the turn of the nineteenth century as a ghastly Bartholemew's Fair. Only a variation in

44. From a letter written by Theodor W. Adorno to Walter Benjamin, in Benjamin, *Gesammelte Schriften*, ed. Rolf Tiedemann and Hermann Schweppenhäuser (Frankfurt am Main: Suhrkamp, 1977), 2 (pt. 3):1178.

45. William Wordsworth, *The Prelude, or Growth of a Poet's Mind* (*Text of 1805*), ed. Ernest de Selincourt (London: Oxford University Press, 1933), VII.695–706, p. 124.

pathos marks this text in Janouch's *Conversations with Kafka*: "Mankind can only become a grey, formless, and therefore nameless mass through a fall from the Law which gives it form. But in that case there is no above and below any more; life is levelled out into mere existence; there is no struggle, no drama, only the consumption of matter, decay" (J 172).

Yet literary Expressionism has survived in its own right through the specific character of its response to the violence and leveling of urban life—a response that Kafka is needed to specify.

*   *   *

What most survives of the Expressionist Kafka? This is a question for the critic who has the floor. My own answer turns on Kafka's consciousness of the metamorphic character of metaphoric language—and of "meaning" as the product of a struggle to arrest such metamorphosis.

The insight that metaphor implies metamorphosis is fundamentally Expressionist. Carl Einstein posited this axiom as central to Expressionist culture in the course of bitterly rejecting the conclusion that in his view followed from it: namely, that "the use of metaphor and fictions, the technique of aesthetic metamorphosis, allows individuals to *escape* social determinations" (my italics).[46] What survives through Kafka is the exact opposite of this thesis: the making of metaphor and fictions does not constitute an aesthetic means to liberate individuals from social determinations. On the contrary, the making of metaphors engenders an uprush of constraint and conflict as an other, not its maker, seeks to arrest the metaphor to serve its will and needs. Kafka shatters the innocence of metaphor, for metaphor is dependent—"on the maid who tends the fire . . . on the poor human being warming himself by the stove" (DII 200–201). "The use of metaphor" provokes interpretations that fix speakers in relations of power. Every metaphor is a provocation to *un*freedom, and a certain freedom from constraint arises from the reader's liberating a little the power of metaphor to produce additional metamorphosis. It is therefore equally correct, following Kafka, to say that the maker is read by his

46. Carl Einstein, *Die Fabrikation der Fiktionen*, ed. Sybille Penkert (Hamburg: Rowohlt, 1973), p. 132.

metaphor: this is the implication of the pragmatic model of metaphorical meaning.[47]

"Expressionists disbarred those rhetorical devices and figures of speech which 'by indirection seek direction out'. . . symbol, metaphor." Thus Ulrich Weisstein, in profiling Carl Sternheim's slogan "war on metaphor [*Kampf der Metapher*]."[48] Kafka is the most gifted Expressionist strategist in this war, more lucid than Herwarth Walden, who wrote: "The concrete element in poetry is always parable [*Gleichnis*] and may not be simile or metaphor [*Vergleich*]. The metaphor or simile depends on the person who does the comparing; hence it is something personal. The parable, however, is impersonal and unbound."[49]

Kafka stresses that metaphor *in literature* cannot be a personal "expression"; literature has to be the "allusion" that discloses the metamorphic impulse of key words. He is more lucid on this point than Ivan Goll, who wrote: "The 'word in itself' is matter—is earth, that wants to be stamped into form, diamond, that wants to be chiseled. It is for the most part noun. Very *realistic*. Word-in-itself-poetry is not expression [*Ausdruck*] but allusion [*Andeutung*]."[50] Here is Kafka's fuller account: "For everything outside the phenomenal world, language can only be used in the manner of an allusion [*andeutungsweise*] but never even approximately in the manner of the metaphor [*vergleichsweise*], since corresponding as it does to the phenomenal world, it is concerned only with property and its relations" (DF 40; H 45). "Literature" is an event outside the phenomenal world.

47. Cf. this recent account of Lacan's "discovery [sic] of the primacy of metaphor in the formation not only of language but of all human institutions": "What Lacan's contribution consists in, however, seems to me to be showing how the negative side of metaphor—its ability to distinguish and discard, cut off, select, etc.—becomes a *determinant* of the social ties (discursive forms) between human beings. It dominates the linguistic mode and it does so in the service of culture. In short, it becomes ideology" (Juliet Flower MacCannell, *Figuring Lacan: Criticism and the Cultural Unconscious* [London: Croom Helm, 1986], p. 91). This was Kafka's perspective before Lacan's!

48. Ulrich Weisstein, "German Literary Expressionism: An Anatomy," *German Quarterly* 54 (May 1981): 276–83. Sternheim used the phrase in his polemical review of Gottfried Benn's *Fleisch* and *Gehirne* (*Gesamtwerk*, ed. Wilhelm Emrich [Neuwied: Luchterhand, 1966], 6:32).

49. Herwarth Walden, "Das Begriffliche in der Dichtung," *Der Sturm* 9 (August 1918): 67; in Anz and Stark, *Expressionismus*, p. 621.

50. Goll, "Das Wort an sich," p. 1084; in Anz and Stark, *Expressionismus*, p. 615.

For Maurice Marache: "The poetic process is in principle exactly the same in the poems of Trakl and in the stories of Kafka. Except . . . Kafka is at once the philosopher recounting incessantly this same story of the metaphor which Trakl is satisfied to live."[51] The story of metaphor that Kafka recounts incessantly is the story of man *as* interpreter of metaphor, of metaphor as a potential field of metamorphosis of local meaning provoking citizen's arrest. The psychoanalytic interpretation is no less an arrest for the fact that the citizen has a search warrant: it is still a matter of securing the metaphor with *one* other somatic meaning, however unheard-of.[52]

Kafka's story of metaphor concludes by invoking the promise of a perfect life as the reward for its perfect extirpation.[53] How essentially original with Kafka the Expressionist, however, is the destruction of metaphor?

Karl Philipp Moritz's great *Anton Reiser* (1785) displays the plainest

51. Maurice Marache, "La métaphore dans l'oeuvre de Kafka," *Etudes Germaniques*, January–March 1964, p. 38.

52. In a general sense, of course, Kafka and the Freud of *The Interpretation of Dreams* share the same project. For Freud, too, "the field of language, of linguistic ambiguity and metaphor, is plainly far more fertile than the field of the patient's lived experience" (Lorna Martens, "Freud, Language, and Literary Form," unpublished MS, p. 7). By literalizing metaphor as symptom, Freud finds a positive expressiveness in metaphor unknown to Kafka; for Kafka, to literalize metaphor is to turn a spinning top into a lump of wood (I owe this aperçu to Kafka's "The Top" and to Anne Carson). In this "field of language," Freud is Joseph K. to Kafka. When, however, Freud connects metaphor to the hermeneutically useless dream's navel, the case improves: here Freud speaks of psychoanalytic dream interpretation as complete when it can point to that "passage in even the most thoroughly interpreted dream which has to be left obscure . . . a tangle of dream-thoughts which cannot be unravelled and which moreover adds nothing to our knowledge of the content of the dream. This is the dream's navel, the spot where it reaches down into the unknown. The dream-thoughts to which we are led by interpretation cannot, from the nature of things, have any definite endings; they are bound to branch out in every direction into the intricate network of our world of thought. It is at some point where this meshwork is particularly close that the dream-wish grows up, like a mushroom out of its mycelium" (Sigmund Freud, *The Interpretation of Dreams* in *The Standard Edition of the Complete Psychological Works of Sigmund Freud*, ed. James Strachey [London: Hogarth Press, 1953–1974], 5:525). For more on the difference between Kafka and Freud, see "Freud as Literature?" in my *Fate of the Self* (New York: Columbia University Press, 1986), pp. 181–195.

53. Janouch wrote: "Franz Kafka sometimes insisted, with a vehemence that reminded one of the passionate obstinacy of fanatical Talmudists, on the narrow literal meaning of ideas, which for him were not sound-symbols for things, but were themselves independent and indestructible truths" (J 145).

274

consciousness of the tendency of metaphor in abnormal states to migrate to the literal: "[Anton's mother] used to say of someone dying that death was already sitting on his tongue; Anton took this literally; and when his cousin's husband died, he stood by the bed and looked very intensely into his mouth in order to make out, roughly as a small black figure, death on his tongue."[54]

Kafka's distinction lies in his power to make the imagination of literalization generative as the principle of an extended narrative. "In the Penal Colony" is an example of its functioning as a source. The story originates from the dismantling of a metaphor more precise than that of the world as a penal colony. As Malcolm Pasley explains:

> The form of punishment adopted, the inscribing or engraving of the transgressed commandment on the offender's body, reawakens the original literal meaning of such phrases as *einem etwas einschärfen* [literally, "to cut or carve something into someone"], to inculcate ["to stamp in something with one's heel"] . . . *etwas am eigenen Leibe erfahren* (to experience something at first hand, feel it on one's own skin). . . . [Compare] "I will put my law in their inward parts, and write it in their hearts" (Jeremiah, xxxi.33).[55]

The brief story *Heimkehr* ("Homecoming") is a lawbook example of how Kafka develops an entire plot—a sequence of informative images—on the basis of the single root *Heim*, which gives rise to the congeners *Heimkehr*, *heimlich* ("homey"; also "canny"), and *Geheimnis* ("secret") but is itself undecidable.[56] "A Country Doctor" appears to be organized around the unwonted significances of the metaphorical clusters *Haus* ('house') and *Schweinestall* ('pigsty').[57] Marthe Robert demonstrates how this irregular literalization of metaphor involves something different from allegorical or Freudian-oneiric gratification;

54. Karl Philipp Moritz, *Anton Reiser* (Munich: Goldmann, 1961), p. 27. The first part of Moritz's novel was published in 1785, the second and third parts in 1786, and the fourth part in 1790.

55. Malcolm Pasley, "In the Penal Colony," in *The Kafka Debate: New Perspectives for Our Time*, ed. Angel Flores (New York: Gordian Press, 1977), p. 302.

56. I owe this example to Sigrid Mayer's excellent "Wörtlichkeit und Bild in Kafkas *Heimkehr*," *Germanic Notes* 7, no. 1 (1976): 6–9.

57. Edward Timms, "Kafka's Expanded Metaphors," in *Paths and Labyrinths: Nine Papers from a Kafka Symposium*. ed. J. P. Stern and J. J. White (London: University of London Press, 1985), pp. 72–73.

it functions as a critique of group behavior and, importantly, as a psychological defense mechanism.

> The autobiographical character of Kafka's story ["Investigations of a Dog"] can be easily . . . inferred from Kafka's special way of treating everyday words and phrases so as to bring out their hidden implications. "Dog," as we know, is a traditional anti-Semitic epithet. Taking the insult literally, Kafka places it in a logical situation that reveals the infinite stupidity of the word and, at the same time, its bitter consequences for the insulted individual. To make matters worse, the insult is not only used by the enemy, but also has currency within the family circle. At the time of Kafka's friendship with Isaac Löwy, director of the Yiddish theater troupe that played so large a part in his development, his father, who despised and loathed Eastern Jews, said to him: "He who lies down with dogs gets up with fleas." This brutal attack on his friend drove Kafka half-mad. But he took his revenge immediately—and punished himself for it: in his art of the instantaneous the two impulses are always connected—by changing the verb "get" to the verb "be," the outcome being two pseudo proverbs, variants of the popular maxim, the one saying roughly, "He who gets fleas is himself a flea," and the other, "He who sleeps with dogs is himself a dog." . . .
>
> Since in Kafka metamorphosis is always *animated metaphor,* it requires no complicated operations, but need only exploit the large selection of pseudo reasonings provided by rhetoric and grammar. If, for example, a Jew is a dog, then the Dog is a Jew; there is no grammatical objection to this second proposition, but since its absurdity is self-evident, while the first proposition passes for plausible, it glaringly exposes the absurdity of the insult.[58]

Marthe Robert's analysis proves how "animating the metaphor" defends against the humiliating social effects of a "literal" use of metaphor, which here amounts to a conventionally figurative understanding of metaphor. Kafka's aggressive/defensive thrust shapes a critique of metaphorical reason. The task of literature is by means of a

---

58. Marthe Robert, *Franz Kafka's Loneliness,* trans. Ralph Manheim (London: Faber & Faber, 1982), pp. 14–15. Among the fragments of Kafka's thought, we find these confirming notations: "The lament is senseless . . . the jubilation is ridiculous. . . . Obviously all he wants is to lead the others in prayer, but then it is indecent to use the Jewish language, then it is quite sufficient for the lament if he spends his life repeating: 'Dog-that-I-am, dog-that-I-am,' and so forth, and we shall all understand him" (DF 297). The reflection beginning "they are strangers and yet my own people" concludes: "I sniff round them like a dog and cannot detect the difference" (DF 304–5).

language of allusion "to raise the world into the pure, the true, the immutable" (DII 187). Failing this, its task is to explode language into the multifarious possible and hidden senses occluded by "the world," the world being the very conventional occlusiveness of metaphor. Here the *metamorphosis* of metaphor has become an allegorical marker, an instituted negative sign, of the impossibility of literature in the higher sense.

Because there is the human family, there is oppression; and as there are families (the Pit of Babel), there is family language (Babel), a negative memorial to the language buried in metaphor. But Kafka stages its exhumation. As a father, like Mr. Bendemann, I may speak of my son (tenor) *as* a devil (vehicle) and make good family sense—as long as I confine the metaphor to the transfer of only certain properties from vehicle to tenor, from devil to son: say, instinctualness, impulsiveness, and defiance. If, however, I carry over from vehicle to tenor properties in excess of the metaphor, such as the automatic adjuration and violent punishment that a *devil* calls forth—if I carry this violence over to a *son,* then I have made the metaphor monstrous . . . but visible.

There is something in this of genuine paternity. "As soon as a man comes along who has something primitive about him, so that he does not say: One must take the world as it is . . . but who says: However the world is, I shall stay with my original nature, which I am not about to change to suit what the world regards as good; the moment this word is pronounced, a metamorphosis takes place in the whole of existence" (L 203).

Certainly it takes place in the whole of language, and Kafka means to be that father to himself. He does not maintain the line of metaphor, he tampers with the difference and in this tampering reveals the spring of a revolutionary force—his force as a critic of ideology, the force of the form of his fiction. If (in Peter von Haselberg's words) "metaphors are the first to wrench paralyzed realities into the possibility of historical transformation,"[59] Kafka marks out that transformation in advance by wrenching metaphors apart. His allegories lay out in time a dangerous metaphorical moment, engendering textlike

---

59. Peter von Haselberg (writing on metaphor in Jean Paul), "Musivisches Vexierstroh: Jean Paul, ein Jakobiner in Deutschland," in *Jean Paul: Wege der Forschung,* ed. Uwe Schweikert (Darmstadt: Wissenschaftliche Buchgesellschaft, 1974), p. 191.

worlds that expose the disfigurement hidden by metaphorical constructions.

Kafka's villains in crisis read metaphor conservatively when they would do better to endure the excess—at least, if it is better to live than to die. It is to Joseph K.'s shame that he reads the figurative word *Prozeß* as the vehicle of the legal term "case at civil law." That is his reading, and by his reading he is condemned. In fact his process is more and less than a civil case: it is different, but he will boast to the chaplain of having finally learned from experience to read metaphors conservatively. It is Gregor Samsa's doom, too, to be read as vermin when he is in fact a new kind of man—sheerly different—but it is a reading to which he accedes. Yet how free is any protagonist (and reader) not to read figures conventionally, not to become the literal stuff (*Zeug*) of metaphor?

We start out, at least in principle, being as free as our "souls" are free. Consider another Expressionist source in Moritz's Sturm und Drang novel *Anton Reiser* (which I cited above for an example of literalized metaphor):

> With respect to some thing [the city of Hanover] about which one knows nothing but the name, the soul labors to conjure an image by means of even the most remote similarities, and lacking all other comparisons, it must take refuge in the arbitrary name of the thing, where it attends to its hard or soft, full or weak, high or low, murky or clean-sounding tones, and institutes between them and the visible object a sort of comparison, which sometimes accidentally hits the mark.[60]

The mark that is then hit, however—the commonly accepted "image"—is finally the mark of an other's will to power. The young Anton Reiser focuses "poetically" on the signifier but with the intent of hitting only one image—its "meaning." The jargon of structuralism says that poetry, more than prose, rivets attention on the self-display of the signifier—the sound/look of the word.[61] But if such a sound/look is once identified as belonging to a language, it is already a word and hence a virtual concept. This is Reiser's second image—the "real" Hanover. What, however, if not another's metaphor, has

60. Moritz, *Anton Reiser*, p. 42.
61. A moment's reflection, however, shows that there cannot be any such thing as a pure signifier within a language.

been hit as a mark when his aim turns out to be correct? There might, therefore, be a foretaste of freedom in tarrying at the signifier, looking elsewhere, or not yet, or against the grain of the field of meanings subtended by every verbal sign. This is what Kafka brings about when he uncovers the illimitably homonymic character of key words.

Arno Schmidt calls such defense against the literal "etymnic," in the course of offering "a bit of basic introductory theorizing" in dialogue:

"*How* are *words* stored in the human brain? . . . Concretely speaking: what does an Englishman . . . think of when he hears the sound 'vail'?"

"'Veil.'. . . Poetically speaking, a 'vale': 'Once more thou fillest shrub and vale.'[62] 'Vale, veil—: wail?' that means 'to lament.' And, taking off from here, in a more dissolute mood, I'd head for 'whale' and the Prince of 'Wales.'"

"Of course there's more—vee-ay-i-ell, the 'vail' that lurks in 'available'—but enough: all that comes to mind, whether you want it to or not. And they're terribly divergent things, which cannot be explained either by the 'homonym' or the philological concept of the 'root'— they can be [gotten at] just as well by means of lettering [*Schriftbild*] or by metaphorical meaning—probably the best thing for us to do is to invent a new term. . . .

"Let's inflict the burden on language itself. What shall we call this densely packed basic linguistic tissue? . . . 'Etymology': the doctrine of the valid: let us baptize these polyvalent fellows simply 'etym'? . . .

"Every word we utter is in more than one way 'overdetermined.' It's a sort of spinning disk or shunting station, so that the branchings of our thoughts, which often seem queer, are in this perspective by no means arbitrary or absurd."

"According to this theory everyone would harbor, so to speak, *two languages*: the one consisting of words, the other of "ay" word-*seeds*, precisely your 'etyms.'"

"Unlike *words*, which are more numerous and also more seriously 'correct,' etyms are far more many-sided, and they lust wittily after copulation. You could try to imagine it more concretely in [the] 'stories' [of a building]: at the very 'top' there is the consciousness that makes use of *words* and also insists, from its dim sense of its laboriously balanced, precarious vulnerability, on strict spelling according to *Webster*'s. The portion of the personality *underneath*—one half quite *capable*

62. "Füllest wieder Busch & Thal" is the first line of Goethe's poem "An den Mond."

of achieving consciousness, one half running wild in the unconscious—
speaks etyms."

"And as both languages can hardly be told apart, the minute one says
anything in words, the other will play along. . . ."

"More accurately: for the ear of the practiced listener a *second voice*
will always be heard singing along—phonetically speaking, per-
fidiously attuned, often painfully divergent from the bourgeois-inten-
tional 'meaning.' That comes about because the well-tempered language of words sounds *above* the threshold of the censor. . . . 'read &
approved by the superego': . . . 'conscience has intervened.' But the
language of the etym responds from *below* that barrier, with something
of that which, as it whizzed past at least once, the singer *truly thinks.*"

"The etyms, then, speak the truest truth. . . ."

"No. They are content, as comedians, for the most part with furnishing admonitory possibilities; bubbling over with dwarfish humor,
they are the representatives of the *homo sum* and renounce the
tiresomely sweaty 'deed.' Still they govern certain details, which
viewed in the perspective of motility, are 'more inconsequential,' viz.
dreams, 'slips,' 'associations'— and so forth. Which to be sure is no
mean thing."[63]

Kafka, however, does not tarry at the level of the etym. He deletes
the distinction between etym and meaning by projecting both onto
another plane, as principals in the enacted conflict within a person or
between persons for whom one or the other etymic signifier is at
stake. Kafka's metamorphic literalization of the metaphor conjures,
along with the atmosphere of comedy, edges of mortal danger:
throughout an extended context, to save themselves, both protagonist and reader must choose for each repetition of a word or phrase a
meaning for which they are unprepared. This is how Kafka disrupts
the unfreedom with which we read and with which we finally fail to
have experience. "Metaphor is more than a stylistic figure: it is an
existential figure," writes Jacques Sojcher. "It brings about a change
in . . . feeling, thinking, and speaking, without which there would be
no such thing as the consciousness of metaphor. This is the *exchange*
between writing and reading, the *reversal* of the direction of the cir-

63. Arno Schmidt, "Das Buch Jedermann: James Joyce zum 25. Todestage," in
Der Triton mit dem Sonnenschirm: Großbritannische Gemütsergetzungen (Karlsruhe: Stahl-
berg, 1971), pp. 278–81 (my translation).

cle."[64] Kafka the writer compels us to maintain this reversal incessantly. This could very simply be the task of Expressionist literature—"the incessant transformation and renewal of the image of the world . . . as the experiences [*Erlebnisse*] of art burst the formula of experience [*Erfahrung*]," in Robert Musil's words. "Literature does this in the most direct and aggressive way, because it works immediately with the very material of the formulation."[65] It is a view consistent with Gottfried Benn's, for whom Expressionism, more than a literary movement, inaugurated "a new historical being [*ein neues geschichtliches Sein*]" on the basis of "words charged with a huge accumulation of creative tension."[66]

In the lamed Expressionist vision, James Rolleston observes, "the language for communicating privileged moments sickens, wears down, becomes culturally unavailable. . . . Yet its failure opens no way back to a viable historical narrative: the stagnation of history merely becomes visible in horrifying intimacy."[67] Kafka often wanted what is called historical renewal, and his liberating gesture might again be found in "The Judgment." By identifying the "intimate" impossibility of historical action with the repressions of "the family beast," he produces a liberating narrative. This dialogue of the pit is built on the plainest consciousness of the animal warmth of family rhetoric: after Georg has put his father to bed, his father wants to know whether he is now "well covered up." But on Georg's responding, "Don't worry, you're well covered up," the father leaps up, hurls the covers away, defies the son: "You wanted to cover me up, my young sprig, but I'm far from being covered up yet" (S 84). Kafka sees all metaphors as potential usurpations of mastery.

Usurpations or humiliated accessions?

"The Burrow" ("Der Bau," 1922) is a late, beautiful work organized by the rhetoric of metaphor, metamorphosis, and chiastic reversal. The narrator-hero describes his construction as arising, at least

---

64. Jacques Sojcher, "La métaphore généralisée," *Revue Internationale de Philosophie* 23 (1969): 68.

65. Robert Musil, *Gesammelte Werke: Essays und Reden,* ed. Adolf Frisé (Hamburg: Rowohlt, 1978), 8:1152.

66. Gottfried Benn, "Expressionismus," in *Gesammelte Werke: Essays, Reden, Vorträge* (Wiesbaden: Limes, 1959), 1:243–44.

67. Rolleston, *Narratives of Ecstasy,* p. 19.

in part, from the "sheer pleasure of the mind in its own keenness" (S 325) and from "intense intellectual labor" (S 327). It is compelling to think that Kafka has coded in the metaphor of the burrow his "house of art"—an imaginary lodging for his being-a-writer (*Schriftsteller-sein*). The connection is strengthened by the link between the scratching, digging activity (*scharren*) of the burrowing creature and the act of writing (*schreiben*); both verbs derive from the common Indo-European root *sker*. As a builder and a narrator, the burrower is a mask of Kafka, at once inside his story (he is an articulate badger digging a palace for pleasure and defense) and outside the story (he is the fabricator of this very burrow metaphor). The burrow can thus be grasped as the metaphor of *metaphor*, as all-embracing.[68]

The story makes a decisive claim on totality, for its main figure has more than a certain rough adequacy to Kafka. In the throes of melancholy, Kafka might consider himself a bedbug or, in merriment, a provincial doctor to a godforsaken world. But as a metaphor of the whole of Kafka's authorial being, the burrow is a radically inclusive figure.

That a story of Kafka's called "Der Bau"—which means, literally, "The Building," "The Construction"—alludes to Kafka's literary enterprise will come as no surprise. *Bauen* is a recurrent figure of writing for Kafka, as is its cognate noun *Konstruktion*.[69] Parabolic houses abound in Kafka's confessional writings. A building arises from his

> plan for autobiographical investigations. Not biography but investigation and detection of the smallest possible component parts. Out of these I will then construct myself, as one whose house is unsafe wants to build a safe one next to it, if possible out of the material of the old one. What is bad, admittedly, is if in the midst of building, his strength

68. The phrase "all-embracing metaphor" is Henry Sussman's, who thus titles his "Reflections on 'The Burrow,'" in his study *Franz Kafka: Geometrician of Metaphor* (Madison, Wis.: Coda Press, 1979). Sussman writes of "The Burrow" as "an end to Kafka's writing, an ending worthy of the body, a culmination of its exploration into the limit disclosed in the process of metaphor. . . . The project under construction is a literary as well as an architectural object bespeaking the same duplicity, illusoriness, impenetrability, and limit characteristic of the literary text" (p. 150).

69. Like the English word, *Konstruktion* can have a negative valence, but at least one astute reader has read it as a consistently creative term in Kafka, meaning "project." Gerhart Baumann (in "Creative Constructions," a radio address, Freiburg broadcasting station, April 13, 1986), gives the example of Kafka "on the hunt for constructions. I come into a room and find them whitely merging in a corner" (DI 311).

gives out and now, instead of one house, unsafe but yet complete, he has one half-destroyed and one half-finished house, that is to say, nothing. [DF 350]

Kafka also composed an aphorism on *graben*, the verb which, more often than *scharren*, describes the activity of the burrower: "We are digging the Pit of Babel" (DF 349). And in a famous letter to Max Brod, he makes the link explicit: "What is essential to life is only to forgo complacency, to move into the house instead of admiring it and hanging garlands around it" (L 334).

"The Burrow" thus projects a plan faithful to the contours of Kafka's inner life, chiefly as this life centers on the act of writing: it is an allegorical burrow of writing. Kafka surveys the shape of his life in art—its design, its urgency (it takes place in dire straits), its obstacles, its reward—in linking writing with tomb building. He alludes to the ecstasy of art and to all its various enemies as parts of the nexus that writing engages with the body, others, the world, anxiety, death. A number of these associations are inscribed at the outset of the story in the sort of deceptively natural landscape found in Romantic works of inner intensity: the scene is a stripped-down *locus amoenus* for the inspiration to "descend," which would have been familiar to Kafka from a poem like Hölderlin's "Der Rhein." We glimpse a hole—"all that can be seen from outside" (it "really leads nowhere" that is, it leads nowhere in reality)—which evokes the "false hole" in Kafka's imagery of the writing process (DI 201; cf. pp. 53–54). The "false hole" contrasts with the vaginalike hole of the "authentic entrance [*eigentlicher Zugang*]," an opening below a bed of moss and, as the most vulnerable place in the burrow, a sort of wound: the image links womb and wound (compare "'You,' I Said, . . ." p. 19). The wound is the way to the life of writing. It abuts against a thing eluding description—"natural, firm rock," suggesting the inexplicable "substratum of truth" of the parable of Prometheus.

Below ground, the creature can be found building and shoring up his castle keep, using, as a sort of earth-pounding tool, his forehead. When he is not digging or caching food, he hunts with gusto the tiny intruders who have stumbled into his burrow—very likely allegorical figures of thoughts and experiences pursued by introspection (compare DII 202, and pp. 99–101 above]. Alongside, the burrow fans out

283

a variety of dainty gangways, connecting this written self with the world. They help compose an allegorical physiology of writing—friendly paths, provided by forest mice—little angels of reading, perhaps, and equally, dendrons of cooperating senses.

Hence, the burrow, while an *oeuvre,* also exhibits the qualities of a sensate body. "You belong to me," the narrator exclaims to his walls, "I to you, we are united. . . . And with its silence and emptiness, the burrow answers me, confirming my words" (S 342). Creature and burrow, being inseparable, are equally sensitive; and indeed Kafka's corpus (of works) would be indistinguishable from his body as habitations of a self nowhere else at home.[70] "Ever ready, his house is portable, he lives always in his native country" (DF 95). As a body of (literary) works and a physical body, the burrow metaphor provokes continual metamorphosis. In this way, the story gives an unsettling account of being a writer under the constraints of the world—that is, of having to be embodied in the double sense of having to produce works and having to have a body. An uncertain vermin dwells in lightless ground under the burden of needing to defend his work against enemies, visible and invisible, drawn to it by its double nature.

He is far from helpless, though. Badger *faber* describes the achievement of his burrow with pride, in a mood of toughness, the mood of a master predator and builder: "I have completed the construction of my burrow, and it seems to be successful" (S 325). This is the voice of the Kafka who regarded himself as the legitimate representative of his epoch. "No coward," he flaunts his powerful intelligence and the pleasure that power takes in its own performance, asserting his single-minded, ruthless lucidity.

And yet at the end of his life, everything threatens, terribly. An uncanny figure, the creature's enemy, has made a figure-eight return.

70. This example of metamorphosis, by which the building—a metaphor of the poetic self—is literally given sensitivity, the power to feel and to obey, is a textbook catachresis, a type of monstrosity of the metaphor. The metaphor of the poetic intention is made to function in a double register: the poetic self is doubled both as building and body, and attributes of the body (e.g., sensitivity) are transferred to the building, to the other vehicle of its tenor. This is the same phenomenon that Walter Sokel, in his psychological reading of "Der Bau," calls an animistic projection of the narrator-creature's narcissism (*Franz Kafka: Tragik und Ironie, Zur Struktur seiner Kunst* [Frankfurt am Main: Fischer Taschenbuch, 1983], p. 419).

Once upon a time it had appeared to the young artist, when he was an apprentice builder, but then it had seemed to fade away definitively. Now "the burrower has changed his intention anew, he has turned back, he is returning from his journey" (S 357). Announcing himself with a sinister hissing or whistling, he shatters "the fountains from which flows the silence" (S 350). Indeed, right along, these images of defensive building have conjured a factor fatal to a life in art. This fatality might be construed as "the world" of distraction and contingency; as Kafka grows older, it might more nearly have the sense of death. The narrator himself has no idea of the substantial identity of this whistling or hissing; for him it is an empty place for interpretation. "Death" tends to be the critics' choice, but it is not a good choice. Though it makes sense as an attack on Kafka's beleaguered body in 1923—and "whistling," too, is the sound that came from poor Kafka's infected larynx—it fails to address a crucial metaphorical dimension of the figure: the building as the constructed corpus of literary works. Death does not threaten such a building, because for Kafka's understanding of the act of writing, writing is as such the production of a kind of death assimilated to life (compare Chapter Five).

The sound has a clear-cut functional identity. It provokes in the narrator a sense of the futility of all his attempts to shore against ruin by continuing to dig, to write. It contests the authority of *this* metaphor, grounded on the resemblance between the work of literature and a dwelling place, in which literature figures as a place of shelter and support. It literally jeers at metaphorical building, its whistling and hissing being the sound an audience makes to indicate disapproval of a performance.

The enemy returns as a chiastic moment of critical thought, threatening the spatial metaphor of the "construction." It signals a return of the excluded difference, introducing into the extended metaphor of the poetic self a repressed agency of unsettlement. Until this moment, the metaphor has been metamorphosed only punctually, wittily, by a reversal of the positions of tenor and vehicle, of burrow and body. Now, the metamorphosis of the metaphor is brought to a destructive finale by a movement of temporal withdrawal and return of the factor that shatters equivalences.

"The Burrow" elaborates Kafka's entire life in work as a metaphor of a building, a house of art, and a second, more rapturous body. But the metaphor is attacked for its own mere constructedness by the chiastic movement of a truth that it has ignored and that resists it. There is a building, and it is pierced by the hissing of an invader; the very signal of its alien presence, in breaking the silence, shatters the building. But more, the building of this story, founded on the extension of metaphor, on the analogy between the burrow and Kafka's life in art, stands derided in its own factitiousness. Critique penetrates the story of an extended metaphor as a disruptive helix announcing the death of reassuring structures of resemblance, jamming the beneficent "rustling" of "warmth and coolness" (S 327) with radical, senseless "hissing" (S 352).

In his earlier stories especially, Kafka staged the metamorphosis of metaphors of art and life as an interpersonal struggle for meaning and mastery. The purpose of reading can be to read one's opposite number, an adversary consciousness, into "literal" being. The creature of the burrow avoids this negative truth by constructing his metaphor in isolation. But the crucial point of this story, which—like every one of Kafka's stories—dramatizes the fate of a metaphor, is that there is no safety even outside numbers. The metaphor elaborated in solitude, seemingly secure against another's urge to shatter the construction and contain its maker, cannot be defended. In "The Burrow," the other person is lacking but not Kafka's truth, which from this late perspective seems right along to have vehiculated persons as human beings: this truth is the will to unsettle metaphor. But if the final effect of "The Burrow" is destructive, it is also works the "living magic" to which Kafka alludes in his last epigrams, "a destruction of the world that is not destructive but constructive" (DF 103).

Max Brod reports that Dora Dymant told him how "The Burrow" ends: the builder would die but only after a struggle with his adversary (B 314). Fought with what weapons? Presumably with the same tools with which he had built his burrow—his digging or writing claws and his brow—beaten into weapons. "You too have weapons," Kafka's diary concludes (DII 233). Is not Kafka, therefore, one with the burrower? Didn't he also go on fighting as the burrower fights, for *his* metaphor against destruction, for his portable house of art?

There is a critical difference: it is the same difference we have seen between Kafka and Georg Bendemann and between Kafka and

Joseph K. Though all, as narrators, are in a sense alike, Kafka's created persons are natural in a way their maker is not. They have only their natural expectations buried in the love of marriage, experience, and metaphorical construction. Yet "the chain of the generations is not the chain of your nature. . . . The generations die as do the moments of your life. In what, then, does the difference lie?" (DF 94). Surely, in "your" duty to die aware: "You have to dive down . . . and sink more rapidly than that which sinks in advance of you" (DII 114). The difference is a "view of life . . . in which life, while still retaining its natural fullbodied rise and fall, would simultaneously be recognized no less clearly as a nothing, a dream, a dim hovering" (GW 267). This view is enacted in the movement of stories that kill off their heroes, while identifying their delusions as ones with which Kafka has "certain connections"; yet the lament that "dies beautifully and purely away" voices the surmise as to their difference (DF 94, DII 102).[71] Kafka projects for writer and reader an unawed consciousness of death.

This awareness is still not a mere affair of contemplation. "Contemplation and activity have their apparent truth; but only the activity radiated by contemplation, or rather, that which returns to it again, is truth" (DF 97). The stake is neither composure nor criticism but an ecstasy of critical composure. "If I wish to fight against this world, I must fight against its decisively characteristic element, that is, against its transience" (DF 95). In Kafka's lexicon what is most transient is most factitious, least designed by thought or least visionary.

Kafka wrote to his fiancée that in the building where he worked, papers were moved from office to office on a little trolley called *die Bahre* (the bier on which corpses are laid). This figure would appear to be creative only in destruction. A trolley turns out to be a vehicle that conveys from one office cell to the next the scripts of a deadly circulation. But the flimsy metaphor also acknowledges its own fatality. In displaying a metaphor that alludes to death—and thus de-

71. "The end of a Kafka-story is the flooding of the text by the excluded dimensions, a definitive silencing of the individual consciousness which renews the dream of unity in the very language, the very process of the collapsing project" (James Rolleston, "Kafka's Time Machines," in *Franz Kafka, 1883–1983: His Craft and Thought,* ed. Roman Struc and J. C. Yardley [Calgary, Alta.: Wilfrid Laurier University Press, 1983], p. 32). The dream of unity may be renewed, but it is with a difference.

stroying it—Kafka points out an exhilarating option. The conscription of trolleys into the circulation of death liberates a different meaning for the thing called "bier." It could henceforth acquire the meanings that trolleys have, including those trolleys which in modern times have carried freedom fighters to the front of their elected fight.[72] At the very least, it attractively redefines a corpse as a letter to the next higher office, as literature.

Kafka's most stringent perception is that the German word *sein* means at once "to be" and "to belong to him," to be another's property (DF 39). Words are in the first place an index of the struggle between ownership, property, proper meaning and that of being, daring, projecting oneself upon the undiscovered, not yet or no longer alive. This call to human renewal in the form of the destruction of specious, inculcated metaphors—of the tribal uses of the word—is the Expressionist enterprise par excellence. Kafka complicates Stefan George's line "Kein ding sei wo das wort gebricht [no thing could be where the word is lacking]" by suggesting that without literature no thing could be even where the word is present.[73]

72. In Barcelona in 1936, in Paris in 1944, in Budapest in 1956.
73. Stefan George, "Das Wort," in *Werke* (Munich: Küpper, 1958), 1:467.

Excursus
on Method

Chapter Eleven

Principles of Kafka Interpretation

In interpreting Kafka, have I behaved like a man of principle? Or more like the reluctant hermeneut who declared, "Certainly I am a man of principle—at least I think I am." I hope to make this question interesting by addressing any reader reading Kafka; the word "I" in the first sentence means "any interpreter." If, in reading Kafka, I uphold principles, what are these principles and what rules do they entail?

The answer is not easy, because the scene of reading is hard to stage. If I am engaged in interpreting a work by Kafka, I cannot easily lay hold of my principles. They are elsewhere; in governing, they do so somewhere offside—and yet they can be situated: they are in the text of what I have written on Kafka in the past, although I can find them there only by following directions leading from the place where I am now reading him.

Grasping that it is by means of the present that I am able to discover my principles elsewhere, in the past, I am pained by the pastness, by the already inscribed character of my principles, and hence I am unwilling to find them there. I want to find them here. I do not want to think that I am determined by my past—that in writing on Kafka I am instantiating no new rule, generating no new scheme—and that a Kafka story has failed to open in me an organ of theoretical perception.[1]

1. The historicist and meliorist sides of this reluctance belong, evidently, to the notion of research in the humanities in general and help explain its resistance to a

Of course, this might be the very point of reading Kafka anew—to defer consciousness of my subjection to past principles of interpretation. And so I will always resist, as disturbing, the requirement of confessing a method: I am not ready; I have not finished reading Kafka; my principles are still forming. I have to advance in the work of specific interpretation before I can shake out the scruples from my shoes.

What emerges as a circle of resistance to confessing principles of interpretation is a variation on the hermeneutic circle, which it behooves me not to get caught in but to get out of in the right way. This means: realize that my principles, wherever they are found, cannot be adequate in advance to the specificity of interpretation, for this is what a text is—the specificity of interpretation; realize that what principles I have can and must be corrected in only one way—by further work of textual interpretation.

These claims evoke some famous disputes and solutions. To grasp that my principles will never be adequate in advance to the specificity of the text is a way of defining what is called the "immanence" of reading.[2] It is a way of marking literature's independence of the circumstances surrounding its production of meaning, including the intention of the reader and the intention with which an author has endowed his raw materials.[3] The immanence of literature stresses

---

structuralist scientism. This is the very attitude that Michel Foucault identifies, in his foreword to the English edition of *Les mots and les choses*, as constituting the resistance to his enterprise: "The other disciplines . . .—those, for example, that concern living beings, languages, or economic facts—are considered too tinged with empirical thought, too exposed to the vagaries of chance or imagery, to age-old traditions and external events, for it to be supposed that their history could be anything other than irregular." On the other hand, mathematics, cosmology, physics—the "noble sciences" allied with philosophy—are "sciences of the necessary" precisely in *not* requiring a continual discovery of principle. And yet "[what] if, in short, the history of nonformal knowledge had itself a system?" Foucault means to establish "the laws of a certain code of knowledge" but deplores the association with "structural analysis" (*The Order of Things: An Archaeology of the Human Sciences* [New York: Pantheon, 1970)], pp. ix–x, xiv).

2. "A literary text . . . merely solicits an understanding that has to remain immanent because it poses the problem of its intelligibility in its own terms" (Paul de Man, *Blindness and Insight: Essays in the Rhetoric of Contemporary Criticism*, rev. 2d. ed. [Minneapolis: University of Minnesota Press, 1983], p. 107).

3. Fredric Jameson, discussing Stanley Corngold, "Kafka's Challenge to Literary History," in *Rewriting Literary History*, ed. Tak Wai-Wong and Ackbar Abbas (Hong Kong: Hong Kong University Press, 1984), pp. 230–31.

instead the completeness with which the work saturates the present act of interpretation. Whatever its genealogy, literature confers on the scene and event of reading a dense, inescapable, local and temporal particularity, making it (writes Manfred Frank) "the critical place where repetition becomes transformation, [proving] the non-simultaneity of the whole of its meaning, the inexhaustibility of its significance," and—stressing now the power of the text to generate an entire succession of readers—"its fundamental ability to be transcended by individuals capable of interpretation."[4] Here we identify at once the literalness of the literary object, its resistance to an extrinsic, generally imputable meaning, and its dependence on the life of the act of interpretation.

As a result, I can never possess the meaning of a text—neither in advance nor as a consequence of a finite act of reading: the text cannot give rise to a completed signifying act. Sartre pointed this out. The literary work, even as it *completes [the life of the author] by expressing it,*" is transcended by the signifying activity it provokes, which is its project, transforming the author into "a synthetic collection of questions."[5] If a method adequate to the work is regressive, for attending to the circumstances of its origination, it is also progressive, for attending to its power to produce the historical moment in which it is interpreted.[6] It is, therefore, as a function of its immanence or literality that the work becomes ontologically richer than the author or the epoch that considers it as its project or otherwise appropriates it.[7]

This principle of literalness sheds light on a feature of Kafka's narration. *The Metamorphosis* is a good example; its narrative struc-

4. Manfred Frank, "Polyvalent Meaning and Nonsimultaneity: Hermeneutical Questions for a Theory of the Literary Text," *Sprache und Literatur in Wissenschaft und Unterricht* 17, no. 57 (1986): 29.

5. Jean-Paul Sartre, *Search for a Method*, trans. Hazel E. Barnes (New York: Vintage, 1963), pp. 142–43.

6. Ibid., p. 154.

7. Here is Paul de Man's early and eminent contribution to this discussion: "The hermeneutic understanding is always, by its very nature, lagging behind: to understand something is to realize that one had always known it, but, at the same time, to face the mystery of this hidden knowledge. Understanding can be called complete only when it becomes aware of its own temporal predicament and realizes that the horizon within which the totalization can take place is time itself. The act of understanding is a temporal act that has its own history, but this history eludes totalization" (*Blindness and Insight*, p. 32).

ture thematizes literal reading. The narrator virtually coincides with the hero, the *Aspektfigur*, the access that narrator, hero, and reader have to the displaced, uncanny world is restricted entirely to its word-by-word unfolding. In this sense a rapt, immersed reading is the chief action of Kafka's stories, which, as Walter Benjamin noted, can never be exhausted by what is explainable in them.[8]

My second point is that principles cannot be corrected or enlarged except by specific acts of textual explanation. This should suggest the urgency of interpreting Kafka anew, despite the only dim lure offered by a history of readings repeatedly affirming that Kafka cannot be interpreted—an urgency which is favored by the critical atmosphere of the 1970s *dit* "semiotic" but to which, in other respects, Kafka is resistant. In the universe of semioticians in which all entities are signs, all groups texts, and all experience interpretations—in which no self exists, except as the series without paradigm of its readings, and the vale of soul-making has been developed into the archive of soul-marking—Kafka's work would seem to occupy a privileged position because of the rigor with which it holds this view to be deranged. The hero of each of Kafka's novels is, of course, on edge as a being whose main mode of existence is interpretive—who, like the author, is an *erschriebenes Selbst,* a self achieved through acts of, or like, writing.[9] But the difference between Kafka's world and "the world of signs" lies in his frustrated sense that the goal even of self-writing is a mode of authenticity, one that would no longer be a mode of reading and would survive precisely when self-enclosed and without signs. The goal gives grounds for despair because, as the prison chaplain in *The Trial* declares, "the scriptures are unalterable and the comments often enough merely express the commentators' despair" (T 272–73). This means, I believe, that the world is ineluctably scriptural; and every

---

8. *The Metamorphosis* thematizes literal reading at the same time, of course, that it indicates its intolerableness. The hero is given the opportunity of a literal reading, which he then rarely takes. What he does see with the intensity of the illusory literal is his "obvious undiscussed assumption" as to what "'stands there.'" (Martin Heidegger, *Being and Time,* trans. John Macquarrie and Edward Robinson [New York: Harper & Row, 1962], p. 192; cf. my Chapter Twelve. At times, it seems, Gregor does rise to the occasion by acting in conformity with the possibilities of his new body; at least the pleasure he has in swinging on the ceiling seems to indicate a sort of joy of reading.

9. Cf. Gerhart Baumann, *Sprache und Selbstbegegnung* (Munich: Fink, 1981), p. 74.

comment, having necessarily the form of a wish to escape from this limit, is additional testimony of despair.

Now at this point it might seem wrong to insist that when I read Kafka, principles can never be facts within specific acts of interpretation. They can be, with this proviso: that they are not my principles but the principles of others—of Kafka and, as I shall explain, of his critics. Kafka has inscribed in specific texts of his own the intention that they be self-reflective of literal writing or reading. I base my view of Kafka's intention on these texts and on the principles guiding the other critic with whom I am forever taking issue, even, or especially, as I cite him or her.

I now speak in my own right. My understanding of Kafka's fiction is of an enterprise that aims to engage to the limit the being wholly centered on writing, whose mode is, in Kafka's word, *Schriftstellersein*, existence as a writer (L 333). Kafka makes the act of writing fiction the middle of an exploration of a life constituted by the awareness of the exile this imposes and the strength that comes from the sense that this exile is perfect. Aspects of Kafka's project invite eloquent redescription from texts by writers like Roland Barthes, Jacques Derrida, and Gilles Deleuze, for whom writing responds to the (non)origin of articulation, difference, and deferral and for whom literature incessantly figures desire and death as writing. As a consequence, Kafka's social alienation follows from a primordial experience of separation which his relation to writing forced on him (including the separation masked by the simple term "primordial experience"). Social alienation may be a sign of this primary relation, but it is a misleading and factitious sign, because this relation cannot be expressed as a prime origin except "allusively," as Kafka says—through a kind of allegory. A sign more faithful to the fact of separation is "metamorphosis," which is more nearly responsive to the catastrophe confining Kafka's existence to acts of writing, acts of preparation for writing, and acts of interpretation made upon his history as writer. If Kafka captures the sense of his destiny as the crow that dares to storm the heavens, it is by means of an image of the *kavka* (jackdaw) that inks in, with transcendental expectations, a sky of blank paper. Kafka's old documents, plans, ordinances, mazes, crumbling walls, and castles that merge into villages are forms of the imagination of life lived palimpsestically, in labyrinthine scripts. This dimension of Kafka's work is unarguably present—a reflection in the mode of allegory upon existence as writing—and this dimension always requires interpretation because the relation of allegorical sign to meaning is not constant.

At the close of Chapter Three I distinguished between symbolical and allegorical readings of *The Metamorphosis*.[10] It followed that there could not be a symbolical representation within a text or a correct symbolic interpretation of a text aiming to constitute *Schriftstellersein*. Symbolic writing and reading are therefore seduction and error. Kafka's works are essentially nonsymbolic in the sense that their meaning cannot be specified by a scrutiny, however intensified and refined, of their material substrate, of the world of objects—"the face of Nature"—that they represent. For this reason Adorno's reading of Kafka in *Prisms* is a brilliant error, a tour de force of refined materialist exegesis but a tour de force only, and one that runs counter to the truth of its own premise. For Adorno declares at the outset that the meaning of Kafka lies in the abyss between the literal and the signifying moments of his work,[11] yet Adorno's actual practice is to find meaning all on the literally *material* side of the abyss, in Kafka's representations of the detritus cast out by a decaying capitalist order: commodity fetishes, subaltern types, abandoned stairwells, cluttered shopwindows, lumber rooms. Here Adorno is heedless, perhaps, of committing with a vengeance the same heresy of immediate interpretation with which he arraigned the materialist, ideological description of the fetishes of Parisian capitalism in Benjamin's early essays on Baudelaire.[12] To take up residence, as a critic, somewhere between the literal and the signifying moment of Kafka's images is precisely, of course, to dwell on the incessant moment of disjunction, the ongoing metamorphosis of image as metaphor—or, in a comparable phrase of Benjamin's, on "allegory as script."[13] It is, therefore, to

10. See further my *Fate of the Self* (New York: Columbia University Press, 1986), pp. 154–55.

11. Theodor W. Adorno, "Notes on Kafka," in *Prisms,* trans. Samuel and Shierry Weber (London: Spearman, 1967), p. 246.

12. Adorno's critique of Benjamin as insufficiently dialectical is discussed in Richard Wolin, *Walter Benjamin: An Aesthetic of Redemption* (New York: Columbia University Press, 1982), pp. 198–204.

13. Walter Benjamin, *Ursprung des deutschen Trauerspiels* (Origins of the German funeral pageant), ed. Rolf Tiedemann (Frankfurt am Main: Suhrkamp, 1982), p. 161; quoted in Fredric Jameson, *Marxism and Form: Twentieth Century Dialectical Thories of Literature* (Princeton, N.J.: Princeton University Press, 1971), p. 72.

affirm the difference between one's reading as a desymbolizer on the one hand and, on the other, as Benjamin's *Grübler*—"the super-stititous overparticular reader of omens" in the allegorical world where things are "sundered from meanings, from spirit, from genuine human existence" (thus Fredric Jameson).[14] Benjamin writes:

> Once the object has beneath the brooding look of Melancholy become allegorical, once life has flowed out of it, the object itself remains behind, dead, yet preserved for all eternity; it lies before the allegorist, given over to him utterly, for good or ill. In other words the object itself is henceforth incapable of projecting any meaning on its own: it can only take on that meaning which the allegorist wishes to lend it. He instills it with his own meaning, himself descends to inhabit it, and this must be understood not psychologically but in an ontological sense. In his hands the thing in question becomes something else, speaks of something else, becomes for him the key to some realm of hidden knowledge, as whose emblem he honors it. This is what constitutes the nature of allegory as script.[15]

"Script rather than language," adds Jameson in his gloss, "the letter rather than the spirit. . . . Allegory is the privileged mode of our own life in time, a clumsy deciphering of meaning from moment to moment, a painful attempt to restore a continuity to heterogeneous disconnected instants."[16]

And yet, as evocative as Benjamin's text is of Kafka's reader—transfixed, say, by Odradek, by the torture apparatus, the castle tower, or the obscene scripture of the court—it is incorrect in its tendency to kill the object, to make it the empty cipher of the brooder's intent: these objects reflect back on the linguistic energy that propels them into existence as the fictive imagings of metamorphosed metaphors torn from context, from the stability of ordinary narrative. Jameson's gloss, though it was never intended to apply to Kafka, would make Kafka's narrative too much the project of recovering a genuine human life of the middle, where Kafka's narrative is concerned above all with enacting the necessary consequences of writing. This is to emphasize the randomness of empirical existence and also to conjure with an existence anywhere out of this world.

In having now evoked the work of some of Kafka's best critics, I

14. Jameson, *Marxism and Form*, p. 71.
15. Benjamin is quoted in ibid., p. 72.
16. Ibid.

conclude by affirming my admiring quarrel with them. I stand in a relation of apparent opposition to but real dependency on Kafka's interpreters, whom I am swift to accuse of having bad principles.[17] "Opposition," because the principles they assert are not radical enough for the centrality of writing in Kafka, but "dependency," too, because my principles are won antithetically from the specific insights of these critics—by the impression of correct insights arising from their momentary disregard of principle, and by the freedom that their mistakes, arising from their fidelity to insufficient principles, engender.

Let us look at the achievement of one of the best of these critics.

17. For a statement of some further disagreements with the implications of Adorno's and Benjamin's work on Kafka with respect to *Metamorphosis,* see my *Commentators' Despair* (Port Washington, N.Y.: Kennikat Press, 1973), pp. 51–53, 76–77.

Chapter Twelve

"The Pure Expression": An Exemplary Reading of Kafka

Jörgen Kobs, a young Germanist at Tübingen, died in an automobile accident in 1968, leaving behind the manuscript of his only book, *Kafka: Untersuchungen zu Bewußstein und Sprache seiner Gestalten (On the consciousness and language of his characters)*.[1] The text was revised for publication in 1970 by Ursula Brech. Her decision was more than an act of piety, for Kobs's book is masterly. The plan to rescue a critical work of such originality, accuracy, and radiance, and in this way bring Kafka's work to light, is not strictly incomparable with Max Brod's original salvaging project. Kobs's philosophical devotion to his subject, seen in the perspective of his early death, recalls the strictness, fragility, and tension of Kafka's literary enterprise.

In the wake of Kafka's mythographers and iconographers came his structuralist critics. His recent canonization as an author of handbook rank and as the object of a critical edition—while certainly a fate his importance merits—tends further to hypostatize the act by which his work arose. Kobs's book and Kobs's death renew a sense of frail energies concentrated on metaphysical design: that of elaborating a language able to analyze life into its visible parts, in order to contend with it and "raise it up" (DII 187).[2]

1. Jörgen Kobs, *Kafka: Untersuchungen zu Bewußtsein und Sprache seiner Gestalten*, ed. Ursula Brech (Bad Homburg: Athenäum, 1970). Quotations from this work are indicated hereafter by page number.
2. "I can still have passing satisfaction from works like 'A Country Doctor,' provided I can still write such things at all (very improbable). But happiness only if I can raise the world into the pure, the true, and the immutable" (DII 187).

Kobs's study, 560 pages long, is the most important panoptic book on Kafka since the works of Emrich, Sokel, and Politzer.[3] It may be the most productive of them all because, apart from its discoveries about Kafka's fictional world, it is exemplary for its method. It exhibits the practices grounding the best work on Kafka of whatever ideological kind. Kobs's studies of the manuscript of Kafka's "America-novel"—which Kafka referred to as *Der Verschollene (The boy who was never again heard from)*—demonstrate, first, the importance of the most exact efforts at establishing Kafka's texts even where the changes are ostensibly few and slight. Kobs can draw astonishingly rich conclusions from the faint variations constituting the authorial history of single phrases, even single participles. His philological intensity supplements Emrich's, Politzer's, and Sokel's high classical interpretive style while proving decisively the need to undo Max Brod's editorial intrusions. If now, in 1988, we have a fair text of *Amerika*, thanks to Jost Schillemeit's work on the new critical edition, it is in good part due to the impulse coming from Kobs's book.[4]

Equipped with an authoritative text, Kobs follows his main principle: intrinsic, "work-immanent" analysis. He examines the semantic implications of variations in word order and types of diction as they emerge from trial transformations of Kafka's sentences.[5] Kobs's data

3. Wilhelm Emrich, *Franz Kafka* (Frankfurt am Main: Athenäum, 1965); Walter Sokel, *Franz Kafka: Tragik und Ironie, Zur Struktur seiner Kunst* (Frankfurt am Main: Fischer Taschenbuch, 1983); and Heinz Politzer, *Franz Kafka: Parable and Paradox* (Ithaca: Cornell University Press, 1962). Along with Kobs's book, Gerhard Kurz's recent *Traum-Schrecken: Kafkas literarische Existenzanalyse* (Stuttgart: Metzler, 1980) must now be reckoned a synoptic work of great distinction.

4. Kobs's work deserves credit for having helped make urgent the sense in the last decade that a critical edition of Kafka's works could no longer be postponed. Two volumes have so far appeared from Fischer Verlag, Frankfurt am Main: *Das Schloß*, ed. Malcolm Pasley (1982), and *Der Verschollene [Amerika]*, ed. Jost Schillemeit (1983).

5. "Simply by the manner in which a speaker arranges the various parts of a *taxeme* [a sentencelike element], by which he structures their succession within the possibilities of variation at his disposal, he reveals distinctions of interest, says (wholly explicitly) what seems significant and what seems less important to him" (p. 350). Kobs's tool for his analysis of the semantics of syntactical variation in sentences comes from the linguistics of Hans Glinz. Kobs's procedure can be viewed as part of the modern project, following Barthes, to reimagine two other senses of the linguistic sign apart from the symbolic—apart, that is, from the alleged power of signs to represent immediately the substance of their meaning. These two other senses are the syntagmatic (the sign is grasped in the linear context of its grammatical arrangement) and the paradigmatic (the sign is grasped as the object of a selection made from among

are the minimally interpreted semantic correlatives of structural anomalies in Kafka's grammar and diction. This analysis presupposes and, by its results, proves a major premise: that Kafka's texts reward scrutiny of the most microscopic nuance, each increase of optical intensity producing an increase in the depth of penetration. It becomes entirely improper to think, for example, that *Amerika* can be read with something less than exhaustive fidelity to word order on the putative grounds that it is after all an imperfect text never intended for publication. Kobs's "Amerika" text is genuine in two senses: it is philologically reliable, and it is also a kind of absolute—an authoritative constitution of worldly consciousness, perfect for what it has left out as much as for what it includes, wider and deeper than Kafka's previous commentators, however patient and ingenious, have imagined.[6] It is no mean sign of Kobs's genius that he is able to dwell for over a hundred pages on some thirty sentences from *Amerika* and not be boring. The extraordinary demand he makes on the reader is lightened by the fluency and clarity of his exposition.

Kobs's main concern is to define the distinctive "way of seeing" (*Sehweise*) produced by the form of Kafka's sentences. This is, in a strict sense, the same project as describing the world of Kafka's main character without the help of categories furnished by the extraliterary systems that Kafka deplored (for example, psychoanalysis). How can the link between his world and the distinctive verbal structure of his vision be made so direct? That is because the world of Kafka's fiction is constituted entirely by perception identical with that of the hero's. "Everything," writes Kobs, "that is narrated and described is seen from the perspective of only a single person," even where there is no explicit signal that this is the case. "Only the thoughts of the main character—not those of other characters as well—can be represented; only those events can be reported at which this person—seeing, hear-

---

a group of substitutable congeners). For a brilliant reading of how Faust's Bible translation "suspended for a century the sign's assignation to the groups of which it is an element," see Friedrich A. Kittler, *Aufschreibesysteme 1800 . 1900* (Munich: Fink, 1985), p. 19.

6. On the matter of the literary work's being perfect for what it keeps silence about, unlike the work of criticism, see Joel Fineman's "The Structure of Allegorical Desire," in *Allegory and Representation: Selected Papers from the English Institute,* (Baltimore: Johns Hopkins University Press, 1983), pp. 49–50, 58.

ing, feeling, and thinking—is present" (p. 25). Kobs's analysis of perspective therefore addresses itself to the whole world of the novel, for in Kafka the verbal texture is the fictive world. In following the assigned forms of consciousness of the hero-narrator, Kobs defines the structures of his worldly experience. The hero's actions issue self-evidently from his way of seeing the world; an account of them can be given without recourse to the universalizing, material motivations supplied him by the exegete (read psychoanalyst).[7]

This is Kobs's enterprise, and I think it succeeds beautifully, in the sense that I can always either consent to what he writes or else feel that it opens up only the advanced form of an enigma. Kobs shows that the principles of the world of Kafka's hero are indeed the a priori forms of his apperception. He uncovers these principles in detail. He shows that they cannot be situated at the level of the hero's material intentions in combat with the supposed norms of an impersonal alterity—with *our* nature or society or law. Hence naturalistic interpretations of Kafka's characters, like those of empirical psychology, are at best speculative.[8] In this order of explanation, as Heidegger puts it, "one is appealing to what 'stands there'" in the text only in order to assert "one's obvious undiscussed assumption."[9] The categories that Kobs addresses, however, are necessary, being linked to language: they constitute the world of Kafka's heroes.

But the special value of Kobs's procedure is more than its wider economy—its generality and coherence—as a method of reading Kafka, supposing, as I do, that his minimally interpreted semantic correlatives do indeed go beyond special pleading. The gain is more

---

7. Kobs insists on another fundamental peculiarity of Kafka's narration that looms large in his findings: Kafka never interpolates future occurrences; the narrative perspective is rigorously confined to the present moment. The utterly unique distinction of Kafka's method is not *Einsinnigkeit*, the so-called coincidence of perspective as between narrator and perspectival figure, but the form of the experience of time—strict linearity, the series of empty and incandescent present instants.

8. Is Gregor Samsa, e.g., a subliminal malingerer and family avenger? Certainly the verbal reality of the work is strikingly bare of named intentions, wishes, motives—conscious or otherwise. *The Metamorphosis* is short on wishes apart from the wish to go under (i.e., to have no wishes). Still, this is not the worst hypothesis. Yet in illuminating certain cruxes, psychoanalysis muddles others: e.g., how can the unconscious wish to be at once aggressive and submissive account for the specific kind of enjoyment that Gregor finds in his sister's violin playing?

9. Martin Heidegger, *Being and Time*, trans. John Macquarrie and Edward Robinson (New York: Harper & Row, 1962), p. 192.

302

than the articulation of Karl Rossmann's, Joseph K.'s, and K.'s way of seeing. What is at stake is the question of whether or not one can admit into Kafka's fictive world the possibility of an edification of persons. In naturalistic readings—whether psychoanalytic, Marxistic, aesthetic, or *Bildungs*-philosophical—Kafka's world is in principle redemptive. That is because these systems, in advancing the superiority of one type of worldly experience over another, have in common a belief in the truthfulness of experience. It follows that just as Kafka's critic at home in natural experience fulfills his or her life through a dismantling of illusions, perceiving with relief the merely delusory sovereignty of the reality that torments him or her, so too Kafka's hero can in principle be redeemed, on the condition that he or she too have the benefit of this training in critical reason.

In Kobs's account, however, there is no (or almost no) possibility of liberation from the a priori constraints on any consciousness that interprets. "As subjectivities," he writes, "Kafka's characters are always already in a state of self-alienation" (p. 411). "To be a subject means just this: to live outside all positive existential definitions, to exhaust oneself in abstract, hence absolute, yet groundless claims" (p. 387). There is no way—none, at least, leading through social experience, through the mutual interpretation of subjectivities—for characters in Kafka's world to arrive at the center of their personality. (I shall explain shortly why I qualify this point by writing, above, "*almost* no possibility of liberation" and, now, "no way—*none, at least*, leading through social experience.") An initial, ineluctable obstacle prevents even a rudimentary hearing, so that revelation through another of the hidden, equivocal, yet propulsive images of oneself is a priori reduced to confusion by the intrinsic shortcomings of interpretative consciousness.

But much worse: the mutual relation of all subjectivities tends actively not toward attempts at illumination but toward annihilation. "Because they are subjects, consciously active beings intentionally directed toward objects, they simply cannot avoid pushing their opposite number further and further into the background, restricting his possibilities, robbing him finally of any sort of free play. . . . In these novels there is actually no possibility of avoiding the turnabout of altruistic strivings into the absolute egoism of subjective being" (p. 315).

Excursus on Method

What, then, are the typical, indissolubly mediating forms of, say, Karl Rossmann's "subjective consciousness"? Kobs describes them as

> the projection of his own inwardness onto the outer world; his unmotivated distrust, which robs itself of its own foundation; his translation of coincidence into causality; his tendency subsequently to seize on impressions having an only subjective validity, as if they were objective facts; finally, his inability to arrive at consistent observations and to interpret his observations without contradiction. . . . As soon as Karl attempts to verify his subjective fore-conception against the concrete situation, he becomes captive of the situation. . . . The concrete case, which is supposed to confirm the general, to lend it visibility and weight, in fact makes it dubious and uncertain. [pp. 47, 132–35]

Karl's troubled seeing, slightly modified, appears again at the beginning of *The Castle* as the failure of the project of determining essence, the inadequate overview, the observer's slide into detail, the distorting effect of minute observation:

> The world that appears to the observing subject as the indifferent contiguity of isolated parts cannot, . . . even through superior acts . . . of relational thought and judgment, come to light as a meaningful and structured totality. Of course, relational thought establishes distinctions of rank, but the connections it is capable of generating always remain "short-circuited." Of course, the subject, in judging, takes up a position . . . : it establishes gradations among values . . . , but the *engagement* that every act of judgment presupposes necessarily misses the object to be judged and leads to the self-negation of the judger, leads back, therefore, into indifference. [p. 350]

Now if Kobs's achievement were simply the discovery that Kafka had revealed the constitutive activity of the subject, then Kobs would have discovered the North Pole for the second time. And if he were to argue only that Kafka's account of his characters' way of seeing always aims at the fundamental nature of cognition and judgment in any consciousness, then neither his nor Kafka's achievement would be decisive. Kafka would be functioning as epistemologist, hermeneut, and philosopher of intersubjectivity without different or deeper effect than, say, Nietzsche. Kobs's power in fact lies elsewhere: in his ability to develop the radical bearings of Kafka's epistemological concerns on the meaning of his fictions, and to turn these principles—an instructive scourge—on Kafka's heedless interpreters.

304

He shows, for example (on the basis of a chapter fragment from the body of *Castle* manuscripts) that Kafka's heroes are never so isolated and outcast in a world not of their making as they, and Kafka's critics, are inclined to suppose. These readers take the subjective impressions of characters as if they were objective givens.

> In fact all subjectivities are alike in their ignorance. The village inhabitants understand K. and themselves exactly as little as K. could understand himself or them. . . . [Here is an initial statement] of the general identity [for Kafka] of all figures who experience the world through the mediation of their consciousness. . . . It is the equivalency [*Gleich-Gültigkeit*] of all events which makes Kafka's world seem not only indifferent to values but strange and unintelligible. The perspectival determinant of permanent alienation can be recognized only in the continual incongruencies and contradictions that run through the ostensibly precise observation. [pp. 198, 205]

In this light it becomes impossible to construe a contradiction that the hero registers within his conscious horizon as the collision between a fact and a mere surmise. Kafka's heroes are not, as is often said, forever tarrying in the domain of pure possibility: K., for example, is constantly at work erecting pseudorealities around him, and it is interesting for him to do so.

When, now, Kobs attempts to grasp the meaning of Kafka's work as a whole, he cannot escape a fundamental enigma. The main outline of his reading is clear: he sees Kafka's fiction as a flow of intentional energies. The poetic will aims to extract from itself and—via the exemplary reduction and schematization of this extract—to create a model of inauthentic, appropriative, striving, ultimately self-devouring consciousness. Kafka remains pure as his work acquires the purity of total but perfectly organized error.[10] "Total" error? This is the

---

10. This could be the place to stress the way in which Kobs's view surpasses Heinz Politzer's account of the paradoxical character of cognition in Kafka's heroes. In *Franz Kafka: Parable and Paradox,* Politzer wrote incisively about Kafka's paradoxes, and indeed Kobs draws on him. But Kobs's work is different by virtue of its stringently antipsychological thrust. Politzer's conception of paradox has a wide, impressionistic governance, whereas Kobs defines and develops Kafkan paradox as a strict circle of contradiction on the model "A Cretan says, 'All Cretans are liars.'" "In this neutralization of tendencies [both toward and away from signification]," writes Kobs, "in the opening up of the hermetic circle, through a movement which itself leads to a void of indeterminate content, lies the real difficulty in understanding Kafka's works" (p. 18). The paradoxical circle introduces, most visibly into the shorter prose, a structural

problem. Kobs's account wavers at this point. Consider the following exhibits (italics throughout are my own):

1. Concerning the process by which subjectivities engaged with one another move toward mutual annihilation, Kobs writes: "Although it is nothing but a phenomenon of consciousness, still the engaged subject cannot himself *in any fashion* understand it or be made conscious of it" (p. 336).

2. "For Kafka's figures, who *never* reflect on the role which their own consciousness plays in the act of understanding, the hermeneutic circle remains a *circulus vitiosus*" (p. 420).

3. "*Everything* narrated was able to be narrated the way it was narrated *only* as mediated by Karl's consciousness. . . . The principle of congruence means that *all* depicted events appear *only* as mediated by a subjective consciousness" (pp. 32-33).

Hence the truth freed by the confinement and reduction of inauthentic consciousness to its own basis could never in this novel be portrayed in itself but only as it appeared for Karl: hence, as untruth.

But consider another series. This series turns on a key term in Kobs's argument, "the pure expression [*der reine Ausdruck*]." The axial point in Kafka's heroes' way of seeing, at which a hypothesis about experience collapses into blank facticity, is a *Leerstelle*, a void for any consciousness, which nonetheless—for Kobs—conceals and shelters a fundamental reality. This reality can actually be experienced, however, by the character who gives himself up to his pure expressive response to it. The pure expression may be a mute gesture: "Nowhere . . . does experience find a purer expression than in the spontaneous unmediated gesture" (p. 412). Or it may be a fit of weeping like that, for example, of the desperate observer of "Up in the Gallery," who cannot fuse what he sees with what he imagines. "The pure expression," continues Kobs, "actually does break through the covering and masking strata of subjective overlays and reaches

principle of indeterminacy. It has the same effect as the principle of narrative congruence in the novels—a principle that operates the reduction to an immediate present and hence to the inescapable mediation of all events within the novel by a subjective consciousness. The rigorous correlation in Kobs of novelistic detail and fundamental interpretation closes gaps in Politzer's intuitive "psychological" speculations.

down to the basis of reality: indeed, it radiates authentically from this basis. Exactly for this reason the pure expression must remain a great rarity in Kafka's work, in a world that is mediated by the principle of the way of seeing" (p. 401). It is a tribute to Kobs's scrupulousness and mastery of the whole of his argument that in the very act of introducing the category that unsettles it, he alerts the reader to the danger. For in the light of the preceding account of Karl's way of seeing, the pure expression cannot be "a great rarity"; it cannot exist at all. "Pure" reality cannot come to light within a work systematically mediated by inauthentic consciousness.

Kobs's discussion of this point only adds further difficulties. Describing Karl's response—his interpretative restraint—in the face of pure expressions by Robinson and by Karl's uncle, Kobs writes: "Precisely because Karl Rossmann stays completely outside the matter as an interpreter [*schaltet sich auf keine Weise deutend ein*], he succeeds in making visible reality transparent. . . . Instead of getting involved in interpretation, instead of weighing the external as the expression of the internal, he follows as attentively as possible only the visible events, and thus he succeeds in uncovering the basic pattern of all social acts" (pp. 401, 403). This basic pattern is tyranny.

How, then, can it be true (as Kobs writes) that the pure expression so described "signifies [*bedeutet*] nothing despite its abundance of meaning [*Sinn*]"? Can it "signify" nothing while disclosing the "basic pattern of all social acts"? The pure expression amounts for him who performs it to a "gratifying and liberating unity of external and internal, of phenomenon and meaning" (p. 412). Merely in "following the phenomenon attentively," Karl Rossmann brings "the inner meaning" of the gesture to the surface as significance. But significance (*Bedeutung*) is precisely what belongs to the object of interpretation (*das zu Deutende*). Hence the distinction vanishes between Karl's customary interpretative way of seeing, which looks for significance, and the rare suspension of perspective, which here discloses significance. Once the absolute prerogative of Karl's way of seeing has disappeared, Karl's experience can in principle be read at all times either as a distortion of reality or as itself the gesture disclosing a deeper reality—"a unity . . . of phenomenon and meaning"—such as social facticity.

Now Kobs insists that Karl does not himself grasp the significance

that he brings to light. The inauthentic consciousness remains sealed
off from truth. But in order to have Karl succeed in bringing out the
"basic pattern of all social acts," Kobs has had to suspend the mediating activity of Karl's ordinary conciousness. The seal is ruptured.
Karl's consciousness can be stopped long enough for him to bring to
light "the authentic basis of reality"—but if this is so, then there is no
reason in principle, no argument possible, to prove that Karl is unable
to grasp the significance of his act.

The notion of the pure expression therefore produces at least these
difficulties: How, in Karl's world, could a perspective be entirely
neutral with respect to an object—an expression? How could Karl's
failure to interpret the expression uncover its significance? How could
a unity of sign and meaning appear within the degraded language of
this fiction: that is, how could an object that Karl names appear as it
is, without disfigurement?

Through these contradictions an even more fundamental one
arises: that of the status of represented consciousness in the novel—of
Karl and, hence, of the narrator. At the outset Kobs writes that Karl
"cannot succeed in attuning to one another" the various determinations of his judgment (p. 124). But now Kobs has Karl succeed in
suspending his interpretative interests for the sake of his object.
Clearly, it is not in Karl's power to decide when to succeed and when
not to; the decision lies outside him. But neither is this decision
arbitrary. Here is the difference between a fiction and reality. Whether a consciousness sees truly or falsely is, in a fiction, the responsibility of *another* consciousness.

Another consciousness? The absoluteness of congruence as a narrative principle is now jeopardized; the perspectival figure stands in
critical relation to a *narrator* who is responsible for his success or
failure, who decides when to suspend the optic of Karl's inauthentic
consciousness. The gap that the "pure expression" broaches in the
narrative of the novels invites further destruction of its unity. To a
putative narrator—for Kobs "the narrator to be postulated" (p. 32)—
now belongs the wider consciousness responsible for fundamental
decisions of composition. It decides when and with what effect
Karl Rossmann's consciousness splits, turns in on itself, and perfectly
betrays its designs. It elects one kind of material substrate in Rossmann's "mere impressions" rather than another, knows the meaning

of certain bookish allusions within the text that Rossmann is unlikely to know, exists as the reticent awareness of the horizon of meaning within which individual moments are situated. There is a narrator perceptible in *Amerika*, despite the congruence of one dimension of his consciousness with that of the main figure. Kobs is wrong to assert that "it can therefore no longer be said that the narrator says something, gives us to understand something, for he is reduced to the function of a *merely registering organ*" (p. 32; my italics).

Kobs does indeed grant the presence of a superior consciousness flowing *around* Kafka's work. He speaks explicitly of "the writer's intention" (p. 258). "The alleged presence [in Karl's world] of a comprehensive horizon of observation is ironically distanced by the writer" (pp. 221, 284). "The writer treats his creation with irony" (p. 255). But Kobs eschews the identification of this superior consciousness with a work–immanent narrator. "It must be stressed once again that there is no superior narrator in these stories who could bring to light his own thought-forms . . . behind the characters' backs" (p. 302).

The key word is "in," "*in* these stories." Kobs wants the superior consciousness to be wholly outside the novel. A wholly truthful authorial consciousness must exist outside the work, keeping itself pure at an "ironic distance"; the work itself exists as the dross of the act of writing. Kobs's model is binary: the writer remains truthful; the work exists as hermetically schematized monological error corresponding to Kafka's "real [i.e., empirical] self." But this model is destroyed by "the pure expression," which postulates a narrator inscribed *within* the text who is not identical with "Kafka the writer."

If Kobs's scheme were genuinely intrinsic or work-immanent, he would be required to cede the binary division of consciousness to one asymmetrically triangulated. His reading is in fact founded on a doctrinal view of Kafka's intention drawn from the confessional writings, which does not deliver the most adequate or interesting theorem. The mediator of the fictive world of *Amerika* is not Karl Rossmann but a narrator only one side of whose consciousness is congruent with Karl Rossmann's and whose other sides set Rossman in a different perspective. The degree to which this different perspective is explicit and visible varies from moment to moment, but it is active even in the moments when it is least perceptible. The work is thus at all times a play of the narrator's presence/absence; the character of the fiction is at all times equi-vocal, for the degree of presence/absence of the narrator's voice belongs to the novel as part of its total interpretation. I stress "interpretation"; the reader has no certain guide. It does not follow, for example, that the work is most truthful when the narrator is most visible, for the explicitness of his presence runs counter to the degree of presence with which, following Kobs, the pure expression could come to light. But neither, of course, is the narrator's apparent absence a guarantee of the truth of the gesture. Indeed the work is dominated by the phenomenon of the apparent absence of narrator and the presence of sheer error.

If, then, the felt presence of the narrator is no guarantee of the truth of the action, it follows that in one important sense the narrator is not reliable. Irony in this work does not flow all one way, from the superior narrator to the deluded hero; in the moments when the narrator merges his perspective with that of the hero for the sake of the pure expression, the hero celebrates an ironical (because unconscious) victory of captivation over the narrator. In such moments the narrator suspends the limitations of the hero's perspective, cedes to the hero the prerogative of his own vision. And yet for what does he relinquish his own sobriety, lucidity, and sense of self? Is not the very temptation of pure expression in the world of the K.s a delusion and a snare?

Kafka's narrator (*pace* Kobs) has to be seen as in a condition neither of truth nor of error but at once of truth and error. His condition mingles stupidity and insight inextricably. But this mingling should not imply that in the narrator both dimensions are reconciled into a unity—certainly not, at any rate, the "unity of contemplativeness and activity [which] exists only in the congruence of narrator and perspectival figure, in the personal unity of 'writer' and 'real self'" (p. 539). The relation of truth and error in Kafka's perspective is not continuous but "allusive"—the allegorical language of allusion meanwhile implying a division between meaning and phenomenon and, more, division within each meaning and each phenomenon.

As a consequence of this state of affairs, it is impossible to decide authoritatively whether at any given moment the language of *Amerika* is to be read literally, as accurately presenting Karl's own erroneous grasp of the world, or figuratively, as proffering Karl's experience as pure expression, as a gesture whose truth undoes the manipulative, "ironically distancing" perspective of the narrator. This zone of indetermination in Kafka—which Kobs, albeit inadvertently, leads us to discover—appears to be the ultimate field of Kafka's paradox.

Postscript

Earlier, in the conclusion to Chapter Ten, I spoke of a moment of "unity" in Kafka—an ecstatic movement of critical activity and contemplation. The form of such a movement is defined in the *Octavo Notebooks* as "the activity radiated by contemplation, or rather, that which returns to it again" (DF 97). Such movements follow the death or virtual death of the heroes of "The Judgment" and "The Burrow" after their will to maintain and reify metaphors has been destroyed. A moment of unity is also present in the fusion of contemplation and critical activity that excoriates the bachelor's frozen fear in "'You,' I Said . . ." or dissolves Joseph K.'s false hold on life in *The Trial*.

Are such moments to be thought of as experiences for a reader? If so, they would indeed close off the field of Kafka's paradox. Yet if they exist, why, then, in the preceding pages, have I taken Kobs to task for affirming moments of unity?

The reason is that our conceptions of Kafka's privileged moment are not actually comparable. Consider the kind of unity that Kobs sees represented in Kafka's work. He speaks of a fulfilled "unity of contemplativeness and activity [that] exists only in the congruence of narrator and perspectival figure, in the personal unity of 'writer' and 'real self'" (p. 539). I cannot agree, however, that Kafka situates such a moment on the level of a narrator congruent with his character. It is equally difficult to envision a moment in Kafka's work bringing about a *personal* unity of the writer and the real self. If such a "pure" yet articulated "expression" exists, it would have to be attributed to Kafka as narrator, occurring in the instant at which his congruence with his character dissolves. Indeed, in his diary, Kafka identifies the high moment of his art as one following the enactment of a character's death and consisting in the narrator's lament that "dies [*verlaufen*] beautifully and purely away" (DII 102; Ta 449).

The truth of unity is certainly not in the pure expressiveness of scenes of dying. Admittedly, Kafka exalts them in saying that they are "secretly a game" for the writer, who means to "lie very contentedly on [his] deathbed" and who consequently has "a much clearer understanding" of death than the distracted sufferer or reader who suffers with him. The writer's distance allows him to "rejoice in [his] own death." Yet such a rejoicing suggests that even as Kafka describes the dissolution of congruence, he is prey to insidious forms of inauthenticity. For the condition of his rejoicing is his character's—*someone else's*—death. And it is not proved that the empirical person Kafka possesses the "capacity . . . to meet [his own] death with contentment" (DII 102).[11] It is only the lament, the radiant passage from the "critical activity" of death to its contemplative recovery, that is "true" (DF 97)—a moment that cannot be called "the personal unity of 'writer' and 'real self.'" In one sense the writer cannot die, for "he is already dead"; in another, the notion that his body will die contentedly is only a hopeful surmise. That death is beautiful, says Kafka, in which the lament dies purely away; neither Kafka's nor any reader's real death is beautiful.

It follows, therefore, that the moment of radiant contemplative activity in Kafka's work is not one that could be experienced by one empirical personality on the strength of another's or instituted by a reader as a source of strength to which he or she could return again and again. These moments arise from acts of dissolution, graspable only as they themselves dissolve into the task of being contemplated. Thus, their radiance is only virtual, like "the radiance that fell from Ulysses's great eyes"; but "if the Sirens had possessed consciousness, they would have been annihilated at that moment" (GW 250). The "truth" is the barely heard music of dissolution, of the death of an illusion that returns to thought. But death is "clearly understood" only in a world already raised into "the pure, the true, and the immutable" (DII 187). If writing gives glimmers of such an understanding, it is, as Kafka said, "only . . . allusively" (DF 40)—that is, by means of the destruction of familar metaphors. This destruction gives rise to new metaphors worthy of dissolution; that is the necessity of form.

11. See Chapter Five.

Index

Index

Index

Index

Index

Library of Congress Cataloging-in-Publication Data
Corngold, Stanley.
  Franz Kafka : the necessity of form.
  Includes index.
  1. Kafka, Franz, 1883–1924.   2. Authors, Austrian—20th century—
  Biography.   I. Title.
PT2621.A26Z664   1988   833'.912 [B]   88-47721
ISBN 0-8014-2199-3 (alk. paper)